Elwood Haynes

Alloys and Automobiles

THE LIFE OF ELWOOD HAYNES

RALPH D. GRAY

Indianapolis
Indiana Historical Society
1979

For Jan,
       whose courageous contributions
       are immeasurable;
         and for Eddie,
              who would have taken great pride

Contents

Tables and Illustrations

Preface

Before I returned to Indiana in 1964 to teach American history at the Kokomo Campus of Indiana University, I knew of only two of Kokomo's many claims to distinction. I was aware that the city had produced many excellent high school basketball teams, and I had a vague impression of a man named Elwood Haynes who had driven one of the earliest American automobiles on the streets of Kokomo in the 1890s. I prided myself on this second bit of information. Many of my acquaintances in the historical profession, as I discovered later, had never heard of Haynes, or Kokomo either, save as one of America's "funny" town names. I attributed my hazy awareness of Haynes to my Hoosier upbringing and a childhood book about the automobile.

After moving to Kokomo, I began to hear more about Haynes. Many people of the city, including my next door neighbor, worked at the "Stellite plant"; others worked at Delco and Chrysler, where automobile radios and transmissions were produced. All of these major plants were related, directly or indirectly, to Haynes. I soon discovered that the Stellite plant, then a division of Union Carbide Corporation, had originated as the Haynes Stellite Company to produce an alloy Haynes had discovered. In addition to being an automobile pioneer, Haynes also had been a metallurgical scientist who had managed to convert his knowledge to practical advantage.

In many other ways too, the Haynes name is impressed upon the newcomer to Kokomo. One of the public schools bears this name, and there is a Haynes room in the YMCA; a fine portrait of Haynes hangs in the session room of the First Presbyterian Church. At this point I recall making a desultory search for printed information about the man, hoping to be able to make reasonably informed comments to my classes about the local contribution to the American automobile. But nothing came readily to hand, and I let the matter drop. Obviously, I thought, Haynes's experiments with his first car were a historical curiosity only, and the man was not worth more than the customary mention he is given in textbooks as one of a number of automotive pioneers before Henry Ford is discussed.

Two things happened to cause me to revise radically this hasty and false impression. One of my students in an evening course was Mrs. Garry (Pat) Springer. From her I learned that a substantial body of Haynes Papers had been rescued from destruction a few years earlier by Mr. Wallace Spencer Huffman, an antique automobile buff. Mr. Huffman was anxious to have this priceless historical source material preserved, and he subsequently arranged to have the papers deposited in the Howard County Historical Society Library, where Mrs. Springer was employed in cataloging and arranging them. She told me of the enormity of the task as well as something of the true significance of the singular and versatile man whose career was revealed in the papers. Before her cataloging job was completed, however, a second important development occurred.

In 1965, the year of Kokomo's centennial as an incorporated city, the fine brick house which Elwood Haynes had built in 1915−1916 came onto the market. A lovely two-story dwelling, ideally located adjacent to the city's well-kept Highland Park, this had been the place where Haynes lived for the last ten years of his life. Subsequently his son, March, had lived there, but then it was acquired by others. When the house became available, the Haynes descendants, many of whom still lived in Kokomo, decided to act. In a generous, public-spirited gesture, the family repurchased the property for conversion into a museum, depicting not only Haynes's achievements but the growth of Kokomo industry, and presented it to the city of Kokomo. The Haynes Museum became the new depository of the Haynes Papers and other memorabilia, including early Haynes and Apperson automobiles.

Another feature of Kokomo's centennial was the re-enactment of Haynes's famous trial run of his first automobile. Mr. Jack A. Frost of Detroit, Michigan, the proud owner of an 1897 Haynes, repeated the trip that Haynes had made on July 4, 1894, even to the extent of having the car towed to the edge of town by horses. Haynes had refused to begin his test run in front of the Riverside Machine Shop, where the vehicle had been constructed, because of the possible danger to the crowd which had assembled.

During a warm spring shower on May 28, 1967, the museum dedication ceremonies were conducted. The day featured an antique car parade, the renaming of Haynes's test route as Haynes Boulevard, and an appropriate address by Mr. Fred L. Shanklin of the Union Carbide Corporation. As a member of the museum dedication committee, I had played a very minor role in planning the day's activities. My chief interest was in having a look at the papers. Thanks to the support obtained through the grant of an Indiana University Faculty Fellowship, this I was able to do in the summer of 1967. My preliminary survey of the papers convinced me that Haynes was indeed an extraordinary man—well-educated, literate, humane, technically competent in a wide variety of endeavors, and deeply committed to science and various social reforms. His brilliance in the natural gas industry, in the design of one of America's first automobiles, and particularly in his discovery of amazingly valuable new alloys and metals was undeniable, and I decided to try to develop the story as fully as possible.

This decision was made before I moved in 1968 to join the history faculty at

Indiana University at Indianapolis, but I was able to carry out the project from a slightly longer range than I had planned. Over the years my studies and my travels have been eased by countless acts of friendship and professional courtesy. One of the joys of authorship is the opportunity to give public thanks for such acts of assistance, encouragement, and constructive criticism. Although it will not be possible to acknowledge each one by name, I am conscious of and grateful for the help of each and I am more than ever aware that the making of books is a collaborative effort.

I am indebted initially to Chancellor Victor M. Bogle of Indiana University at Kokomo for suggesting and supporting my first investigations of the Haynes papers. I am also deeply grateful to Mr. Wallace Spencer Huffman of Kokomo for his interest and assistance in this project and to the late Mr. John Cupp, former caretaker and curator at the Elwood Haynes Museum, for his willing acceptance of all my impositions. The Stellite Division of Cabot Corporation, particularly Mr. William D. Manly and Mr. A. M. Edwards, materially strengthened the metallurgical sections of this book, first, by employing me during the summer of 1971 to write a history of the Stellite company and, second, by supplying me with metallurgical information, insights, and interviewees.

Indiana University at Indianapolis supported this research project with a sabbatical leave, and several of my colleagues, especially Professors Donald Kinzer and Bernard Friedman in Indianapolis and Donald F. Carmony and Martin Ridge in Bloomington, have read and evaluated portions of this study. There are also dozens of librarians, law clerks, newspapermen, and others who assisted me in locating materials and answering questions. I am particularly grateful to Mr. Richard Ardrey, librarian at Indiana University at Kokomo, Mr. Francis L. Brey, reference librarian at Indiana University at Indianapolis, and the entire staffs at both the Indiana Division and the Archives Division of the Indiana State Library. Mr. James J. Bradley, head of the Automotive History Collection in the Detroit Public Library, helped make my visits to Michigan pleasant and productive, and Mr. Henry E. Edmunds, director of the Ford Archives, answered several queries for me.

Finally, I want to acknowledge the graceful forbearance of my family during my long association with Elwood Haynes and his family, and I want to express my gratitude to the Indiana Historical Society, and to its highly efficient and professional staff, particularly Executive Secretary Gayle Thornbrough and Lana Ruegamer, a cheerful yet competent, even demanding, editor who is a joy to work with, for seeing this book through its final stages. I lay sole claim, however, to the responsibility for all the errors and shortcomings that remain.

Alloys and Automobiles

Chapter 1

Portland Days

Natural gas was discovered in Portland, Indiana, in 1886. Two middle-aged artisans of Portland, stimulated by the developing gas boom in neighboring Ohio and convinced that gas and oil resources lay beneath their feet in Jay County, raised the money for sinking a trial well. It had not been easy. The two, Henry W. Sees, a foundryman, and William N. Current, a mason, worked throughout the winter of 1885–1886, walking the streets of Portland to solicit the subscriptions. Many persons subscribed, it was reported in the newspaper, simply "to get rid of them, for they 'hung on like leeches,' and wouldn't take no for an answer. . . ."[1]

By early March the two entrepreneurs organized the Eureka Company. A Lima, Ohio, contractor, an experienced gas well driller, was hired to drill the first natural gas well in the state of Indiana.[2] The work began on April 8, and twenty days later, at a depth of 700 feet, a weak vein of shale gas was struck. News of the early morning strike spread through the town like wildfire, and hundreds dropped what they were doing to visit the well. The workmen obligingly ignited the gas and let it burn for several hours before resuming their drilling. The main source of gas was believed to be deeper.

Even a preliminary indication that gas would be located in Portland, however, was enough to touch off a spontaneous celebration. That evening the gas was again ignited before a crowd estimated at between 2,000 and 3,000 people. As the flames leaped upwards nearly as high as the derrick itself, the onlookers were entertained by several of the "best selections" of the Port-

---

[1] Portland (Ind.) *Commercial,* March 17, 1887.

[2] There are records of natural gas having been discovered in Indiana prior to 1886, but these finds were made accidentally, while drilling for oil or water, and the gas was not commercially developed. The early discoveries came in the 1860s (Pulaski County) and the 1870s (Delaware County), but the Portland well was the first one sunk as a commercial enterprise for the purpose of locating natural gas. Later in 1886 gas was discovered in other parts of the state, particularly at Kokomo, in Howard County, and Eaton, in Delaware County, and the boom was on. See the chapter on "Natural Gas" by Elwood Haynes in *Biographical and Historical Record of Jay and Blackford Counties, Indiana* (Chicago: The Lewis Publishing Company, 1887), pp. 217–26; Margaret Wynn, "Natural Gas in Indiana: An Exploited Resource," in *Indiana Magazine of History,* IV (1908), 31–45; Clifton J. Phillips, *Indiana in Transition: The Emergence of An Industrial Commonwealth, 1880–1920* (Indianapolis: Indiana Historical Bureau and Indiana Historical Society, 1968), pp. 192–97. The rise and decline of the Indiana gas fields can best be followed in the annual reports of the Indiana Department of Geology and Natural Resources; see especially the reports of 1887, 1898, and 1915.

land City Band and expansive visions of future industrial greatness for their city.[3]

During the next few days, as the drilling continued, a young professor of chemistry at the recently established Eastern Indiana Normal School visited the site regularly. He kept careful records of the drilling operations, analyzed samples taken from the successive strata penetrated, and tested the gas and then the oil taken from the well. Later he journeyed to the Ohio gas fields near Findlay and Lima, armed with a notebook and his steeltrap mind, to learn all he could about the gas business. When Professor Elwood Haynes returned to Portland and delivered a public lecture on natural gas and oil before a large, enthusiastic audience, he was the man of the hour. By then Portland's initial well was known to be nonproductive and the Eureka Company had collapsed, but the money was readily forthcoming, upon Haynes's recommendation, to organize a new company. The popular teacher-scientist agreed to resign his teaching post to become superintendent of the Portland Natural Gas and Oil Company.

This decision had been a most difficult one. Haynes, a graduate of Worcester Polytechnic Institute, possessed exceptional talents as a teacher, lecturer, and research scientist, and he was strongly attracted to the academic world. "I like school teaching first rate," he wrote in 1881, "and the more I teach the better I enjoy it."[4] Later, exciting new vistas had been opened to him through a year's study at Johns Hopkins University. There, under the tutelage of Professor Ira Remsen in chemistry and Professor H. Newell Martin in biology, he earned a reputation among his colleagues as the "best research worker of the bunch,"[5] and he applied for a university fellowship to finance continued graduate study. But his request was denied and Haynes, called home in May, 1885, by the death of his mother, decided not to return to Baltimore. Instead he accepted an eagerly proffered position at the Portland Normal School where he became one of the most popular and respected members of the faculty.

Haynes never explained his reasons for leaving the teaching profession in 1886, but at least three may be suggested. The gas opportunity represented a considerable scientific and technical challenge, and Haynes was eager to test his ability to establish a workable gas plant. Secondly, the future prospects for the Normal were not bright. As Haynes must have perceived, the school would eventually succumb to financial and competitive pressures.[6] Certainly various personal considerations also went into the decision. Haynes was approaching his thirtieth birthday and had not yet secured for himself a place in the community comparable to those of his older brothers. It is not mere coincidence that less than a year after entering the business world Haynes married Bertha B. Lanterman, whom he had courted for nearly a decade.

By 1887, Haynes could look back with some pride upon his achievements. He enjoyed a solid local reputation as a teacher, a scientist, and a gas plant manager. Under his bold and imaginative leadership, Portland had acquired an excellent gas facility. It was expected, moreover, that Professor Haynes, as he was still known, would help channel and stimulate Portland's antici-

[3] Portland *Commercial,* March 17, 1887.

[4] Elwood Haynes to Bertha B. Lanterman, December 29, 1881, Haynes Papers, Elwood Haynes Museum, Kokomo, Indiana.

[5] Charles S. Palmer to Elwood Haynes, December 24, 1919, *ibid.*

[6] Elwood Haynes, "Autobiography," May 15, 1918, typescript, five pages, *ibid.*

pated industrial growth in its second half-century, just as his father had been a leading force in the community during its first fifty years. Much as Haynes was admired and respected, however, no one could have predicted the even greater effect the energetic young businessman and scientist was to have upon the country at large in his next thirty years, the period of his major metallurgical and mechanical contributions.

Elwood Haynes was the grandson of a Massachusetts craftsman who manufactured weapons during the War of 1812. After the war Henry Haynes manufactured harness and carriage trim, bought land, and fathered twelve children, among them Elwood's father, Jacob March Haynes, born April 12, 1817. Jacob helped with his father's manufacturing business as a boy but chose a legal career for himself. Educated at Phillips Academy in Andover, he read law from 1842 to 1843 with Linus Child in Sturbridge and then headed west in 1843, looking for opportunity.[7]

When Jacob Haynes arrived in the straggling village of Portland in east-central Indiana in 1844 to begin a law practice, the town consisted of perhaps twenty-five log houses in the middle of a heavily wooded area along the Salamonie River. The territory had belonged to the Miami Indians and had been organized into Jay County, with Portland as county seat, in 1836, only eight years before. The surrounding countryside was composed of gentle hills that were well-watered and fertile, and the town became a modest trading center for the growing number of farmers around it.[8] Supplementing his attorney's fees by farming and teaching, Haynes married Portland resident Hilinda Sophia Haines in 1846, and in the next twenty years they parented a family of ten children, eight of whom lived to maturity and became business, civic, and religious leaders of the community. The first two children to survive infancy were girls, Eleanor Josephine (Josie) and Susan Isabel; they were followed by six boys, Walter, Sumner, Elwood, Frank, Calvin, and Edward.[9]

By the time Elwood Haynes was born on October 14, 1857, Jacob Haynes was one of Portland's most distinguished citizens. He had been Jay County School Commissioner and School Examiner between 1846 and 1852 and took the county census in 1850 along with another man. In 1856 he was elected judge of the court of common pleas for Jay and Randolph counties, an office he held until 1871, after which he served a six-year term as judge of the twenty-sixth judicial circuit. A Whig/Republican, a Presbyterian, and a pro-

Portland Days

5

---

[7] The Haynes family traces its origins in America back to the earliest period of New England settlement. Walter Haynes, his wife, and five children immigrated to the Massachusetts Bay colony in 1698 from Wiltshire, England. His descendant Judge Jacob March Haynes is the subject of several biographical sketches in county and state histories, and there is a Haynes family genealogy. *Biographical Memoirs of Jay County, Indiana* (Chicago: B. F. Bowen Company, publishers, 1901), pp. 291–92; Milton T. Jay (ed.), *History of Jay County, Indiana* (2 volumes. Indianapolis: Historical Publishing Company, 1922), I, 225; Frances Haynes (ed.), *Walter Haynes (1583–1665) of Sutton Mandeville, Wiltshire, England, and Sudbury, Massachusetts, and His Descendants, 1583–1928* (Haverhill, Mass.: Record Publishing Company, 1929), especially pp. 150–51; Joseph S. Powell, "History of Elwood Haynes and Automobile Industry" (master's thesis, Indiana University, 1948), pp. 1–2. See also Martha C. M. Lynch (ed.), *Reminiscences of Adams, Jay and Randolph Counties* [Fort Wayne, Ind.: Nelson & Singmaster, 1896?]; Chapter XV was written by Judge Haynes.

[8] Jay, *History of Jay County*, I.

[9] Haynes (ed.), *Walter Haynes . . . and His Descendants*. Altogether there were ten children: Henry William (1847 [b. December 18, d. December 29]); Eleanor Josephine (1850–1918); Susan Isabel (1851–1901); Walter March (1853–1929); Sumner Watson (1855–1936); Elwood (1857–1925); John (1859 [b. September 28, d. December 7]); Frank (1861–1950); Calvin Herbert (1864–1949); and Edward Maurice (1867–1944). The death dates after 1928 were supplied from newspaper obituaries.

Judge Jacob March Haynes, circa 1880

hibitionist, Judge Haynes was a pillar of his community. He was also a homebody, a strong family man, and a stern father. He succeeded in imbuing his children with his convictions, and they too were all Republicans, Presbyterians, and prohibitionists—except for those whose prohibitionism was even stronger than their Republicanism, so that they deserted the Republican party for the Prohibition party until the enactment of the Nineteenth Amendment. Austere but not humorless, the judge was a middle-sized man, clean-shaven, and neat. His neighbors called him the "Yankee lawyer," and his colleagues at the bar remembered him with high praise when he was gone.[10]

Elwood was the fifth child and the third boy. He was born the year of the Dred Scott decision, and sectional tensions were on the increase. Some of Elwood's earliest recollections included scenes of soldiers assembling in Portland, preparing to enter the war. Until he was nine, the Hayneses lived in a two-story frame house, with only two rooms on each floor available to house the rapidly growing family. A large kitchen was attached to the south side of the dwelling, and the whole building fronted on High Street, without yard or fence to afford privacy. However, a sizable orchard containing a variety of fruit-bearing trees stood at the side of the house.[11]

The judge was required to travel a great deal as his family grew up, so that an even greater than usual share of the responsibility for childrearing lay with Hilinda Haynes. Many years later Elwood's older brother Sumner, who became a lawyer like his father, described her as "all that a mother could be" and his memory endowed her with all the Victorian virtues. In fact she is nearly anonymous, so far as records are concerned, although it appears that she was a local founder of the Woman's Christian Temperance Union and seems to have helped to instill a high order of self-confidence in many of her offspring.[12]

As Haynes remembered it many years later, his early childhood was spent roaming around a primitive forest teeming with game on the outskirts of Portland, accompanied by a dog and a cherished bow and arrow. Young Elwood's excursions apparently caused his mother frequent anxiety as she searched from neighbor to neighbor for the child. And Mrs. Haynes's worries were not over when the roamer turned into a reader, since the quiet and studious "Wood" developed an early interest in chemical experiments. His family moved to a new house in Portland in 1866, located on thirty-five acres of land, and Wood was expected to do his share of farm chores. But his brother Sumner complained sixty years later that Elwood "would always make promises, just as soon as he got through with this experiment." The sources for the boy's experimentation were two textbooks his older sister brought home from college courses in chemistry and science,[13] especially

---

[10] In 1869 two more counties, Delaware and Blackford, were added to Haynes's jurisdiction, and he held special sessions of court as far away as Kokomo, two or three days by horseback from Portland. In 1871 the common pleas court was replaced by the circuit court. Hurd Allyn Drake manuscript, undated, Haynes Papers. Reverend Drake undertook a biography of his famous former parishioner Elwood Haynes in the mid-1930s, of which three chapters are extant. Judge Haynes died in 1903 at age eighty-five. See also Powell, "History of Elwood Haynes," pp. 6–7; remarks of attorney John M. Smith, quoted in Jay, *History of Jay County,* I, 191; Portland (Ind.) *Semi-Weekly Sun,* February 28, 1903.

[11] Haynes, "Autobiography," Haynes Papers; Sumner W. Haynes, "Address," October 9, 1932, *ibid.*

[12] Sumner W. Haynes, "Address," October 9, 1932, *ibid.* Sumner Haynes claimed that Elwood built a crude steam engine before 1866.

[13] Haynes, "Autobiography," *ibid.*; Elwood Haynes to Jane Rowe, March 11, 1920, Jane Rowe to

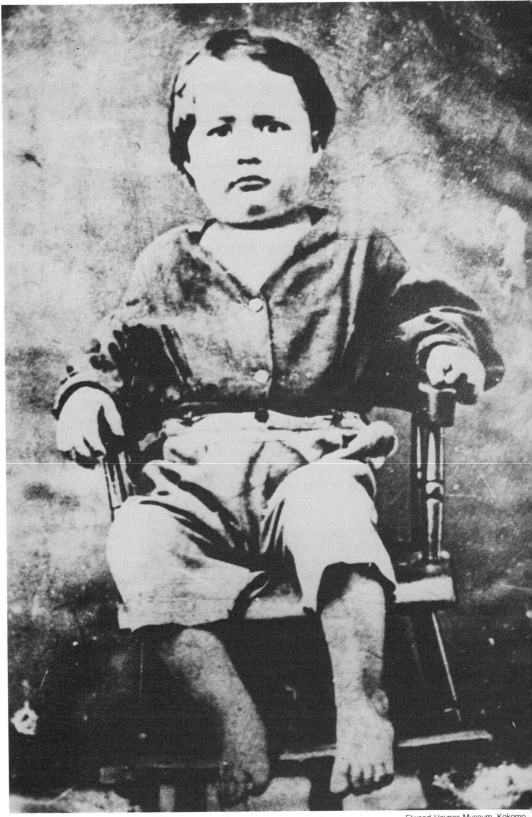

Elwood Haynes, four years old

David A. Wells, *Principles and Applications of Chemistry,* first published in 1858.

Nearly fifty years later Haynes was still able to describe in vivid detail his first scientific experiments. Using a crude apparatus of his own design, the young experimenter produced hydrogen gas and chlorine. His tenacious resourcefulness is clear from his account of other early experiments:

> The preparation of oxygen presented a ... problem, inasmuch as it required the use of a retort, which must withstand sufficient heat, and a delivery tube for carrying off the gas. I possessed neither of these articles, nor even so much as a common test tube. I was obliged to make a retort by molding it from clay in the interior of a small flower pot belonging to my mother. By lining the flower pot with soft clay and putting on a cover of the same material, and afterward allowing the lining to dry, I obtained a clay vessel with a sealed cover. This "retort" was carefully dried, and the materials for making the oxygen put in through a small hole in the cover. For a short delivery tube, I used a piece of parasol handle which I filed from a discarded sunshade. Over the end of this tube I placed a small rubber tube which I obtained from a baby's nursing bottle.
>
> A furnace for heating this retort was made from a piece of stove pipe, much after the fashion of the furnace used by the tin smith. A pressed-ware pan served for the top. Two holes were cut through this. Into one of these pieces a piece of rain spouting was inserted, and into the other the small clay retort. The furnace was fed by chips obtained from the wood house. To my delight, I was always able to make oxygen in this manner, and I shall always remember the pleasure afforded me by burning iron wire, charcoal, sulphur, etc., in this gas.[14]

But Haynes insisted in an autobiographical sketch that his chief interest, even in his youth, was metals, and he claimed as an old man that the usefulness of pure forms of rare metals like nickel, chromium, cobalt, aluminum, and tungsten had intrigued him in his teenage years. A former neighbor recalled that the boy had repeatedly checked "to see if I had broke any pewter spoons" because he said he wanted to melt them. Wood also cultivated a friendship with the Portland druggist, partly to gain access to the *Druggist's Pharmacopeia,* a significant reference work for the young chemist.[15]

His melting operations were performed in a furnace, built in his parents' backyard when he was about fifteen years old. The blower

> was constructed from a cheese rim, two large boards, and some pieces of shingle for fans. With this furnace I succeeded in melting brass and cast iron, but was unable to melt steel successfully on account of the high temperature required. I tried several times to alloy tungsten with iron and steel, but was unable to do so, owing to the limits of the furnace.[16]

Despite the ingenuity Elwood demonstrated in these experiments, he was not an especially good student and found it difficult to decide on an occupation. His family apparently felt real concern that he might never amount to anything. Although at least one of his older sisters and both older brothers

---

Elwood Haynes, March 13, 1920, quoted in Mary Ellen Harshbarger, "Elwood Haynes: Scientist with a Social Conscience" (doctoral dissertation, Ball State University, 1964), p. 3.

[14] Haynes, "Autobiography," Haynes Papers.

[15] *Ibid.*; Harshbarger, "Elwood Haynes," p. 3; Powell, "History of Elwood Haynes," p. 9 (interview with March Haynes, June 1, 1948).

[16] Haynes, "Autobiography," Haynes Papers.

attended college (Walter, the future banker, attended Eastman Business School in Poughkeepsie and Sumner, the lawyer, went to Earlham and the University of Michigan), Elwood simply stopped his formal education when he completed grammar school. Portland had no public high school until 1876, so between 1871 or 1872 and 1876 Elwood Haynes was not in school. For the most part he spent this time performing routine chores at home, reading, and conducting chemical experiments. His youngest brother remembered that Wood was "unhurried, always unobtrusive, always considerate of others, always a bit of a dreamer, always pursuing strange fancies and always putting together odd and se[e]mingly useless contrivances. . . . He was regarded as more of a plodder than anything else. . . ." His oldest brother reportedly remarked during these years that "Father will always have to keep Elwood."[17]

The family was also concerned about the dangers involved in Wood's occupations, both in this period and throughout his life as an experimenter. Many times his solitary researches led to explosions. "He made many mistakes and received many hurts," his next younger brother later remembered; "that he should have remained active and not a cripple is one of the things of his life that have never been explained."[18] Their anxiety was well founded. Wood demonstrated a reckless ingenuity as a teenager by building a railroad vehicle that he and his friends operated illicitly on the tracks around Jay County, after the railroad was completed in December, 1871. The "car" was built mainly with parts from abandoned threshing machines and had open bearings so that it could be lifted quickly from the tracks when necessary. The boys were frequently chased by a wrathful railroad foreman, and the machine was eventually discovered and destroyed by a railroad crew.[19]

In the years between his grammar school and high school studies, Elwood did manage to make himself somewhat useful, despite his family's uneasiness about his future. He performed janitorial services for the Presbyterian Church for a while, including ringing the bell, and later was promoted to teaching a Sunday school class for boys. The coming of the railroad offered him an opportunity to earn money for his later education by working as a teamster; he hauled gravel for track ballast with a team of horses and a dump-bed wagon provided by his father.[20]

Finally in 1876, in response to the town's spurt of railroad-inspired economic growth and the consequent increase in population from 500 to 3,000 in the decade of the 1870s, Portland expanded its public school system to include the first two years of a high school course. Elwood was nearly nineteen years old; nevertheless, he enrolled in the high school and, despite the four- or five-year lapse in his formal studies, he found the course rather easy. He became a good student and attended classes regularly. Elwood also began to participate more in community activities. He joined the church choir, revealing a fine tenor voice, and began to take a special interest in the church organist, Bertha B. Lanterman. Both Elwood and Bertha were shy and saw each other only in group activities at first. Even so, by the time the

Lanterman family moved to Alabama in March, 1877, their friendship had grown strong enough to prompt a regular correspondence.[21]

In the summer of 1877, in a move that must have pleased his father, Elwood became an eager recruit in the "Murphy Movement," a temperance drive which swept through Indiana. Founded by Francis Murphy, a "reformed" alcoholic from Portland, Maine, the organization used the techniques of evangelical religion to persuade people to sign a pledge of total abstinence. Elwood reported enthusiastically to Bertha that in the first week in Jay County the Murphy Movement had obtained over seven hundred pledges, and among the signers were "a large number [of] tiplers & tap[p]ers." Haynes went on to tell the history of the movement:

> An Irishman by the name of Francis Murphy having caused a man's death by intemperance in the City of Portland (Maine) was cast into prison; and upon being visited by a man (who was a minister I think) he promised if he was released that he would do all in his power to prevent intemperance; having obtained his freedom he went to Pittsburgh Penn. & commenced a series of lectures exhorting the people to sign the pledge; in a short time a large number had signed the pledge; and sufficient money was raised to carry the work forward and extend it into other states; and it is indeed a grand institution. The speakers are almost all men who have had experience with spirituous liquors, and are well acquainted with their horrible effects.

Elwood promised to send Bertha one of the Murphy pledge cards and noted that those who took the pledge wore a blue ribbon as a symbol of their promise of total abstinence.[22]

After the Blue Ribbon organizers left Jay County, Elwood and his close friend Perry Creager, along with two other enthusiasts, conducted their own three-day "Murphy Meeting" in the countryside in July. Haynes put his pleasant tenor voice to work for temperance in this camp meeting, and he also did "part of the speaking." Ninety-two persons signed the pledge, encouraging Haynes and Creager to sing again in August at a Murphy picnic.[23]

Elwood continued to keep Bertha informed about the temperance movement in Jay County, and through this common interest their friendship deepened. "Dear Friend Bertha," Haynes remarked in 1878, "[we are] becoming better acquainted through correspondence ..." than ever before. He also reported with satisfaction that an attempt to acquire a license to sell liquor in quantities smaller than a quart had failed in December, 1877; "Portland will not have a saloon," Haynes announced.[24]

When Haynes finished the two-year high school course in 1878, he was nearly twenty-one years old and still not at all certain what he should do

---

[21] Portland *Commercial*, May 16, 1878; Elwood Haynes to Bertha B. Lanterman, July 26, 27, 1878, Haynes Papers. The Lantermans lived in Morgan County, Alabama, from March, 1877, to 1883. Bertha B. Lanterman to "Josie" Haynes, April 20, 1877, *ibid.*; Portland *Commercial*, May 31, 1883.

[22] Elwood Haynes to Bertha B. Lanterman, June 19, 1877, Haynes Papers. The Murphy pledge card is not found in the Haynes Papers. The cards read "I, the undersigned, do *pledge* my word and honor, GOD HELPING ME, to abstain from ALL intoxicating liquors as a beverage, and that I will by all honorable means, encourage others to abstain." Beulah B. Gray Papers, in possession of the author. A Grant County historian estimated that there were perhaps ten million persons in the United States who took the Murphy pledge. Rolland Lewis Whitson (ed.), *Centennial History of Grant County, Indiana, 1812 to 1912* (2 volumes. Chicago and New York: Lewis Publishing Co., 1914), I, 557. See also Jay, *History of Jay County*, I, 248.

[23] Elwood Haynes to Bertha B. Lanterman, July 10, August 29, 1877, Haynes Papers.

[24] *Ibid.*, February [17?], 1878, December 16, 1877.

Murphy Movement pledge card

next. It seems clear, however, that his success in the high school course encouraged both Elwood himself and his family to seek more schooling for him. Suddenly, late in the summer of 1878, the appropriate school was found—perhaps through the advice of the Massachusetts Hayneses or perhaps by Judge Haynes himself at the Philadelphia Centennial Exposition, where Elwood's new school had installed a large display—and Elwood found himself on the way to Massachusetts to enroll in the Worcester County Free Institute of Industrial Science (later Worcester Polytechnic Institute).[25]

He was not the most promising college freshman ever to venture forth, and his brother Walt was convinced he was wasting his time. He would be four years older than most of his fellow students, and his preparation in Jay County public schools was ragged at best. Still, Elwood the "slow boy," as a brother was later to call him, and the precocious experimenter was getting a second chance to join his brothers and sisters in acquiring the middle-class education appropriate for the son of a professional man.

---

[25]*Ibid.*, June 3, September 9, 1878; *Worcester County Free Institute of Industrial Science, Worcester, Massachusetts. Prepared for the Industrial Exhibition, 1876* ([Worcester, 1876]), pamphlet. An eleventh grade was instituted in Portland in 1878, but Haynes chose Worcester instead, where only two years of high school were required for matriculation. Portland *Commercial*, June 6, 1878.

Chapter 2

The Education of
a Scientist

Elwood Haynes left Portland in September, 1878, and was not to return home until after his graduation from Worcester County Free Institute of Industrial Science in 1881. In order to enable the slender resources of his father's purse to meet the needs of a large family it was essential that expenses be kept to a minimum. During the brief school holidays he usually would stay with relatives and friends in New England. Haynes was to find the academic work difficult and demanding but exhilarating once he had mastered the fundamentals. He had been poorly prepared in the Portland schools. Ill-trained teachers, a severely limited curriculum, and inadequate facilities were all responsible for the minimal opportunities in education available to rural and small-town Hoosiers in the 1870s.

Although perhaps Haynes had second thoughts about it at times during his college years, it is clear by hindsight that his choice of colleges was a particularly good one. The offerings at Worcester were exactly what Haynes needed, and his training served him well during his subsequent careers in natural gas engineering, automobile manufacturing, and metallurgy. The school attempted to combine technical training with a liberal arts curriculum—still a relatively new idea even in Europe—and there were few other schools in the United States with offerings comparable to those at Worcester.[1]

The Worcester Free Institute was located in a growing industrial community in east-central Massachusetts. Forty-five miles from Boston, Worcester was the largest city in the county and boasted nine railroads, twelve banks, seven insurance companies, and several small manufacturing establishments. There was also a public library, two newspapers, and some forty thousand people. Haynes found it "a very beautiful City. . . ."[2]

[1] An Indiana technical school was established in Terre Haute in 1874 by Chauncey Rose, but its doors were not opened until 1883. Frankly based upon the Worcester example, Rose Polytechnic Institute, now Rose-Hulman, even appointed Professor Charles O. Thompson as its first president. Thompson had guided Worcester Polytechnic Institute during its formative years and had been Haynes's chemistry professor. Thompson's premature death in 1885 deprived the new Indiana school of a wise and experienced administrator. Mildred McClary Tymeson, *Two Towers: The Story of Worcester Tech, 1865–1965* (Barre, Mass.: Barre Publishers, 1965), p. 41; Indianapolis *Star,* January 7, 1971.

[2] Tymeson, *Two Towers,* pp. 18–20; Elwood Haynes to Bertha B. Lanterman, September 9, 1878, Haynes Papers. See also *History of Worcester County, Massachusetts* (2 volumes. Boston: C. F. Jewett and Co., 1879), II, 614–18, 651–52, 653–54.

Worcester, Massachusetts, Main Street, circa 1878

Worcester County Free Institute of Industrial Science, circa 1884

The technical institute was one of the first of many industrial science and engineering schools established in the United States immediately after the Civil War. Massachusetts Institute of Technology, which opened its doors in 1865 and soon rivaled the oldest such school in the United States, Rensselaer Polytechnic Institute (1824), was to become the outstanding school of this type. A number of land-grant colleges also established programs in science and engineering during this period. In comparing the early curricula of MIT, RPI, and the University of Illinois with the course of studies Elwood Haynes undertook in the 1870s, one finds considerable similarity. The WFI program, however, required much more practical or laboratory work than the other schools; MIT, for example, did not institute shop work until 1877.[3]

The Worcester school had evolved from a gift of John Boynton, a Templeton, Massachusetts, manufacturer. Boynton had wanted to establish a new type of school, one in which emphasis would be placed upon practical as well as traditional learning. His initial gift of $100,000 in 1865 was supplemented by an equally munificent gift from Ichabod Washburn of Worcester. Washburn's special interest was in establishing a well-equipped machine shop to be operated by the school, both as a training device and a business enterprise. The citizens of Worcester raised the additional money required for the school, with one of its leading citizens, Stephen Salisbury, donating the elevated acreage for the campus. As a result of the local fund-raising efforts, the school was tuition-free to residents of Worcester County.[4] Haynes benefitted from this policy after his first term, when he turned twenty-one and declared Worcester as his residence.[5]

When the school opened its doors in November, 1868, it boasted two buildings. Boynton Hall was a three-story granite structure housing a four-hundred-seat chapel, lecture rooms and offices, and science laboratories; the Washburn Machine Shop was a three-story brick building equipped with the latest industrial machinery. The buildings stood back to back on the hill above a row of faculty houses. Despite the school's newness, a competent faculty had been assembled, headed by Principal Charles O. Thompson, a young Dartmouth graduate with a special interest in chemistry. Other faculty members included George E. Alden in applied mechanics, George Gladwin in drawing (known to students as "T-Square George" and "Freehand George"); John E. Sinclair and Thomas E. N. Eaton in mathematics; Edward P. Smith in English and modern languages; and Alonzo Kimball in physics. Kimball was an acquaintance of the Haynes family who befriended Elwood while he was at Worcester. Elwood often stayed with the Kimballs and did odd jobs for them, including house-sitting when the Kimballs were away. Walter U. Barnes, a Worcester graduate who assisted in the chemistry program, tutored Haynes for a time.[6]

In 1878, the entrance examinations for the Worcester Free Institute were held on September 10, covering "common English branches" (United States

[3] Charles Riborg Mann, *A Study of Engineering Education* (Bulletin No. 11, Carnegie Endowment for the Advancement of Teaching. New York: n.d. [1917?]), pp. 9–14.

[4] Tymeson, *Two Towers*, pp. 13–18.

[5] The school catalogs list Haynes as a resident of Worcester in his first two years; for his final year he is listed as a resident of Portland, Indiana. The residency requirement interpretation is attached in a handwritten statement to the 1881 catalog in the collection of the Worcester Polytechnic Institute Library. The rule is also published in *Eleventh Annual Catalog of the Worcester County Free Institute of Industrial Science* (Worcester, 1881), p. 46.

[6] The faculty members are listed in the annual catalogs. Their nicknames appear in the controversial yearbook published by the class of 1881, not in Haynes's letters. *Antenna*, Volume I, No. 3 (Worcester, 1881).

history, geography, and grammar) and "Algebra as far as quadratic equations."[7] The sample questions in each area, published in the annual catalogs, indicate a rather stiff examination. Evidently Haynes had no difficulty passing the examination since his first letters home make no mention of it. Nevertheless, Elwood would find many of his courses at Worcester extremely difficult, particularly those in mathematics. His preparation in the Portland schools left him far behind even the weakest graduate of a Massachusetts school. In 1879, in a letter to his youngest brother Edward, Haynes ruefully advised him to "try to learn all you can [in school] and you will be glad of it when you are as old as I am."[8]

The Worcester three-year curriculum allowed few electives. Students were only permitted to choose a major from among five degree programs and whether to take French or German in the last year.[9] The former was extremely important, since the "practice" periods, consisting of laboratory, field, or shop work, constituted a large part of the curriculum and all practice periods were taken in the major department. For Haynes, a chemistry major, practice would involve at least ten hours a week in the laboratory during five of the six twenty-one-week terms, plus eight hours a day during the month of July following both his first (called "junior") and middle years.

Haynes and his classmates faced an imposing curriculum when they entered Worcester in the fall of 1878. Although the initial term was light, with mathematics, science, language, and drawing classes totaling only twenty hours per week, during the final five semesters the students would average more than thirty-two hours in the classroom and laboratory.[10] Classes began at 7:00 AM and ran through the day. Chapel closed the regular day's work at 5:55 PM, and attendance was taken at every exercise.[11]

Haynes was a conscientious student and missed few, if any, classes. Keenly aware of his inadequate preparation for college work, the Hoosier seized every opportunity to make up his deficiencies. "My occupation is a little monotonous," he reported in 1879. "Nothing but Study! Study! from one week's end to another." This self-description was confirmed by Dwight Goddard, one of Haynes's classmates, who remembered him as "very slow and methodical and sober minded," but also as one who was "wholly absorbed in his studies and laboratory tasks. . . . We all honored and respected him and laughed about his slow ways," he added, "little dreaming he was to be the outstanding personality of our class."[12]

Even in one of his few recreational activities, playing in the traditional football game between Tech's junior class and the local high school, the unathletic, rather slender Haynes found the game hard going. It was his first and last football game, and it prompted him to remark, "I do not believe I ever worked harder at anything than at that game of ball."[13]

[7] Worcester County Free Institute of Industrial Science, *Eighth Annual Catalog* (Worcester, [1878?]), p. 31; Elwood Haynes to Bertha B. Lanterman, September 9, 1878, Haynes Papers.

[8] Elwood Haynes to Edward M. Haynes, Worcester, January 31, 1879, Haynes Papers.

[9] The five degree programs, or majors, were mechanical engineering, civil engineering, chemistry, physics, and drawing. Mathematics and modern language courses were supplementary to the major programs.

[10] Worcester County Free Institute of Industrial Science, *Eighth Annual Catalog,* pp. 15–16.

[11] Herbert Foster Taylor, *Seventy Years of the Worcester Polytechnic Institute* (Worcester, Mass.: The Davis Press, Inc., 1937), p. 58.

[12] Elwood Haynes to Bertha B. Lanterman, March 2, 1879, Haynes Papers; Drake Manuscript, *ibid.*

[13] Elwood Haynes to Bertha B. Lanterman, November 12, 1878, *ibid.; Antenna,* pp. 61–64. Mrs. Bernice Hillis, Haynes's daughter, recalled her father's comment in the 1920s that the game of

Elwood also worked hard at his studies and developed an eye twitch "because I am not accustomed to studying so much at night." Later in the first term he confided to his mother his worries about the first term examinations. These were crucial, since all students were admitted on probation, subject to doing satisfactory work during the term. "My lessons are quite difficult & I am quite fearful about the approaching examinations," he admitted. "I am obliged to study early and late in order to get my lessons & then I do not have them very well." On the brighter side, he reported that he had had his first chance at "chemical manipulation in the labratory [sic] a few days ago. I liked it very much; tried some of the same experiments that I used to try at home."[14]

As the time for the first term examinations neared, Haynes grew increasingly depressed and nervous. "Some of the seniors say it is the time which tries men's souls," he moodily recorded on the eve of his first test. "Well, I am going to do the best that I can to pass & of course if I am not successful I will be terribly discouraged." He took some consolation in the fact that, at any rate, he could "do a great deal more now in the same time than I could when I came here . . . ," but added, "I should like very much to pass the examination as I like the school full well if not better than I expected."[15]

The school maintained high standards in all departments, symbolized perhaps by Professor Sinclair's oft-repeated remark: "There is no such thing as nearly right. . . . If you solve a problem correctly, I mark you perfect; if there is the slightest error, I mark you zero."[16]

A passing mark of 60 was required for the juniors to carry on into the second term. Haynes compiled an average of 59.2 percent for his first term, primarily as a result of "the wicked algebra," but he was permitted to remain in school because of "recent progress."[17] When the grade report reached home Haynes received a blistering letter from his father, charging him with not making good use of his opportunities and with trying merely to "squeeze through." Haynes remonstrated at length, pointing out his seriousness of purpose and his dedication to his studies, which he claimed was almost always more than the two hours per lesson recommended by the professors. "I felt uncomfortable enough before I got your letter," he replied to his father; afterwards

> I felt almost like giving up going to school any more and trying to find a place to work somewhere. I tell you it came pretty hard. . . . I did not come to Worcester simply to squeeze through the Institute but to learn. . . . I thought you had a better opinion of me than to think I would slight the advantages that I enjoy. That is what makes me feel so miserable. . . . I know I am not quite as bright as some boys but do not think I am wholly to blame for that.

After a recitation of the steps Haynes had taken recently to economize and a dutiful promise to "try to do better next term if possible," the letter ended with the typical college student's request for more money.[18]

During the second term majors were declared, and the chemists were introduced to "Blow Pipe Analysis," studied the first four chapters of El-

---

football had changed drastically since his schooldays. "We just kicked the ball around when I played," he sighed. Kokomo *Morning Tribune,* May 15, 1965.

[14] Elwood Haynes to Hilinda H. Haynes, September 28, December 22, 1878, Haynes Papers.

[15] Elwood Haynes to "Sister" [Josie Haynes], January 19, 1879, *ibid.*

[16] Tymeson, *Two Towers,* p. 56.

[17] Elwood Haynes to Bertha B. Lanterman, January 26, 1879, Haynes Papers.

[18] Elwood Haynes to Jacob M. Haynes, February 3, 1879, *ibid.*

derhorst's laboratory manual, and undertook the determination of fifty unknown minerals. They studied qualitative analysis and identified additional "unknown substances" during the month of July. In their middle year, the chemists would take up "wet analysis," quantitative analysis, and the separation of bases and acids. The final year's work featured an introduction to metallurgy, ore analysis and assaying, and one aspect of Professor Thompson's specialty, the analysis of liquids such as water, milk, and beer. Each student also prepared a senior thesis. As Haynes reported to Bertha, "This school requires almost as much of its students in three years as is usually required in four."[19]

After declaring his major and commencing laboratory work in chemistry, at which Haynes was always a strong student, there was a slight improvement in the second term's grade average. As the end of the year approached, Elwood again tried to prepare his family for the worst. The results revealed that this was not false modesty. "I passed and am no longer a Junior," he reported with evident relief to Bertha, although he had little margin after making up the deficiency from the first semester. Presumably he accumulated an average of 60.8 percent or slightly above. Again it was algebra which did most of the harm; he received a mark of 15 percent in that subject.[20]

At the end of his first nerve-wracking year in Massachusetts, Haynes spent the six-week summer vacation with an uncle, Henry Haynes, and his family in nearby Sturbridge. His summer companions were his fifteen- and sixteen-year-old girl cousins, whom he described to Bertha as "young ladies (or say they are at least)," and his thirteen-year-old cousin George. George later earned a Ph.D. in history and political science and was to spend his entire teaching career at Worcester Polytechnic Institute.[21] While visiting with this family Elwood obligingly pitched in to help with the farm chores; he found plowing in New England's rocky soils unlike anything he had ever done at home. He also joined the Sturbridge Hayneses in worship and at temperance meetings, where he occasionally spoke. But he did not put aside his experimental work altogether, even during vacation times. Elwood continued to experiment with his graphite crucibles at the local blacksmith shop in Sturbridge.[22]

Despite his poor grades and the fact that he was several years older than the average student, Haynes was popular with his classmates. When he returned to Worcester for his second year, he was elected president of the Middle Class for the fall term, entitling him to preside over the traditional "Half Way Through" banquet in January, 1880.[23] Moreover, Haynes improved steadily in his classroom performances and excelled not only in chemistry but also in German and freehand drawing. Mathematics, however, continued to plague him, as one of Haynes's classmates recalled many years later in describing the challenge of Sinclair's class in descriptive geometry. Success in this class, wrote William Lowe, depended "largely upon visualizing the

---

[19] Worcester County Free Institute of Industrial Science, *Eighth Annual Catalog*, pp. 23–24; Elwood Haynes to Bertha B. Lanterman, January 26, 1879, Haynes Papers.

[20] Elwood Haynes to Bertha B. Lanterman, June 29, 1879, Haynes Papers.

[21] George H. Haynes was a member of the Tech faculty for over forty years, serving for a while as acting president. His sister Emily was the school librarian from 1902 to 1942. Haynes authored numerous articles and monographs, including biographies of Charles Sumner and Charles G. Washburn and a history of the United States Senate. See Taylor, *Seventy Years of the Worcester Polytechnic Institute,* and Haynes (ed.), *Walter Haynes . . . and His Descendants.*

[22] George H. Haynes to Elwood Haynes, October 20, 1919, Haynes Papers.

[23] *Antenna,* pp. 17–19.

problem, and if you can do this, descriptive geometry is simple. . . . Haynes took the problems so seriously, was stumped, could not work them, actually cried he was so discouraged. . . . We used to call him 'slow.' "[24] Nevertheless, at year's end Haynes proudly reported to Bertha that his marks were "better than I have ever received . . . since I entered the school." True, the calculus grade for the second term was very low, but then calculus "is considerably like algebra."[25]

Elwood was not disposed to speak proudly of his improved grades to his critical sister, however, a teacher in Jay County, and was obliged in fact to defend his performance:

> I freely admit that my grades were rather low but I never received low marks at home. If you will take the trouble to examine the marks which I received while in high school you will find that there are few below 90%. Now the percents which I sent you are (with the exception of calculus) here considered fair if not *good,* and are just about the average if not a little above. If you take a teachers examination and multiply it by ten, (i.e. such as is ordinarily given by the county examiners) you will then form an approximation of what we have here. I would send you an examination paper but it would do no good as you could not probably understand what it meant. I would be willing to wager almost anything that, though Sum has been almost through college that he could not solve half of the examples which we had in the algebra examination at the end of the Junior Year.

He added that even his marks in German and English were lower than he expected, but this had not been caused by lack of study. "When I was attending the high school at home I only studied during the school hours; now I study almost all the time through the day and almost every night. I am no doubt naturally dull especially in some things but there is one consolation: when I have once learned a thing I can generally retain it." The family should understand, he concluded, "that there is some difference between getting high marks here and at the Portland schools."[26]

After his second year at Worcester Haynes spent part of the summer with his roommate of the first two years, Stephen Roberts of Birmingham, Connecticut, also a chemistry major. Before embarking on a week's camping trip, the two visited Birmingham, where Roberts's father and uncle were employed in a paper mill, and toured several manufacturing establishments in addition to the paper mill, much to Haynes's delight. He was able to indulge both his interest in manufacturing and in metallurgy as he visited the various industries. The young chemists were able to reciprocate their host's kindness by demonstrating for him "how to analyze bleaching powder, which is used in large quantities for bleaching the pulp from which paper is made." The same summer the two unemployed young men made up a quantity of artist's colors for sale in Worcester and earned a sizable return on their small investment. Although the demand was great, their business was hampered by the fact that only during vacation periods did they have enough time to manufacture the product.[27]

Haynes was impressed by the variety of manufacturing enterprises in Connecticut, but the factory that impressed him most was the Ansonia Brass

---

[24] Drake Manuscript, Haynes Papers.

[25] Elwood Haynes to Bertha B. Lanterman, July 3, 1880, *ibid.*

[26] Elwood Haynes to "Sister" [Josie Haynes], July 15, 1880, *ibid.*

[27] Elwood Haynes to Hilinda H. Haynes, August 12, 1880, *ibid.;* Drake Manuscript, *ibid.*

and Copper plant. The precision and chemistry involved in pin production fascinated him, and he described the process in minute detail to Bertha, who may have found the technical language somewhat baffling.[28] Earlier he had described his visit to a corset factory to her, wondering "where all the corsets went to as it seemed as though they could make enough in a week to supply a state at least."[29] The contrast between the volume of industry in cities like Birmingham and Worcester and Portland's two small manufacturing enterprises made a great impression on the small-town boy.

By the time Haynes began his senior year, he had made considerable improvement, both in learning how to study effectively and in preparing himself for a career. Despite his painfully hard work and relatively small success during the first two years, as Haynes pointed out, once he learned something it stayed with him. Moreover, the quiet, methodical Haynes had earned the respect and affection of his classmates. Only medium-sized at 5'7½" and 142 pounds, Haynes even subjected himself to occasional class sporting events, especially baseball.[30]

He also debated and sang with the glee club. He especially enjoyed singing but declined an invitation to join a light opera company for Gilbert and Sullivan's *H.M.S. Pinafore* because he could not spare the time. In the debating society he tested his views on politics and history. Coming from a strong Republican family and area he was obliged to consider the views of intelligent northern Democrats for perhaps the first time. This clash of opinion seems not to have altered Haynes's political or social views in any substantial way, but it did require him to re-examine and articulate his own views with greater care.[31] Occasionally he asked Bertha in Alabama for her observations on conditions in the South, seeking reinforcement for positions he took in debates on southern politics and the Negro. In an 1879 debate on whether fear or reward was the best incentive, Haynes argued, for example, that black men were naturally indolent and usually "would do no more work than was strictly necessary to sustain them." He wrote for Bertha's opinions on this issue and was delighted when she agreed with him.

Haynes similarly reflected widespread midwestern prejudices when he deplored the "increase of foreigners" in New England. Immigrants, he averred, were a threat to Yankee institutions and would lead to New England's utter decline. In Worcester Haynes reported that "the Irish vote together . . . almost to a man and when they *do* get the upper hand the free school system (which is as it were, the keystone of the power and intelligence of this people, of N.E.) will be short-lived indeed."[32] Despite his prejudices, however, Haynes was never a zealous racist or nativist; indeed, he strongly criticized the Ku Klux Klan in the 1910s and 1920s during the apex of its popularity in Indiana.

In his daily activities Haynes continued to follow long-established patterns during his years at Worcester. He attended Sunday school and church regularly—"almost always . . . once a week and usually twice"—and continued to promote the cause of temperance. For entertainment he attended public lectures and concerts frequently. In his personal life he coupled good study

[28] Elwood Haynes to Bertha B. Lanterman, August 23, 1880, *ibid.*

[29] *Ibid.*, July 27, 1880.

[30] *Antenna*, pp. 61–64.

[31] *Ibid.*, pp. 22–23.

[32] Elwood Haynes to Bertha B. Lanterman, April 20, 1879, October 31, 1880, April 21, 1881, Haynes Papers.

habits with thrift and economy. He filled his letters home with accounts of his efforts to save money on room, board, clothing, and books. For a time he cooked his own meals, mended his clothes, shared expensive science books with fellow students, and rarely bought new clothes. He had had a suit made when he left home, and after a year he reported that he would soon need a new pair of pants, because the original pair was getting frayed around the hem and had a hole in one knee, "or rather they did have until I sewed it up." Even so he assured his mother that his clothes looked "as well as some of the boys'."[33]

A reinterpretation in 1880 of the residency requirement eliminated recent arrivals to the county from the free tuition benefit, so that Haynes was required to pay the tuition fee for his last year. This extra expense was perhaps the reason for Haynes's rather unusual rooming accommodation that year. During 1880–1881 Haynes lived in the public library, where he served as night custodian and guard. This arrangement not only gave him an income during the school year, rare in itself since the school policy was to require all of a student's time for study, but it also gave him access at night to the library's collection of some fifty thousand volumes. Haynes believed it was "one of the best reference libraries in the country."[34]

During Haynes's senior year his class clashed with the school's administration on two occasions and thereby won a certain mild notoriety for the group in Tech history. The episodes created some difficulties for Haynes, since his loyalty to his classmates placed him in the uncomfortable position of being forced to stand up against his strong-willed father. In the first instance the senior class was celebrating the new year with a traditional bonfire and volleys from makeshift cannons. One of the cannons exploded and broke the school president's window. Thompson was irate, and the students were told, in Elwood's words, that "if we wished to fire powder we must go outside the school grounds, where the Faculty has no jurisdiction over us."[35]

This statement of supposed immunity from faculty control outside school property was tested a few weeks later when seventy-five members of the student body attended an Amherst College glee club concert, held in Worcester's Horticultural Hall. The students were dressed in identical stovepipe hats and carried canes, a combination which led irresistibly to some rowdiness, as hats were knocked off by canes. A faculty member rushed to the students in an attempt to quiet them, failed, and ordered one culprit to step outside immediately. The student refused and was suspended from school the following day. Almost the entire student body met to consider the situation and voted to petition Professor Thompson to reinstate the suspended student or to explain "why he was suspended while nothing was said to so many others who were similarly situated." Instead the student was required to sign a statement admitting his guilt. Seventy-five students, including Haynes, rose up in revolt. They sent resolutions to the faculty denouncing its action, and in retaliation the school refused to allow the petitioners to use the laboratories. Moreover, the administration threatened

---

[33] *Ibid.,* May 15, 1881; Elwood Haynes to Hilinda H. Haynes, November 15, 1879, *ibid.*

[34] *Eleventh Annual Catalog of the Worcester County Free Institute of Industrial Science,* p. 46; Elwood Haynes to Bertha B. Lanterman, December 12, 1880, Haynes Papers; Worcester County Free Institute of Industrial Science, *Eighth Annual Catalog,* pp. 28–29.

[35] Elwood Haynes to Hilinda H. Haynes, January 2, 1881, Haynes Papers; Elwood Haynes to Jacob M. Haynes, February 29, 1881, *ibid.*

to expel every student who refused to rescind his name from the petition.[36]

Haynes wrote to his father about the situation and the threat of his imminent expulsion. He announced that he could not in good conscience remove his signature "unless the school as a whole agree to do the same." In his own defense he pleaded that "Public sentiment as far as I can learn is with the students," but he warned the judge to expect a letter from the faculty "if I do not withdraw my name." He also suggested that his mother not be told of the crisis "as it may worry her."[37]

Eventually, after another exchange between students and faculty, the students backed down, and within a week of the episode the signatures all were withdrawn. But Haynes's father was understandably upset by the incident. Elwood remonstrated with him for his lack of confidence. The judge should know, Elwood wrote, "that I will not do anything which will bring disgrace nor dishonor upon any of my relatives nor friends." To reassure his father Elwood reported that everything was entirely back to normal two weeks after the episode, but he reasserted his conviction that the students had been right. "My conscience does not reproach me for anything I have done. . . . The only thing which troubles me in the least," he wrote, "is that you should feel so disturbed about the matter."[38]

Haynes overcame his disapproval of Professor Thompson's handling of the disciplinary action enough to continue working on his thesis topic under Thompson's direction. Thompson was not only a strong administrator, he was also a practicing chemist who consulted for a number of firms in Massachusetts. He specialized in analyzing city water supplies and beverages manufactured with those water supplies, especially beer. Fortunately for Haynes, Thompson was interested in metallurgy, and though not expert in that field he was willing to supervise Haynes's senior thesis.[39]

Haynes's topic was "The Effect of Tungsten upon Iron and Steel," an investigation he had initiated in Portland in about 1877 with only limited success because of inadequate equipment.[40] When Haynes announced his topic to Bertha, he teased, "Of course you will readily understand what the subject means; but if you do not you will not be more ignorant than most of my class mates and most of the Professors. I shall endeavor to explain the subject at some future time." The promised explanation came on May 15, 1881, when Haynes summarized his research topic as follows:

> *Carbon* is what is termed an allotropic element (i.e. one which exists in more than one form) and is found in nature in three distinct modifications, viz: Diamond, Charcoal and graphite. These substances though differing widely in their physical properties are chemically identical.
>
> When carbon combines with iron in various proportions it forms cast iron or steel according as the amount of carbon is large or small.
>
> In just what form the carbon exists in the iron is unknown though it always imparts hardness to that metal when caused to combine with it.
>
> But the subject of this thesis is the treatment of a steel which differs from what is commonly known by that name.
>
> The steel in question is a compound of *tungsten* and iron instead of carbon

---

[36] Elwood Haynes to Jacob M. Haynes, February 29, 1881, *ibid.*; student petition to the faculty, February 25, 1881, quoted in *Antenna,* p. 31.

[37] Elwood Haynes to Jacob M. Haynes, February 29, 1881, Haynes Papers.

[38] *Ibid.,* March 1, 13, 1881.

[39] Tymeson, *Two Towers,* pp. 31–32, 41; Richard G. Boone, *A History of Education in Indiana* (New York: D. Appleton and company, 1899), pp. 431–32.

[40] Elwood Haynes to C. M. Miller, December 29, 1920, Haynes Papers.

and iron. Metallic tungsten, which is obtained with difficulty, is a very heavy metal of a steel grey color and of sufficient hardness to scratch glass. The ores of this metal, though not so abundant as those of some of the more common metals, are found in sufficient abundance to enable the steel-maker to use them without seriously increasing the price of the steel containing this metal.

In manufacturing steel containing tungsten it is not necessary to obtain the metal itself; but if an ore of this metal such as wolframite is mixed with iron and the mixture fused the tungsten of the ore unites with the iron and forms a *"steel"* of varying properties depending upon the quality of the iron used and the percent of tungsten employed.[41]

This statement was perhaps an early draft of the thesis abstract Haynes read at the commencement exercises in June.

During the spring of 1881, Haynes worked diligently on his research project, without much direction from his professor. As the project developed, Haynes wanted to broaden the scope and study the effect of chromium, as well as tungsten, on iron and steel, but Thompson refused to allow this because chromium had not been mentioned in the original topic proposal. Perhaps Thompson wanted to avoid the superficial research which might have resulted in view of the pressure of time. When Haynes returned to the project many years later and did finally examine the effect of chromium on steel, he discovered that it produces stainlessness.[42] However, in 1881, limited to investigations of tungsten, Haynes was pleased with the results of his research. He was able to produce several small samples of tungsten steel and to test its qualities. He was able to make a few razors from his samples and presented one to his friend Professor Kimball, who reported years later that he had used it often with good results. The tungsten steel blade would take and retain a keen cutting edge, but it also had a tendency to tarnish and eventually to rust.

When Haynes's parents and one of his brothers arrived in Worcester in July, 1881, to attend Elwood's graduation, Mrs. Haynes found her son unchanged in his appearance, except for the customary student beard and mustache. The difference most apparent to his family was Elwood's New England accent. Haynes, for his part, decided that Hoosiers do indeed "drawl their words wonderfully." The Haynes family stayed with their friends the Kimballs while in Worcester, and Professor Kimball told the judge that he was greatly pleased with the young metallurgist's thesis, as well as with the razor he had recently received. Kimball assured the judge that Elwood had acquitted himself proudly during his years at Worcester.[43]

Haynes spoke fourteenth in a class of twenty-one in the graduation ceremonies, probably indicating his class standing; if so, he had made considerable improvement at the end of his college career. Of the forty-one students who had started with the Class of 1881, only twenty-two completed the course of study, and one of these did not graduate. The graduation ceremonies were also memorable for the ode Haynes composed for the class of 1881.[44]

---

[41] Elwood Haynes to Bertha B. Lanterman, February 20, May 15, 1881, *ibid.*

[42] Elwood Haynes to C. Clarence Poole, April 18, 1912, cited in Harshbarger, "Elwood Haynes: Scientist with a Social Conscience," p. 10. Poole, a Chicagoan, was Haynes's patent attorney at the time of the correspondence.

[43] Elwood Haynes to Bertha B. Lanterman, July 21, 1881, Haynes Papers; Hilinda H. Haynes to "Dear Folks at Home," June 29, 1881, *ibid.*

[44] Worcester County Free Institute of Industrial Science, *Twelfth Annual Catalog* (Worcester, 1882), pp. 32–33.

24

Elwood Haynes, class of 1881

Following commencement, the Haynes family moved on to Sturbridge for a few days' visit. They returned to Indiana via New York City and Washington, spending a day in each place. In Washington Haynes took pains to visit both the Patent Office, which the incipient inventor especially wanted to see, and the Capitol. The White House could not be visited because President Garfield was dying from an assassin's bullet.

At home the Portland *Weekly Sun* hailed Elwood's return in a regular news item:

Elwood Haynes, who has been absent three years acquiring an education at a Worcester, Massachusetts, college, finished his course and arrived home Friday morning. We are pleased to learn that Wood acquitted himself with honor as a student and stood among the foremost of his class. He has a future of great promise before him.[45]

Despite its trite and expected form, including the exaggeration about class standing, the prediction contained in the report was at best an understatement. Haynes's technical training at Worcester Free Institute had come to a happy end. He had suffered many disappointments and had had his ego trampled occasionally, but on the whole the experience was invaluable to him. He remained a proud and loyal alumnus of Worcester throughout his life; he cherished his college friendships and occasionally visited the school.

Haynes had acquired a respect for formal training, but his educational philosophy included a wholesome skepticism about the system. The important thing, he believed, was what one had learned, not the marks one received; and he knew, too, that education did not stop at graduation. Haynes indicated his independent spirit in a comment to his future wife written while researching his thesis: "Many of our eminent men, scientific as well as others, have had, for the most part, only Nature and experience for their teachers. I may be a little radical on this subject but what I say I believe." He concluded his remarks by quoting these lines: "Who never walks save where man's tracks makes no discoveries. Show me the man Who leaving God and Nature and himself Sits at the feet of masters, *Stuffs* his brains with Maxims, notions usages and rules And yields his fancy up to lead-strings And I shall see a man who never did a deed worth doing."[46]

These self-confident remarks reveal a person far from being a "plodder," not much good at either books or athletics. Although initially considered "slow," Haynes had struggled mightily to achieve a professional credential, the symbol of middle-class status expected and revered in his own family. Through the Worcester technical school the judge had found a way to enable his tinkering son to acquire an appropriate education and, hence, to take a place along with his siblings as a leader in the community. Elwood Haynes might have lived a useful life without his formal training at Worcester, but it would not have been a fully self-respecting one without the parental approval his education won for him.

---

[45] Portland *Weekly Sun,* July 15, 1881.

[46] Elwood Haynes to Bertha B. Lanterman, April 4, 1881, Haynes Papers.

Chapter 3

Professor Elwood Haynes

Haynes set about at once to find suitable employment when he returned to Portland in July, 1881. As a graduate of Worcester's technical institute, he offered unusual qualifications as a teacher. Consequently Will J. Hauck, the Jay County school superintendent, quickly tendered Haynes a position in his school system, at first in a small district school known as the "Hanlin school." As part of his special preparation for this post and in order to take the mandatory teacher's examination, Haynes attended the Jay County Teachers' Institute in August. His sister Josie, also a teacher in the local system, was there too, and the two Hayneses were elected secretary and recording secretary of the 1881 institute.

At the end of the brief session, when Haynes took the licensing examination administered by Superintendent Hauck, he scored 93 5/16ths percent, "not as high as it might have [been] but as good as I expected."[1] This qualified him for at least a two-year license.[2] Moreover, at many of the subsequent teachers' institutes held in Jay County during the next few years, Haynes was used as an instructor and lecturer on topics like "Chemical and philosophical experiments relating to the facts of practical life."[3] His first such labor came in October, 1881, when he was on the program of the institute for Wayne, Pike, and Noble townships.

In the meantime Haynes was learning firsthand the art of classroom teaching at Hanlin, some five miles south of Portland. For the first week or two, Haynes walked the distance twice a day, convening school at 9:00 AM and teaching until 4:30 PM. Early in October, however, he began to board "a little nearer" the school, which, he said, was in "a very good neighborhood and the people are generally pretty intelligent."[4] He had twenty-two pupils in

---

[1] Elwood Haynes to Bertha B. Lanterman, October 5, 1881, Haynes Papers.

[2] This is an assumption, based upon regulations published in 1884 by the Indiana State Board of Education, which required a general average of 70 percent, with no grade below 60 percent in any of the eight statutory branches of learning or the theory of teaching for the six-month license; 80 and 65 were the percentages required for a twelve-month license, 90 and 75 for a twenty-four-month, and 95 and 80 for a thirty-six-month license. See the Portland *Commercial*, January 11, 1884.

[3] *Ibid.*, November 3, 1881.

[4] Elwood Haynes to Bertha B. Lanterman, October 5, 1881, Haynes Papers. According to Reverend Hurd Allyn Drake, Haynes boarded with the John Prillaman family while at Hanlin. The Prillamans remembered the way Haynes looked after their youngsters as they walked to school

his school, ranging from six-year-olds to teenagers, and this initial experience of teaching proved mutually satisfactory. Haynes rather cautiously allowed after a full month had passed that "I find teaching pleasanter than being taught . . . ," and after another month he made a more definite judgment: "I like school teaching first rate and the more I teach the better I like it."[5] Haynes then compared his student days at Worcester with his present situation. "As far as work and worry are concerned," he told Bertha, "I should much rather teach than be taught at the WTI. School teaching was pictured to me by most of those who have had experience as something difficult and trying in the extreme. But as far as my experience has gone it is much easier than learning the difficult lessons in mathematics which we had in school. But I recognize the benefit of the drill received in mathematics for any problems in arithmetic which once seemed very hard are now plain almost at a glance."[6]

One suspects that because of some of his rather painful experiences as a student, Haynes was a kind and understanding teacher. This view is reinforced not only by Haynes's lifetime pattern of strong affection for children but also by the remarks of his former students. "Elwood was a dandy!" exclaimed one former pupil to Reverend Drake when asked about the young teacher. "He would come in a-whistling, then he would say, 'Let's sing!'; and we would sing 'What a Friend We Have in Jesus,' 'Throw out the Life-line,' and other religious songs. He would then read a chapter from the Bible, or just a Psalm, but would make no comment because that wasn't allowed. We would then pray the Lord's Prayer in concert and then Elwood would say, 'Now go to your lessons.' . . . I was old for that class but went to have Mr. Haynes. He mixed with us, he was just like us."[7] Other former students recalled his kindness, especially his gentle ways with the younger ones, and the fascinating chemical experiments he occasionally performed after school.

Haynes spent only part of the year at Hanlin; for the term which began in April, 1882, he was transferred to the Coulson district school, only two miles from Portland. He resumed living at home and walked to and from school daily, a task he found "only a pleasant exercise."[8] Before this term started, he used some of his earnings to finance a trip south. Bertha Lanterman met her beau in Chattanooga, Tennessee, for a brief reunion after their five-year separation. The probably anxious Haynes came down with a cold, and his first letter to Bertha afterwards carried apologies for being "stupid and dull" when they met.[9]

Again at Coulson Haynes enjoyed unusual success as a teacher, and he was well pleased with his choice of a profession, although he aspired to high school or even college teaching. One pupil at Coulson remembered Haynes as "pleasant but reserved. . . . There was nothing frivolous about 'Wood,'" and she also praised his ability to control the older boys, something his predecessors had found impossible.[10]

---

together and how he entertained their preschool children while Mrs. Prillaman prepared the evening meal. Drake Manuscript, *ibid.*

[5] Elwood Haynes to Bertha B. Lanterman, November 5, December 29, 1881, *ibid.*

[6] *Ibid.*, November 5, 1881.

[7] Quoted in Drake Manuscript, *ibid.*

[8] Elwood Haynes to Bertha B. Lanterman, April 15, 1882, *ibid.*

[9] *Ibid.*, April 8, 9, 1882. Harry Lanterman, Bertha's younger brother, recalled in 1948 a visit of Haynes to the Lanterman home in Alabama, but no mention of such a trip appears in the correspondence. See Powell, "History of Elwood Haynes," pp. 16–17.

[10] Drake Manuscript, Haynes Papers.

Just after beginning the April term, Haynes learned that his mentor, Professor Charles O. Thompson, had come to Terre Haute, Indiana, to implement industrialist Chauncey Rose's plans for a technical school. Haynes wrote immediately to Thompson seeking a place on the Rose Polytechnic Institute faculty and was most disappointed when Thompson replied that all the necessary appointments had been made. Thompson's assurances to Haynes that he would be considered when a demand for more instructors developed failed to console him, but he resolved to apply for the position of principal at Portland High School.[11] Haynes had scant hopes of being selected. "[W]e must not be discouraged by one failure but 'try again,'" he moralized after the Terre Haute rejection; as for the job as principal, at least "it will do no harm to make the application."[12]

In July Haynes received two job opportunities, both of which pleased him immensely. Somewhat to his surprise, the school board offered him the position as principal, an office that carried primarily teaching responsibilities. He was to have charge of the entire high school program, except for Latin and general history. These two subjects were taught by "Professor Caraway," the new county superintendent. For the balance of the program, Haynes managed to include substantial amounts of science, even a course in astronomy. He particularly enjoyed the latter because "it affords such a broad field for the imagination."[13]

Haynes's other offer came from a young educational entrepreneur, George Suman, a recent graduate of Otterbein College in Ohio with experience at the normal school in Valparaiso, Indiana. Suman arrived on the Portland scene in June, 1882, and immediately interested various community leaders, including Judge Jacob M. Haynes, in his plan to establish a teacher training school in Portland. Almost as quickly Suman offered the judge's son a position teaching physics and chemistry, "the two branches which, of all other," Haynes stated, "I would rather teach." Suman also told Haynes he could have the privilege of selecting the apparatus for these two departments. Greatly interested, Haynes responded to the invitation but wisely refrained from declining the offer as principal until the prospects for the normal school were determined. Haynes explained his offers and options in some detail to Bertha Lanterman, who still resided in Alabama. In what may have been a first and tentative marriage proposal, he suggested she might be interested "because you know these things may ere long concern us *both* if they do not already."[14]

The city of Portland welcomed Professor Suman with open arms. As the editor of the Portland *Commercial* pointed out, "this paper has urged for five years a permanent normal at Portland," and he rejoiced at the public spirit of those soliciting funds for the project. Nearly $1,500 had been raised already, and Judge Haynes, now retired from the bench and dabbling in real estate, had offered two and one half acres of centrally located land along Arch Street for the school. Only an additional $1,500 was needed to begin construction.[15] This sum was raised during the next month; on August 10, 1882, the paper proclaimed success for the campaign and stated, a bit over-

*Professor
Elwood Haynes*

29

[11] Elwood Haynes to Bertha B. Lanterman, April 24, May 15, 1889, *ibid.*

[12] *Ibid.*, May 15, 31, 1882.

[13] *Ibid.*, October 9, 1882.

[14] *Ibid.*, July 3, 1882.

[15] Portland *Commercial*, July 6, 1882; Hilinda H. Haynes to Calvin Haynes, February 26, 1883, Haynes Papers.

optimistically, that the school would "positively open" in the fall. Instead, it opened the following summer.

In the meantime, as had been the case for several years previously, temporary "normals" were conducted in Portland in the summertime. Haynes again attended and lectured to the group on "the atmosphere" early in June. This was Haynes's first experience before a large gathering and he reported feeling "considerable anxiety for the result. However, everything resulted very well and what was said seemed to be appreciated."[16] He found it difficult to study during the hot August days, but he charitably reported that "the recitations are full of interest and good work is being done."[17]

As soon as the normal sessions ended, the annual teachers' institute convened. Those few days were extremely busy ones for Haynes, as he attended the sessions, lectured once on chemistry to an audience of three hundred, and prepared to begin his new teaching duties at the high school. "I think I have never before felt such a pressing responsibility and corresponding incompetency, in my life," he despaired in a letter, but he was being uncharacteristically alarmist. He was to serve as Portland's principal for two years, as well as teach part-time at the new Normal, which eventually opened in June, 1883, and he excelled in both positions. As he recognized later, "it is not generally work but worry that injures people."[18]

When Haynes took over teaching duties in the high school, he found thirty pupils in his room. He expected two or three of them to graduate at the end of the year, as there were three seniors. Less than two months later, his room's enrollment was up to thirty-four, "about as many as I care to teach," and he was more enthusiastic than ever about his work. "No I do not think I shall become tired of teaching," he responded to a query and repeated "in fact, the more I teach the better I enjoy it." His confidence in himself and his school had been bolstered by a trip in September, 1882, to Richmond, which boasted one of the larger high schools in east central Indiana. Haynes believed that "we were doing about as good work in our own town as was done in Richmond, which conclusion was quite a consolation." He was also favorably impressed with the personnel and the "substantial air" of Richmond's Earlham College, where his brother Sumner had gone to college and where the Portland teachers had taken tea.[19]

Haynes was nevertheless looking forward with great eagerness to moving from the high school to the Normal in 1883. When Superintendent Caraway learned of this, he tried to persuade Haynes to remain at the high school and promised to seek an increase in pay for him by "at least one half. . . ." Haynes reluctantly declined, for he considered Caraway "a splendid man! and it is pleasant to teach with him as superintendent." That the community was equally pleased with its principal was indicated by a year-end newspaper report: "Mr. Haynes is quite a young teacher; but he is a thorough student, and his character and habits of life fit him in an eminent degree for successful instruction and school work. He enjoys the confidence and esteem of his pupils, all of whom are thoroughly imbued with the importance of securing an education."[20] The students also gave evidence of their respect

---

[16] Elwood Haynes to Bertha B. Lanterman, June 15, 1882, Haynes Papers.

[17] *Ibid.*, August 4, 1882.

[18] *Ibid.*, September 3, 1882, March 31, 1883.

[19] *Ibid.*, October 9, 29, 1882.

[20] Portland *Commercial*, December 31, 1882. This story stated that Haynes then had forty students in his care, twenty-one in the high school grades and nineteen in the "A grammar grade."

and admiration for their new teacher after the June graduation, when a delegation from high school presented their surprised and embarrassed principal with a silver watch and an autograph album. "I will never hold the somewhat popular opinion among teachers," Haynes averred, "that a teacher's work is never appreciated."[21]

Such community acceptance had its drawbacks. By January, 1883, Haynes had an enrollment of sixty-six in his room; more accustomed to his job, he said he liked it "almost as well as when I only had forty; though it keeps me pretty busy." Busy as he was, though, he became even busier when Portland's Eastern Indiana Normal School completed its two buildings in the spring and Haynes embarked upon double duties by assisting in the preparations for a June opening.

Four days after high school commencement in June, 1883, formal opening ceremonies were conducted at the Normal. Several hundred persons crowded the new lecture hall to hear Professor Suman speak and introduce his faculty. Much to Haynes's chagrin, Suman called upon each faculty member for impromptu remarks. Haynes was recorded as saying "he could hardly impress upon himself the fact that he was a teacher, as it had been so short a time since he had been a student." He later suggested to Professor Suman that it had been unfair to the teachers not to tell them they would be asked to speak, but Suman replied "that he had hired his teachers to work for him and he expected them to do whatever he asked them to."[22]

The school, located at Arch and Middle streets, consisted of two two-story buildings, one of which was a dormitory of approximately forty rooms owned and operated by Professor Suman and his brothers. The other structure housed the classrooms, laboratories, and offices. Approximately 110 students enrolled for the first term, about 40 more than expected, and the student body increased to 150 before the term ended; 130 enrolled for the second term, which began August 28. Soon it appeared that the normal school, Portland's "most prominent educational institution," would succeed. In the middle 1880s as many as 600 students were in attendance there, and the school, according to one Jay County historian, was "an admirable factor in the social development of the community. . . ."[23] Within five years, however, the Sumans were to abandon the institution, and subsequent attempts to revive it proved futile. The last effort to operate a normal school in Portland would come in 1898, after which the buildings were converted into private residences. Jay County teachers subsequently were trained elsewhere, eventually at Ball State Teachers College (now Ball State University) at nearby Muncie.

At the school's outset, however, the prospects were bright, and Haynes was pleased with the situation. He taught a variety of courses besides chemistry, including "advanced algebra, higher arithmetic, and Higher lessons in English & geometry, giving an hour to each recitation." He was also occupied the first summer in negotiations with the school board about the next year's arrangements at the high school. Much to Haynes's sorrow, a group of "democrats" had come onto the school board and had discharged Superintendent Caraway "on account of his politics." Haynes, however, was retained "at the same price with the privilege of teaching one class in the

---

[21] Elwood Haynes to Bertha B. Lanterman, June 10, 1883, Haynes Papers.

[22] Portland *Commercial*, June 7, 1883; Elwood Haynes to Bertha B. Lanterman, June 6, 1883, Haynes Papers.

[23] The writer continued that "it was long regretted that it [the normal school] could not make a permanent place for itself." *Biographical and Historical Record of Jay and Blackford Counties* (Chicago: The Lewis Publishing Co., 1887), p. 247; Jay, *History of Jay County*, I, 225.

32

Bertha B. Lanterman

Normal. . . ." A good Democrat was appointed as the new superintendent—"needless to say I don't like the change."[24]

A change he did like was the return in the summer of 1883 of the W. D. Lanterman family from Alabama. Bertha was now a grown woman of twenty-five, strong-willed and independent although usually shy and soft-spoken in groups. Although she had been separated from Haynes for six years, a special relationship between the two had developed nevertheless. Short and still slender, Bertha was neat, hard-working, and witty. She had taught for a while in Alabama and hoped to teach in Indiana before marrying and raising a family. Her father, frequently down on his luck, had been a farmer and handyman but took a job as clerk in a grocery upon returning to Portland. Later Lanterman opened his own butcher shop. Harry Lanterman,

---

[24] Elwood Haynes to Bertha B. Lanterman, June 10, July 25, 1883, Haynes Papers.

who was Bertha's brother and thirteen years her junior, remembered that Haynes became a frequent caller at the Lanterman home in the evenings, and Harry also recalled that he had taken an immediate liking to his sister's suitor. He remained close to Haynes and was a lifelong associate in all of his business undertakings. Unfortunately for the historical record, however, Bertha's return to Portland meant a hiatus in her long, revealing correspondence with Haynes until he left town again in 1884 for a year's study in Baltimore.

Consequently, very little is known or has been uncovered that directly reflects upon Haynes's first experience as a teacher at the Normal or upon his approach to his subjects there. Haynes's basic educational philosophy, however, can be seen by examining his participation in the annual Jay County teachers' institutes in 1883 and 1885. Indications of his pedagogical style and his theory of teaching emerge from the recording secretary's reports of the daily activities at the institute in 1883 and 1885, both published in the Portland newspapers at the close of the sessions.[25]

Jay County's 1883 institute included four faculty members from the Eastern Indiana Normal School on its instructional staff and a few outside professionals. For a session in arithmetic Haynes demonstrated an approach to the teaching of the metric system, explaining in particular the meaning of the prefixes of unit names. To a class on physiology, he urged the teachers to grasp a firm overview of the subject and maintained that if a general idea of physiology were learned at the beginning, then "the science as a whole will be easily and profitably studied."[26]

His other services involved additional mathematical sessions, with at least one in geometry and one in figuring interest. That he may still have had some difficulty here himself is indicated by the reporter's cryptic comment for Thursday afternoon: "The problem that was given the teachers before noon was discussed then, after which Mr. Haynes gave a demonstration with which most of the teachers agreed." Undoubtedly Haynes enjoyed most the scientific experiments he performed for the institute; on one occasion he melted a silver dime and demonstrated its composition to be 90 percent silver, 10 percent copper.[27]

Haynes's belief in the efficacy of experimentation, of learning by doing, was explicit in the 1885 institute, held shortly after Haynes had returned from a year of graduate study at Johns Hopkins University. He stressed that teachers should "first teach the thing, then the name of the thing." Definitions, he insisted, should not be the first thing taught "to young pupils," and he advocated a broad use of visual aids and actual experiments. To illustrate the point of "how useless" a study such as physiology is "without experiments," he read a number of physiology examination questions, followed by some actual answers given by students:

---

[25] Portland *Commercial*, April 14, 1887; Powell, "History of Elwood Haynes," pp. 16–17, 18. Powell interviewed Harry Lanterman on May 5, 1948. For some months prior to the Lanterman family's return to Indiana, Bertha made inquiries about a teaching position in the state. Haynes in April, 1882, sent her a book on the state teacher's examination, plus an institute manual containing a section he had written on chemistry. There is no evidence, however, that Bertha taught in Indiana as she had done in Alabama. See the Haynes-Lanterman correspondence, November, 1881–April, 1882, Haynes Papers.

[26] Portland *Commercial*, August 30, 1883. Haynes had divided this subject into six categories: bones, muscles, nerves, digestion, circulation, and respiration. It should also be noted that Haynes became a strong advocate of the United States' adoption of metric measurement, even testifying in favor of this before a congressional subcommittee in Washington, D. C., in 1921.

[27] *Ibid.*

Q. Describe the heart? A. It is a comical shaped bag.

Q. Mention some occupations considered injurious to health? A. Occupations which are injurious to health are carbonic acid gas, which is impure blood.

Q. Is a bootmakers trade injurious to health? A. Yes, very injurious, because the bootmakers press the boots against the thorax and therefore presses the thorax and it touches the heart, and if they do not die, they are crippled for life.

Q. Describe the process of digestion? A. When food is swallowed, it passes through the windpipe and the chyle passes up through the backbone and reaches the heart, where it meets the oxygen and is purified.

Q. What is said of the influence of climate and season on the amount of food to be taken? A. It should be well seasoned.[28]

Haynes concluded "We should always teach practical truths [and] Teach as much as possible by experiments."[29]

That Haynes was the most popular institute speaker in 1885 is clear from the report; that he was also one of the most respected is indicated by the attention given his suggestions by the institute secretary. Haynes's "practical way . . . in conducting recitations" was praised, as was the clarity of his lecture upon fermentation: "The subject was treated in a way so simple, that the whole audience could not fail to understand fully all that the speaker intended to illustrate. He showed by experiments all the chemical changes which take place in fermentation, and for this reason we believe that the entire subject was better understood, than if the lecture had been delivered without any experiments to accompany it."[30]

This topic too, of course, was related to one of Haynes's chief passions—the temperance movement. He strongly opposed drinking not only on moral and economic grounds but because of his understanding of chemistry and the way alcohol affected the human body. Haynes had resumed his support of the Jay County temperance movement immediately upon returning to Indiana in 1881, and he occasionally spoke and conducted experiments for small groups on this subject. His correspondence, indeed the entire Haynes family correspondence, is full of comments on the latest developments in the temperance field.

As the Jay County experience indicates, the educational system in the state of Indiana was undergoing an important series of changes in the 1870s and 1880s. Brave attempts were made by the state legislature, and by the state superintendents of public instruction, to upgrade the caliber of teachers and teaching, to improve school curricula and facilities, and to increase and regularize the length of the school term. In 1873, the legislature had replaced the county examiners with county superintendents and enlarged their powers. These officers virtually controlled education within their jurisdictions—they licensed and appointed the teachers, visited the schools, influenced the curriculum and textbook selections, and operated the county institutes. On another level, the average number of school days per year had been increased from 87 in 1868 to 120 in 1870, and this number averaged 131 for the next few years. Yet the range remained unacceptably broad, going from 86 days in Dubois County to 200 in Vanderburgh County. Jay County ranked near the bottom of the state in both the length of the school year (seventieth out of the 92 counties in 1878) and in average daily compensation to the teacher. Although there was considerable variation in the pay

---

[28] *Ibid.*, August 20, 1885.

[29] *Ibid.*

[30] *Ibid.*

scale in rural as opposed to urban areas—the state average for males was $1.93 per day, $1.72 per day for females—Jay County in 1878 had paid an average of $1.63 to its male teachers (ranking eighty-third in the state), and $1.48 to its female teachers (ranking seventy-fifth). With these figures as a standard, it is possible to evaluate Haynes's compensation. He received only $1.40 or $1.50 per day during his first year, approximately the same as laborers in Indiana were then receiving, and his pay during his two years as principal of Portland High School was $2.25 a day.[31]

During the summer of 1884 Haynes sat down and wrote a letter to Johns Hopkins University. He explained that he was a graduate of Worcester and that he wanted "to take a year's course in some good institution in order to make myself more proficient in organic chemistry and in one or two studies not taught at W." By then Haynes had saved enough money to finance "a partial course" at a graduate school.[32] His ultimate intentions were not spelled out exactly, but Haynes probably still planned to pursue a teaching career, either at the Portland Normal or elsewhere, and he wanted to upgrade his qualifications. Perhaps he expected eventually to hear from Professor Thompson in Terre Haute and wanted to improve his chances for a position there. It is clear too that Haynes wanted more training in chemical research also in order to carry on with his promising metallurgical studies of tungsten and chrome steel. He was admitted to the university.

September, 1884, found Haynes in Baltimore, following an uneventful journey eastward. In the last-minute rush for the train, Haynes had forgotten his Bible and his instruments, but his mother forwarded them. In all other respects, the twenty-seven-year-old scientist was prepared for his studies at one of the best, though one of the newest, universities in the country. Given his goals and aspirations at the time, Haynes again had made an excellent choice of institutions.

Although Johns Hopkins was even younger than Worcester, the two were similar in that they represented significant changes and improvements in American higher education. The Baltimore university had introduced European style graduate training, particularly the German seminar method, and it was already, in its first decade, an outstanding graduate school. The school's initial bequest had been large enough and it was well enough conceived in details to create almost an instantaneous university, complete with numerous graduate programs and a medical school. President Daniel C. Gilman, formerly the president of the University of California, had agreed to shoulder the burden of organizing the university.

Beginning in 1875, he assembled a faculty of international reputation before the first students were enrolled. Most significant for Haynes were Ira Remsen, a brilliant young American with a German Ph.D. in chemistry, and Henry Newell Martin, a twenty-eight-year-old assistant to Professor Thomas Huxley, with whom he had co-authored a successful textbook; both Remsen and Martin headed their respective departments and Haynes worked closely with them in 1884–1885. Haynes also studied conversational German with Professor Adolph Gerber. This required little work outside the classroom, but Haynes occasionally immersed himself in the subject. One Sunday he attended a German church in the morning, read a German novel in the

---

[31] Boone, *History of Education in Indiana*; Harshbarger, "Elwood Haynes: Scientist with a Social Conscience," p. 11.

[32] Quoted in Harshbarger, "Elwood Haynes: Scientist with a Social Conscience," p. 12. For a complete listing of the courses for which Haynes registered in 1884–1885 see *ibid.*, p. 13n.

afternoon, and afterwards took a stroll with Professor Gerber, conversing in German. Haynes reported that in the evening even his thoughts came to him in German.[33]

An outstanding new chemistry laboratory designed by Remsen was available to Haynes upon his arrival in Baltimore. The biology department also had its own building and laboratory, and both were fully equipped. When Haynes met Professor Remsen for the first time, he liked "his appearance very much." It was Remsen's daily practice to visit the laboratory and talk to each student.

Haynes found a place in the center city, near the university, where he received room and board for $5.00 a week. City noises disturbed him at first, but he soon grew accustomed to them, as he did to his new study routine. As a grown man he found Johns Hopkins a much more agreeable institution than the boy had found Worcester and soon came to consider Johns Hopkins University "about the best in the United States."[34]

Another of Baltimore's attractions was cousin Frank Haynes and his four children, whom Haynes frequently visited. He also found two other Worcester graduates enrolled in the university, and during his first week in school Alonzo Kimball, his former professor, arrived to attend a series of lectures by the brilliant William Thomson of the University of Glasgow. Men from all over the United States gathered to hear the Scotsman, later Lord Kelvin, deliver what President Gilman was to call "one of the most remarkable courses ever given in this University." The professor's topic was announced as "molecular physics," but he limited his remarks to the "wave theory of light."[35]

Haynes attended some of the lectures but found them difficult to comprehend. "Sir William is a very ordinary looking man, and has a very poor delivery," he wrote, "but there are few men in the world who can understand his lectures." Later in the year Haynes heard Lieutenant Adolphus Washington Greely, just back from an incredibly difficult and tragic three-year expedition to the Arctic.[36]

In many ways Haynes found his year in Baltimore exciting and interesting. He did not feel "driven" by his course of studies, as he had at Worcester, and he felt a great sense of accomplishment in all of his work. In the chemistry laboratory he perfected his technique in analyses of soils and clays and in preparing various metallic compounds. In his free time he qualified for the male glee club—"they were probably scarce of tenors," he explained—and he found a strange new political climate. Most of his fellow boarders were Democrats, and, during the heat of the presidential contest between Cleveland and Blaine, they rode Haynes hard about his Republican views. ". . . I

---

[33] *Ibid.*, p. 13n; Hilinda H. Haynes to Elwood Haynes, [October] 1, 1884, Elwood Haynes to parents, September 27, October 5, 1884, Haynes Papers. The Drake Manuscript, *ibid.*, contains the quotation about the day of studying German. A fine introduction to the origins and early years of Johns Hopkins University is John C. French, *A History of the University Founded by Johns Hopkins* (Baltimore: Johns Hopkins Press, 1946); see also Hugh Hawkins, *Pioneer: A History of the Johns Hopkins University, 1874–1889* (Ithaca, N.Y.: Cornell University Press, 1960).

[34] Elwood Haynes to parents, October 5, 1884, Haynes Papers.

[35] French, *History of the University*, p. 91. For a remarkably lucid and concise discussion of Kelvin's scientific contributions see also C. Watson, "William Thomson, Lord Kelvin (1824–1907)," in R. Harre (ed.), *Some Nineteenth Century British Scientists* (Oxford: Pergamon Press, 1969), pp. 96–153.

[36] Elwood Haynes to parents, October 5, 1884, March 8, 1885, Haynes Papers. For an account of Greely's arctic adventure, which saw his party of twenty-five reduced to six when rescue ships were delayed for two full years, see A. L. Todd, *Abandoned; The Story of the Greely Arctic Expedition, 1881–1884* (New York: McGraw-Hill, 1961).

defend myself as best I can," he wrote, "and try to answer their arguments against the Republican party. I must say, however, that they always treat me in a kind and gentlemanly way."[37]

Haynes also found time to tour manufacturing establishments in Baltimore. In October he accompanied a female cousin to a pottery works. "We saw it all," he wrote, "from the grinding and sifting of the clay to the baking and burning of the ware. . . . Strange to say nearly all of the work, except the grinding, is done by hand." Later he visited a copper works and a sulphuric acid plant, and he planned to make a more extensive tour of the Baltimore manufactories during the Christmas vacation. His plans changed, however, when he was invited by Professor Harmon N. Morse, Remsen's associate, to assist in investigating the atomic weight of aluminum, a topic of considerable importance at the time. For all its commonness today, in 1884 aluminum, "the silver made from clay," had only recently been discovered, and its economical extraction from the clay-like ore bauxite had not yet been developed. Haynes, excited by the potential significance of the project, was equally enthused by the Hopkins facilities and the opportunity to work closely with leading scientific researchers. "I had the entire laboratory at my disposal during most of the vacation," he marveled. "My expectations in regard to coming in contact with the principal men of the various departments have been fully realized."

He worked side by side with Morse for several days and felt highly complimented and a bit tired at the conclusion. "Never before have I done such searching and careful work on any subject," he observed.[38] Certainly this experience in the procedures of a significant research program proved invaluable to Haynes. He was to emulate it years later in lengthy searches between 1895 and 1901 and again between 1911 and 1915 for new types of metal alloys.

Haynes allowed himself a break from his labors in March and attended the inauguration of President Grover Cleveland. The long day began under leaden skies with a morning rail trip to Washington. Haynes and his companion, a redheaded Jewish fellow Hopkins student, were forced to stand for the entire ninety-minute trip, but they arrived in good spirits and were welcomed by the sun breaking through the clouds and shining down brilliantly during the noon ceremonies. Haynes reported the day's events to his family, employing his best literary style: "Directly in front of this platform stood a tremendous crowd of assembled thousands, each apparently eager to catch every syllable that was soon to fall from the lips of the nation's chief." He carried on in this vein for many paragraphs, describing the pomp and procession and his own encounter with some men from Portland with whom he exchanged news. Elwood and his friend ate their sack lunches on a balcony outside a Senate parlor room, enjoying the view, and then watched the inaugural parade while sitting on the platform from which the President had spoken earlier. They visited the Washington Monument and watched an enormous display of fireworks. On the way home on the train a ruefully chivalrous Elwood stood again when two young women entered the car, while his friend kept his seat and chatted with the girl in Elwood's place.

Haynes's experiences at Hopkins encouraged him to apply for a prestigious university fellowship to continue his graduate work and prepare himself

---

[37] Elwood Haynes to brother [Frank], December 10, 1884, Elwood Haynes to Mother, October 26, 1884, Haynes Papers.

[38] Elwood Haynes to parents, October 5, 1884, January 5, 1885, *ibid.*

for a career in research and college teaching. His application was unsuccessful, possibly because he did not complete the second term, leaving several weeks early in response to a family emergency. Years later a former classmate, Charles P. Palmer, told Haynes that the "Hopkins boys" knew he was "the best research worker of the bunch, and it was you who should have had one of those fellowships. However, Providence did more wisely, and made you what you are." Still, it must have been a blow to the aspiring researcher to be turned away from the advanced scientific work he most enjoyed and sent back to teach chemistry at the Portland normal school.

This blow came on the heels of the terrible news that his mother, the most supportive person in his life, was dead. Mrs. Haynes died on May 11, following a brief, eleven-day illness. She had lived in Portland since childhood, and had lived to see eight of her children, to whom she was wholly devoted, grow to young adulthood. Elwood arrived home from Baltimore in time for the funeral on May 14th. The Normal suspended classes—Judge Haynes was then president of its board of trustees—and the WCTU chapter in Portland later paid special tribute to the memory of Mrs. Haynes, one of its most faithful members.[39]

Haynes's Baltimore years thus came to a sad and sudden end. Because it was late in the term and no degree was involved, Haynes decided not to return to complete his year's work. Yet the memory of his days there and the impact of what he had learned at the university remained with him. As he informed one of the Baltimore Hayneses in 1921, it was the research work he did in Baltimore that led to the discoveries that later made him a rich man. Whether a fulltime career as a "pure" scientist would have offered him even greater opportunities than those he created on his own is an intriguing, and unanswerable, question.[40]

A week after Haynes returned to Portland he buried his grief for his mother and disappointment for his ambitions by getting ready for the next term.[41] Suman's offer to have Haynes head a chemistry department had been quickly accepted, and Haynes soon found himself back into an enjoyable routine. As noted earlier, he participated in the 1885 county institute and then settled down in September for his first and only year as a college professor.

His success as a teacher continued, and Haynes endeared himself to his students both because of his devotion to his subject and his interest in teaching. In the first published biography of Haynes, which appeared in the 1887 edition of a Jay County history, he was described as having given services "highly esteemed and appreciated by the students and faculty."[42]

Such feelings were mutual, and Haynes seemed firmly established as a teacher when his attention first focused upon the newly discovered natural gas in Portland. By inclination and training he was drawn to this intriguing substance, and before long he had become one of the eminent gas men in the state of Indiana. Laboriously, Elwood Haynes was searching for his place in the world, and the fortuitous discovery of natural gas in his own hometown provided the next opportunity to use his unusual talents.

---

[39] A brief obituary of Mrs. Haynes was carried in the Portland *Weekly Commercial*, May 14, 1885; see also *ibid.*, May 21, 1885.

[40] Elwood Haynes to Frances Haynes, November 8, 1921, Haynes Papers.

[41] Portland *Weekly Commercial*, May 21, 1885.

[42] *Biographical and Historical Record of Jay and Blackford Counties*, p. 525.

Chapter 4

A Premier Gas Man

When natural gas was discovered in Portland, Indiana, it set in motion a train of events which radically altered Elwood Haynes's life. His participation in the "gas boom" that hit first Jay County and then other counties in the state led to his abandonment of teaching for the business world.[1] And this step led in turn to his early searches for a mechanically-operated road vehicle and to a nearly continuous search during the remainder of his life for improved industrial and domestic alloys. Haynes's career as a scientist and inventor was inaugurated, paradoxically, when he left the school laboratory for a gas company office.

Natural gas had a strong impact on Indiana's economic development. In just a matter of months after the strike in Jay County in April, 1886, gas was discovered throughout an arc of counties extending from the Ohio state line between Richmond and Fort Wayne westward and southwestward to Howard, Tipton, and Hamilton counties. The Hoosier cities most advantageously located to benefit from the gas literally beneath their feet were Muncie, Marion, Anderson, Kokomo, and scores of nearby smaller villages. In September, 1886, important gas strikes were made at Kokomo in Howard County and Eaton in Delaware County (the latter an 1876 well redrilled), and for the next ten years strikes occurred at frequent intervals. The gas, contained in the Trenton limestone underlying a nineteen-county area northeast of Indianapolis, lay approximately nine hundred to a thousand feet below the surface.[2] The initial rock pressure was more than 320 pounds per square

---

[1] The authority for the statement crediting Portland with the first commercially drilled gas well is Haynes himself, in the chapter he contributed to the 1887 history of Jay County. He alluded to the fact that "one frequently hears of gas being discovered in Indiana before it was discovered in Portland; but in every instance thus referred to, when the bottom truth is ascertained, it will be found that the gas was either shale gas, discovered accidentally, not used, or something else, still leaving to Portland the credit of first purposely drilling for gas to be utilized." Elwood Haynes, "Natural Gas," *Biographical and Historical Record of Jay and Blackford Counties,* I, 223. Nor did he change his views after many years in the gas business; in 1896 Haynes chided the citizens of Portland for permitting the Delaware County community of Eaton to claim priority in wells without challenge. Portland *Sun,* July 24, 1896, quoted in Harshbarger, "Elwood Haynes: Scientist with a Social Conscience," p. 16n.

[2] The "Gas Belt" covered an area of 3,750 square miles in parts of nineteen counties. The chief gas-producing counties were Blackford, Grant, Howard, Delaware, Hamilton, Madison, Hancock, Henry, Randolph, Rush, and Tipton, but gas was also found in Adams, Decatur, Jay, Marion, Shelby, Wabash, Wayne, and Wells. Phillips, *Indiana in Transition,* pp. 192–93. See also Phillips's map of the Indiana natural gas field, *ibid.,* p. 195.

inch (psi), but the pressure steadily declined as the field was exploited. As exasperated manufacturers would point out in 1900 in an effort to conserve the fuel, the gas field was "single, continuous, connected, and limited," and it was in dire danger of complete exhaustion unless user practices changed.[3] By 1900, however, it was already too late for such warnings, and the gas boom was over less than two decades after it began.

Within these two decades, however, the widespread and virtually unlimited use of natural gas led to a remarkable spurt of growth in the state's economy in the 1880s and 1890s. As the competition to attract industries stiffened, some communities offered prospective manufacturers access both to free gas and to free factory sites. The initial results delighted boosters. As historian Clifton J. Phillips has pointed out, the gas belt was almost immediately transformed into a "scene of intensive industrial activity," as scores of eastern manufacturers built plants to manufacture glass (e.g., the Ball brothers), wire, tinplate, strawboard, and other products. New towns, such as Gas City, were founded while older communities doubled and redoubled in size, and real estate values, both in the city and the countryside, rose rapidly. In 1890, the

> Department of Statistics calculated that 162 factories capitalized at nearly $10,000,000 had been located in the Gas Belt since the first strike, creating more than ten thousand jobs. Three years later it was estimated that the number of factories built in Indiana as a direct result of the discovery and development of natural gas was 'not less than 300.'[4]

In addition to industrial use, natural gas was employed then as now for domestic heating and lighting, to replace wood and coal stoves, candles, and kerosene lamps. The charges at first consisted of a flat annual rate based upon the number of outlets, or burners, in each home, not the amount of gas consumed.

While the first Jay County well was being drilled in a northern section of Portland in April, 1886, Haynes was a frequent visitor to the site. He offered his services to the drillers and was soon busy analyzing soil samples and constructing tables showing the underlying strata. On April 14, just six days after the drilling began, the drill became stuck only one hundred feet down, but a local merchant, B. F. Fulton, who boasted he could "do anything he ever saw done," improvised a sand pump with some local assistance and freed the drill in a few days. On April 28, 1886, a vein of shale gas was hit about seven hundred feet down, touching off a large, impromptu celebration.[5]

When the drilling resumed, indecision and confusion led to a number of mistakes. Despite the advice of the drillers to stop at 1,150 feet, where a small oil vein was found, the company managers insisted upon going deeper. Finally, at 1,650 feet, all agreed not to go farther; instead, they decided to "shoot" the well as close as possible to the place where oil had been found. The well was plugged, and nitroglycerine was lowered into it. A specialist

---

[3] *Manufacturers Gas and Oil Company* et al. v. *The Indiana Natural Gas and Oil Company*, 57 Northeastern Reporter 912 (1900).

[4] Phillips, *Indiana in Transition*, p. 194.

[5] Portland *Commercial*, April 29, 1886. This account concluded with a geologic report by "E. Haynes, Normal School." As indicated earlier the first well in Jay County was drilled by a company formally organized in March, 1886. Two Portland artisans, H. S. "Hank" Sees and William N. Current, had raised money by subscription to finance the project. The drilling contract was granted to Baxter & Porter of Lima, Ohio. *Ibid.*, March 17, 1887.

hired for the delicate task placed forty-five quarts of the explosive, topped by a percussion cap, in the well, and then dropped a "go-devil," a pointed metal rod, onto the containers. After a few seconds a sharp crack was heard, followed by a rumbling noise and then an outpouring of water, crushed rocks, and pieces of equipment, which lasted for several seconds.[6] The "shot," which took place on May 29, only temporarily increased the flow of gas; gradually the well filled with salt water to within two hundred feet of the surface and hardly enough gas remained "to light one jet."[7]

Despite the obvious disappointment with the "dry" well, there were encouraging aspects to this failure. "No. 1" served as a useful test well, giving drillers "a correct knowledge of the formations in this field, as Prof. Haynes kept an accurate record and analyzed every variation in the stone." He had also refined some of the oil discovered and declared that it was excellent.[8] Consequently, no Portlander interested in the project considered his investment fruitless or censured the inexperienced company managers. Instead they raised additional money to put down a second well in the fall of 1886.

In the interim Haynes took it upon himself to learn all that he could about natural gas operations, both in field and office management. In addition to these efforts his teaching responsibilities were quite heavy during the spring of 1886, and he frequently spoke to student groups on the weekends. On May 20, combining his two occupations, he discussed "The Gas Well" he had studied so carefully in a talk to the Normal's Philodicean Society. He concluded with the cryptic remark that any additional information they might want would be found "in a big book," evidently a reference to Haynes's chapter on "Natural Gas" in the forthcoming county history. A week later Haynes spoke to the Jay County Teachers' Association, this time lecturing on "Chaucer's Age and the Present Compared."[9] Apparently, however, Haynes did not teach during the summer of 1886; instead he began his intensive investigation of the gas business by visiting the gas fields in Ohio near Findlay and Lima. Upon his return, he delivered a well-received public lecture about his findings. It was largely upon Haynes's recommendation that the money was raised for drilling the second well.

This well, northeast of the first one and just beyond the corporate limits of Portland, was drilled by another experienced Lima, Ohio, driller, Jack Robinson. It came in on October 21, after three weeks of work, with impressive results. Headlines in the Portland newspaper proudly announced the strike: "Gas At Last.—The Bowels of the Earth Successfully Tapped, and Made to 'Come Down Liberally' in Behalf of the Demands of the Energetic and Plucky

---

[6] Haynes, "Natural Gas," *Biographical and Historical Record of Jay and Blackford Counties,* I, 220. Haynes pointed out in describing the "shooting" process that its purpose was to disintegrate the Trenton rock and, "by thus increasing the wall surface and creating crevices, correspondingly increase the flow of gas." *Ibid.* See also Harold F. Williamson and Arnold R. Daum, *The American Petroleum Industry: The Age of Illumination, 1859–1899* (Evanston, Ill.: Northwestern University Press, 1959), pp. 149–56.

[7] Portland *Commercial,* March 17, 1887.

[8] *Ibid.,* May 20, April 29, 1886. Substantial parts of the county history were preprinted in a special edition of the *Commercial* on March 17, 1887, which Haynes helped to edit. The lead article featured a review of Portland's natural gas developments during the previous year with engravings of portraits of the men prominently involved in the story, i.e., Sees, Current, and "Prof. Haynes." Other illustrations depicted the first wells, showing the derricks and the flaming gas.

[9] *Ibid.,* May 20, 1886. This issue also carried the notice of the forthcoming lecture at the teachers' meeting.

Citizens of the Most Enterprising and Prosperous Little City in Eastern Indiana."[10]

A controversy arose immediately over the quality, quantity, and utility of the gas. Haynes immodestly explained a few months later that

> Then it was that the services of one of Portland's most thoroughly educated and brainy young men proved of inestimable value to the city. Every one could see there was a large flow of gas; but was it worth piping, with the well forty rods from the corporation, and how many stoves would it heat or jets light? These were important questions, . . . Only one person could give the desired information, and that was Professor Elwood Haynes.[11]

By capping the well and measuring the rate of increase in pressure, Haynes was able to estimate the well's capacity (100,000 cubic feet a day) and the number of stoves it would serve. Then, by his own testimony, he "solicited the citizens to organize a company to pipe the city and utilize the gas. The people had confidence in the correctness of his tests and estimates, and a company was soon organized."[12]

The Portland Natural Gas and Oil Company was incorporated in November, 1886. Capitalized at $20,000, with provisions for increasing that amount, the initial holders of the $100 shares included Judge Jacob M. Haynes (10), Charles C. Cartwright (10), and Elwood Haynes (5), no stockholder having more than ten shares.[13] The stated purpose of the company was "to conduct the business of mining for oil and gas and furnishing the same for propelling machinery and for heating and lighting purposes," and among its officers was Elwood Haynes, superintendent. Haynes was delegated the task of actively managing the company. He resigned from Portland Normal and drew up preliminary plans for piping the city.[14]

The new company first purchased well number two from the bankrupt Eureka Company, which had expended all of its funds in drilling the well. Then the gas company planned to drill at least six other wells and contracted to purchase pipes and equipment. The city council granted permission to install mains along city streets, and the company proceeded at once with drilling and piping. Haynes carefully oversaw all the operations, particularly the drilling of the third well, which he watched "with an 'eagle eye,' analyzing the formations frequently."[15] This well, completed in February, 1887, proved to be an extremely good one. The local paper with pardonable pride called it "the best in the state—a gusher," with "enough gas for the dwellings, business rooms, mills and factories" of Portland. When the drill had pierced the Trenton rock initially, the gas had rushed out with such force "that a number of anxious lookers-on imagined there was an earth-

---

[10] *Ibid.*, October 28, 1886, as quoted in the issue for March 17, 1887; Haynes, "Natural Gas," *Biographical and Historical Record of Jay and Blackford Counties,* I, 220–21.

[11] Haynes, "Natural Gas," *Biographical and Historical Record of Jay and Blackford Counties,* I, 221. This section was repeated in the newspaper account on March 17, 1887.

[12] *Ibid.*

[13] Articles of Association, Portland Natural Gas & Oil Company, Archives Division, Indiana State Library, Indianapolis. The capital stock was increased to $40,000 in 1887 and to $70,000 in 1889.

[14] There is no record of exactly when Haynes resigned from the Normal. The newspaper account indicates that he did so "as soon as the Company was organized," but it is unlikely that he waited until late November, 1886, when it was formally organized. Portland *Commercial,* March 17, 1887; Haynes, "Autobiography," Haynes Papers.

[15] Portland *Commercial,* February 10, 1887, quoted in *ibid.,* March 17, 1887.

quake," and when it was piped outside the derrick and ignited, "the blaze leaped forth from 20 to 40 feet." Again, thousands of Jay County citizens journeyed to the well to view the magnificent sight.[16]

By this time, considerable progress had been made in providing service to individual houses and businesses. The same issue of the newspaper that reported the strike at the third well contained other stories about the popularity of "turning on the gas" and listed numerous customers of the Portland company. Between twenty-five and fifty "plumbers and laborers" were busy installing the "mixers" (burners) and jets.[17] Free gas to the city building and all the churches had already been provided, and a month later the Portland *Commercial* claimed to be the first newspaper "printed in Indiana with natural gas."[18] Haynes estimated that by April, 1887, when five miles of main pipe had been laid, that 400 stoves, 500 jets, and 50 large torches or street lamps were being supplied by wells two and three, with more wells coming. By then at least two other gas companies had been organized in Portland.[19]

The newspaper's glowing report on the history and prospects of natural gas in Jay County concluded with an article by Haynes on the subject, again an extract from his chapter for the county history. It contained a clear statement upon the geology and chemistry of natural gas. Haynes was particularly impressed with the balance between the carbon and the hydrogen in the Portland gas, which resulted in a product that "not only yields great heat, but affords an excellent light which is remarkably free from smoke." As he pointed out, natural gas usually affords great heat but not good light, "since it contains a large amount of hydrogen." He also remarked on the relative purity of the gas, the trace of sulphur it contained being actually a "valuable property" which would permit its ready detection in a room. Haynes wisely concluded his remarks with a plea for sensible and economical use of this "valuable fuel," the total quantity of which was unknown. "Let us not waste it," he cautioned, "by ignorance of its use nor carelessness in its management. . . ."[20]

At the time Haynes was writing these comments, the natural gas boom in the state was in full swing. "The interest in natural gas is well-nigh universal," exclaimed the Indianapolis *News* in April, 1886. "Gentlemen discuss the prospects on the streets, at the lunch-rooms, in business hours in offices, and even at prayer meetings and all entertainments. . . . It's a poor town that can't muster enough stock for a gas company just now." Muncie, in Delaware County, boasted of seven producing wells by June, 1887, with at least that many companies organized in the county. In Howard County the movement to organize a drilling company had begun in March, 1886; gas was struck in October, touching off a boom in that section of the state.[21] Within months a very substantial field had been located there and its exploitation was begun. In all, some 5,400 gas wells were opened in the state of Indiana by 1898.

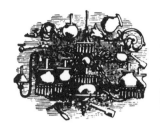

A Premier Gas Man

---

[16]*Ibid.*

[17]*Ibid.*

[18]*Ibid.*, March 17, 1887. The editor claimed this made "our devil . . . the happiest juvenile in the land."

[19]Haynes, "Natural Gas," *Biographical and Historical Record of Jay and Blackford Counties*, I, 222–23.

[20]Portland *Commercial*, March 17, 1887.

[21]Indianapolis *News*, April 28, 1887; Frank D. Haimbaugh (ed.), *History of Delaware County, Indiana* (2 volumes. Indianapolis: Historical Publishing Company, 1924), I, 383–86; Mrs. John F. Richardson, "Discovery of Natural Gas at Kokomo," in *Indiana Magazine of History*, LIV (1958), 279–80.

The initial Howard County strike was recalled in a 1915 newspaper article:

In less than an hour, the news that gas had been struck, had traveled to every home in town. . . . At the well, people became hushed in the presence of the mystery they found there, and stood with tense faces while the old driller, a veteran from the Pennsylvania field, told how gas had been struck and that the flow was of sufficient strength to insure that Kokomo was in a field abundantly supplied with the fuel. The quiet of the little country town was replaced with feverish activity. Two or three more gas companies were organized within a week. Steps were taken to pipe the gas from the one well into the business district. Real estate values began to soar. Talk of factories filled the air. The gas was going to bring to Kokomo untold riches. All through winter and spring things boomed. Early in the spring the factories began to arrive. The first was a window glass plant. . . . The next was the straw board mill. . . .[22]

This proved to be a much more substantial field than the one in Jay County. It was, in fact, the greater abundance of gas in the Kokomo area that would draw Haynes there in the 1890s.

Haynes's involvement in the Indiana "gas boom" made him part of one of the most important developments in the state's history. He worked long and hard to build and operate the Portland gas utility, and in so doing he established one of the finest municipal plants in the state. The fact that he "frequently works till midnight looking after the interest of the company" was duly noted in the press.[23] There had been countless problems to overcome, the major one being to obtain an adequate supply of gas. The wells in the immediate Portland area proved weak and small and had to be supplemented. Additional gas was located in the Pennville-Camden area, several miles outside of Portland, and pipelines from wells there to the Portland mains had to be constructed. Haynes supervised not only the drilling operations and the pipeline construction, but also the home and business installations. All of this required a great deal of travel over the heavy, sandy roads of Jay County, particularly those between Portland and Pennville, some ten miles apart. It was at this time that Haynes first conceived the idea of building a self-propelled "road vehicle." He was concerned less about speed or the time required to travel by horse and buggy than about the terrific strains this placed upon his horses, a function both of the distances and the long hours involved. Haynes's inherent sympathy for animals, evident since his early childhood, led to his initial thoughts about the "horseless carriage," but he was much too busy in the late 1880s to give serious attention to the idea.[24]

His more immediate problems concerned acquiring or designing the proper equipment for the gas business and protecting it from vandals. The high field pressure of the gas had to be reduced from several hundred pounds psi to only a few ounces in order to use it commercially; this was accomplished by regulators. Malfunctions were extremely hazardous. For years Haynes slept with a self-designed alarm at his headboard, set to go off whenever the gas pressure in the city changed two-tenths of a pound or more. Occasionally he was called out to supervise the repair of breaks

---

[22] Kokomo *Dispatch*, September 19, 1915, quoted in Powell, "History of Elwood Haynes," p. 30.

[23] Portland *Commercial*, March 3, 1887.

[24] Haynes, "Autobiography," Haynes Papers; Jacob Piatt Dunn, *Indiana and Indianans: A History of Aboriginal and Territorial Indiana and the Century of Statehood* (5 volumes. Chicago and New York: The American Historical Society, 1919), III, 1216–17.

in the line or to repack a leaking well. On other occasions he was required to remedy acts of vandalism, such as the instance in April, 1887, when a well was shut off. The pressure in the well increased enough to blow out the packing and raise the casing by ten feet. When Haynes reached the scene and relieved the pressure, the casing dropped down suddenly and snapped off its "T" connector, which allowed the casing to sink into the well. The repair crew was obliged to "fish" for the casing in order to restore it to its proper place before the well could be repacked. "Supt. Haynes,"˙announced the newspaper, "says he has frequently been put to considerable bother by meddlesome people, and that it must be stopped." Haynes estimated the company's loss in this incident at between $150 and $200 and proceeded to offer a reward "for information in regard to parties meddling with the gas, street posts, mains, regulators, or any other property belonging to the company."[25]

In other ways, too, Haynes demonstrated considerable ingenuity in his work. He invented a meter to measure the flow of gas in various sized pipes and at variable pressures (1886) and an "automatic gas regulator" or thermostat (1887). The only available contemporary description of the thermostat comes from a reporter's account, happily a rather detailed one. The regulator consisted of

a lever connected with one of two metal cups, in size we should judge, about two-thirds of a pint, the top cup or receiver being inverted and slightly smaller than the bottom one into which it fits rather loosely; the top of the upper cup or receiver is attached by a cord to the lever which regulates the supply of gas to the stove.

The lower cup was filled with a fluid, "the composition of which is a secret known only to the inventor," so that temperature changes caused "an expansion or contraction of its content, thus raising or lowering the lever to suit the requirements. Its construction is novel and simple and it works to perfection. He will get it patented."[26] Haynes later recalled, however, that his patent application was delayed and "another appeared before it was granted."[27] Haynes did use his thermostat to regulate the temperature in his own home for several years.

Haynes's new position in life as the manager of a prosperous public utility may have inspired him at last to establish his own household—or perhaps it was his father's example, since the judge remarried in June of 1887. For whatever reason, at age thirty and after a friendship of ten years, Elwood Haynes married Bertha Lanterman on October 21, 1887. A strong woman, pleasant and matronly, Bertha possessed a quiet wit and an accommodating spirit, although she could be stubbornly independent upon occasion. She made Haynes an excellent wife and companion, reinforcing both his reli-

---

[25] Portland *Commercial*, April 21, April 28, 1887. For a report on three breaks in the line between Camden and Portland in February, 1889, see *ibid.*, March 1, 1889. Haynes, awakened by his special alarm, was up and on his way to Camden at 3:30 AM. By 9:00 PM two breaks had been repaired; a third break occurred twelve hours later. Haynes theorized that they were caused by the rising and falling of the ground and proposed to install a high pressure regulator at Camden to reduce the pressure on all the mains and the likelihood of a recurrence.

[26] Portland *Jay County Bazoo*, April 1, 1887. In 1924 Haynes commented in an interview on his "gasometer," which had been made by the Portland tinsmith from Haynes's plans and specifications. " 'He made a good instrument, too,' the inventor chuckled, 'but he didn't know what it was.' " Quoted in Kokomo *Daily Tribune*, April 14, 1925.

[27] Quoted in Harshbarger, "Elwood Haynes: Scientist with a Social Conscience," p. 19.

This Certifies

That Elwood Haynes. of Portland. State of Indiana.

Bertha B. Lanterman. of Portland. State of Indiana.

What therefore GOD hath joined together let not man put asunder.

It is not good that the man should be alone Gen 2.18

I will make him an help meet for him. Gen 2.18

WERE UNITED IN

MARRIAGE

By Me

According to the Ordinance of GOD and the Laws of the State of Indiana, at Portland, on the Twenty First day of October, in the year of OUR LORD One Thousand Eight Hundred and Eighty Seven.

J. Iley. Indiana. Minister.

Witnesses

Marriage is honorable in all. Heb. 13. 4

HOLY BIBLE

Copyrighted by David M. Crocker 1882

gious and his temperance views. A capable musician, Bertha frequently served as church organist in Portland and later in Kokomo, and she worked closely with various women's organizations in the church. Judging from later newspaper reports, the wedding was not announced publicly and caught their friends by surprise. The Portland *Sun* announced on November 4 that the two "were quietly married last week at the home of the bride's parents, and left on their wedding tour before many of their friends were 'on to the racket.'" After a weekend honeymoon trip to Cincinnati, the couple returned to Portland where Elwood faced the growing fuel shortage of 1887 – 1888 and the first public criticism of his management of the gas company.[28]

Although Haynes's management of company affairs had generally been applauded as expert and conscientious, two Portland hardware merchants named Fulton strongly objected to the gas company's attempt to monopolize the installation of gas pipes and mixers and to Haynes's claim that only the gas company could install this equipment properly. The Fulton Brothers raged in the Portland newspaper in November and December, 1887, against "the scientific (?) knowall who holds down the Superintendent's chair" and about "the Portland N. G. Company (which probably stands for No Good)."[29] Haynes had placed a continuous notice in the newspaper, announcing that

Persons wishing plumbing put in their buildings should give their orders to the Gas Co. at once. All work done by the Company will be under the direction of an expert workman, who has had a great deal of experience in the business. We will give you all necessary information concerning the size of pipe the building requires, cost, &c. It is very important that the pipe should be the proper size, to insure good service. We guarantee satisfaction in every respect. Elwood Haynes, Supt.[30]

Haynes's competitors charged that he had made false statements about installation and equipment provided by them, and they threatened legal action against him. Moreover, the Fulton Brothers claimed that problems in gas service resulted nine times out of ten from an inadequate gas supply, caused in turn by inefficient gas plant management.[31]

This attack on Haynes did not suffice to shut off the offensive newspaper notice, so the Fulton Brothers struck again a few weeks later. Pointing out that they had equipped more than three hundred houses and businesses with gas fixtures, they ridiculed both Haynes's reputation as "the only and infallible natural gas authority in Eastern Indiana" and the claim that only his company had the "great intelligence" to install gas equipment. They challenged Haynes's company to prove that their work measured up on the average to that of the Fulton Brothers.[32]

Neither Haynes nor other members of the gas company responded directly to the public attacks, which were in fact symptomatic of the already declining gas supplies in the immediate vicinity of Portland.[33] Instead the

---

[28] Portland *Sun,* November 4, 1887; Portland *Commercial,* October 27, 1887; Portland *Semi-Weekly Sun,* February 28, 1903.

[29] Portland *Commercial,* November 24, December 15, 1887.

[30] *Ibid.,* February 24, 1887. This notice had been printed repeatedly in the paper.

[31] *Ibid.,* November 24, 1887.

[32] *Ibid.,* December 15, 1887.

[33] Expressions of concern about the early exhaustion of the city's wells even cropped up in a local department store's advertisements: "There may be some doubt as to the quantity of gas Portland has, but there is none as to the quantity and quality of Holiday goods you can find at Sebring Bros." *Ibid.,* December 29, 1887.

company concentrated on bringing new, ever more distant wells into their system, and Haynes retained the generally good image he had created as a gas expert. In the spring of 1889, the young new editor of the Portland *Commercial* reported on the gas company's recent progress and Haynes's management in glowing terms. Calling at the gas office one Monday morning to pay his bill, "a habit we have to keep the gas on," Editor G. M. Holloway interviewed Haynes, "the clever 'High Pressure Regulator' of the Gas Company." Haynes reported that there had been no complaints at all about service during the previous winter's cold weather. Three breaks in the line in late February had come during good weather and had been quickly repaired. Twenty-two miles of three-, four-, and six-inch mains were bringing gas into Portland, providing an adequate supply. With five regulators situated throughout the city, a relatively constant pressure was maintained which made night usage of the gas "absolutely safe." Holloway concluded that Portland's gas plant was "second to none in Indiana" and that the city was rightfully "proud of the gas company and its service."[34]

The previous winter the Hayneses had been eagerly looking forward to the birth of their first child. Haynes was a fatherly man and fond of children; he was delighted when his daughter Marie Firth Haynes was born January 28, 1889. The community welcomed the new addition with a humorous birth announcement in the Portland *Sun*:

> Professor Elwood Haynes, the gas company's clever superintendent, enjoys a wide reputation as an expert chemist, and since the oil and gas boom reached Indiana his skill has been frequently invoked to analyze and test specimens of rock and minerals taken from every strata from the azoic age up. But the prettiest specimen that has been placed in his hands was left at his residence Monday morning, and he became so interested in his analysis that he stayed away from the gas office all day, and extended his tests on till the small hours of the morning before mastering the rarest subject ever placed in his keeping. Tuesday afternoon the SUN met Elwood on the street. He looked pale, careworn and yet smiling, and when we asked the result of his analysis he pulled us to the curb-stone and whispered: "*A mighty fine little girl!* Lung pressure six pounds to the square inch, and I'm on my way to the office to get a regulator for it."[35]

The teasing quickly turned to condolences, however, for the infant daughter died within a few months, as did their second child, a son born a little over a year later. Although deeply affected, Elwood and Bertha responded to these tragedies courageously, accepting them as the will of God. And Haynes, of course, had his work as well as several positions of responsibility in the community to console him. He was both an elder of the First Presbyterian Church of Portland (since 1888) and strong supporter of the temperance movement.[36]

While Haynes was building a respected gas system in Portland, events in other parts of the state and in Chicago were leading to the formation of a large gas corporation that would play an important part in Haynes's life. The Indiana Natural Gas & Oil Company—usually referred to as 'the Chicago company'—was incorporated in 1889, in order to supply the city of Chicago

---

[34] *Ibid.*, March 15, 1889.

[35] Portland *Sun*, February 1, 1889.

[36] Marie Firth Haynes died July 30, 1889. Haynes (ed.), *Walter Haynes . . . and His Descendants*, p. 176; Sumner W. Haynes, *History of the First Presbyterian Church, Portland, Indiana [1872–1922]* (n.p., n.d. [1922?]). The author of this pamphlet succeeded his younger brother as church elder in 1890.

with gas piped in from the rich Indiana fields. The mastermind of this plan was Charles T. Yerkes, a classic representative of the urban monopolist and corruptionist active in the latter part of the nineteenth century. He proposed to add to the Chicago Gas Trust's fuel supply gas from Howard and Grant counties in Indiana.

Yerkes was a relative newcomer to Chicago, having arrived there after a flashy financial career in Philadelphia, which had led to a brief imprisonment for embezzling. Abandoning the East and his first wife upon his release, Yerkes remarried and launched a new life for himself in Chicago. He is primarily known for his successful takeover of the traction lines in Chicago and London, while his role in establishing the Chicago gas monopoly, though equally decisive, is less well known. Even Theodore Dreiser, who wrote three novels based on Yerkes's life in Philadelphia, Chicago, and in Europe, failed to document Yerkes's gas career as fully as he did other aspects of "Frank Cowperwood's" life.[37]

Municipal government in Chicago entered "a period of incredible corrup-tion," according to Charles E. Merriam, during its leap forward after the 1893 Columbian Exposition.[38] In the two decades after 1880, Chicago tripled its population to one and a half million, and there was a corresponding increase in the demand for city services and franchises. The opportunity for wrong-doing in the granting of such franchises was also present. At this point the Chicago city council was dominated by the "Gray Wolves," venal aldermen who readily sold their votes to the highest bidders.[39] Yerkes understood this kind of chicanery well and used money borrowed from his former associates in the East to establish himself as the traction king of Chicago. His final efforts in this field led to the city's famous "loop" elevated railways. Termed a "skillful manipulator" by Chicago's noted historian Bessie L. Pierce and "a cheerful corruptionist" by author W. A. Swanberg, Yerkes soon became one of the most powerful men in the city. "You can't get elected to the council unless Mr. Yerkes says so," reported alderman Johnny Powers, himself "the prince of boodlers."[40]

After establishing himself in the traction field, Yerkes broadened his inter-ests to include another public utility—gas. At the beginning of the 1880s only two gas companies were operating in Chicago, selling their manufac-tured product in separate parts of the city. Then, in the early part of the

---

[37] There is no satisfactory biography of Yerkes, a powerful figure in Chicago's financial and political life during the 1880s and 1890s. Yerkes's activities are covered in part in Bessie L. Pierce, *A History of Chicago*. Volume III: *The Rise of a Modern City, 1871–1893* (New York: A. A. Knopf, 1957); Lloyd Wendt and Herman Kogan, *Lords of the Levee: The Story of Bathhouse John and Hinky Dink* (Indianapolis and New York: The Bobbs-Merrill Company, 1943); and [Carter H. Harrison II], *Stormy Years: The Autobiography of Carter H. Harrison, Five Times Mayor of Chicago* (Indianapolis and New York: The Bobbs-Merrill Company, 1935). See also Sidney I. Roberts, "Portrait of a Robber Baron: Charles T. Yerkes," in *Business History Review*, XXXV (1961), 344–71; Max Lerner and Mary Frances Holter, in *Dictionary of American Biography*, (1964 ed.), s.v. "Charles T. Yerkes"; Theodore Dreiser, *The Financier* (New York: Boni & Liveright, 1912); Theodore Dreiser, *The Titan* (Garden City, N. Y.: Garden City Publishing Co., 1914); Theodore Dreiser, *The Stoic* (Garden City, N. Y.: Doubleday, 1947). Useful information on Dreiser's research techniques and his admiration for Yerkes's use of power and his way with women is in W. A. Swanberg, *Dreiser* (New York: Charles Scribners' Sons, 1965).

[38] Charles Edward Merriam, *Chicago: A More Intimate View of Urban Politics* (New York: Macmillan Co., 1929), p. 21.

[39] Forrest McDonald, *Insull* (Chicago: University of Chicago Press, 1962), p. 84. The "Gray Wolves," holders of the balance of power on the council, sold their votes "according to a regular schedule of bribes, ranging from $300 to $25,000." *Ibid.*

[40] Pierce, *History of Chicago*, III, 216; Swanberg, *Dreiser*, p. 26; Wendt and Kogan, *Lords of the Levee*, pp. 36–38, 40.

decade, a number of additional companies quite literally purchased franchises from the city council, permitting them also to supply gas within the city. In November, 1886, Yerkes acquired control of one of the new gas companies, renaming it the Consumers' Gas Company, and five months later the Chicago Gas Trust was formed, sponsored chiefly by Philadelphia money. Each of the eight companies brought into the trust kept its corporate identity, but control passed to one central organization. Even after the trust was dissolved by the Illinois supreme court in 1889, a high degree of unified control continued. In 1896, seven years after the trust was declared illegal, the Illinois Bureau of Labor Statistics reported that it was "flourishing," and questioned whether the gas combination was "greater than the State of Illinois."[41]

Soon after the gas trust was organized Yerkes implemented his plan to increase its available gas supply by piping fuel in from north-central Indiana. Two gas companies were organized for this purpose, in addition to an "outside" construction company. These Yerkes-sponsored companies were based upon broad gas field leases obtained by a prescient gas prospector in Howard County soon after the onset of the gas boom there. Jacob A. Smith, known in Howard County as "Silent Smith" because of "his taciturnity in the face of universal eagerness to know all about his business," had obtained those early lease rights in 1886 and 1887 and subsequently granted them to the Indiana Natural Gas & Oil Company (INGO), formed in October, 1889. In time he became general manager, then president of the company.[42]

INGO, incorporated to "acquire petroleum, natural or other gas, or both" and to "pipe, store, distribute, sell or otherwise dispose" of it to consumers for heating and lighting, was capitalized at $2.1 million.[43] An Illinois company, the Chicago Economic Fuel Gas Company, was formed in 1890 to meet the Indiana company at the state line and distribute the gas throughout Chicago. Although the terms of the city franchise forbade an alliance with any other company, control of the Chicago Economic Fuel Gas Company was soon announced to be in the hands of the Chicago Gas Company.[44]

By the summer of 1890, the plans to bring in the Indiana gas were sufficiently advanced to begin construction. As the company cast about for a person to direct field operations, the name of Portland's gas company superintendent came up repeatedly. According to Elwood's younger brother Edward, the Chicago men "discovered that Elwood Haynes knew more about natural gas than anybody else in the state, so he was

[41] Pierce, *History of Chicago*, III, 221 – 24. See also Louis Stotz and Alexander Jamison, *History of the Gas Industry* (New York: The Press of Stettiner Bros., 1938), pp. 100 – 107, for an account of the Chicago Gas Trust.

[42] Kokomo *Dispatch*, November 6, 1897. Earlier, as president of the firm of Smith & Zeigler, he had obtained his options to vast acres of gas territory in Howard and Grant counties.

[43] Articles of Incorporation, Indiana Natural Gas & Oil Company, Lake County Recorder's Office, Crown Point, Indiana. The five incorporators were from Chicago, where the papers had been drawn up, and the company was commonly known in Indiana as the Chicago company. Its first directors were Patrick A. McEwan, John B. Cohrs, Aniceto Hoyos, Frederick S. Winston, and Robert C. Bell. At least the latter two were attorneys retained by Yerkes. Swanberg records that Yerkes kept a battery of fifteen lawyers on his staff to look after his interests and "protect him from women and other threats." Swanberg, *Dreiser*, p. 166. The 1891 Chicago city directory lists Yerkes as president of INGO, but this office was soon passed on to William J. Campbell and, in 1896, to Jacob A. Smith. Larry A. Viskochil, Reference Librarian, Chicago Historical Society, to author, November 6, 1970.

[44] Pierce, *History of Chicago*, III, 223n. The Chicago Gas Trust was technically dissolved in 1889.

hired."[45] One likely source of this information was Charles E. Hequembourg, an experienced gas man from Bradford, Pennsylvania, who had helped to install a short pipeline leading from Jay County into Ohio in the late 1880s. Hequembourg moved to Chicago soon afterwards to join the Yerkes operation and was certainly aware of Haynes's ability as an imaginative and resourceful gas man, since the two had been close friends during Hequembourg's stay in Portland.[46]

When Haynes accepted the challenge of constructing what was to be the nation's first long-distance, high-pressure natural gas pipeline, he was responding to the same factors which had brought him into Portland's gas business: the chance to make new and exciting use of his technical and scientific training, the opportunity for advancement, and the realization that his present position was a precarious one because of the limited gas reserves in Jay County. He seems not to have been aware of Yerkes's leadership in the pipeline project; certainly he was not aware of his character or moral standards. Haynes's contact with the Chicago company was Hequembourg, and that connection with the project satisfied Haynes as to its propriety.

Characteristically the young gas engineer minded neither the temporary hardships his new position imposed upon him nor the need to move away from Portland and the close Haynes family ties. For Bertha, however, the move to Greentown sixty miles west of Portland loomed as a formidable and unpleasant necessity, one that she postponed for as long as possible. Haynes left Portland for his new post in June, 1890, while his wife remained in Portland at least until September. There is even some evidence that his wife's reluctance to live in Chicago later influenced Haynes to refuse a higher-ranking position with the INGO Company after the pipeline was completed.[47]

Haynes's new employer was actually the Columbus Construction Company (CCC), a Yerkes corporation which had the contract to build the double line of eight-inch pipes extending 120 miles across northwestern Indiana. Charles E. Hequembourg was president of this company, and an 1890 contract between INGO and CCC stipulated that the pipeline, complete with pumping stations, would be constructed by November, 1891. In return for this, the construction company would receive $5.5 million, $1.5 million in gas company stock and the balance in 6 percent mortgage bonds.[48] By April, 1891, when construction was temporarily delayed by an extremely complicated lawsuit, more than $2.5 million had been expended on the work and an on-time completion date was anticipated.

When Haynes arrived in Howard County to assume his position as field superintendent, he immediately plunged into the manifold duties required to oversee the drilling of a number of new wells, the construction of a pumping station on Greentown's west side, and the laying of pipe. He was obliged to

---

[45] "The Slow Boy," clipping, Kokomo *Tribune,* Elwood Haynes File, Library, Indiana University at Kokomo.

[46] Charles E. Hequembourg Affidavit, June 3, 1891, *Egbert Jamieson* v. *Indiana Natural Gas & Oil Company* File, Archives Division, Indiana State Library. See also *The State of Indiana on the relation of Cornelius Corwin* v. *Indiana and Ohio Oil, Gas, and Mining Company* File, *ibid.*

[47] Interview with Spencer Huffman, December 8, 1970.

[48] *Egbert Jamieson* v. *Indiana Natural Gas & Oil Company* File, Archives Division, Indiana State Library. See also the decision rendered in this case at 128 Indiana 555.

travel much more than his previous duties had entailed, and the idea in the back of his mind about a mechanical vehicle to replace the overworked horse and eliminate the time spent waiting for trains grew stronger. His overwork disturbed his wife, who demanded that he rest on Sundays, rather than draw maps and write business letters.[49]

The work was neither unpleasant to Haynes nor without its comic relief. "I often think of the old days in the gas business at Greentown, Fairmount and vicinity," Haynes wrote to an old friend in 1923, reminding him of an amusing incident:

> A certain farmer, having a strong German accent, came into the office and told you it was time to drill a vell on his land; calling your attention to the lease, he said, "Der party of der first part, dats de company, aind it?—agrees to drill a vell widin one year—dats Tomorrow." You asked him for the lease and read the same passage he had quoted but proceeded a little further in your quotation, "The party of the first part agrees to drill a well within one year or thereafter." "Oh," said the old farmer, "or thereafter—that thereafter is quite a word, aind it?"[50]

Haynes was boarding in Greentown, occasionally traveling back to Portland. In mock seriousness in July he wrote to his wife not to let the chickens drown again, "as I may not be there to bring them round." Mrs. Haynes for her part fretted considerably about her husband being away; "I think," she once remarked, "I shall put in a bill to the company for about seventy-five a month for taking you away from me." But she was also preoccupied with the difficulty of moving. She mulled over the matter with members of the Haynes family, who generally advised her to move, for perhaps different reasons. Elwood's oldest brother Walter still doubted that Elwood could look after himself. His sister Sue argued that a wife's place is with her husband. "I thought perhaps she would think of me, and with me," Bertha commented drolly, "but no, her thoughts are all for her brother! Whatever her brother does is perfectly right and proper in Sue's sight. Now I have a mind of my own, and am not so easily led about, by this brother of hers. . . ." She consented to make the move "if you think it would be of *real* advantage," but worried about it considerably. "Just how your chemicals and the special things of yours were to be moved" kept her awake at night and delayed the actual event.[51]

During this time Haynes and his crew of workmen were making good progress on the wells and pipelines, and a huge pumping station, described in 1901 as "the largest plant of the kind ever erected," was well underway at Greentown. It consisted of thirty-four boilers, eighteen feet by six feet, with engines to correspond, and twelve large compressors.[52] This progress was

[49] Bertha Haynes to Elwood Haynes, July 13, 1890, Haynes Papers. Haynes wrote to his wife from Alexandria, repeating his request that she join him in Greentown. He also had offered his brother-in-law Harry Lanterman a position with the gas company, which Harry accepted in July, 1890. Elwood Haynes to Bertha Haynes, June 26, 1890, *ibid.*

[50] Elwood Haynes to William H. Mosier, June 4, 1923, *ibid.*

[51] Elwood Haynes to Bertha Haynes, June 26, 1890, Bertha Haynes to Elwood Haynes, July 9, 13, 19, 24, 1890, *ibid.* Bertha was debating whether it would be of "advantage" to move to Greentown rather than simply to board there. Bertha postponed the move until after she visited her hometown of Paulina, New Jersey, with her mother in September. Portland *Sun*, September 4, 1890.

[52] *The State of Indiana and the Indiana Natural Gas and Oil Company* . . . ([Chicago], 1901), p. 3. This anonymous pamphlet, a copy of which is in the Indiana Division, Indiana State Library, is an outraged recital of supposed violations and circumventions of Indiana law by the "Chicago company." It also condemns state officials for failing to enforce natural gas provisions in the state statutes.

interrupted in the spring of 1891 while a legal test was made of the company's right to carry out its plans. The case developed into an involved series of court actions, the complete story of which may never be known. Haynes himself was uncharacteristically terse in all his autobiographical writings and reminiscences about these events, although his actions appear to have been above board and in keeping with his own high personal moral code. Indeed, it appears that Haynes's uneasiness about the illegality of building the pumping station and the pipelines led to the litigation of 1891–1892. Haynes's discomfiture was based on the recently-passed McHugh law, an Indiana statute prohibiting artificially increased pressures in gas pipelines, a law Haynes and INGO proceeded to test in the case of *The State* v. *Elwood Haynes*.[53]

---

[53] The first known mention of Haynes in the Kokomo *Dispatch* reports on the progress of *The State* v. *Elwood Haynes* on June 18, 1891. For a brief discussion of the related Jamieson case and the temporary crossing of paths by Haynes and Yerkes, see Ralph D. Gray, "The Puritan and the Robber Baron: An Episode in the Exploitation of Indiana's Natural Gas," in *Proceedings of the Indiana Academy of the Social Sciences*, 3rd Series, VII (1972), 102–10.

Chapter 5

Legislation and Litigation

The root cause for much of the opposition to Haynes and INGO was concern for the dwindling gas supply of the state. Although Indiana then boasted the largest known gas field in the country, one far more extensive than Ohio's or even Pennsylvania's, its capacity was not unlimited and the average field pressure had already dropped alarmingly. It was feared that continued rapid exploitation of the field would completely destroy its productive qualities. That a decline had already taken place was dramatically illustrated by the pipelines reaching from cities on the periphery of the field towards the heart of the field in Grant, Madison, and Delaware counties. Particularly alarming to Indiana consumers was the advent of a double pipeline draining gas from the rich heartland to meet the needs of a metropolis outside the state. In the course of its survey of the nation's natural gas supply, published serially in August, 1891, the Indianapolis *News* expressed particular concern about the proposed use of pumps on the Chicago pipelines:

> It is believed that the pumping process will hasten the destruction of wells to which it is applied by drawing water into them more rapidly; and this will help on the speedy exhaustion of the field. On every hand destructive agencies are at work, put in operation and maintained by the very people whose most vital interest it is that the gas supply should be prolonged as much as possible.[1]

Indiana authorities had already taken preliminary steps to conserve gas. As early as 1887, less than two years after the natural gas boom started, official statements of concern about the inefficient and wasteful use of this resource began to appear. In the fall of 1887 state geologist S. S. Gorby calculated the probable daily waste of the gas to be at least one hundred thousand cubic feet, worth $10,000, every twenty-four hours. Between April and October, 1887, he reported, more than $1.5 million worth of gas had been lost. Much of the waste was clearly avoidable, coming as it did from such foolish practices as using flambeaux in the fields as an advertisement of

---

[1] Indianapolis *News*, August 24, 1891. This series, which appeared daily from August 19 to August 26, stressed the need for economical use of the limited gas supplies that remained; it concluded with a reasoned appeal for the widespread adoption of meters, which had been shown to reduce consumption by one third to one half. *Ibid.*, August 25, 26, 1891.

a well's productivity, packing and anchoring the wells carelessly and inefficiently, and consuming the fuel extravagantly. As long as charges were based upon the number of outlets in the home or factory rather than upon the actual quantity of gas consumed, there was little incentive to consumers for conservation. Gorby ridiculed the gas companies' use of flambeaux, asking them to imagine a coal mine operator who set his mine afire to prove he had coal in his mine and that it would burn. The geologist gloomily predicted the complete exhaustion of the gas fields at an early date unless reforms were made.[2]

Gorby's report was published in 1889, the year in which the Indiana General Assembly attempted to protect the state's natural gas fields by prohibiting the transportation of the gas out of the state. This law was immediately challenged by a company engaged in piping natural gas from Jay County, Indiana, into Ohio to supply the village of Fort Recovery, and the Indiana supreme court upheld the challenge. The court ruled that the state law affected interstate commerce and violated Article I, Section 8 of the United States Constitution.[3] Consequently, at the next biennial session of the Indiana General Assembly a less direct method was devised to achieve the same end. For "safety reasons" then, by an act of March 4, 1891, known as the McHugh law, the legislature prohibited the artificial increase of the pressure under which natural gas would be allowed to be transferred from one point to another. The law was designed to put an effective end to long-distance transmission of natural gas, in the conviction that such safety legislation was clearly within the normal police powers of a state. The same legislature also prohibited the use of flambeaux for illumination and authorized the appointment of a state inspector of natural gas. But the state inspector found it most difficult, indeed impossible, to enforce the flambeaux prohibition. The gas was there, it belonged to its finders, the flambeaux had been erected, and the towns continued to use them. The law was a dead letter long before it was declared unconstitutional in 1896.[4]

The law forbidding the artificial increase in pressure was also challenged, in this case by the INGO company. The challenge was initiated by Elwood Haynes, much to the discomfort of his employers, because he wanted a ruling on the constitutionality of his actions in building the Chicago pipelines. He instigated the action to test the validity of the McHugh "anti-pumping" law within a month after its passage. At Haynes's insistence the state filed suit against him in Howard County Circuit Court in April, 1891. The information in the suit, based upon the sworn testimony of Martin H. Mosier, a Howard County landowner, stated that Haynes unlawfully used "a certain artificial device for pumping, commonly called a pump, for the purpose of increasing the natural flow of said natural gas through the said line of pipe"; by such means he had increased the pressure from 320 to 420 psi. Haynes, assisted by gas company attorneys, admitted "all the matters of fact stated therein to be true as alleged," but he suggested that the state should

---

[2] State of Indiana, Department of Geology and Natural History, *Sixteenth Annual Report, 1888* (Indianapolis, 1889), pp. 202–203. According to R. R. Russel, "Down to World War I, it is safe to say, more natural gas was wasted than was utilized." Robert R. Russel, *A History of the American Economic System* (New York: Appleton-Century Crofts, 1964), p. 354.

[3] *The State of Indiana, on the relation of Cornelius Corwin* v. *Indiana and Ohio Oil, Gas, and Mining Company* File, Archives Division, Indiana State Library. The supreme court decision in this case is at 120 Indiana 575.

[4] Indianapolis *News*, August 24, 1891; Phillips, *Indiana in Transition*, pp. 195–96. This decision came in *Townsend* v. *State*, 147 Indiana 624.

not prosecute him. First of all, his defense argued, he was merely an agent of the natural gas company, which owned a large number of other gas wells and gas territory for the purpose of transmitting the gas to various towns and cities, including Chicago. This was the "only way in which the said natural gas could be made a source of any benefit or profit to the said owner"; moreover, the company's plans had been made long before the statute in question was enacted, and more than $2.5 million had already been spent to acquire gas properties, rights of way, iron pipe, and to begin the work. Over twenty miles of pipeline had been laid, and the pipe had been distributed "ready to be laid and connected" for another sixty miles.[5]

Haynes pointed out, furthermore, that the pipe in question was capable of supporting a pressure of at least 1,000 psi; the slight increase in pressure which the company intended to make was "in all respects safe." In a revealing statement, the gas company, through the Haynes brief, admitted that without such an increase in pressure it would be impossible to transport the gas profitably to the places intended. The defense therefore claimed that the company had an "absolute vested right" to proceed. Chicago was 130 miles from Mosier's well in Howard County, and the gas there could not be carried in "commercial quantities" over such a distance without the use of pumps.[6]

These arguments were persuasive to Judge Lex O. Kirkpatrick, who quashed the information against Haynes and discharged him. The state, however, appealed the case to the Indiana supreme court and made strenuous efforts to have the circuit court ruling overturned. That the gas company considered this outcome a distinct possibility is indicated by its quick action in getting another case before the supreme court, challenging the same law. This second case, a civil rather than a criminal action, stemmed from stockholder Egbert Jamieson's apparent attempt to void the contract between INGO and CCC because it required unlawful actions, that is, violation of the antipumping statute.

All of the facts surrounding this most curious example of jurisprudence will never be known, but a compelling argument against the disinterested involvement of INGO is suggested by the extant evidence. Obviously the antipumping statute threatened the very existence of the company and would eventually have to be challenged. The evidence indicates, however, that the company had been disturbed, to say the least, by the insistence of its highminded field superintendent on having an immediate determination of the constitutionality of his duties. The possibility that the court would enjoin them from building the pipeline and pumping station as planned was frightening. Consequently, when company officials and attorneys convened in Kokomo to answer the complaint against Haynes, they decided to arrange another legal test under more controlled conditions. Their hopes were to overturn the antipumping law in a civil suit before it could be used to destroy the company.

INGO acted swiftly. Mosier's complaint against Haynes was drawn up on April 7, 1891, citing "violations" as of April 4. By April 9, only two days after Mosier had signed his complaint and two days before the first suit was filed in court, the second suit, the so-called Jamieson case, was on its way to the Indiana supreme court. During a single, busy day in Valparaiso, Indiana, Jamieson's "complaint" had been filed and answered, a decision rendered,

---

[5] *State v. Elwood Haynes,* File No. 16,124, Office of the Clerk of the Indiana Supreme Court, State House, Indianapolis.

[6] *Ibid.*

and an appeal to the state supreme court granted.[7] These highly unusual proceedings were investigated at length during the course of the appeal hearings, and from this investigation it is possible to piece together most of what had transpired.

The case originated when Egbert Jamieson, identified as a stockholder of the INGO company, filed a complaint against INGO and CCC in the Porter County Circuit Court in Valparaiso on April 9, 1891. Jamieson described the contract between the two companies, the amount of money involved, and the work completed to date. He then asked the court to cancel the contract and prevent INGO from paying either its stock or its bonds to CCC, because compliance with the agreement would require violation of the McHugh law. Jamieson's complaint was answered at once: INGO did not deny the allegations but pointed out that the pressure in the pipes would not exceed 600 psi and that the operation would be entirely safe. The court then ruled that the answer was good, the complaint faulty, and rendered judgment accordingly, but it also granted Jamieson's request for an appeal. All of this, to repeat, took place in a single day, and considerable wonderment was expressed when these rapid-fire events were scrutinized. An intervenor's brief charged that "the real purpose of this case" was to attack one of the state statutes:

> The coming together at Valparaiso of three attorneys from Chicago, Fort Wayne and Indianapolis on April 9—where no party or client resided—reminds one of the first chapter in Ben Hur. They traveled with one prescience, the parties were moved by one purpose, and that was to destroy the law the legislature had made.

In short, the intervenors maintained that it was a "fictitious suit" and moved its dismissal on that ground.[8]

Judge William Niblack, a leading member of the Indianapolis bar, and his law partners A. C. Harris and Luther Cox were the attorneys for the intervening gas companies. They had been retained by the Consumers' Gas Trust Company and other interests "which desire to have the law sustained."[9] In their long, cogently argued brief, they contended that "the case was made by parties alike interested in overthrowing the statute," and that the parties "have agreed to the existence of controlling facts which are known of all men to be untrue." They based these statements, first, on the fact that Charles T. Yerkes, the organizer of INGO and CCC, was also the employer of Egbert Jamieson, who served as corporate attorney for the North and West Side Systems of Street Railways in Chicago, another Yerkes company. Second, Niblack and his colleagues challenged the sworn statement regarding the complete safety of a pipeline at a pressure of 600 psi. In a series of affidavits accompanying their brief, these attorneys also pointed out 1) that Walter D. Holt, Jamieson's attorney of record in the original suit, was another of Yerkes's employees, with offices at CCC; 2) that the original bill of complaint and the answer to it had been typed on the same machine, on identical paper, with corrections in both in the same handwriting; and 3) that natural gas operations were inherently dangerous, that leakage and explosion were common, and "that any artificial means that may be em-

[7] *Jamieson* v. *INGO* File, Archives Division, Indiana State Library.

[8] *Ibid.* The "intervenors" on behalf of the state were several natural gas companies within Indiana, especially the Consumers' Gas Trust Company of Indianapolis.

[9] Indianapolis *News*, June 16, 1891.

ployed to increase the pressure and accelerate the flow will increase the danger of explosion."[10]

To reinforce the final point not only were affidavits taken from several experienced gas men, each of whom reported on the hazardous nature of their work, but also newspaper accounts of tragedies and scientific reports on natural gas operations in other states were introduced. William H. Shakleton, the superintendent of the Consumers' Gas Trust Company of Indianapolis, testified that he had worked in the gas business since 1865, in Pennsylvania and then Indiana, and that gas mains tested to 700 psi were known to break under 300 pounds of pressure only months later. Three other affidavits related to a serious explosion near Peru, Indiana, on October 31, 1888.[11]

These disclosures, especially the evidence indicating that the suit was fictitious, created a sensation and temporarily halted the proceedings. The court, anxious to have the charges investigated, appointed lower court Judge Livingston Howland as a "special Master Commissioner" and empowered him to hear the evidence and to make a full report. Although he was only given five days to do this, Howland met the deadline.[12] His report explained the suit's origin, relating it to the Haynes case in Kokomo. According to testimony elicited by Judge Howland, when Charles E. Hequembourg, president of CCC, and attorneys Ferdinand Winter and John Bell learned in Kokomo that the prosecution of the Haynes case had been delayed, they arranged for an immediate test of the law by means of a civil suit. They originally planned to have the construction company sue the gas company, thereby putting the facts of the contract and the new law before the court in order to decide the constitutionality of the law. The place and date for filing the suit were to have been determined by Hequembourg, who was to telegraph his decision to the attorneys. In the meantime Winter had proceeded to draw up the bill of particulars. Shortly thereafter, according to Hequembourg's instructions, the three men met again in Valparaiso on April 9, along with other employees of CCC, and decided to file the suit on behalf of an individual gas company stockholder, rather than the construction company, so Winter amended his complaint accordingly. Jamieson's name was to be used, but since no one knew his first name they wired to Chicago for it and received both the name and express permission to use it. A court stenographer then typed the amended complaint, and Walter D. Holt signed it as the attorney for the plaintiff. John Bell as attorney for the defendant then dictated the answer to the same stenographer according to information given him by Hequembourg. Judge Howland reported:

> Mr. Winter and Mr. Bell both stated that, from their acquaintance with [Mr. Hequembourg] and their knowledge of his experience and reputation as a gas man, they had implicit confidence that the facts contained in the answer were the actual facts, and [were placed] in the answer for that reason and none other, and with no purpose to shape the case so as to induce any particular decision. . . .

He concluded, "I believe and find that to be the fact."[13]

Following these steps, the case had been argued before Judge Johnson on that single, busy day of April 9. Winter and Bell spoke for the defendants,

---

[10] *Jamieson* v. *INGO* File, Archives Division, Indiana State Library.

[11] *Ibid.*

[12] *Ibid.*

[13] Special Master's Report, *ibid.*

submitting and discussing authorities; Holt spoke for Jamieson, the plaintiff, without citing any authorities. Having seen the complaint and answer for the first time that day, he obviously was not prepared to present a case. At the close of the arguments, the judge sustained the complaint and entered judgment accordingly sometime between 5 and 6 PM. The appeal was filed immediately thereafter.

The information Howland obtained from his oral examination of attorneys Winter and Bell was supported by affidavits filed by most of the other *dramatis personae:* Charles T. Yerkes, Egbert Jamieson, Walter D. Holt, and Charles E. Hequembourg. Yerkes as president of INGO swore that the parties and the suit were real, that his company's reply was factual and complete, and he expressed his belief that only a speedy resolution of the case on its merits would prevent his company from suffering "great loss and damage."[14] The other statements taken in Chicago were similar in import. Howland submitted the affidavits, a transcript of the oral testimony, and certain sworn statements supplied by the intervenors with his report. His conclusions were that "the parties to the suit . . . are actual and not fictitious parties," but that "the purpose and intention of all parties to the proceeding were to take the case to this court and obtain a decision . . . upon the validity of the statute set out in the complaint." It was a fact, he continued, "that the case was advised to be brought, the form of it decided, the pleadings framed as a whole and the questions of law discussed, practically, alone by the attorneys for the defendants below. Mr. Holt's connection with the case was wholly perfunctory."[15]

The special commissioner stopped short of making any recommendations based upon his findings, but most observers considered the report damaging to INGO. The Indianapolis *News* headlined its account of Howland's report as follows: "Was There Collusion? . . . Defendants Inspired the Case and Employed All of the Attorneys, Etc." Some participants in the case, especially the Consumers' Gas Trust Company, also believed the charge of collusion had been sustained. The supreme court, however, merely took the report under advisement and proceeded with the hearing of the case. This surprised one of the attorneys for the gas trust company, A. C. Harris, who remarked, "If a case in which all of the attorneys are employed by the same side can be held good, I'll have to unlearn what I have thought I knew about law."[16]

The problem this strange set of circumstances posed for the court was twofold: if, as the newspaper report boldly stated, the purpose of the McHugh law had been "to prevent the transportation of gas from the Indiana field into Illino[is]," then the law was unconstitutional. This question had been determined some two years earlier. On the other hand, the indications of an arranged or fictitious case were certainly strong. Within four days, nevertheless, the court handed down its decision, Judge Walter Olds dissenting. In an opinion written by Judge Byron K. Elliott, the court surprisingly sustained the McHugh law, but it also ruled that pumping was permissible so long as the natural field pressure of the gas was not exceeded.[17] This ruling in effect invalidated the law, as disgruntled observers pointed out, because there was no way to enforce it. "This Something's

[14] *Ibid.*

[15] *Ibid.*

[16] Indianapolis *News,* June 16, 1891.

[17] *Ibid.* The decision of the court appears at 128 Indiana 555.

Nothing," grumbled a Kokomo editor, "The McHugh Law is Valid But Chicago Will Get Gas."[18] Indeed, the end result accorded with the views of Judge Olds, who had dissented from the majority opinion because he considered the statute unconstitutional. The state had erred in trying to do by an indirect method what the court had only recently ruled it could not do directly—i.e., to prevent the transmission of natural gas to points outside the state. The Chicago company, although patently in violation of the antipumping law, was in accord with the fundamental law of the land.

Because it was essentially superseded by the Jamieson case, the Haynes case lingered in the supreme court for eighteen months. Arguments were confined to briefs filed by both parties and by interested third parties, but the eventual outcome was that Haynes "confessed judgment" in December, 1892, i.e., the lower court's ruling was reversed and the antipumping statute upheld. By this time, however, the ruling was meaningless. The vital issues of the case had already been resolved in favor of the gas company.[19]

INGO of course announced its satisfaction with the Jamieson ruling. Company spokesmen reported that the three hundred pound limitation would not prevent them from sending gas to Chicago, and plans were made to resume construction immediately. Despite the prediction of an Indianapolis *News* reporter that the intervenors would file either an injunction or an appeal to the United States Supreme Court, no further impediments to the pipeline materialized. For Haynes, who had started it all, the hiatus in construction occasioned by the litigation meant some personal free time. He used the opportunity to take up in a more serious fashion his earlier idea of a self-propelled road vehicle. He gave careful consideration to some of the problems involved with various types of motive power—steam, electricity, and gasoline—, and he began to make detailed drawings of the components of such a vehicle regardless of power source. Greentown lacked a machine shop, so his work did not proceed beyond the planning stage at this time.[20] And soon he was back at work supervising the laying of the two main pipelines, the completion of Greentown's pumping station, and the construction of a branch line to Kokomo. As early as July 16, 1891, the Kokomo paper reported that "a great force of men is at work completing the lines through the Kankakee flats and through the low lands between Logansport and Winamac."[21] A November completion date was still planned.

The Kokomo branch line was also being rushed to completion. The Chicago company had determined, both for legal and political reasons, that it needed to provide local service to smooth the way for its major purpose of supplying gas to Chicago. The company was having difficulty obtaining a right of way across state land at the site of the Wabash and Erie Canal and needed the local franchise to strengthen its position in the state. The Kokomo franchise also served to fortify the company in its battle with other gas companies in the state. There was some problem in arranging the terms of the franchise, because of local opposition, spearheaded by editor Henderson, to the hard bargain driven by the company; but the city fathers were impressed with what they were offered. Not only did INGO's new eight-inch

---

[18] Kokomo *Dispatch*, June 25, 1891.

[19] *Ibid.*, June 18, 1891, December 16, 1892.

[20] Indianapolis *News*, June 22, 1891; Elwood Haynes to David Beecroft, April 22, 1915, Beecroft Papers, Automotive History Collection, Detroit Public Library.

[21] Kokomo *Dispatch*, July 16, 1891.

main enable Kokomo to tap some of the richest gas properties in the state, it also provided the possibility (largely unrealized) of effective competition between rival gas companies in the city. The "Chicago Gas Company," reported the state natural gas supervisor in 1893, "owns a large amount of the best producing gas territory in the State, upon which they have drilled a great number of wells. With the facilities at their command, they, also, can furnish gas in quantity to supply the needs of Kokomo."[22]

The franchise agreement between company and city was concluded in late January, 1892, following weeks of heated public and private discussion. At length the terms dictated by the company for the most part were accepted. "The Bars Are Down"—"Kokomo aids the Chicago project, possibly at her own great cost," cried the newspaper headlines. "For good or for ill," began editor Henderson's angry report, the city council "acceded" to the "last and fullest demand" of the gas company. No performance bond was given, and other guarantees on rates, service, and competition were missing. Henderson interpreted the eight-to-two vote in favor of the new gas ordinance as a reflection of the council's belief that the ordinance was in accord with the popular demand, not from

> a conviction of right, or even expediency. . . . To the observing mind, it looked very much like a play—and a dangerous play—to the galleries. But the galleries are fickle. What they applaud today they hiss tomorrow.[23]

In Henderson's view Kokomo had done everything it could possibly have done "to aid the project to pipe gas to Chicago." Passage of the ordinance disposed of pending litigation requiring local service from the Chicago company; it also established rates for service that a year before had prompted public outcry, and it did nothing to assure effective or sustained competition between the two gas companies serving the city. "Every prudential and reasonable demand" had been waived, and he feared that "there are grave reasons to fear that a grievous mistake has been made."[24] Even so, Henderson hoped that he was wrong and adopted a "wait and see" attitude. By May, 1892, he was pointing with pride to Kokomo's enviable supply of gas. Even though he credited the "constant legal fire" against the Chicago company for the service to Kokomo, he was pleased that it had resulted in connecting the city with "the largest gas territory controlled by a single corporation on the face of the earth," and made it the "most advantageously situated city in the natural gas region."[25] Rate competition between Kokomo's two gas companies, moreover, temporarily benefited the consumers considerably.

In August, 1892, when the pipeline system was nearly completed, the Chicago company began to advertise the availability of service, offered free of charge until September 1, after which the ordinance rates would apply.[26] A rate war between the Kokomo Gas Company and INGO, however, led to

---

[22] State of Indiana, Department of Geology and Natural Resources, *Eighteenth Annual Report, 1893* (Indianapolis, 1894), p. 203. The "also" referred to the Kokomo Gas Company, which had fourteen wells within seven miles of the city.

[23] Kokomo *Dispatch*, January 21, 1892.

[24] *Ibid.* This issue of the paper reprinted the gas ordinance in its entirety on the front page, spelling out, among other things, the specifically authorized rates for summer and winter cooking and heating.

[25] *Ibid.,* May 14, 1892.

[26] *Ibid.,* August 1, 1892. The first notices placed in the newspapers were signed by "George A. Yuile, Supt." Beginning in October they were signed by Haynes as superintendent. His services for CCC had ended with the completion of the pipeline and pumping station, and he had "transferred" to INGO. See Elwood Haynes, untitled, undated transcript of testimony, Haynes

free gas being supplied by both companies until December 1, when the competitors agreed to charge the full rates authorized in the January, 1892, ordinance. When gas company customers came into the offices to make arrangements for continuation of service, they were disturbed, to put it mildly, at both companies' new "single-stove" policy. The gas suppliers had decided to bill customers with only a single mixer both for cooking and heating, i.e., to charge them $3.00 per month rather than $1.50. The alternative was no service at all. Some consumers also complained that the Chicago company's pressure in the city lines was less than that required by both the ordinance and gas users.[27]

Given these supposed violations, several angry gas consumers descended upon City Attorney C. C. Shirley's office to "get the law" on the two gas companies. This "surging mass of humanity," so described by a Kokomo reporter, was "just about as mad as it is possible for American people to become," and they were demanding quick action.[28] When Shirley declined to act until he had received instructions from the city council, the attention focused there. Not since the gas ordinance excitement early in the year had such a crowd attended a council meeting. There the citizens were pleased to learn that each of the ten councilmen was "with the people," for they quickly adopted a resolution condemning the gas company practices and directed the city attorney to prosecute all violations of the earlier ordinance. The action was taken with "such a vim, and every member voted with such decided emphasis, that there was no mistaking the feeling of the council."[29]

Following these emphatic demonstrations of sentiment, various specific complaints were filed with City Attorney Shirley, and prosecutions followed. The plaintiffs won most of the cases; however, the damages assessed against the companies were trivial, ranging from $2.00 to $5.00. But such proceedings, however insignificant in dollar sums, were damaging to the community's confidence in the gas companies, a circumstance further exacerbated by Charles E. Hequembourg's conference with the Kokomo city council. "Baron H.," as the newspaper referred to him, replied to the council's complaints that his company would comply with the ordinance regarding pressure "as soon as they found it convenient to do so," and he invited any dissatisfied patron to have his service disconnected (for a two dollar charge).[30]

Editor Henderson could not refrain from an "I told you so" editorial in December, quoting liberally from his earlier warnings. He reminded his readers that many had fought vigorously to prevent Indiana gas from being piped out of the state and pronounced that Kokomo had foolishly "transferred its fealty to a non-resident corporation" without safeguarding its own interests.[31] Ten days later, when the case of the *State* v. *Elwood Haynes* was

Papers. The front pages of the document are missing, but the interrogation of Haynes appears to be related to the injunction issued at the instigation of Tom Conway to prevent the gas company from drilling and piping wells near his home. Kokomo *Dispatch,* October 13, 1892. Haynes testified briefly concerning his background and relationship with the company and at greater length about the customary proceedings for laying pipelines. The attorneys for the plaintiff handled him rather roughly during cross-examination, and he proved to be a somewhat hostile, uncommunicative witness. These suits were common. See Kokomo *Tribune,* April 28, 1968, "75 Years Ago" column.

[27] Kokomo *Dispatch,* December 5, 1892.

[28] *Ibid.*

[29] *Ibid.,* December 6, 1892.

[30] *Ibid.,* December 14, 1892.

[31] *Ibid.,* December 6, 1892.

finally concluded by Haynes's confession of judgment, the editor renewed his attack upon the gas company and its representatives. Because of this action, he claimed that the company was still violating the law. Henderson, unwilling to accept the law's unenforceability, demanded that the McHugh law be vigorously enforced and Elwood Haynes be immediately arraigned. Since Howard County was "firmly and eternally opposed to the Chicago project, . . . it should be stopped."[32]

At this juncture, when the Kokomo editor was all but demanding his arrest, Elwood Haynes and his extremely pregnant wife moved to Kokomo. Although the Hayneses had been contemplating the move from Greentown for several months, they waited until after the construction Haynes was supervising had been completed and after he had assumed his new position as manager of INGO's Kokomo operations. Probably Haynes was still needed in Greentown for final adjustments to the pumping station after it was put into service in mid-November, but the impending birth of the Hayneses' third child may have dictated that they move as soon as possible after November 15. At any rate, Elwood and Bertha Haynes arrived in Kokomo to take up residence sometime in December, 1892. They occupied a house belonging to the gas company on North Washington Street, property that also accommodated one of the gas company's large pressure regulators for the city's mains. Just days later Bertha gave birth to a daughter, Bernice, the first of the Haynes children to survive infancy.[33]

Because of the rather hostile climate of opinion regarding the gas company and its officers, it is perhaps not surprising that the city newspapers took no notice of the new residents other than to publish a notice from a Greentown reporter lamenting the fact that the Hayneses had moved away. In the early years of their residence, in fact, there are no notices about Haynes and his family outside the business columns. It is ironic that the man later referred to as "Kokomo's First Citizen" was so ignored in the early years. Men who knew Haynes respected his learning and his technical and scientific competence, and he quickly assumed a responsible leadership role in the affairs of the First Presbyterian Church of Kokomo. But he would not become "copy" for the city newspapers until long after he and Elmer Apperson had produced their first automobiles.

By the time Haynes moved to Kokomo, the Chicago company finally had begun to supply Chicago with gas. The two eight-inch mains had been completed during the summer of 1892, but no Indiana gas had been delivered to the Chicago Economic Fuel Gas Company's lines until November 15, when the pumping station was finally completed. The Economic, another Yerkes company, had employed more than five hundred men in October and November to install or connect gas appliances for its customers. When the gas was turned into the Economic's mains in mid-November, more than thirty thousand Chicago consumers "were in direct connection with the great gas fields of Indiana."[34]

Haynes's new duties both as supervisor of the Kokomo branch of INGO and of its Chicago pipelines posed some interesting challenges. One of his first problems dealt with the wintertime transmission of the gas through the pipelines; because the pipes in northern Indiana were either shallowly buried or exposed, the moisture-laden gas in the pipes often froze. When the company appealed to Haynes for a solution, he advised the dehydration of

64

[32] *Ibid.*, December 16, 1892.

[33] Bernice was born December 7, 1892. There was no notice of her birth in the local press.

[34] Kokomo *Dispatch*, November 1, 16, 1892.

the gas before it was shipped northward. As Haynes later pointed out in his autobiography, "Not only did the ice stop the flow of gas in the line, but it endangered the people of Chicago, as it rendered it dangerous to turn on the supply after the trouble was over, since the gas, of course, went out, and the valves were left open."[35] Given the go-ahead by his employers he designed a workable refrigeration unit and assembled it. The process which he used worked most satisfactorily; however, it not only removed water vapor from the gas, but also condensed some of the lower boiling constituents in the gas, thereby producing casinghead gasoline. Since there was no market for it at the time, the gasoline was discarded as a waste product.[36]

Haynes also agreed to write an article on natural gas for inclusion in the natural gas supervisor's annual report for 1895. The supervisor was a Kokomoan, J. C. Leach, who called Haynes "an expert chemist, as well as a natural gas engineer of large experience. He is constantly experimenting along the line of natural gas economy, and his paper will be read with interest, especially by those acquainted with his work in the Indiana gas field."[37] Haynes's article on "Utilization of Natural Gas" included some discussion of the composition of the gas as determined by his own careful analysis, but its chief emphasis was the recommended method to follow in achieving both safe and economical use of natural gas.[38]

Haynes revealed many of his capabilities in the natural gas field. He was a loyal and competent employee and gave efficient management to company affairs. Nevertheless, the nature of his duties allowed him to devote a good deal of time to his other interests. Haynes's important discoveries in both the automotive and metallurgical fields were made during the time he worked for the gas company, the most productive period in his life. In a small laboratory above the office and with the gas company's permission he conducted numerous experiments, wrote various technical reports and scientific papers, and supervised the creation and manufacture of an automobile in the 1890s. His last service for the gas company was to come in 1901, at the time of another popular outcry against the company. This time consumers were opposed to the mandatory installation of meters and the initiation of charges based on the amount of gas used, rather than the number of outlets.

After an informal merger of INGO and the Kokomo Natural Gas and Oil Company in the late 1890s, in effect a single gas utility served Kokomo. It notified the city in April, 1901, that unless meters were authorized for individual use it would cease operation in Kokomo on November 1, the date winter rates were scheduled to begin. Haynes was interviewed by the Kokomo *Dispatch* after the announcement of the "ultimatum," and he defended it as a necessary means of informing the public that the days of "natural gas by 'lump contract' in Kokomo were at an end"; this situation was caused by the "gas field condition." Supply no longer equalled demand, company sales were being limited already in Chicago, and economical use would have to be enforced everywhere. Meters, he continued, were the only way to accomplish this, and at the proposed rate of thirty cents per thousand cubic feet he believed that the "frugal householder" would actually pay less than the current rates. He declared that the company "would certainly

---

[35] Haynes, "Autobiography," Haynes Papers.

[36] Harshbarger, "Elwood Haynes: Scientist with a Social Conscience," p. 23; Dunn, *Indiana and Indianans*, III, 1217.

[37] State of Indiana, Department of Geology and Natural Resources, *Twentieth Annual Report, 1895* (Indianapolis, 1896), p. 372.

[38] *Ibid.*, pp. 399–405.

withdraw" if meters were refused it, " 'turning the key' and leaving the city without a gas supply from this source." Haynes declined to speculate about the legal situation this would create; an attorney who was asked to comment also evaded the question, describing it as an intricate issue and suggesting that the higher courts would have to settle the matter.[39]

Haynes also spoke to representative manufacturers in the city about the gas shortage crisis and the need for conservation, and he spoke out again in defense of meters at a city council meeting called to consider the problem. The question facing the council was whether or not to accept the gas company's request for a new ordinance, allowing the installation of meters in order to regulate supply. Domestic customers wondered whether this new policy would mean that industrial users would be supplied in preference to individual homes. The Kokomo *Dispatch* called it "the most momentous question with which the city has had to deal in its entire history," and again a standing-room-only audience filled the council chambers. The popular feeling was clearly opposed to the use of meters, but this offered no solution. Haynes suggested to the gathering that they face two salient facts: one, the gas was "giving out" and two, the waste from a single outlet would supply a 400-horsepower factory. He also invited the wrath of the audience by suggesting that corporations were "not always in the wrong" and that the question of the obligation of the company to furnish gas would become moot if the supply of gas vanished. Finally, and at the heart of the matter for most people, Haynes promised that the meters would not result in a "tremendous bill" monthly, as critics maintained. With reasonable use Haynes predicted that there would be little change in the cost to consumers.[40]

When the council voted the next week, it rejected the meter ordinance. The mayor had recommended this action, arguing that "If there was to be no gas, then there was no need of a new contract," and, "if there was plenty of gas, the contract was good enough."[41] As expected, the gas company continued to operate on the same basis for some time to come. Haynes, however, was soon to resign in order to devote himself to his growing automobile business, already recognized by the latter part of 1901 as the oldest in the United States.

By 1906 the Indiana gas boom was over; a decade later, the Chicago company's eight-inch mains were abandoned, and its ten-inch line was used to carry manufactured gas *into* north-central Indiana. The reverse flow was needed to replace the resources that had been so flagrantly wasted.[42]

For Haynes's career, the relationship with the gas company in some ways substituted for the academic affiliation he had sought earlier: his services as an expert were exchanged for a modest competence and the opportunity to pursue his own research. Missing from this equation, of course, was the academic atmosphere and challenge of other research that a college would have provided. In a research laboratory Haynes might have addressed himself to the burning scientific problems of his day; on his own, he worked to solve more immediate problems.

---

[39] Kokomo *Dispatch*, April 27, 1901. INGO was supplying the other Kokomo company "with all the fuel passing through its mains," and nominally the two companies "are one." *Ibid.* A formal merger occurred on November 19, 1906. "Historic Review" [1965?], in the office files of the Kokomo Gas and Fuel Company, Kokomo, Indiana.

[40] Kokomo *Dispatch*, May 13, 1901.

[41] *Ibid.*, May 21, 22, 1901.

[42] "History of the Kokomo Gas and Fuel Company," History File, Kokomo Gas and Fuel Company, Kokomo, Indiana.

Chapter 6

"How I Built
the First Automobile"

Elwood Haynes had begun to think about a self-propelled road vehicle as early as 1887 or 1888. As Portland's gas company superintendent he had spent many long hours traveling Jay County's sandy roads with a horse and buggy. "The great trouble with the horse," Haynes wrote in 1918, "was his lack of endurance and this became more apparent when he was driven day after day. I accordingly laid plans for the construction of a mechanically propelled vehicle for use on the highway."[1]

He first considered using a steam engine but abandoned this plan as unsafe because of the danger of fire. He next considered electricity and abandoned that idea because he believed that a battery capable of producing enough power would also be too large and heavy for his purposes. The gasoline engine presented a similar problem: "Even the lightest made at the time were very heavy per unit of power, and rather crude in construction."[2]

At Greentown in 1891, where his traveling duties were again heavy, Haynes made several sketches for his proposed vehicle; but the pressure of his gas company responsibilities during the construction of the pipelines and pumping station postponed further work. Greentown also lacked a machine shop, a handicap Haynes overcame when he moved to Kokomo in December, 1892. But the greatest impetus to his plans was the discovery of a usable, available gas engine at the Chicago World's Fair in the summer of 1893.

He might also have seen, but apparently did not see, an automobile at the Chicago fair, since models of both a Karl Benz gasoline vehicle and a Sturgis electric vehicle were exhibited for a time.[3] The "first automobile," after all, was not built in America—not by Haynes or anyone else. Operable steam-powered road vehicles were built in Europe in the late eighteenth and early nineteenth centuries, but these developments led to the steam locomotive

---

[1] Haynes, "How I Built the First Automobile," in *Haynes Pioneer,* July, 1918, p. 5.

[2] *Ibid.*

[3] Haynes repeatedly claimed that he did not see an automobile on display at the fair, although one of the Benz models and a Sturgis electric were exhibited for a time. He was, of course, familiar with gasoline engines before his visit to Chicago. In 1879, for example, at commencement exercises that Haynes attended Edward Barnes read a thesis abstract on "The Otto [four cycle] Silent Gas-Engine." *Tenth Annual Catalogue of the Worcester County Free Institute of Industrial Science, 1879–1880* (Worcester, 1880), p. 32.

and railroads rather than to the automobile. Beginning in the mid-nineteenth century, however, there was a series of developments in Europe that led to the internal combustion engine. In 1860 a Belgian mechanic, Etienne Lenoir, patented a two-cycle engine in Paris, and eighteen years later Nicholas Otto, a German engineer, built an operable four-cycle engine. The major step forward came in the mid-1880s when two Germans, Karl Benz and Gottlieb Daimler, constructed vehicles using the new engine. From their first two- and three-wheeled machines flowed a continuous stream of innovations leading to the motor vehicles of the 1890s.[4]

On the other side of the Atlantic countless American mechanics and inventors tinkered with their own ideas of self-propelled vehicles in the 1890s. Haynes was one of many such men, most of whom worked independently of the Europeans, and of each other, to produce workable automobiles during the decade. It is inconceivable that Haynes, college-educated (and therefore almost unique among American automobile pioneers) and a visitor to the 1893 Chicago fair, was totally unaware of the European achievements in automobiles, although he later implied as much; but it is also abundantly clear that he designed his own automobile. The feasibility of self-propelled vehicles must have been known beforehand, but in all other matters the first American automobiles were built through trial-and-error design and invention. As Haynes declared forthrightly,

> When I set about making my first car I did not know that anything was done by any one at any place along this line, and whatever blunders or mistakes I made were due to my own shortcomings, as I did not copy the machine from any one else.[5]

Haynes's fellow pioneer Hiram P. Maxim later affirmed the relative isolation in which he and other inventors worked and wondered at the remarkable coincidence of near-simultaneous invention in the United States. In 1892, when the idea of a self-propelled vehicle came to Maxim, a young man from Massachusetts, while pedaling home from an evening's courting in a neighboring town, he considered various power sources, especially the Otto engine, and entertained bright visions of being the first person in the world to use a "gasoline-engine to drive a vehicle." He later confessed to being "blissfully ignorant" of the work of Benz and Daimler in Germany, of DeDion and Panhard in France, of Napier in England, of the Duryeas, Haynes, the Appersons, Winton, and many others in the United States, all of whom were deeply involved in inventing gasoline-propelled vehicles. Maxim continued: "As I look back, I am amazed that so many of us began work so nearly at the same time, and without the slightest notion that others were working on the problem."[6]

---

[4] An excellent survey of the development of the automobile in Europe and America up to 1915 is in Allan Nevins and Frank Ernest Hill, *Ford: The Times, the Man, and the Company* (New York: Scribners, 1954). See also John B. Rae, *The American Automobile: A Brief History* (Chicago: University of Chicago Press, 1965); Edward D. Kennedy, *The Automobile Industry: The Coming of Age of Capitalism's Favorite Child* (New York: Reynal & Hitchcock, 1941); G. A. Niemeyer, *The Automotive Career of Ransom E. Olds* (Lansing, Mich.: Michigan State University, 1961); William Greenleaf, *Monopoly on Wheels: Henry Ford and the Selden Automobile Patent* (Detroit: Wayne State University Press, 1961); James J. Flink, *America Adopts the Automobile, 1895–1910* (Cambridge, Mass.: MIT Press, 1970); George S. May, *A Most Unique Machine: The Michigan Origins of the American Automobile Industry* (Grand Rapids, Mich.: William B. Eerdsman Publishing Company, 1975).

[5] Elwood Haynes to Charles E. Duryea, July 2, 1915, Beecroft Papers, Automotive History Collection, Detroit Public Library.

[6] Hiram Percy Maxim, *Horseless Carriage Days* (New York: Harper & Brothers, 1937), p. 3.

American pioneers of the internal-combustion automobile include J. Frank and Charles E. Duryea (1893), Elwood Haynes (1894), Alexander Winton (1896), R. E. Olds (1896), Charles B. King (1896), and Henry Ford (1896). J. Frank Duryea by his own account produced his first operable machine in September, 1893, in Springfield, Massachusetts. The evidence for this includes a contemporary story in the Springfield *Republican,* September 22, 1893, describing the initial, rather disappointing, test run. The younger Duryea admitted he was working on an idea given to him by his brother Charles, who had left Massachusetts and returned to Illinois, but he claimed that many of the plans and designs drawn up by Charles had to be discarded as unworkable. Charles Duryea, on the other hand, claimed not only a greater responsibility for the vehicle but also an earlier date (April, 1892) for it, and in later years he spent considerable time and effort attempting to substantiate these now discredited assertions.[7] By either reckoning, however, the second successful automobile in America, and to Haynes's way of thinking the first complete and satisfactory model, was the one he test drove along Pumpkinvine Pike, on the outskirts of Kokomo, Indiana, on July 4, 1894.

That model began with the Sintz engine Haynes discovered at the Chicago World's Fair in the summer of 1893. A flyer issued in 1893 by the Sintz Company of Grand Rapids, Michigan, now among the Haynes Papers, describes the company product and the advantages of the stationary gas engine over small steam engines for manufacturing. Greater safety, economy, and cleanliness were promised, and details on the construction and operation of the complete line of Sintz engines, both stationary and marine, were spelled out. Prices began at $200 for a one-horsepower 500 rpm stationary engine or $225 for the similar marine model and rose to $875 or $975 for the fifteen-horsepower models. Haynes ordered the $225 engine sometime early in the fall of 1893, and it was delivered in late October or early November.[8]

The engine was mounted on sawhorses in the Hayneses' kitchen, and the gasoline and battery connections were installed. When Haynes turned the crank nothing happened. He tried again, and again, until finally after much cranking the motor started. Then a new problem developed; the machine "ran with such speed and vibration that it pulled itself from its attachments. Luckily, however, one of the battery wires was wound around the motor shaft and this disconnected the current."[9] No one has recorded Mrs. Haynes's reaction to the 180-pound piece of machinery writhing on her kitchen floor, but shortly afterwards Haynes made arrangements with Elmer Apperson to work in the privacy of Apperson's Riverside Machine Shop. Moreover, the intense vibration of the engine prompted Haynes to design

---

[7] James Frank Duryea's claims are contained in his booklet, *America's First Automobile; The First Complete Account of Mr. J. Frank Duryea of How He Developed the First American Automobile, 1892–1893* (Springfield, Mass.: D. M. Macaulay, 1942), and two other pamphlets: *Data Relative to the Development of America's First Gasoline Automobile* (Springfield, Mass., 1942) and *Who Designed and Built Those Early Duryea Cars?* (Madison, Conn., 1944). All three publications are in the Indiana State Library. Charles E. Duryea's publications are more scattered, but see, for example, "It Doesn't Pay to Pioneer," in *Saturday Evening Post,* May 16, 1931, p. 30; "The American Motor Car Industry," in *Motor,* March, 1909, p. 33; M. J. Duryea, "America's First Automobile Controversy," in *Antique Automobile,* December, 1953, pp. 25–48; M. J. Duryea, "The Haynes—Indiana's First Car (The Battle of Kokomo)," in *ibid.,* December, 1943, p. 19.

[8] Haynes, *How I Built the First Automobile,* in *Haynes Pioneer,* July, 1918, p. 5; A. A. Barber to [Elwood Haynes], August 16, 28, September 13, 1893, Haynes Papers. The letters from Barber of the Sintz Company indicate that Haynes inquired about the engines early in August, 1893, and followed up with another inquiry on August 10.

[9] Haynes, "How I Built the First Automobile," in *Haynes Pioneer,* July, 1918, p. 5.

Edgar Apperson   Elmer Apperson

Elwood Hayne

and build a much heavier carriage frame than he had planned originally.[10]

Haynes asked a friend, a Mr. Lafferty, where he could get "some work done which I did not want made public" and was told about the Riverside Machine Shop on South Main Street where no one was allowed in during the day. The shop was run by Elmer Apperson, a thirty-two-year-old mechanic who had been in business in Kokomo with his younger brother Edgar since 1888, specializing in the construction and repair of bicycles, farm machinery, and swedges. Apperson had been born on a Howard County farm and was educated in the local public schools and at the normal school in Valparaiso. Haynes called on him, and they immediately agreed upon terms. The work would be done during "slack time," i.e., it would not take priority over Apperson's normal business, and on an hourly basis. Haynes would pay Apperson and his men the standard rate for such work, forty cents an hour. Haynes further agreed not to hold Apperson responsible for the outcome, although he expected the work to be done well.[11] Thus began an association that was both historic in significance and profitable to the two men.

This is Haynes's partial description of his first car:

> The framework in which the motor was placed consisted of a double hollow square of steel tubing, joined at the rear corners by steel castings, and by malleable castings in front. The hind axle constituted the rear member of the frame and the front axle was swiveled at its center to the front end of the "hollow square" in which the motor and countershaft were placed.

In order to determine the amount of power necessary to move the machine, and thus to determine the gear ratios, Haynes had a bicycle rider towed behind a "light buckboard by means of a cord and a spring scale." The "draw-bar pull" registered on the scale indicated the amount of power necessary per hundred pounds to move a vehicle equipped with ball bearings and pneumatic tires. Using this crude data, Haynes worked out the pitch of the sprockets and other engineering details. Then he ascertained the torque of the Sintz engine (nine pounds) to arrive at the gearing required.

> I arranged for two speeds, the low speed just strong enough to move the machine up a 4 per cent. incline. It could barely do this. On the other hand, it moved right off on the level road, carrying three men.[12]

Top speed in the second gear was between seven and eight miles per hour.

---

[10] Charles B. King of Detroit also attempted to adapt a Sintz engine to a vehicle. He too had discovered the engine at the Chicago fair, where he was exhibiting machinery himself. King purchased his engine earlier than Haynes and recalled that he too had "considerable trouble" with it. Both King and Haynes soon abandoned the two-cycle for a four-cycle type. King also passed along a story about Haynes that was cherished by the Sintz management and which not only verifies Haynes's account but adds some interesting details. Harry Kraft, the "trouble shooter" for Sintz, was sent to Kokomo in the winter of 1894 (1893?). Kraft and Haynes moved the engine into Mrs. Haynes's kitchen, mounted it on sawhorses, and finally got it started. The vibration brought it off its supports, and the engine "chased around the room." Fortunately, no fire resulted. According to the Sintz version, Mrs. Haynes never allowed either Kraft or the engine into her house again. Memorandum by Charles B. King, April 4, 1944, Beecroft Papers. Whether this incident occurred once or twice is moot; certainly the kitchen calamity happened at least once.

[11] "A Sworn Statement by Elwood Haynes," 1920, Haynes Papers. A. G. Seiberling, the general manager of the Haynes Automobile Company, published this statement during the height of the controversy with the Apperson Brothers Automobile Company over who had built the first car in Kokomo.

[12] *Ibid.*

Various men employed at the Apperson shop worked on Haynes's mechanical novelty during the next several months. Because of the subsequent controversy between the advertising departments of the Haynes and the Apperson Brothers automobile companies and because of the inherent importance of the pioneer vehicle, many of the workmen were later called upon to make sworn statements about their labors and to judge who deserved credit for the machine produced in 1893-1894. Although claims and counterclaims continued to be made for years, a rather consistent story emerges. Haynes had conceived the idea, drawn up the plans, purchased the engine, worked out the engineering problems—using the higher mathematics he had acquired so laboriously at Worcester—, and financed the entire project; the Apperson brothers and their workmen had *built* the car. The Appersons made modifications and offered various suggestions as the work progressed, which Haynes always acknowledged, but there can be no serious doubt as to where the primary credit for the "Pioneer" should go.

Haynes himself distinguished between the first car, built in 1893-1894, and the second one, which he and Apperson produced jointly for entry into the 1895 Chicago race, by calling the first a Haynes and the second a Haynes-Apperson.

Among the workmen on the first car were William Adrian, Warren Wrightsman, Edgar Apperson, and John D. Maxwell, the latter a youngster not yet on the Haynes-Apperson payroll and whose participation in the "closed door" project was apparently unknown to Haynes.[13] Haynes himself often joined the men at the shop and spent long hours working out technical problems. His primary interest was in the engine itself, which was mounted on a sturdy log buried in the dirt floor of the building. One Apperson employee recalled not only the frequent ice cream treats Haynes brought for the men but also an occasion when the inventor was nearly overcome with carbon monoxide after several hours bending over the balky engine.[14]

Only one financial statement of the earliest arrangements between Haynes and Apperson has survived, and it confirms Haynes's recollection of the agreement. For 59½ hours of work performed during the first eight days of June, 1894, Apperson billed Haynes for $23.80, i.e., at the rate of forty cents an hour. The bulk of the labor covered by this invoice was being done "on Frame," but there was also one charge for six hours of work "Designing Wagon." Probably the work was related to the clutch or the wheels, since Edgar Apperson wrote to automobile historian David Beecroft in 1924 that "I can remember very distinctly that Elmer worked out the clutch mechanism" on the first car and that Edgar himself created the wheels:

I made the patterns for the hubs, machined the hubs, made the cups and cones out of tool steel, made wire spokes and nipples, as there was nothing larger at that time than bicycle spokes, which were insufficient in size and strength, so I probably made the first set of wire wheels that were [e]ver built, and certainly the first ever built in the United States, for a motor car.[15]

[13] Kokomo *Dispatch,* April 3, 1921; Statement by John D. Maxwell, 1905, in Duryea Papers, Automotive History Collection, Detroit Public Library. Jonathan Dixon Maxwell (1864–1928) began construction work on the first Haynes car in 1894. After five years in Kokomo, Maxwell assisted R. E. Olds in Detroit; later he organized the Northern Automobile Company, Maxwell-Briscoe Company, the U. S. Motor Company, and finally the John D. Maxwell Company. *National Cyclopedia of American Biography* (1936), s.v. "John D. Maxwell."

[14] Indianapolis *Star,* July 1, 1913.

[15] Edgar Apperson to David Beecroft, October 17, 1924, Beecroft Papers.

By an interesting coincidence the vehicle they had been working on intermittently since November, 1893, was ready for testing on July 4, 1894. Despite the continuation of the Pullman strike in Chicago, which had precipitated a general railway strike, an unusually large gathering was expected in Kokomo that day; in addition to the customary holiday celebrants, a veterans' encampment, the eighth annual convention of the Sons of Veterans of Indiana, was scheduled to begin on the fourth. The city was handsomely decorated for the occasion, with gay bunting streaming from the downtown buildings and many private residences along the parade route. A full day's activity was planned, including baseball games and bicycle racing in the morning, an early afternoon parade, and "a great pyrotechnic display" at night.[16]

When the day was over and a stocktaking had been made, the Kokomo *Dispatch* expressed some disappointment at the size of the public turnout, the smallness of which was attributed to the reluctance of local farmers to forsake a good weather day in the field at corn plowing time and to the rail strike. In reviewing the day's events, however, the newspaper failed to mention the most significant one. Midway through the afternoon of the fourth, three men had silently rolled a strange-looking carriage out into Main Street in front of the Riverside Machine Shop. A crowd gathered almost immediately, convincing the men, Elwood Haynes, Elmer Apperson, and Warren Wrightsman, that it would be unsafe to begin the test of the machine there. As Haynes put it, "Not one of the persons intending to operate the machine had ever seen anything of the sort before, much less having driven one." They arranged, therefore, for a team of horses to pull the vehicle out into the country. Approximately three miles from the center of town, along a twisting but practically level stretch known as Pumpkinvine Pike, the men stopped, unhitched the carriage, and started the gasoline engine mounted on it. The three men clambered aboard and, to everyone's delight, the vehicle "moved off at once at a speed of about seven miles per hour. . . ."[17]

After approximately fifteen minutes and a mile and a half into the country, Haynes, who was driving, brought the machine to a stop. He and his passengers turned it around manually, since there was no reverse gear, and they chugged back to Kokomo, running

> all the way into the city without making a single stop. . . . I remember as the little machine made its way along the streets [Haynes recalled in 1918] we were met by a "bevy" of girls mounted on wheels. I shall never forget the expressions on their faces as they wheeled aside, separating like a flock of swans and gazing wonder-eyed at the uncouth and utterly unexpected little machine.

The car was driven all the way back to the Apperson shop without mishap or interruption, although the engine died while Haynes was negotiating the gutter and slight incline into the shop. Following this historic drive, Haynes went home for supper. Years later Mrs. Haynes commented that the only thing extraordinary about this day in her memory was that her husband was late for his evening meal.[18]

[16] Kokomo *Daily Dispatch,* July 4, 1894.

[17] *Ibid.,* July 5, 1894; Haynes, "How I Built the First Automobile," in *Haynes Pioneer,* July, 1918, p. 6.

[18] Haynes, "How I Built the First Automobile," in *Haynes Pioneer,* July, 1918, p. 6; Haynes to W. A. P. John, September 14, 1921, Haynes Papers. John had asked what time of day the first trip was made. Haynes, unable to remember, asked his wife; "she remembered it distinctly because we had company that evening and I was late for supper."

Haynes's July 4, 1894, drive along Pumpkinvine Pike has made its way into Hoosier, if not national, folklore, and those who know anything at all about Elwood Haynes know of this journey. Several roadside markers from time to time have been placed to identify the spot where this stirring event took place. But what has seemed like triumphal success to people of a later generation seemed quite different to Haynes at the time. Although he was pleased that the car ran, he was also dissatisfied with it, especially its weak engine and dangerous steering device. The latter device was neither a tiller nor a wheel; instead, the first Haynes vehicles were equipped with a vertical rod to which a horizontal handle was attached. The mechanism, similar to a bicycle crank and pedal, moved forward and backward, not from side to side. The rule of steering was "forward to the right, backward to the left." Charles Duryea later suggested that the awkward steering device might have been responsible for the skidding accident which was to prevent Haynes and Apperson from participating in a race in Chicago in 1895. Haynes himself admitted in the Selden-Winton patent suit in 1901 or 1902 that his first car's steering was "just the reverse of satisfactory—it was positively dangerous," and Mrs. Bernice H. Hillis, daughter of the inventor, recalled somewhat sadly in 1970 that she had never been allowed to ride in the "Pioneer"—"Father thought it was too dangerous."[19]

The engine was unsatisfactory both because of its low power and its extreme vibration. Within two weeks of the initial trial run, Haynes was writing to the Sintz company seeking a replacement engine. The Sintzes declined Haynes's suggestion that they lend one to him, but they soon agreed to take in the old engine on trade for a new two-horsepower model. This transaction was made in August, and Haynes was in some respects better satisfied with his car's performance; he had, however, even more trouble getting the second engine to function properly than he had with the first. Later, in building the second car, he and Apperson designed and made their own "double-opposed" two-cylinder engine.[20]

The Sintzes were pleased to learn of the new use to which Haynes was putting their engine and asked for pictures of his vehicle in November, 1894. They advertised the use of their engine for a motorized vehicle and generously responded to Haynes's requests for assistance in operating the engine.[21] But Haynes considered at least briefly the merits of converting to electrical power before he and Elmer Apperson embarked upon the task of building their own engine.

In a 1915 series of letters to David Beecroft and Charles E. Duryea, Haynes contributed some valuable details about the production of his first car. Beecroft and Duryea were in the midst of preparing the most authoritative possible account of pioneer American automotive work for publication in *Automobile* magazine, and they had submitted a questionnaire to Haynes. He responded with a letter in which he reiterated the sequence of events culminating in the "Pioneer": the idea in the late 1880s, the choice of motive power in 1890, preliminary sketches in 1891 and 1892, construction in 1893-1894, the road test on July 4, 1894, and the substitution of a larger engine and pneumatic tires in the fall of 1894. At that point Haynes reported the

---

[19] Interview with Bernice Haynes Hillis, December 8, 1970.

[20] H. A. Winter to Haynes, July 18, August 6, September 20, November 3, 7, 15, 1894, Haynes Papers.

[21] Theo F. Upson to Elwood Haynes, December 3, 1894, *ibid.* Upson, a would-be automobile maker from Elkhart, wrote to Haynes for advice at the suggestion of the Sintz company.

car's top speed was twelve to fourteen miles per hour. In 1895 a "good muffler" was added, and thereafter the machine "ran very quietly, particularly when in high gear."[22] In response to follow-up questions from Duryea, Haynes went on to describe the car's clutch and gearing in great detail:

> Power was transmitted from the motor by means of 3 driving chains to a countershaft which crossed the frame about 18″ forward from the engine shaft. On the countershaft were placed 2 clutches of the lake type, which were at that time in common use on lathe countershafts. These clutches were connected by means of a sliding collar on the countershaft, which was moved longit[u]dinally on the shaft by means of a cable which could be drawn taut in either direction by means of a vertical post near the driver's seat, which could be turned in either direction by means of a cross bar something like the handle of an ordinary auger.
>
> The slowest speed mechanism consisted of a small loose sprocket on the engine shaft and a large sprocket keyed to the countershaft. The small sprocket on the engine shaft could be locked at will by a small cone clutch operated by a separate lever. I will say, however, that this slow speed did not work well and was seldom used excepting under very hard conditions. The engine when first placed in the car was not provided with a starting crank, but was supplied with one shortly afterward. The power from the countershaft was conveyed to the rear wheels by means of 2 sprocket shafts in the usual manner now employed upon trucks. No differential was used in the car, but one of the sprockets on the end of the countershaft was attached to . . . a conical clutch. This clutch was always in action, the cone being held in the socket by means of a spiral spring on the countershaft. In turning a corner this cone would slip sufficiently to prevent any undue stress on the working parts. For the light power used, this arrangement worked very well.[23]

*"How I Built
the First Automobile"*

75

As indicated, there was no reverse gear on the car. It could be driven backwards, however, by reversing the motor. This could be done, as Haynes explained,

> by setting the engine free and allowing it to slow down nearly to the stopping point and suddenly applying the spark. A little practice enable[d] the operator to accomplish this nearly every time, though it must be admitted that he was never absolutely sure whether the car would run backward or forward when the clutch was applied.

This interesting feature of the car "gave but little trouble," Haynes averred, confessing that he "was more concerned about getting the machine to run forward than about manipulating in close places."[24]

In a separate, personal letter of the same date to Duryea, Haynes set forth his views on the growing controversy over who was entitled to American automobile priority and glory. He was concerned with neither of these, he claimed, but merely wanted "future students of the automobile" to "know exactly what was done by the writer and when it was accomplished." Haynes summarized his position, repeating first his denial that he copied anyone else's machine, whether European or American:

> I simply determined the horse power of the motor under the brake and calculated the stress obtainable on the rear tires at different speeds and determined

[22] Elwood Haynes to David Beecroft, April 22, 1915, Beecroft Papers.

[23] Elwood Haynes to Charles E. Duryea, July 2, 1915, *ibid.*

[24] *Ibid.*

as nearly as possible the tractive effort necessary to draw the machine over a common road, and proceeded to build the machine accordingly. Some modifications were made in the machine principally to render it more easy to construct.[25]

Haynes estimated that he drove the "Pioneer" perhaps a thousand miles in all, chiefly in the evenings with his wife when the streets were unoccupied. He noted that he averaged 56 miles per gallon of gasoline with the little vehicle at a time when the fuel cost six cents per gallon, but he also admitted to friends that his first car "was never much account."[26]

It is doubtful that Haynes would have begun to manufacture automobiles except for the stimulus provided by the Chicago race of 1895, which was inspired in turn by the first European automobile race from Paris to Rouen in 1894. As Haynes repeatedly remarked, the first little car was intended for his personal business use, and he continued to devote his primary energies to his gas company duties in the 1890s. When H. H. Kohlsaat announced that his newspaper, the Chicago *Times-Herald,* was sponsoring an automobile race—the first one in America—, Haynes and Apperson could not resist the opportunity to participate. They formed an informal partnership and set about building a new car especially for the race.

Franklin Upson Adams, the young *Times-Herald* reporter who had sold the race idea to his publisher, toured the country seeking entrants for the race. He was delighted when he reached Kokomo and found an actual working model of an automobile as well as plans for a second entry.[27] Most of the people Adams talked to in the fall of 1894 had ideas and high expectations but no workable vehicles. In fact the original race date of July 4, 1895, had to be postponed twice in order to give aspiring contestants more time to prepare their automobiles.

By July 16, 1895, however, the *Times-Herald* had proceeded so far as to announce tentative "Horseless Carriage Contest" rules, with the final rules to be announced later by a panel of judges yet to be selected. The *Times-Herald* promised prizes totaling $5,000, $2,000 of which was to be awarded to the winner of the race. Seventy-five entries were expected, and the race was planned to run from Chicago to Milwaukee on November 2, 1895. The purpose of the whole affair was "to promote, encourage, and stimulate the invention, development, perfection and general adoption of motor carriages."[28] It was stipulated that the vehicles were to have their own mechanical (not muscular) motive power, three wheels or more, and be of a safe and practical design. Speed was only one of the criteria to be considered by the judges in awarding prizes; "general utility," initial and operating costs, and "general appearance" would also be taken into account.

To drum up interest in the contest and to promote newspaper circulation, the *Times-Herald* offered $500 for the best name suggested for the new vehicles, hitherto known in America as "horseless carriages." Many people were displeased with this rather negative designation and were looking for

---

[25] *Ibid.* See also Elwood Haynes, "Just a Little Bit Historical," in *Motor,* February, 1908, p. 53.

[26] Foster, "How Elwood Haynes Came to Build First 'Horseless Carriage,'" in *Forbes,* March 1, 1925, p. 682; clipping, January 17, 1923, Haynes Papers.

[27] G. H. Winders, "The Great Motocycle Race," in Indianapolis *Star,* May 28, 1967; H. H. Kohlsaat, "America's First Horseless Carriage Race, 1895," in *Saturday Evening Post,* January 5, 1924, p. 21; Bellamy Partridge, *Fill 'er up! The Story of Fifty Years of Motoring* (New York: McGraw-Hill, 1952), pp. 10–19.

[28] Chicago *Times-Herald,* July 16, 1895.

something more positive, generic, and indigenous. A New Yorker, G. F. Shaver, won the $500 for the suggestion of "motocycle," which the *Times-Herald* then adopted and attempted to introduce into general circulation.[29] An early automobile journal actually was called *Motocycle,* but the name was soon discarded in favor of "automobile" or "car."

By September the expected seventy-five entrants had dwindled to fifty-five ("unless gross misrepresentations and false claims" had been made), and by October the number was reduced to between thirty and fifty. The contest judges were announced (an army officer, a manufacturer, and a professional man) along with the final contest rules. The route was changed and shortened to begin and end in Chicago, and preliminary tests of the vehicles were to be conducted on October 29, 30, and 31 at the Jackson Park race course.

In the meantime the paper proceeded with its cheerful announcements about the race and printed stories on many of the entrants, but it was increasingly obvious that the number of entrants on November 2 would be very small indeed. In fact, only one vehicle had shown up for the Jackson Park tests—a German-made Benz owned and operated by H. Mueller of Iowa—and even this had been accomplished only with difficulty. A Chicago policeman who heard "the 'chuck, chuck' of the engine . . . concluded it was neither a bicycle nor an ordinary carriage" and ordered it off the boulevard leading to the park, much to the chagrin of the race sponsors.[30] Special orders were issued thereafter to permit motor carriages to use the boulevards, but even so Mueller was stopped a second time on October 31 and ordered off Michigan Boulevard, a fate Haynes was to share a few days later in the "Pioneer."[31] Mueller made it to the racetrack on both occasions, however, and each time his vehicle was able to make a circuit of the mile oval. On October 29, the Benz did a mile in 4:07.5; on October 30, its time was 5:40. Rather uncharitably the newspaper pointed out that the racehorse Joe Patchen had covered the same distance in 2:06.1 a few weeks earlier.[32]

Since the trials had produced only one contender, the *Times-Herald* decided at the last minute to postpone the race until Thanksgiving Day. Not wishing to disappoint spectators altogether on November 2, however, the judges decided to run a special trial over the ninety-mile course for a prize of $500. Only Mueller's Benz and the Duryea machine, which had just arrived from Springfield, Massachusetts, entered the trial race, and only the Mueller vehicle finished it. Duryea swerved into a ditch to avoid colliding with a wagon, and though the damage was minor it prevented him from completing the race.[33]

In the weeks after November 2, more race entrants trickled into Chicago. Elwood Haynes shipped his improved "Pioneer" from Kokomo on November 19. "This buggy is now a familiar sight to everyone about town," commented the Kokomo *Dispatch,* and a second one was about to be completed. The *Dispatch* also reported that both vehicles had been built by the Apperson brothers and that great results were expected from the new machine. The reporter was unable to describe it, however, because the new two-cylinder

---

[29] *Ibid.,* July 25, 1895.

[30] *Ibid.,* October 30, 1895.

[31] This event was restaged and photographed years later and is a familiar item in the Haynes folklore (which does not recognize the earlier Mueller arrest). See Charles B. King, *A Golden Anniversary, 1895–1945: Personal Side Lights of America's First Automobile Race* (New York: privately printed by Super-power Printing Company, 1945), p. 40.

[32] Chicago *Times-Herald,* October 31, 1895.

[33] *Ibid.,* November 3, 1895.

78

Elwood Haynes in the 1894 "Pioneer"

engine (an "invention of Elmer E. Apperson") was still unassembled. Nevertheless, the Appersons planned to leave for Chicago five days later to make the race on November 28.[34]

Reflecting on the future of the motor vehicle in the midst of final race preparations, the Kokomo *Daily Dispatch* editorialized that—whatever the outcome in Chicago—the automobile would not replace the horse. Both, the editor predicted, were "here to stay." Machines might replace the horse in the streets, as railroads had replaced him on the turnpikes, but outside the "narrow areas of trade and money making" the horse would grow in use and favor as society gained in wealth and intelligence.

> Life is much easier under the principle of merely "touching the button" and summoning the powers of nature to do the rest. But the desire of ease is not the ultimate aspiration of humanity. . . . [P]hysical exertion and mastery is a need of

---

[34] Kokomo *Dispatch,* November 20, 1895. As this report indicates, albeit somewhat exaggeratedly, the Appersons were the primary force in building the second car and in operating the Haynes-Apperson firm in its early days from their Riverside Machine Shop. In 1915 Haynes admitted to Beecroft and Duryea that he could not give them detailed information about the earliest sales and production records of his automobile company because Elmer Apperson "was in active charge of the manufacture when the early cars . . . were placed on the market." Haynes to Charles E. Duryea, July 2, 1915, Beecroft Papers.

the American of to day. And no other form of pleasure or trial of skill so well meets this need as the fiery spirit of the horse.[35]

When Haynes arrived in Chicago with the "Pioneer," he was given an unexpected reception. "I remember very well when the little machine was unloaded for the Times-Herald contest in 1895 at Englewood, a suburb of Chicago," Haynes wrote in 1918:

> I was riding down Michigan Ave., intending to drive to the central portion of the city, and had scarcely proceeded more than six or eight blocks, when I was accosted by a policeman who ordered me to leave the boulevard at once, as nothing like "horseless carriages" were permitted. I remonstrated with him what harm the machine could do the boulevard, since it was equipped with rubber tires and made but little noise. He simply replied that it was "Arders, Sir," so I could do nothing but obey.[36]

This encounter was later restaged and photographed by Haynes's automobile company for an advertisement stressing the pioneering background of their product.

Haynes took his car by another route to the exhibition and testing rooms on Wabash Avenue, where he was joined by Elmer Apperson and the other exhibitors/contestants early the next week. Haynes had not planned actually to enter the race with the older vehicle but brought it to Chicago in order to exhibit it. Many spectators visited the site, examining the machines and witnessing the careful performance tests each underwent. But more than just race spectators arrived in Chicago during Thanksgiving week; a blizzard came too. Snow several inches deep blanketed the city only days before the race, and it was still on the ground as the starting time approached. Although the snow was likely to create considerable difficulties for the primitive vehicles, a third postponement also seemed out of the question; so the promoters and judges decided to carry on. This proved to be a most unfortunate decision for Haynes and Apperson, since their new automobile skidded in the snow while making its way towards Jackson Park and the starting line on race day morning. The vehicle swerved to avoid colliding with a streetcar and slammed into a curb at the corner of Indiana Avenue and Thirtieth Street; a wheel was broken, and there was no spare. For Haynes and Apperson the race was off.[37]

In fact only six "motocycles" were on hand to begin the race, and only two finished the course to Evanston and back. The Duryea entry won the race, finishing ahead of Mueller's Benz by approximately one and a half hours. J. Frank Duryea drove the winning car, with an umpire riding along, while Charles Duryea watched from a horse-drawn sleigh. Mueller collapsed from exhaustion an hour from the finish line, and his umpire, Charles B. King, drove the remaining distance. The *Times-Herald* report on the race began as follows:

> Against tremendous odds, which perhaps demonstrated conclusively the practicability of the horseless carriage, the *Times-Herald* motocycle race was run

---

[35] Kokomo *Daily Dispatch,* November 22, 1895. This editorial may have been inspired by a rash of expressions of support for the horse that appeared in other newspapers at this time.

[36] Haynes, "How I Built the First Automobile," in *Haynes Pioneer,* July, 1918, p. 7.

[37] Chicago *Times-Herald,* November 29, 1895. The Kokomo *Daily Dispatch* reported on November 30, 1895, that the car collided with a streetcar just after the race began, but this is clearly wrong.

yesterday. Through deep snow, and along ruts which would have tried horses to their utmost, six motocycles raced.

The paper's editorial that day cautiously predicted a bright future for the motocycle, "still in its experimental stage," and praised the impetus this new development would give to the "good roads movement."[38]

A week later the judges announced the prize awards. The Duryeas, unsurprisingly, collected the first prize of $2,000 and Mueller the second prize of $1,000, but many others were recognized also with special awards. The Haynes-Apperson entry received $150 for its "meritorious design feature"— the reduction of vibration by "balancing the engine."[39]

Buoyed by this rather limited success and by the ideas picked up in Chicago, Haynes and Apperson decided to go into the business of manufacturing automobiles. For Apperson this would be a full-time undertaking; for Haynes it would be only part-time in the beginning, since he would continue with his work at the gas company.

The Chicago race had an additional significance for automobile history: acting upon Charles B. King's suggestions, the American Automobile League was organized on November 1, 1895, and Haynes became one of its charter members.[40] This organization was the forerunner of the present National Association of American Automobile Manufacturers. The race also established a certain beginning point in American automobile development; as the *Times-Herald* editorial properly indicated, the industry in 1895 was still in its experimental stage, but the half dozen American builders of that year became several score by 1900. The contemporary impact of the nation's first automobile racing event is perhaps underscored by Henry Ford's remark years afterwards: "I never wanted anything so much in my life as to attend that race, but I couldn't raise the money."[41]

In 1908 the city of New York staged a celebration to honor the American automobile industry, and Elwood Haynes and the "Pioneer" were chosen to lead the historical section of the parade. Ten years had passed since the automobile had first appeared in New York, and several events were planned to celebrate the occasion—a parade, a hill climb, and a trophy race. The "Pioneer," already promised to the Smithsonian Institution, was immediately followed by ten other Haynes cars. They represented the period marked by the celebration and illustrated the progress in the industry over the preceding decade. Thousands of people lined Broadway and Fifth Avenue on the evening of April 7 to witness the spectacle.[42]

To Haynes's delight his first car performed well during the evening. It had been removed from storage at the Haynes Automobile Company plant in Kokomo and shipped to New York only three days earlier; understandably Haynes was concerned about its running condition. During the afternoon before the parade Haynes and his chief engineer Frank Nutt had taken the old car out for a trial run. It responded beautifully, and Haynes forgot about the city's speed control laws as he gaily drove along upper Broadway. A city patrolman promptly arrested him for "fast driving" and "driving a machine

[38] Chicago *Times-Herald*, November 29, 1895.

[39] *Ibid.*, December 6, 1895.

[40] King, *A Golden Anniversary, 1895—1945*, p. 41.

[41] Quoted in Kohlsaat, "America's First Horseless Carriage Race," in *Saturday Evening Post*, January 5, 1924, p. 89.

[42] Kokomo *Morning Dispatch*, April 4, 8, 1908; New York *Times*, March 1 through April 10, 1908.

without a number." After full explanations were made in magistrate's court the charges were dropped, and Haynes and the "Pioneer" reappeared as planned that evening on the city streets. The inventor was more proud than embarrassed by the fact that his fourteen-year-old "Pioneer," "now little more than a relic," could travel fast enough to warrant a speeding charge. After their return home he and Nutt assured doubting Kokomo friends that "It was a for sure enough arrest . . . by a real policeman."[43]

The New York parade recognized Haynes as the builder of America's "first" successful automobile, a questionable although not entirely unsupportable assertion. For his own part, Haynes knew he had built one of the first automobiles in America, that he had done the design and engineering work—but not the actual construction—himself, and he eventually allowed himself to be persuaded that it was the very first successful machine in the country. "Regarding the first Haynes gasoline automobile," he wrote to a journalist in 1911,

> I will say that I do not know whether it was the first machine of this character constructed in America or not. On the other hand, I do not know of an earlier operative machine of this sort. I believe, however, that it was the first *complete, practical* gasoline machine built in America.[44]

Haynes allowed himself to make this statement on the grounds that the earliest Duryea models were merely motorized buggies, whereas his own vehicles were built from the ground up, with wire wheels, pneumatic tires, and a tubular (gas pipe) frame. Duryea argued, on the other hand, that Haynes's vehicle also lacked many essential features to make it a prototype of the American automobile: the "Pioneer" lacked a differential and an adequate steering device. The "Pioneer" Haynes drove in New York in 1908 was, of course, a modified version of the 1894 vehicle, and Duryea was justly infuriated that the display tag on the car in the Smithsonian Institution failed for years to acknowledge the modifications and implied that the vehicle was the 1894 machine as originally constructed.

Ten years later, in 1918, Haynes was to become involved in a dispute provoked partly by an article he wrote entitled "How I Built the First Automobile" and partly by advertising his company as the oldest gasoline-powered automobile manufacturer in America. Although his claim to have built the first automobile is simply false, the latter claim was incontestable after the Duryea Motor Wagon Company folded in 1898. The Haynes and Apperson manufacturing operation was followed by Alexander Winton, who built a two-cylinder automobile in Cleveland in 1896, and Winton soon marketed a single-cylinder model that he claimed was the first automobile sold in America. R. E. Olds also built his first gasoline-powered automobile in 1896, and he became the first large-scale producer of cars in America when he manufactured 1,200 of the curved-dash Oldsmobiles in 1900. In the meantime Henry Ford, who later rather casually claimed 1892 as the date of his first car, was experimenting and produced his first automobile in 1896; but his success did not arrive until after the turn of the century and the forma-

---

[43] Kokomo *Morning Dispatch,* April 14, 1908. The *Dispatch* reported this as Haynes's second arrest for speeding; the previous year he had been stopped in Kokomo while hurrying to catch a train. *Ibid.,* April 9, 1908.

[44] Elwood Haynes to J. E. Homans, October 5, 1911, Indiana Historical Society Library, Indianapolis. A facsimile of this letter appears in Indiana Historical Society, *Annual Report 1969–1970* (Indianapolis, 1971), p. 40.

tion of his third automobile company, the Ford Motor Company, in 1903. Even in Detroit Ford was anticipated by Charles B. King, the first man in Michigan to drive an automobile.[45]

In spite of all that is known of the early stages of the development of the automobile, it is difficult to express precisely the contributions that Haynes and his partners made to that enterprise. While part of the job of constructing the first cars was simply a matter of assembling the proper parts, both invention and innovation were required as well. Haynes not only imagined and designed his own first vehicle, using engines and machinery commonly available at the time, but he also worked out gear ratios, power transmission systems, and a steering mechanism—admittedly an inferior one. Haynes and his workmen solved design and construction problems as they encountered them. Later Haynes and Apperson successfully designed and manufactured a powerful and reliable two-cylinder engine, introducing both the use of aluminum in its construction and a muffler to decrease the deafening noise of a gasoline engine, and they patented a number of other improvements in clutches, carburetors, and lubrication systems.

Still, it must be emphasized, as the Selden patent case eventually was to establish legally, that no one person or small group of persons was responsible for the automobile; it was the product of the combined genius of countless mechanics and engineers on both sides of the Atlantic. The Haynes contribution was a significant one primarily because of its timing and a variety of technical advances, to which should be added those of Haynes's later metallurgical discoveries that were automobile-related. It is clear, however, that the American automobile did not stem from Haynes's work, nor did he make automobile manufacturing his primary pursuit except for brief periods.

82

[45] Rae, *American Automobile,* p. 11. There have been numerous claims, and more yet may come, that automobiles were built in America before either the Duryea or the Haynes prototype. So far these claims have lacked convincing contemporary evidence to support them and do not in any event change the history of the development of the automobile industry in America. Examples of supposedly pre-1893 automobiles in America include the Charles D. Black vehicle of Indianapolis (1891?) and the John W. Lambert vehicle of Ohio (1890?).

The Black car, now on display in the Children's Museum in Indianapolis, has obvious post-1895 features. It was first mentioned in Indianapolis newspapers in 1913 when Black discussed his car and the date of its construction in an interview, but there is no contemporary support for the 1891 date. Black, a carriage manufacturer, did produce a Benz-type vehicle in 1899, but he did not enter automobile manufacturing on a commercial scale. See Indianapolis *News,* December 27, 1913, March 21, 1929, and April 3, 4, 5, 1940; "Charles H. Black's Horseless Carriage," in *Indiana History Bulletin,* XVI (1939), 191–93; and Phillips, *Indiana in Transition,* pp. 311–12. See also the C. H. Black Manufacturing Company file, Automotive History Collection, Detroit Public Library. A reference in the Black file indicates that he had a Benz automobile in Indianapolis in 1891, which he drove around the city with disastrous results—three wrecks—and that he built a vehicle of his own in 1894 but did not produce other vehicles.

Similarly the Lamberts, who eventually went into production in Indiana after 1900, have claimed an early 1890s first vehicle, but the claim has not been substantiated. According to a rumor that once circulated in the state, Haynes paid the Lamberts to keep quiet about the date of their first vehicle, so that he could retain his reputation as the oldest American manufacturer, but the story is too preposterous to be credited. Nevertheless it has re-emerged without attribution in *The American Car Since 1775: The Most Complete Survey of the American Automobile Ever Published* (2d ed. New York: L. S. Bailey, 1971), p. 55, published by the editors of *Automobile Quarterly.*

Chapter 7

Automobile Manufacturing: The Early Years

The automobile industry was born in the waning years of the nineteenth century. Clearly self-propelled vehicular travel was an idea whose time had come, and literally hundreds of firms were organized during the late 1890s to manufacture automobiles. Many of these companies did not get beyond the planning stages, but 327 automobile assembly plants, each with an annual output in excess of three products, have been identified as being in existence in 1900.[1] Probably the first such firm was the Duryea Motor Wagon Company of Springfield, Massachusetts. Winner of the 1895 Chicago race, the Duryea company produced twelve cars in 1896, "the first attempt at quantity production of passenger automobiles by an American industrial firm."[2] The Haynes-Apperson partnership, dating from 1894, yielded at least one automobile a year for the first three years, and then "quantity" production was initiated. By 1900 nearly two hundred Haynes-Apperson automobiles were being produced annually.

When Elwood Haynes hired Elmer Apperson to build his first automobile in 1893-1894, it marked the beginning of a long association, at first as partners and eventually as competitors. The two men, together for eight years, established a new industry in the state of Indiana; afterwards, going their separate ways, they continued to manufacture automobiles for another two decades. At first Haynes and Apperson operated on a simple partnership basis, producing and selling only a very small number of machines. It would be more accurate, in fact, to say that they sold and then produced their earliest automobiles, the orders coming as a result of advertisements in newly established trade journals or from exhibitions of Haynes-Apperson carriages at county and state fairs in Indiana and Ohio. The initial response, an encouraging one even though it appeared the market for their product would be limited, led to two major developments in 1898: incorporation of the Haynes-Apperson Company and erection of a new factory. Initially capitalized at $25,000, with Kokomo and Portland businessmen as stock-

---

[1] Charles W. Boas, "Locational Patterns of American Automobile Assembly Plants, 1895–1958," in *Economic Geography*, XXXVII (1961), 221–22.

[2] *Ibid.* R. E. Olds, who manufactured 4,000 curved dash Oldsmobiles in 1903, deserves recognition as the originator of true mass production of identical models. Niemeyer, *Ransom E. Olds*, p. 52. See also George S. May, *R. E. Olds: Auto Industry Pioneer* (Grand Rapids, Mich.: William B. Eerdmans, 1977).

holders, the company increased its production dramatically after 1898. Nearly two hundred automobiles were delivered in 1900, the year in which total United States production amounted to 4,192, and Haynes-Apperson maintained an annual production of approximately 250 automobiles during the next seven years.[3]

Table 1

Haynes-Apperson Company Production, 1894–1905*

1894–1	1897–3	1900–192	1903–250E
1895–1	1898–5	1901–240	1904–250E
1896–1	1899–30	1902–250E	1905–250E[4]

* Source: Haynes Papers.

Although neither Haynes nor Apperson ever felt it was necessary to record their reasons for undertaking to manufacture automobiles in 1896, quite clearly it was the enormous interest shown in their "experimental" vehicles, capped by their appearance in Chicago, that prompted the endeavor. The first issue of *Horseless Age,* a publication begun in November, 1895, to serve the new industry, announced the Haynes-Apperson Company's plans to build automobiles even before the race was held. The Haynes-Apperson entry at Chicago had been a pre-race favorite and attracted much attention. In many ways this car, more than the winning Duryea "buggyaut," foreshadowed the motor car of the future. Not a motorized buggy, the Haynes-Apperson vehicle featured wire wheels, a tubular chassis, a unique and efficient engine (for which a $150 prize had been awarded), and other "modern" designs. As with the first car, the "Chicago" car was the product of joint effort between Haynes and Apperson, but the exact contributions of each man are unknown. This car, like its predecessor, was built in the Appersons' Riverside Machine Shop, which thus became one of the first automobile plants in America, and a Kokomo newspaper report credited Elmer Apperson with designing the engine. But the work of Haynes is clearly evident there too, for this engine was made of an aluminum alloy (93 percent aluminum, 7 percent

---

[3] Precise production figures for the Haynes-Apperson Company are not available. There are no extant corporate records, and various sources cite various figures. After making a comparison of all the known and contradictory data, the figures presented in Table 1 seem reasonable and reasonably accurate. See Elwood Haynes to Heber D. Williams, April 23, 1920, Haynes Papers; Foster, "How Elwood Haynes Came to Build First 'Horseless Carriage,' " in *Forbes,* March 1, 1925, p. 682; Powell, "History of Elwood Haynes"; and Jackson Morrow, *History of Howard County, Indiana* (2 volumes. Indianapolis: B. F. Bowen & Company, 1909), I, 248–49. For the national production figures, see Alfred Dupont Chandler (comp. and ed.), *Giant Enterprise: Ford, General Motors, and the Automobile Industry* (New York: Harcourt, Brace & World, Inc., 1964), p. 4.

[4] The sources for these figures are the items listed in the previous footnote and other miscellaneous references in the Haynes papers. After single cars were produced in 1894, 1895, and 1896, some contradictions exist within these records. An oft-repeated remark, that five cars were produced "the first year," has been variously interpreted, but the total evidence indicates that this figure applies to 1899, the first year of operation following incorporation. Elmer Apperson, in his affidavit in the Selden case, stated that there was no automobile manufacturing in Kokomo "on a commercial scale" until 1898, and it obviously took some time after that to build up volume production.

The 1894 "Haynes" was his famous "Pioneer"; the 1895 "Haynes-Apperson" was built specifically for the Chicago race; and the 1896 car, also an experimental model, was exhibited at fairs alongside its two predecessors. The 1897 models were the first ones marketed, and in 1916 two of these cars—one in Jeffersonville, Indiana, and the other in Bound Brook, New Jersey—were still being used. The early Haynes-Apperson owned by Mr. Jack Frost of Detroit, Michigan, is also an 1897. The first firm production figures after this are for 1900 and 1901, with the totals after 1901 giving the *average* annual production for the middle years of the decade.

copper) developed by Haynes during his search for a lightweight, sturdy substitute for cast iron.[5]

The relative success of the Kokomo entry at Chicago, despite its failure to compete in the actual race, confirmed the two men in their decision to carry on in the automobile manufacturing business. Their venture, jointly financed and with a logical division of labor and responsibility based upon the unique talents of each partner, began slowly and cautiously. As with the first two vehicles, the automobiles were built under the immediate supervision of Elmer Apperson in his machine shop. Haynes remained in his gas company position, continuing an important series of metallurgical experiments in the small laboratory above his office, but he worked closely with Apperson in designing the vehicles and solving engineering problems. He also assumed the primary responsibility for advertising and promoting the product. The hand of Haynes is clearly seen in the company's promotional literature and its advertising appeals. Both were heavily weighted with technical and sci-entific data, and the references to Haynes personally, while stated in the third person, contained information only he could have provided. The style of writing, moreover, was clearly and uniquely his own.

As early as July, 1896, the *Horseless Age* carried a notice about the Haynes and Apperson "new carriage," which would be "considerably in advance of their previous models." The new model would continue to feature an engine made of aluminum except for the cylinders of steel tubing, as had been the case with their racer. "Their experience," stated the notice, "has demon-strated the superiority of aluminum over cast iron in carriage motors, a truth which they claim to have been the first to discover." It concluded by announcing that the new Haynes-Apperson, capable of averaging fourteen miles per hour on a "good, level road," would be on display at the Ohio State Fair in Columbus in September.[6] Indeed, three carriages were to be on exhibition there, but the notice was intentionally ambiguous, implying that the three were new carriages assembled in 1896. Actually, they represented the total production of Haynes and Apperson up to that point.[7]

The 1896 Haynes-Apperson model was both pictured and described in the November issue of *Horseless Age.* The article, unsigned but obviously written by Haynes, also contained the Haynes-Apperson philosophy of motor con-struction and reviewed their experience with automobiles. The one-cylinder Sintz gasoline engine had vibrated so much that the carriage had to be built much heavier than intended. Consequently, although a satisfactory speed could be maintained "on a level pike," the engine was not "sufficiently pow-erful . . . , even when geared at low speed, to surmount hills. . . ." The one-horsepower engine had been replaced with another, rated at two horse-power, and much better results were obtained. "The carriage is still in use in

Automobile Manufacturing: The Early Years

85

---

[5]*Horseless Age,* July, 1896, p. 10. This is the first recorded instance of using aluminum in automobile manufacturing, a substance widely used today. Haynes made use of other special alloys in his earliest cars, including nickel steel. It appears that Haynes later discovered Stellite while searching for the right alloy to use in spark plugs.

[6]*Ibid.*

[7]*Ibid.* A letter to Elwood Haynes from his brother, Walter, relating to plans for exhibiting Haynes-Apperson cars at the Jay County Fair in Portland, Indiana, later in September seems to confirm that only three such cars were then in existence. Haynes's older brother inquired about freight charges on the "old carriage." "We have made this our attraction & are anxious to make the show a success—and if any thing should happen to either of the other two carriages we would still have *two* to e[x]hibit." Walter Haynes to Elwood Haynes, September 13, 1896, Haynes Papers. Printed on the back of this letter's envelope, obviously fair board stationery, were these words: "Grand Special Feature. HORSELESS VEHICLES. Introduced and Exhibited each day on track at *Jay County Fair.* September 28, 29, 30, October 1 & 2."

Kokomo, and makes a maximum of ten miles per hour on a good level pike. It is fitted with 1½-inch solid rubber tires and rides very easily, as the motor is set on the frame of the carriage and transmits no vibration to the passengers." Their next vehicle, however, was powered by a motor "of original design and manufacture," the Chicago prizewinning "double-cylinder horizontal gasolene [sic] engine." A two-cycle engine, rated at four horsepower "under the brake," it weighed 300 pounds, including the 110-pound flywheel. The cast portions of aluminum, however, weighed only 56 pounds. Haynes and Apperson also had another two-cylinder motor; it used the Otto, or four-cycle principle and produced eight horsepower. Two-inch pneumatic tires were used on this model, "obviating the necessity of setting the motor on springs."[8]

Haynes then went into a discussion of the advantages of cast aluminum over cast iron in gasoline engines—lightness, strength, ease of casting, but he pointed out the continued need for "full-weight" motors, with good heavy flywheels, "so that the motor will run more steadily when thrown into gear," and to assist in maintaining a steady pace while "traversing undulating roadways which are frequently found in rural districts." Haynes also advocated very strong crankshafts, so that "all the shocks and jars communicated from the momentum of the carriage as well as the force of the sudden explosions of the gaseous mixture in the cylinder" could be withstood. He maintained that "the entire motor should be constructed for durability and reliability, qualities far more important than high speed."[9]

Haynes then described some of the features on the "latest carriage" produced by Haynes and Apperson, an open, six-passenger vehicle fitted with 2½-inch pneumatic tires. Although its speed had not yet been "fully tested," Haynes believed "it should run at least 20 miles per hour on a good level roadway. It is fitted with an 8-horsepower motor which makes 500 revolutions per minute and weighs 340 pounds, including balance wheel." Power from the engine was "transmitted through friction clutches to a countershaft, and thence by sprocket chains to the rear wheels." There was a differential gear, "which permits the rear wheels of the carriage to accommodate themselves to the roadway. This carriage has four speeds of 4, 8, 12, and 18 miles per hour, and weighs without passengers about 1,500 pounds."[10]

The fair exhibitions of the Haynes-Apperson mechanical marvels had been arranged by an agent of the John Robinson circus, who offered Haynes $150 a month for the use of a car and driver. Roy Jones of Portland left his job as a railroader to tour with the circus during the 1896 season and demonstrate the wonders of horseless travel to sideshow audiences.[11] A special bonus of $200 was offered by the Ohio State Fair officials to have all three Haynes cars on exhibit in Columbus during the second week of September.[12]

[8] *Horseless Age,* November, 1896, p. 18.

[9] *Ibid.*

[10] *Ibid.* This article was accompanied by three illustrations, including a close-up of the prize-winning "double-opposed" engine, p. 19.

[11] Edgar Apperson (1870–1959), reminiscing in 1952 about these days, said that the 1896 car was leased to the Jack Robinson circus to lead parades. "The rented car business is not so damn new," he commented. Quoted in Robert E. Pinkerton, "Ed Apperson and the Horseless Carriage," in *True Magazine,* March, 1952, p. 85. A Duryea car was also exhibited in 1896 at the Barnum & Bailey circus. John K. Barnes, "The Romance of our Automobile Makers," in *World's Work,* April, 1921, p. 561.

[12] Elwood Haynes believed this exhibit was the first such showing of more than one car by the same manufacturer. Haynes, "How I Built the First Automobile," in *Haynes Pioneer,* July, 1918, p. 4; Powell, "History of Elwood Haynes," p. 81.

Anticipating the experience of thousands of future motorists, the circus tours led to considerable trouble. While in Wooster, Ohio, Jones's car was hit by the driver of a "big pole wagon," bending the front axle, and the "new carriage" was damaged while being shipped by rail to Columbus, Ohio, having "bumped against the sides of the car."[13] The three-car exhibition was successful, however, and the 1896 model was shown afterwards in Bucyrus, Ohio, enroute to its Portland, Indiana, appearance later in the month.[14]

Shortly after the fair exhibits, Haynes and Apperson recorded their first sale—that is, an order for a carriage was received. A brief, undated memoir by Ralph C. Lewis in the Detroit Public Library describes the event. Lewis believed this marked the "first sale of a new gasoline automobile by a recognized American manufacturer." In the fall of 1896, P. C. Lewis, a pump manufacturer of Catskill, New York, and father of the memoirist, purchased a Haynes-Apperson. The machine arrived in the early summer of 1897 and was removed with difficulty from a narrow-doored freight car. The younger Lewis, then a teenager, recalled the "mystery of starting the engine, and the alarm with which we all jumped back when the first explosion came." He described the automobile as a "well-painted dos-a-dos model with red panels, artillery type wheels, and red rubber pneumatic tires." The two-cylinder, water-cooled engine "was well balanced and ran smoothly," using a "make and break" ignition system and no carburetor, just a generating valve. The car had two forward speeds, operated through clutches and "sliding keys" to lock in the desired gear. Chain-driven and steered by a center tiller, "This Haynes [sic] was lower tha[n] experimental horseless carriages of the day. It was well-finished and looked more like a motor car than the other two horseless vehicles my father bought in the spring . . . of 1897."[15] P. C. Lewis, who raced these "wagons" to advertise his pump business, went on to establish one of the first automobile dealerships in America—the Empire State Motor Wagon Company. An advertisement of this firm, using a cut of his first Haynes-Apperson "wagon," appeared in *Horseless Age* in May, 1898.[16] According to Edgar Apperson, men like Lewis and Dr. Sweany, another early Haynes-Apperson buyer, were the true unsung heroes of automobile pioneering. "The ones who *bought* those first cars," he stated afterwards, deserved the most credit for the development of the automobile.[17] They took the risks of financial loss, ridicule, and frequent utter frustration in purchasing the untried vehicles, but the appeal of the automobile, then as now, was a powerful one.

The first Haynes-Apperson automobiles usually were delivered by the manufacturer directly to the customer, who was then taught to drive and care for the vehicle. Edgar Apperson, Elmer's younger brother, frequently performed this task. It was he, for example, who traveled to New York in 1897 to introduce P. C. Lewis to his machine, and he accompanied Dr. Sweany, who had come to Kokomo to pick up his automobile, back to Chicago.[18]

In order to stimulate further interest in the automobile, as well as to prove

---

[13] Roy Jones to Haynes & Apperson, August 14, 1896, Haynes Papers; Kokomo *Daily Dispatch,* September 19, 1896.

[14] Kokomo *Daily Dispatch,* September 19, 1896.

[15] Ralph C. Lewis File, Automotive History Collection, Detroit Public Library.

[16] *Horseless Age,* May, 1898, inside cover. P. C. Lewis died in 1903, the victim of a racing accident in Lewiston, Maine.

[17] Kokomo *Tribune,* May 13, 1959.

[18] Pinkerton, "Ed Apperson and the Horseless Carriage," in *True Magazine,* March, 1952, p. 86; *Horseless Age,* October, 1898, p. 11.

Haynes Pioneer, July, 1918

Haynes-Apperson factory, circa 1899

its reliability and capabilities, a great number of races and endurance runs were staged in the late 1890s and early 1900s. Haynes-Apperson cars participated in many of these events and did quite well in the competition. The early advertising of the firm featured the performances of its vehicles in such events, always making the point that its "racing machines" were standard models available to the general public.

Haynes and Apperson entered the "speed trial" in Boston in August, 1897, one of a series of races booked for the fall.[19] Their entry, driven by Edgar Apperson, was designed for only two passengers and "high speed" (up to 30 miles per hour). The engine, referred to as a "high speed balanced top," was light, powerful, communicated no vibration to the carriage, and ran "almost noiselessly." It also ran successfully, winning and setting the "speed record," unspecified, at the Charles River track. Later the car was exhibited and raced in Worcester, Massachusetts, the college home of Elwood Haynes, where it was "at the front again."[20]

By this time the Haynes-Apperson business was firmly established, and the men had difficulty in keeping up with their orders for cars. The Kokomo press reported in August, 1897, that the Riverside Machine Shop has "been kept running as late as 10:30 at night the last sixty days," and plans to enlarge the plant were underway, including the installation of woodworking facilities. (At that time, the woodwork was being sent out to a shop in Peru, Indiana.) Haynes and Apperson continued to use the "high grade pneumatic tires which are made by the Kokomo Rubber company," the best available, and they anticipated giving the tire manufacturers a "great deal of business."[21]

---

[19] The 1904 catalog of the Haynes Automobile Company also lists a "speed record" set in Louisville, Kentucky, in 1895, but no additional information about this has been found.

[20] Kokomo *Dispatch*, September 4, 1897.

[21] *Ibid.*, August 28, 1897. The newspaper reported orders on hand from buyers in New York, Massachusetts, and Montana. At first, it appears that the Riverside Machine Shop kept its old business separate from that of manufacturing carriages. There exists in the Haynes Papers a bill from the shop to the "Haynes & Apperson Company," dated January 15, 1898. It lists such charges as "Labor, October 17 to November 20 inclusive, $179.30," and "Labor on 4 H. P. Engine 4 Passenger Carriage and 2 Passenger Carriage castings and speed device from November 20, 1897 to January 17, 1898, $281.25," and a number of smaller items. The bill totaled $646.30, on which $300 had been paid.

As a result of the promising response to their product, Haynes and Apperson decided to incorporate the business, using new capital to finance the planned expansion. The well-publicized trip the two men and the Haynes family made to Portland in their "big machine, with its double seats," early in May, 1898, was probably intended as an inducement to potential investors in Portland. They traveled seventy-four miles in less than seven hours, and only six hours were needed for the return. The top speed attained was estimated at eighteen miles per hour, since they traveled from milepost to milepost in just over three minutes. Haynes described the comfort and exhilaration experienced during the trip: "The sensation of riding through the country at a speed which frequently reached 18 miles an hour, in a rubber-tired vehicle, which when running at the speed is nearly noiseless, is pleasant in the extreme. The smell of gasolene," he added, "was not noticeable during the entire trip," which "included some extremely rough dirt road, over a part of which a bicycle could not have been ridden a distance of 50 ft."[22]

The trip was pleasant in other respects, too. According to a Portland newspaper, the Haynes-Apperson "horseless carriage" had "attracted much attention while here, a number of our people . . . being treated to a trial trip. The machine is perhaps the most complete and modern ever made, and is a beauty and success in every particular."[23] More significantly, a number of Portlanders agreed to purchase stock for $25,000 in the expanded Haynes-Apperson enterprise. Of the initial nine stockholders besides Haynes and Apperson, seven lived in Portland, only two in Kokomo. A Kokomo newspaper reported that "some [Portland] capitalists" had offered to take stock on condition of its location in Portland, but the article correctly predicted that the automobile company would not leave Kokomo.[24]

The incorporation papers for the Haynes-Apperson Company were filed with the Indiana Secretary of State on May 25, 1898. These indicate that the company was organized to "manufacture Motor Carriages, Gasoline Motors and gearing for motor vehicles." Its five directors—Elwood Haynes, Elmer Apperson, G. W. Charles, J. W. Polley, and W. H. Reed—were all businessmen from Kokomo and Portland.[25] The decision was made immediately upon incorporation to produce fifty cars as soon as possible. Some directors expressed considerable trepidation that there would be no market for such a large production of such a high priced commodity ($2,500), but the majority view prevailed and capacity production was initiated at once.[26] They also decided upon what terms the automobiles would be sold. Since delivery without payment was deemed risky, the directors adopted a policy, still followed within the industry, requiring payment in full upon delivery. "It was an up-hill job," Charles reminisced in 1921; "models were changed so often

---

[22]*Horseless Age,* October, 1898, p. 10.

[23] Portland *Sun,* May 3, 1898, quoted in Jay, *History of Jay County,* I, 177.

[24] Kokomo *Dispatch,* May 7, 1898.

[25] Articles of Incorporation, Haynes-Apperson Company, Archives Division, Indiana State Library. The only Kokomo stockholders, exclusive of the two founders of the company, were G. W. Charles and his brother, A. A. Charles. The seven Portland stockholders included two of Haynes's brothers. The eleven persons, together with the number of shares purchased, were as follows: from Portland, C. C. Cartwright, 12; Walter M. Haynes, 21; Calvin Haynes, 10; Charles F. Headington, 12; Lewis W. Hoover, 3; J. W. Polley, 10; and W. H. Reed, 15; from Kokomo, Elmer Apperson, 73.5; A. A. Charles, 10; G. W. Charles, 10; and Elwood Haynes, 73.5. In May, 1901, the capital stock was increased to $100,000.

[26] "The question was," G. W. Charles recalled in 1921, "could they sell 50 cars after they were made. 50 cars! At $2,500 each? Would anyone really buy them?" Kokomo *Dispatch,* April 3, 1921.

in those days that it was a hazardous business. But we all pulled hard and all believed in its ultimate success."[27]

News of the incorporation was carried in *Horseless Age,* along with a description of the new factory under construction. The new facilities would increase the company's production capacity to one a week; in the old location, production was limited to one car every three weeks. The company line then included two-, four-, and six-passenger vehicles, and the latter two types "are frequently provided with four and six passenger trailers to be attached when desired."[28] These trailers were simply open carriages fitted with regular automobile seats and pneumatic tires and were easily towed. In July, 1898, one of the Haynes-Apperson carriages-with-trailer was driven to Chicago, and details of the trip were published in *Horseless Age.*[29]

By 1898 the company was producing "two carriages a week" and already advertising itself as one of America's oldest and most experienced firms. "Devoting themselves exclusively to the manufacture of motor carriages, and being one of [the] pioneers in the business," Haynes and Apperson stated that they were "able to turn out a vehicle which they can guarantee will give satisfactory service on the road."[30] The issue of *Horseless Age* bearing this announcement also carried a lead story on "Motor Vehicles in the United States To-Day." The company-by-company narrative was timed to coincide with the "first exhibition of motor vehicles in the United States" at Boston. In presenting the story, the editor pointed out that he had "followed his usual custom and allowed every inventor to tell his own story." Under "Gasolene Vehicles," the "Duryea Motor Wagon Co." was listed first. One short paragraph, without dates, claimed for the Duryea brothers the distinction of being "the first to bring out a commercial gasolene wagon in the United States." The result of "four or five years' labor," it "resembled a buggy in general shape, and was propelled by a 4-HP gasolene engine." The rest of the section described the 1898 Duryea. It had a two-cylinder, water-cooled engine, pivoted hub steering, wire wheels, a friction clutch and gears (not belts), and two forward speeds and one reverse. "The control of the vehicle," wrote the Duryeas, "requires three operations—steering with the right hand, changing speed with the left hand, a button in the end of the lever also regulating the speed of the motor, and braking with the foot."[31]

The second company listed was the Haynes-Apperson, accompanied by a long article describing its progress. In business for "a number of years" since their first "experimental carriage commenced in 1893 and completed in 1894," the company had built numerous vehicles, but its founders were not ready "to put them on the market until they had produced a thoroughly practical and reliable machine. This they have done and are now offering it to the public on its own merits." The author, obviously Haynes, then described again some of the technical features of the motor, their own design, before discussing the ease with which the Haynes-Apperson vehicle could be driven. He sought to dispel the belief that only a "mechanical expert" could operate automobiles. "The carriage will perform its work if properly speeded

---

[27] *Ibid.*

[28] *Horseless Age,* July, 1898, p. 7.

[29] *Ibid.* Haynes reported that the "first run of 50 miles, to Lafayette, in 3½ hours," required only 30 cents worth of gasoline. This type of carriage and trailer is pictured in *ibid.,* September, 1898, p. 1.

[30] *Ibid.,* September, 1898, p. 26.

[31] *Ibid.,* October, 1898, p. 9.

and guided," he stated, "and these two operations can be quickly learned by a person of ordinary intelligence. The motor is expected to take care of itself so far as running is concerned, while the speed is controlled and the carriage guided by the operator."[32] Haynes reported that Dr. Sweany of Chicago, after only two hours of practice at "running a carriage," made a successful trip, with a trailer attached, to Chicago. Later Sweany had journeyed into northern Indiana, "where the roads are merely tracks through wastes of sand," and on to Kokomo, Indianapolis, and Franklin. The motor "never got out of order a single time during any of the above journeys," even though once on the road between Kokomo and Indianapolis a small river had to be forded, the water almost reaching the body of the carriage.[33]

One of the new features on these 1898 models was the ability to somewhat vary the speed of the carriage in each of the gears. One lever, connected to the motor by "steel spur gearing," controlled the speed in all four gears (three forward, one reverse). "These speeds are variable from maximum to minimum within the range of each, thereby making a gradual variation from the slowest to the fastest speed without friction or loss of power."[34]

Unhappily, the corporate records of the Haynes-Apperson Company have been destroyed and various types of secondary evidence must be used to learn about the activities of the company. Obviously the increased production made possible by the move to a new factory resulted in increased sales. *Horseless Age* reported in February, 1899, that the Haynes-Apperson people were working fifteen hours a day, that they had orders enough to keep them busy until at least the first of May, and that another factory expansion was being planned. Two months later, in April, the company announced that those who desired an 1899 model should place their orders "at once," because "our output for this year is about sold."[35] Among their earlier sales in 1899 had been a "delivery wagon for C. B. Knox, the gelatin manufacturer of Johnstown, New York, which has been running for advertising purposes in Buffalo, Rochester, and other eastern cities the past month," and a fifteen-passenger machine (a six-passenger carriage, a nine-passenger trailer) for a party in Daytona, Florida.[36]

Undoubtedly the company's most publicized sale of the year was made to Dr. Ashley A. Webber, a physician from Brooklyn, New York. Dr. Webber had stipulated that the reliability of the machine he purchased be proven by driving it from the factory in Kokomo to New York. This led to the first one-thousand-mile automobile trip in the United States, an event which has remained inexplicably obscure in general automobile history.[37] Haynes joined Edgar Apperson in delivering Webber's car, and the two left Kokomo

[32] *Ibid.*, p. 10.

[33] *Ibid.*, p. 11.

[34] *Ibid.*, p. 10.

[35] *Ibid.*, April, 1899, p. 32.

[36] *Ibid.*, February, 1899, p. 16. The Kokomo *Dispatch* in 1899 also reported sales of a three-seated "motocycle" to a government mail agent in Puerto Rico and a delivery wagon, "almost as pretty as a woman and much more tractable," to a Chicago firm. Kokomo *Dispatch*, April 26, June 17, 1899. Later the paper reported the sale of a Haynes-Apperson carriage intended as a replacement for a stagecoach in Arizona.

[37] By contrast, Alexander Winton's 1897 trip from Cleveland to New York and Roy D. Chapin's 1901 trip from Detroit to New York in an Oldsmobile have been widely hailed. For example, see Rae, *The American Automobile*, pp. 30–31. Rae here mentions the Haynes-Apperson journey but postdates it by two years. There was a second Kokomo-to-New York trip by a Haynes-Apperson car in 1901.

on July 17, 1899. They traveled first to Portland, making the run in less than seven hours despite wet roads. An onlooker said the wheels "carried fully fifty pounds of mud" upon their arrival in Portland, where Haynes and Apperson stayed overnight.[38] The next day they were prevailed upon to remain in Portland and exhibit their vehicle at the street fair then in progress, but the following day they entered Ohio, having no planned itinerary except to follow the best roads. In Marion, Ohio, east of Columbus the two motorists encountered two cyclists en route to Niagara Falls from Cincinnati, one of whom subsequently described this and several other meetings as the two parties traveled eastward. The cyclists, Michael G. Heintz and a companion identified only as Judge Murphy, were checking out of the Marion Hotel early in the morning when two other men, not in bicycle clothing, stepped up to check out. "I knew that they could not leave Marion by train at that hour [5 AM]," Heintz wrote later, "and my curiosity overcame good manners." Upon inquiring as to their mode of travel, one of the gentlemen took Heintz to a side window and pointed to the street.

> There stood the horseless carriage. It had all the appearance of the buggy model called a runabout. It had a dashboard like a buggy, a seat for two passengers . . . and no top. . . . Apparently the only thing needed to make it go was a pair of shafts and a horse.[39]

After learning that both parties were headed next to Cleveland, the cyclists "stood by until the strange contraption chuck-chucked" out of sight, probably forever. To their great surprise, however, since they had not seen Haynes and Apperson along the way, they heard the automobile pull into the next town, Caledonia, while they were breakfasting there. Its arrival caused quite a commotion, and a local newspaper reporter interviewed the motorists, who explained that they were delivering the carriage to Dr. Webber's "front door" in Brooklyn, New York. "This is the longest cross-country run ever undertaken by a motor buggy," Heintz quoted one of the men as saying. The reporter then turned to the cyclists for their comments. Judge Murphy "introduced himself and me, and said with his usual Irish humor, 'We go ahead on our bicycles and order meals for the gentlemen in the gasoline buggy.' "[40]

Again the riders "watched and heard" their new-found traveling companions leave Caledonia for Mansfield, Cleveland, and points east, expecting never to see them again, but their paths crossed repeatedly as both traveled slowly into western New York. On one occasion, as the broadly smiling cyclists prepared to go around the stalled vehicle, Apperson looked out from beneath the car and said, "Judge, don't laugh, we didn't laugh when we passed you." The men last met and dined together in Angola, a few miles west of Buffalo, where a crowd surged "around the motor, just as elsewhere."[41]

The complete Heintz account, while humorous and well intentioned, was

---

[38] Kokomo *Dispatch*, July 22, 1899. This statement was picked up from the Portland correspondent for the Indianapolis *Journal*. See also the Portland correspondent for the *Weekly Commercial*, July 20, 1899.

[39] This memoir, written by Michael G. Heintz, a Cincinnati attorney, was contributed to the Howard County Historical Society in 1960 by Heintz's daughter, Mrs. Lester E. Francis. The society subsequently transferred its collection of Haynes material to the Elwood Haynes Museum.

[40] Heintz Memoir, Haynes Papers.

[41] *Ibid*.

written some years after the 1899 journey and contains some obvious errors about the appearance and construction of the Haynes-Apperson vehicle. It also exaggerated the motorists' mechanical difficulties, which Heintz thought was the reason for the leapfrog pattern of the trip. But Haynes and Apperson themselves reported no engine trouble and only one tire blowout during their leisurely trip of twenty-one days, only ten of which were spent in actual travel. When the Kokomo *Dispatch* carried its story of the unprecedented cross-country journey, it was accompanied by a three-column wide picture of the "Kokomo Automobile Phaeton" which held the "Long Distance Record for America." Proclaiming the machine the "most talked-about 'horseless' machine on the continent," it noticed the full coverage given "every stage of the journey . . . in all the great newspapers of the land." It also pointed out that an electric automobile had left Chicago for New York several days before Haynes and Apperson left Kokomo, but that it "was rattling into Erie, Pennsylvania, fairly distanced, or, as some of the papers put it, 'a week behind the flag,' " at the time that the Kokomo machine was being exhibited in New York City.[42]

"We have every reason," Haynes announced to the New York reporters, "to feel fully satisfied with the machine. The test was made solely to prove the durability of the carriage. Had we desired to make high speed we could have come through in half the time." He pointed out that "all of our running was done in the day-light," with the "fastest run" occurring between Buffalo and Syracuse, "where our average was eighteen and four-tenths miles an hour." The only potentially troublesome incident, Haynes reported, had occurred in Ohio, early in the trip, when he and Apperson were climbing a steep grade at high speed and passed a buggy.

> A man in the buggy was leading a horse behind. Both horses took fright, and as we looked back we saw the buggy and horse dash up on a platform in front of a house. As no one appeared to be hurt, we went on, and thought nothing more of the matter until we reached Buffalo where we learned that the police had been asked to arrest us for causing the accident.

Haynes subsequently learned that a mounted policeman had followed them for two days "but was unable to overhaul us."[43]

Obviously Haynes was proud of his own and his automobile's performance. In all of its subsequent literature, Haynes's automobile company mentioned the feat of the 1,050-mile trip in 1899, as did Haynes personally in frequently-published autobiographical chronologies.

What was not mentioned, and what no student of Haynes has yet pointed out, is that Dr. Webber was unable to master the art of handling his famous phaeton, and that he returned it to the manufacturers. This information is contained in an article Webber contributed to *Horseless Age* in 1903 describing his use of the automobile in his profession. Webber first explained that he had spent his spare moments during the winter of 1898 investigating the merits of all the automobiles in the United States, finally ordering "a gasoline runabout from a Western manufacturer, to be delivered in the spring of '99."[44] Webber did not name this "Western manufacturer," but

---

[42] Kokomo *Dispatch*, August 9, 1899.

[43] Quoted in *ibid.*

[44] Ashley A. Webber, "The Automobile in a City Practice," in *Horseless Age*, January 7, 1903, p. 3.

there can be no doubt about his identity, even though the delivery occurred in the summer, not the spring, of 1899.

The physician anxiously awaited the arrival of his new purchase, and admitted to being "mighty downhearted" when he first saw it. "I had never seen anything like it before," he wrote, and "the photograph did not begin to do it justice. . . . The manufacturer said that it was not very pretty, but it would do the work, and I tried to become reconciled." Dr. Webber noted that "the manufacturer" spent an entire week teaching him and an associate "how to care for and run the machine" and that things went well for several days. Then "something happened that I could not adjust or repair," and Webber "lost faith in the machine. The things that I was on the lookout for didn't happen and those that I was not prepared for did." Eventually he decided he simply

> did not know enough about the machine to make it do good work and so informed the manufacturers, who, not wanting to write, wired me to put it aboard the cars at once, as they had several customers who wanted it. In a few days I received a check for the amount I had paid them. I was more than surprised at this for I had never had any similar experience with a horse dealer.[45]

Although Dr. Webber was surprised at the integrity of the "Western manufacturers" who bought back the unwanted vehicle, it would not have surprised those who knew Haynes and Apperson personally. Both were men of character, honesty, and growing reputation within the state. Theirs was a rapidly expanding industry, and both men were recognized leaders within it. They wanted only customers who were able to benefit from and use their product and knew that, if a Brooklyn doctor was unable to master automobile operation, there were plenty of other people who could. In fact, as Webber charitably pointed out, he subsequently met the second purchaser of his Haynes-Apperson and learned "that the machine had been doing duty every day. This convinced me that the trouble I had was due to lack of knowledge and not to the machine."[46] Webber's report, it may be noted, was part of a special "physician's number" of *Horseless Age*.

By the time these early reminiscences of physicians appeared, the Haynes-Apperson company was well established. It had come a long way during the 1890s, making and marketing approximately forty automobiles. This number was considerably fewer than company advertisements implied, but the promise of relatively large-scale production in the 1890s became the reality of the early twentieth century. After 1900 the company's annual production exceeded 240, which meant sales totaling between $300,000 and $500,000. At the turn of the century, at least twenty persons were employed in what Haynes once described as a modern fireproof building, equipped with the latest tools and equipment. This description, however, is somewhat at variance with that provided by Alfred P. Sloan, Jr., whose salesman had visited the Haynes-Apperson plant in 1899 to take an order for wheel bearings. Sloan said that Pete Steenstrup, who traveled to Kokomo in response to an inquiry from Elwood Haynes, reported that the "Haynes-Apperson machines . . . were made in a dirty little factory about as primitive as our own

---

[45] *Ibid.* The physician then turned briefly to steam automobiles, finally buying a "three wheeler" and then a "four wheeler" of the same make, both manageable and serviceable. He concluded that his move from horse to mechanical power was a brilliant one.

[46] *Ibid.*

place," with most of the work "being done on a dirt floor."[47] As Sloan pointed out, however, it was in such "hidden places, . . . obscure little shops scattered through the East and Midwest" that the automobile pioneers were working. Automobiles then, he noted, "were adaptations of vehicles made in carriage, wagon and buggy factories. The rest of the machines were improvised of parts made in a variety of shops. The men who were doing this pioneer work were, in the main, rather simple people on the surface. For example, Elwood Haynes."[48] While this generalization is a valid one, Sloan's choice of a specific is poor. Almost alone among the automobile pioneers of America, Haynes was college educated and had a sound scientific training upon which to base his innovative work in both mechanical and metallurgical fields. The proof of this became public knowledge during the first years of the new century.

---

[47] Alfred P. Sloan, Jr., and Boyden Sparkes, *Adventures of a White Collar Man* (New York: Doubleday, Doran & Co., 1941), pp. 25–26. Sloan and Steenstrup were then employed by the Hyatt Roller Bearing Company, later taken over by the Timken company. Sloan added that "we were not as excited as we should have been by the Haynes inquiry, though we were vigorously hunting new fields in which to apply John Hyatt's invention." But after visiting Kokomo and getting the order, "our real adventures" began. "It woke us up," he continued. "If one automobile manufacturer wanted something better than ordinary greased wagon axles, why not sell all of them?" *Ibid.*, pp. 24–25. See also the microfilmed "Memoirs of William E. Sidney," Indiana Division, Indiana State Library. Sidney, employed at the Haynes-Apperson plant in 1898-1899, primarily relates here the serious injuries he suffered in a gasoline explosion in the shop, but his account reinforces the primitive image of the undertaking.

[48] Sloan and Sparkes, *Adventures of a White Collar Man*, p. 25.

Chapter 8

Into the
Twentieth Century

The new century opened auspiciously for Elwood Haynes. Still pursuing three careers—gas company officer, promising experimental metallurgist, and president of one of the first automobile companies in the United States—he was beginning to make his mark on the world. His family, in which he took much delight, now included two children; his daughter Bernice had been born shortly after moving to Kokomo in 1892 and his son March in early 1896. Haynes was an elder in his church, attending services usually twice a week and increasing his civic activities. He still lived in the small cottage at 305 N. Washington Street, near the gas company office and the church. The convenience of the location mattered more to him than the ostentation of a large house.

The Haynes children adored their father and cherished the time he managed to spend with them. Somehow as Elwood juggled his many enterprises, he rarely failed to read or tell his children a bedtime story, and at least once he mailed a story to them, complete with a freehand illustration, when he was away from home overnight. Haynes also engaged in playful banter with neighborhood children, occasionally drawing pictures for them. "Let's see what will come out of this pencil today," he would say, drawing an animal or a funny figure. He unwittingly alarmed one neighborhood child, however, by an enthusiastic greeting and a serious-sounding request to the mother to let the little one come to live with him.[1]

Automotive matters began to take a greater part of his time. He continued to work closely with Elmer Apperson in the design, engineering, and production aspects of the business and handled the promotion of the Haynes-Apperson "carriages" through an extensive advertising campaign.[2] He also engaged in a spirited debate, conducted in the pages of the *Horseless Age,* on the superior merits of the hydrocarbon (gasoline) engine over rival sources of motive power, particularly steam and electricity. The question over which type of power was best suited for automobiles would last at least until 1905, when the flexibility and easy operation of gasoline engines finally established

---

[1] Interview with Mary Cedars, Kokomo, December 8, 1970.

[2] The extent and expense of Haynes-Apperson advertising had drawn local newspaper comment in 1899. The company believed in advertising and backed their "conviction with coin"; a four-inch notice in *Scribner's* had cost $125, and the rates for *Cosmopolitan* and other national magazines were "equally altitudinal." Kokomo *Dispatch,* April 5, 1899.

The Haynes family home in Kokomo, ca. 1898

March Haynes and Bernice Haynes, ca. 1902

their superiority. Haynes-Apperson advertisements continued to stress the advantages of gasoline-powered vehicles,[3] as they had from the very beginning. In 1900, in "The Hydrocarbon Engine as a Source of Energy," Haynes spelled out technical reasons for the superiority of the gas engine and furnished a table of performances recently obtained from a series of experiments with "steam, electric, and gasoline carriages." He determined that the test vehicles, weighing respectively 1,115, 2,520, and 1,480 pounds and generating six to eight horsepower each, could travel varying distances between necessary stops—forty-five miles for the steam car, thirty-five miles for the electric car, and one hundred miles for the gasoline car. The maximum speed of both the steam and gasoline cars was thirty miles per hour (only fifteen miles per hour for the electric), but the gasoline car could average twenty miles per hour during its run compared to fifteen miles per hour for the steam. An examination of his nineteen-point table, he observed, "will show that for long distance travel the gasoline carriage easily takes first place, as it will maintain a full 8-h.p. for 5 hours at a time on a single set of supplies. . . . This characteristic shows why the gasoline carriage has always defeated all competitors in long distance runs."[4]

Earlier Haynes had noted the "rapid substitution of the gas engine for the steam engine in the natural gas district" of Indiana, an "almost phenomenal" development which had occurred "in almost every case . . . for purely business reasons, such as economy, safety and diminished cost of attendance." He concluded his essay by describing the enormous power capabilities of the gasoline engine. Most people were unaware, he stated, that "there is far more energy developed by the combustion of a pound of gasoline than by the explosion of the same weight of nitroglycerine. In fact, weight for weight, gasoline is capable of developing about eight times as much power as nitroglycerine." In practical terms, this meant that gasoline delivered more energy for its weight than any other substance in general use, "notwithstanding the fact that our best gasoline motors utilize only about one-fourth of its total energy."[5]

Haynes admitted that gasoline engines were hampered by "inflexibility," i.e., the lack of power at low speeds and the difficulty of changing speeds easily (shifting gears was considered to be beyond the capacity of ordinary people). But he predicted the problem would be easily overcome by building an engine sufficiently large and powerful. And he could not resist the boast: "The objection so often raised by the critics of the gasoline motor, such as vibration, odor and noise, are most effectively silenced by taking a ride in one of the latest models of the Haynes-Apperson carriage, for example, which are fitted with balanced motors that run with but little noise and no vibration."[6]

The "flexibility" problem, moreover, was solved even more satisfactorily by adopting carburetors. Following this improvement, one for which Haynes and Apperson applied for a patent in January, 1901 (receiving it in 1904),

---

[3] A March, 1901, advertisement, for example, claimed that "People who have had 'experience' with other forms of power are all buying gasoline carriages now." The advertisement also warned: "Do not spend your money on experiments. It will take any manufacturer from three to five years to get a first-class machine ready for the market. *Notice When We Commenced —1893." Horseless Age,* March, 1901, n.p. (unpaginated advertising section).

[4] *Ibid.,* January 17, 1900, pp. 14–15; the quotations appear at p. 15.

[5] *Ibid.,* pp. 14–15. This article had been submitted by Haynes in response to an appeal from the editor of the journal for information on the gasoline engine.

[6] *Ibid.,* p. 14. This paragraph appeared over the signature of R. I. Clegg, the editor, but a correction was printed in the next issue. *Ibid.,* January 24, 1900, p. 11.

Haynes submitted another communication to the editor of the journal, answering specifically a question raised by a reader and again supplying experimental test data. J. E. Baldwin had inquired why the gasoline engine "has not been made more adaptable to automobile requirements than it has. By adaptable I mean to have the properties of steam engines or electric motors, which are flexibility, reversibility and the power of self-starting."[7] A brief reply from the editor accompanied the Baldwin inquiry, pointing out that the gasoline engine did have great flexibility between 200 and 1,200 rpm and questioning the self-starting capabilities of the steam engine. Then Haynes, in a letter printed two weeks later, praised the editor's response but believed that "the results of some practical tests in this line may add some force to what you have said." He offered the results of a recent test on a gasoline engine which demonstrated that its power could be varied from a minimum of one-half horsepower to a maximum fourteen times as great. Conversely, the test also demonstrated that "uniform power" could be maintained through a range of speeds. "It is evident," wrote Haynes, "that in respect to flexibility of power and speed," the gasoline engine "is a close rival of the steam engine." He defended its lack of reversibility as unimportant and stated that the use of a starting crank needed no further defense. "What person of ordinary muscular strength," he asked, "would not rather put forth sufficient effort to start a gasoline carriage in less than a minute than to 'potter about' for perhaps half an hour getting a steam boiler ready for use?"[8]

"An Electrical Engineer" answered this communication. He said the Haynes letter, "a good one, . . . shows very clearly just what the defects of the gasoline motor are" and actually proved the point Haynes wanted to refute. Engineers wanted a gasoline motor which would give full-load torque, he said (and chided Haynes's use of the term "pull"), at all speeds and, preferably, an increased torque at low speeds; the engine should also be reversible and start from a standstill with good torque. He charged that the hydrocarbon engine was simply the old Otto engine of 1867, unimproved, and that it ran better in recent years because "more people understand it. The gasoline engine has still a long ways to go before it can properly be called a flexible motor."[9] Again the editor responded to these comments, explaining why he felt the engineer's reasoning and conclusions were faulty.

Haynes, however, provided his own defense to the engineer's criticism. His letter of December 12, 1901, published as "The Characteristics of the Gasoline Motor," argued again that torque and speed could be varied separately and supplied some additional test data. Haynes suggested that the reason his critic had trouble understanding his table, and the methods used to obtain it, "is probably due to the fact that he is an electrical engineer and not because of any fault in the table or in my explanation of it," and he concluded that the ultimate test was performance. He argued that the use of electricity for carriage propulsion, unlike the gasoline engine, remained unproved.

Also unproved, however, was the right of the automobile to be used at all. Whether automobiles could travel on city streets in Kokomo had been challenged by a city ordinance in 1898, when a bicyclist, Claude Bennett, collided with a steam traction engine operated by Edward Bogue and

[7] *Ibid.*, November 13, 1901, p. 713.

[8] *Ibid.*, November 27, 1901, p. 754.

[9] *Ibid.*, December 4, 1901, p. 780.

100

demanded Bogue's arrest on the grounds that a city ordinance prohibited steam-propelled vehicles from traveling on city streets and alleys. The Grant County Circuit Court upheld the ordinance, in its decision in April, 1901, but the Indiana Supreme Court disagreed:

> Highways and streets are not for the exclusive use of vehicles propelled by animal power, nor are travelers confined to the use of such power and ordinary carriages upon highways. The use of any new and improved means of locomotion must be deemed to have been contemplated when the highways and streets were laid out or dedicated, whenever it is found that the general benefit requires it, and such new means of locomotion cannot be excluded therefrom merely because their use may tend to the inconvenience or even to the injury of those who continue to use the highways and streets by former methods.

As Haynes later told a journalist in 1925, one of his biggest problems in the earliest years of the automobile age was dealing with "the strenuous objections of the drivers of horses. At that time I carried in my pocket constantly the decision given by the Supreme Court judge which declared the road was open to all types of vehicles used for transportation."[10]

The way was now open for rapid development, and the 1901 Haynes-Apperson models were remarkable automobiles. The line now included one-, two-, and three-seated carriages, the latter accommodating eight persons and intended for "stage lines, hotel, depot and winter and summer resort purposes." Its twelve-horsepower engine and three-speed transmission made it "especially adapted to country roads and long trips."[11] The company also began more extensive advertising, with full-page spreads being used to point to their long experience in the business, their improved "gasoline system" machines, and their endurance run performances. "We are the pioneer automobile manufacturers of America," announced a 1901 advertisement (without known rebuttal from the Duryeas or others), and another claimed years of experience.[12] An article in the April 3, 1901, issue of *Horseless Age* aided the year's promotional efforts by carrying a full description of the two-seated Haynes-Apperson. A vehicle of this type purchased by a "wealthy merchant" of New York had been seen in a storage company warehouse by one of the magazine's reporters. His technical account analyzed the ignition system, the "considerably simplified" engine and carburetors, the transmission, the bearings, and the wooden-spoked wheels. A lever was used to steer the vehicle, which was "tastily trimmed, well finished, provided with a top extending over both seats, and [had] fenders for the rear wheels."[13]

---

[10] Foster, "How Elwood Haynes Came to Build First 'Horseless Carriage,'" in *Forbes*, March 2, 1925, p. 682. The court went on to cite an Illinois case (1859) and a Michigan case (1876), quoting from the latter: "Persons making use of horses as the means of travel or traffic by the highways have no rights therein superior to those who make use of the ways in other modes.... Improved methods of locomotion are perfectly admissible, if any shall be discovered, and they cannot be excluded.... A highway is a public way for the use of the public in general, ... without distinction." *Bogue* et al. v. *Bennett,* 156 Indiana 478–86; the quotations are at pp. 482–83; see also *Horseless Age,* April 24, 1901, pp. 76–77, for a comment upon the Indiana decision. Cities may regulate public travel upon their streets in the interests of safety, the editor pointed out, but they may not prohibit it because "some new and unusual motive power is used."

[11] *Horseless Age,* February 6, 1901, p. 76.

[12] *Ibid.,* April 3, 1901, p. iii (advertising section).

[13] "The Haynes-Apperson Two-Seated Road Carriage," in *ibid.,* pp. 5–6. The reporter pointed out that the "simple carburetors, which can be controlled from the seat by means of a foot button," permitted the engine speed to be varied "within wide limits." He also noted that "air admission ports" for the two carburetors were so connected and designed that the "noise of the

It was this model—the two-seated, eight-horsepower surrey—which the company entered in the Long Island test run of April, 1901. The car, driven by Edgar Apperson, covered the one hundred miles without mishap, using less than five gallons of fuel and again winning a "blue ribbon" award. The car, with its four mud-splattered occupants, was pictured in the *Horseless Age* article describing the run, which had taken place in unusually bad, wet weather. Given the number of cars encountering delays or failures because of the poor conditions, the tour promoters suggested that automobiles in the future should be designed for successful operation under adverse conditions as well as on pleasant days.[14] A Kokomo newspaper emphasized that the contest was an endurance run, not a race, and that the Haynes-Apperson vehicle was not the first to finish. But "it outranked all others in special awards," because of its power, endurance, reliability (the bad weather, the paper noted, had forced out all the steam and electric vehicles), and superiority of construction. Edgar Apperson called the results "a great triumph for Kokomo."[15]

Late in 1901, a Haynes-Apperson car also won the New York-to-Buffalo Pan-American Exposition run, an event which was saddened (and shortened) by the assassination of President William McKinley in Buffalo.[16] Approximately one hundred automobiles had participated in the run, including three Haynes-Appersons, one of which had been driven to New York from Kokomo. This trip via Buffalo (where they spent two days at the fair) was made by the Apperson brothers in only seventy-three hours of running time. They still arrived in New York only one day after the delivery of a second Haynes-Apperson, shipped "fast freight" on rush orders. This performance "eclipsed all former efforts in time and endurance," noted a Kokomo newspaper, observing that the 1899 trip over the same distance had required ten or eleven days.[17]

Other noteworthy performances during the year were a thirteen-hour run from Kokomo to Chicago in August, 1901, and a first place finish in an actual race in October. It was held in Detroit, with Edgar Apperson the victorious driver. He had covered the ten miles of the course in seventeen minutes, forty-three and one-fifth seconds, a speed of approximately thirty-four miles per hour.[18]

In December, 1901, *Horseless Age* published a photograph of "An Historical Automobile," the Haynes "Pioneer" of 1893-1894. The sideview pictured Haynes, a smug looking, nattily attired young man in a black bowler, sitting in the vehicle. The caption pointed out that the machine, "which embodies in a crude way most of the mechanical principles embodied in the modern

---

suction" was reduced. See also the description of the Haynes-Apperson Company's two "very fine machines" displayed at the New York Automobile Show in Madison Square Garden in the fall of 1900. P. B. Rawson, "The Show in General; Gasoline in Particular," in *ibid.*, November 14, 1900, pp. 22–24.

[14] *Ibid.*, April 24, 1901, p. 82. The photograph appears at p. 81.

[15] Kokomo *Dispatch*, April 27, 1901. The vehicle Apperson drove was not company-owned, but had been "in service as a public conveyance from Harlem to Broadway for a number of months."

[16] For information on the McKinley assassination (with but little mention of the exposition), see Margaret Leech, *In the Days of McKinley* (New York: Harper and Brothers, 1959), pp. 589–601.

[17] Kokomo *Daily Dispatch*, September 9, 1901. The Haynes-Apperson Company had a sizable display of at least six automobiles at the exposition, under the immediate supervision of H. Davis. *Ibid.*, April 24, 1901.

[18] *Ibid.*, October 11, 1901.

Haynes-Apperson machine," was claimed by Haynes to be "the first gasoline carriage ever built in the United States."[19] Additional comments referred to the "enormous progress" in automobile manufacturing made since 1894, as was evident upon "comparing this vehicle with any modern construction." The comparison was particularly

> recommended to those who delight in speaking disparagingly of the efforts of automobile manufacturers. It is true that in principle the Haynes "Pioneer" vehicle is quite similar to a majority of modern machines (except for the two-cycle engine), and the great difference lies in the relative arrangement of parts and their proportion. One striking feature is the great amount of space given to the sparking battery, and this would point to a considerable advance in electric ignition.[20]

The performances and attendant publicity of the 1901 models were reflected in company sales. More Haynes-Appersons were sold in 1901 (240) than had been sold in all previous years. Not surprisingly, when a Kokomo newspaper reporter visited the automobile plant in the spring of the year, he was impressed by the bustle of the place, terming it "one of the very best industries of which this city can boast"; its 280-foot long building was "filled with busy mechanics . . . engaged in the making of horseless carriages of all sizes, styles, and designs." Between eighty and one hundred persons were then employed at the plant, and by fall, the company found it necessary to expand the plant slightly more.[21]

For reasons that were never explained by the men themselves, Haynes and the Appersons decided to dissolve their partnership in November, 1901. The Apperson withdrawal was a friendly one, and the two former partners remained on good terms, despite an intense company rivalry developed later by their aggressive advertising departments. Each sought to establish priority for its own firm in building "America's First Car," the slogan the Haynes Automobile Company was to use after 1912, while the Apperson Brothers Automobile Company used the phrase, "Building Cars Since 1893." Several observers have given explanations for the Haynes-Apperson separation, usually suggesting that the two men disagreed about the type of cars the company should produce. According to these accounts, Apperson, who was more interested in racing than Haynes, wanted to develop a small, sleek, inexpensive, fast automobile, whereas Haynes was content to build a larger, more luxurious car for a limited market. Historian David Beecroft wrote in 1924, "Mr. Haynes visualized the luxury car, the finely finished vehicle at a price to put such a vehicle into the hands of the most people who expected something social with transportation [whereas] The Apperson brothers saw speed and power in the vehicle of their dreams." Perhaps the basis for this division was in the personalities of the men involved. As Beecroft had noted earlier, Haynes "drove overland tours [not races], got himself ordered off the streets of cities and participated in learned discussions as to the art of making motor vehicles and of their future place in the civilization." A scholar and a metallurgist, he "shone best in the controversies of the day."[22] The Appersons, by contrast, were practical mechanics, not theoreticians,

[19] *Horseless Age*, December 4, 1901, p. 776.

[20] *Ibid.*

[21] Kokomo *Dispatch*, September 25, October 12, 1901. Charles Sanders of Portland was given the contract for the factory addition. *Ibid.*, April 27, 1901.

[22] "They Laid the Cornerstone," in *Automobile Trade Journal*, December 1, 1924, p. 79.

Elwood Haynes driving a Haynes-Apperson in the Long Island non-stop contest of April, 1902

and they participated in a number of road and track races, including two Indianapolis 500-mile races.

Subsequent developments give only partial credence to this explanation for the Haynes-Apperson separation. Some of the Apperson "Jack Rabbits" were quite expensive, and the smaller Haynes cars were in the medium price range. The more likely reason for the split is that Apperson simply wanted his own company. At the same time Haynes was finally willing to devote full time to the automobile business because of the approaching depletion of the natural gas supply in Howard County. According to the local newspaper, rumors of the Appersons' withdrawal began to circulate in early November, coupled with reports that they would start a similar factory "under their individual control."[23] Both Elmer and Edgar Apperson were in New York at the first of the month, where they reportedly had obtained a large number of orders. When they returned to Kokomo, the rumors were confirmed. Elmer Apperson's resignation from the Haynes-Apperson Company was effective November 15, 1901, following which he and his brother would manufacture "automobiles on their own account," making the Riverside Machine Shop their headquarters once again.[24]

The Apperson Brothers Automobile Company produced its first car in 1902, building perhaps a dozen for the year. Their production grew steadily after that, reaching a peak of approximately 2,000 a year in 1916 (the Haynes company peak of 7,100 was also reached in 1916). Emphasizing quality rather than quantity production, the Appersons adopted the "Jack Rabbit" name for one of their models in 1906, and subsequently all the Appersons were "Jack Rabbits." These cars were to become famous for their speed, simple lines, and durability.[25]

[23] Kokomo *Dispatch*, November 6, 1901.

[24] *Ibid.*, November 13, 1901. Elwood Haynes, when asked early in the month about the rumors, merely stated that the company "will be found 'doing business at the old shed,' but declined to talk further." *Ibid.*, November 6, 1901.

[25] The best brief overview of the Apperson company is Wallace S. Huffman, "The Apperson Brothers and Their Automobiles," in *Indiana History Bulletin*, XLI (1964), 195–202; see also

A. G. Seiberling, a major figure in the later history of the Haynes Automobile Company, was hired by the Appersons as their general manager in 1907, where he stayed for five years before returning to the Haynes company.[26] During his tenure the Apperson company established itself firmly, and its position as an industry leader was maintained by such men as Burtt J. Hubbard, a clever designer from Detroit who built a V-8 for the Appersons in 1914 (their 1915 model) and later, in 1917, made the famous "8 with 80 less parts." Hubbard also designed the Apperson's popular "Chummy" roadster, featuring bucket seats with an aisle between them for access to the back seat.[27] Following Elmer Apperson's death in 1920, Edgar Apperson would manage the company for a few more years. In 1924 it was taken over by eastern interests and renamed, but the company went bankrupt in 1925.[28]

When the Appersons left in 1901, Haynes resigned as manager of the Indiana Natural Gas and Oil Company and took over the active direction of the Haynes-Apperson Company. Although the Appersons soon were in competition with him, Haynes retained the original company name until 1905. Perhaps he felt it had considerable recognition within the industry and among the public. At any rate, not until a general reorganization in 1905 did the corporate title change to the Haynes Automobile Company.

In the meantime, 1901 to 1905 was the only period in its thirty-year existence in which Haynes gave his full, personal attention to the affairs of the automobile company. Although the company made a series of technical improvements in its product, considerably broadened its line of models, and increased its capitalization from $100,000 to $300,000 during these years, its total annual sales remained on the plateau achieved in 1901 (the precise figures are unknown).[29] Despite the expansion of the plant, the production of automobiles did not increase significantly. The 1901 output was the average production through 1906. Obviously Haynes felt the loss of the Appersons and probably disliked the management responsibilities that fell to him.

Beginning in December, 1902, Haynes wrote a series of advertisements featuring the technical improvements in the new Haynes-Appersons. These ads provide an interesting and useful cumulative description of the 1903 models. "Watch this space for the good points of the Haynes-Apperson" was the continuing caption of the series.

National Cyclopedia of American Biography (1935), s.v. "Elmer Apperson"; Pinkerton, "Ed Apperson and the Horseless Carriage," in *True Magazine,* March, 1952, pp. 20–21, 84ff.; Kokomo *Dispatch,* March 30, 1920, April 3, 1921; Kokomo *Tribune,* May 13, 1959; New York *Times,* May 14, 1959.

[26] A. G. Seiberling, born in Akron, Ohio, in 1865, came to Kokomo in 1887, drawn there by the natural gas boom. He subsequently joined his father in a bicycle and rubber business in Peoria, Illinois, but returned to Kokomo in 1905 to join the Haynes Automobile Company as factory superintendent. After his service with the Apperson company, he was the general manager of the Haynes company from 1912 until 1923. Kokomo *Dispatch,* January 6, 1918, September 26, 1920, June 19, 1921.

[27] Interview with Burtt J. Hubbard, Kokomo, Indiana, December 8, 1970.

[28] Huffman, "The Apperson Brothers and Their Automobiles," in *Indiana History Bulletin,* XLI, 200.

[29] Articles of Incorporation, Haynes-Apperson Company, Archives Division, Indiana State Library. The capitalization, which was raised from $25,000 to $100,000 in 1901, jumped to $200,000 in 1903, $300,000 in 1905, and $600,000 in 1908. This last increase coincided with an increase in sales from approximately 250 to 350 units a year. A "trial balance" sheet for the company, dated September 20, 1902, indicates total assets then of $265,262.07. It also shows sales of $79,145.50, commissions of $5,131.01, an advertising budget for the year of $4,065.92, and general labor expenses of $19,139.70, plus $1,583.00 for "bodies labor," a total of $23,671.81 for labor. Charles Sanders had received $2,024 that year, evidently for constructing the plant addition, and the expenses of the "New York Run" and the "Kansas City Run" were $30 and $150, respectively. "Trial Balance, The Haynes-Apperson Company, September 20, 1902," paper enclosed in a letter, John Ellis Fall to March Haynes, July 18, 1947, Haynes Papers.

On December 3, *Horseless Age* carried a notice describing the "famous double cylinder balanced motor" used in all Haynes-Appersons; the following week the three-speed transmission was described as being the "most flexible of any speed changing device in America," completely free of the jerks "characteristic of the French gear." It had been developed through "10 years of hard service." Subsequent reports explained the advantages of the "single lever control" for speed changes, from four to thirty miles per hour (steering was also by lever, although in 1903 a steering wheel was available as an option and soon became standard), the patented "new carburetors," one for each cylinder and operated by a button in the floor of the car, and the "hub pivots" on all Haynes-Apperson cars, which produced "exceptional steering qualities."[30] Later advertisements featured the adjustable steering wheel "of our own invention," described the full elliptical springs used, both front and rear, on all models, and pointed to the use of roller bearings "throughout the entire driving mechanism of all [our] cars."[31] Other company statements continued to stress the antiquity of the Haynes-Apperson Company, that it had won "every endurance contest held in America, every contest or race ever entered, [and] more records than any other [automobile] made in the United States." They also quoted the editors of *Scientific American* as stating that "the Haynes-Apperson vehicles are probably the handiest and most reliable small size, high power automobiles as yet produced in this country."[32]

When the 1903 cars were displayed at the Third Annual Automobile Show in New York in January, the Haynes-Apperson Company had three models on exhibit—a surrey, a runabout, and a standard. "The production of this concern has been so well standardized for a number of years," reported *Horseless Age*, "as to render any description superfluous. Some few changes, however, have been made," and these were detailed. Not only had a steering wheel replaced the lever, but it was so designed that the entire steering column could be tilted forward out of the way of driver or passenger upon entering or leaving the vehicle (a device recently re-incorporated in some luxury model automobiles). The 1903 models also had permanently attached starting cranks "of very neat appearance," aluminum radiators, gear-driven oil pumps (the belt-driven pump on the Haynes-Apperson entry in a non-stop contest in 1902 had given problems), and the redesigned "bonnet . . . now contains ample carrying space."[33] The public response to these features was pleasing, and the demand for Haynes-Apperson automobiles far exceeded the company's ability to manufacture them.

The company notified its potential customers that most Haynes-Appersons "have practically been sold before they were built" and advised them to place their orders early. Indeed, the Haynes agent in Brooklyn announced that 23 percent of the deposits accepted on orders had had to be returned in 1903, but he guaranteed delivery on orders as promised for the next year.[34]

By this time the company was designating its models with a letter, a

---

[30] *Horseless Age*, December 3, 1902, p. v, December 31, 1902, p. ii.

[31] *Ibid.*, January 14, 21, 28, February 4, 1903.

[32] Haynes-Apperson Company advertisements, Risley Collection, Automotive History Collection, Detroit Public Library.

[33] *Horseless Age*, June 4, 1902, pp. 674–75; *ibid.*, January 28, 1903, pp. 161–62. See *ibid.*, pp. 172–73, for a table of technical data on the gasoline cars in the show, including two Haynes models (8 and 12 horsepower, still with rear-mounted engines) and a 24-horsepower Apperson, with a front-mounted engine.

[34] Haynes-Apperson Company advertisement, Risley Collection.

Ralph Gray

1903 catalog

practice begun in 1902. In 1900 and 1901 the models were simply designated by name—standards, surreys, or runabouts. In 1902, the surrey became Model A, the standard Model B, and the runabout Model C. The next year, these models were, respectively, G, H, and I. Only two models were produced in 1904—a four-passenger tonneau (Model F) and a runabout (Model J), but the next year the company produced its first four-cylinder automobile (Model K), as well as its conventional two-cylinder runabout (Model L) and surrey (Model M). For the next few years, the company concentrated on either thirty- or fifty-horsepower touring cars (Models O and R respectively in 1906, S and T in 1907 and 1908), although in 1908 a medium-sized touring car—Model W—was added to the line.[35]

Handsome catalogs issued by the company repeated the points made in newspaper and journal advertisements. The 1903 catalog, which appears from internal evidence to have been the last one written by Haynes himself, emphasized the technical features of the new models, the history of the company, its long experience with gasoline engines, and its record of performance. Haynes stated his belief that the carriage begun in 1893 and completed on July 4, 1894, was "the first complete gasoline carriage built in America," and pointed out that the next carriage he and Apperson constructed was powered by the "first balanced gasoline motor with opposed cranks ever constructed in the world. This motor has now become world famous and has [been] copied by a number of American and foreign builders. Its smooth-running qualities have been universally recognized and it is now one of the world's standards in this line."[36] Haynes noted that this motor had won a prize of $150 at the *Times-Herald* contest in 1895, and then he commented on subsequent honors received by the company.

[35] Price List of Parts, Haynes-Apperson Company, 1908, Automotive History Collection, Detroit Public Library. The price list extends back to 1897, the first year of actual manufacturing, but the data do not distinguish between the "standard models" of 1897, 1898, and 1899.

[36] *Haynes-Apperson Company Catalog, 1903*, p. 6.

Prize after prize has been awarded the Haynes-Apperson carriage until it now has the longest list of records of any carriage in America, either of foreign or domestic manufacture. . . . *We have never failed* to receive the highest record obtainable in any contest we have ever entered.

He boasted that "these records were not made by machines of special construction, ones [that] have been 'doctored.' 'The machine you buy is the one that makes the record.' "[37]

The various parts and features of the Haynes-Apperson were then discussed in turn, many of which had been publicized separately in the advertising campaign of 1902-1903, and reassurances about the ease and simplicity of operating a Haynes-Apperson carriage were included. The text ended by listing the "points" prospective buyers should consider in making their decision about an automobile purchase. Haynes recommended two cylinders over one, a three-speed transmission, a car free from excessive vibration, time-tested running gears and transmissions, and slight attention to a car's paint and varnish. "You may look at the *outside* of your car before you buy it but you are sure to look at the *inside* before you have had it long," he observed. "If after making the above comparisons of the prime essentials you find any car that is superior to ours," he added wryly, "we would advise you to buy it. *It is a good one.*"[38]

The catalog for 1904 contained much the same kind of information, but it stressed that the Haynes-Appersons were manufactured more completely "in our factory" than any other make, that is, that the Haynes-Appersons were not merely assembled from parts produced elsewhere. Moreover, Haynes claimed to have originated the following "standard features" of the automobile: the magneto generator, make-and-break spark ignition, throttle control, the "double cylinder opposed balanced motor," an aluminum alloy engine block, a "perfectly satisfactory" transmission, and the muffler, adding that "the foreign makers have just 'discovered' the muffler we originated and always use."[39]

The 1904 publication also emphasized the reliability of the Haynes-Apperson car. "Every automobile manufacturer advertises a 'star performance,' " but usually these were made "under conditions governed by his own operator, and often with specially-built machines. This confuses intending purchasers." In the case of the Haynes-Apperson car, however, the tests have come "under conditions officially imposed by others, not once or twice, but 1, 2, 3, 4, 5, 6, 7, 8, 9, 10, 11, 12, 13, 14, 15, 16, 17 separate times, winning first honors: every time with stock cars—always stock cars. This means reliability (in the machine you purchase) of the kind no one else has PROVED." The argument continued by mentioning specifically a recent run from New York to Boston and back, a total of some five hundred miles:

The official report showed that the Haynes Apperson was the only gasolene car that ran the entire contest without repairs or adjustments *of any kind,* either on the road *or in the garage.* The value of this cannot be overestimated. It is certainly very annoying to be obliged to work on a car for nearly half a day in order to get it ready to run the other half.[40]

---

[37] *Ibid.,* p. 8.

[38] *Ibid.,* pp. 21–22.

[39] *Haynes-Apperson Company Catalog, 1904,* p. 6. None of these improvements was patented, however, except the transmission, which Haynes claimed to be "not only the most perfect known, but is found only in Haynes-Apperson cars."

[40] *Ibid.,* p. 19.

In addition to their amazing record in endurance or reliability runs the company continued to participate occasionally in speed contests. These early races were held on horse racing tracks and acted as demonstrations as well as races. In July, 1903, at Marion, Indiana, on the day when Barney Oldfield set the new mile record (on a half-mile track) at 1:16.4 minutes, nearly 50 miles per hour, Elmer Apperson, in an Apperson, won a three-mile race "open to the world." Nelson McClain, driving a Haynes-Apperson, won the handicap event against a field of six in 5:19.5, averaging just under 40 miles per hour for the distance.[41] The end of the Haynes company's racing efforts came in 1904 and 1905, when it entered the first two Vanderbilt Cup races, both of which were won by French drivers.

The strongest showing for the Haynes car came in 1905, when Frank Nutt drove the fifty-horsepower racer, an exact duplicate of the 1906 Model R Touring Car except for the racing body, to a fourth place finish in the 113-mile qualifying run. Nutt, who was then the chief engineer of the company, averaged 59.58 miles per hour on his last four laps and appeared to have qualified the car for the American team. The understanding had been that the top five finishers in the qualifying heat would represent the United States in the cup race to be run on October 14. The third-, fourth-, and fifth-place cars in the Elimination Run, however, were replaced by other entrants in the big race for the Vanderbilt trophy. Reporters as well as company officials were mystified by the action, which was explained belatedly as necessary because the three cars in question—a Royal, a Haynes, and a Thomas—were "underpowered" and probably would not fare well in the race against the European entrants with one hundred or more horsepower. The officials of the qualifying runs maintained that the preliminary trials were designed to give each entrant a chance to run and were not actual races. The substituted cars (a Pope-Toledo, a Christie, and a White) were high-powered but had broken down during the qualifications. Despite strong protests voiced by the ousted participants and threats of lawsuits to recover entry fees ($500) and other expenses, the arbitrary decision held.[42]

As the Haynes Automobile Company's new general manager, V. E. Minich, stated in his appeal for reconsideration, the company had made considerable effort and expenditures in preparing its entry. The car, a stock 1906 model then under production, had been built "at a time when we were very much engaged with our 1905 product." Moreover, considerable training had been undertaken to prepare both car and driver for the race after the invitation to enter was accepted. Then, when the car was driven to a fourth-place finish, "we immediately retained our old training quarters and completed preparations to enter the race October 14, never dreaming but that our car would be a member of the American team." Upon hearing rumors to the

---

[41] Kokomo *Daily Dispatch*, July 10, 1903.

[42] That the Vanderbilt Cup represented a major effort by the company is indicated by correspondence between W. J. Clark and Elwood Haynes in 1920. Clark, who had been employed at the Haynes plant from 1903 to 1908, wanted a job recommendation and he reminded Haynes that he, "in the two Vanderbilts, that we participated in," had been chosen "to build the motors and rode as macinition [sic]." Haynes supplied some additional details about the 1905 run in his recommendation. Clark, the "mechanician" chosen for both the preliminary trial and the final run, had also superintended "the building of the car and motor, and the splendid record made by this machine indicated the pains-taking care exercised by Mr. Clark in building up the machine." On the day of the race, "nothing whatever happened to the mechanism, though the filling tube on the top of the radiator came loose during the run, thus occasioning a certain amount of water loss from splash. Mr. Clark was equal to the emergency. He leaped from the car at Krug's Corners, and obtained a wide strap, which he lashed over the top of the radiator, thus enabling the machine to complete the run without delay. . . ." W. J. Clark to Elwood Haynes, April 3, 1920, Haynes Papers.

contrary, however, Minich had written the race commissioners, appointed by the Automobile Club of America, requesting a hearing. When his first appeal was rejected, he appealed again, "in the name of fair play, as representative sportsmen, that we be given the place on the American team we so fairly earned by the liberal expenditure of our time, money, best efforts and the successful performance of our car" but to no avail.[43] This episode soured the company on racing, and thereafter Haynes contented himself with participating in reliability runs, particularly the famous Glidden Tours.

These tours were the work of retired industrialist Charles J. Glidden of New England and began in 1904. Glidden offered a trophy each year to the winner of a tour over a preselected route of at least one thousand miles. Members of the Automobile Club of America and any club recognized by it were eligible to participate. Glidden wanted to promote private touring rather than to provide an opportunity for manufacturers to compete for publicity, so he insisted that each entry be driven by its owner. Nevertheless, contestants who were also manufacturing executives greatly outnumbered private automobile enthusiasts.[44]

Thirty-three cars started in the first Glidden Tour, which traveled round-trip from New York City to Bretton Woods, New Hampshire. Percy Pierce, driving a Pierce-Arrow, won the first Glidden Trophy; Elwood Haynes also participated in the initial run, and his car finished with a good score. In 1907, when the Glidden Tour traveled from Cleveland to Chicago and then to New York, via Kokomo and Indianapolis, Haynes was with the group until it reached Kokomo. Frank Nutt drove the car on to New York, his Haynes getting one of the perfect scores for the entire run.[45] These tours continued annually until 1914, and Haynes enjoyed the sociability afforded by the "motor picnics." He was not, however, one who celebrated with the glass, and he frowned upon his employees who did. Dr. J. R. Morgan tells of saving the day for one of the Haynes men with whom he was sharing a table following one day's run. When Haynes himself walked in, the employee carefully pushed his drink over in front of his companion, who lamely explained to the bemused Haynes, a well-known prohibitionist, that he was uncommonly thirsty because of the heat.[46] If the glint in Haynes's eye indicated that he had sized up the situation correctly, he did not mention it to his employee afterwards.

In spite of the many rewards, both personal and financial, that Haynes found in the automobile industry during its earliest years, he was eager to devote his primary attention to his laboratory. Not an outstanding business executive, Haynes's major interests were in research rather than management. He relinquished direct control of the automobile company in 1905, and returned to an active role in its affairs only in later times of crises, like

---

[43] "The Haynes Racer," General Folder, 1906, *ibid.* This was a four-page leaflet containing reprints of newspaper reports on the remarkable events on Long Island in September, 1905. One story was headlined: "Auto Racers Re-eliminated. Committee Likes Cars Which Did Not Qualify. Weird Work in Selection. Three Machines that Finished in Vanderbilt Elimination Trial are replaced by Cars that Broke Down." See also David J. Wilkie, *Esquire's American Autos and Their Makers* (New York: Esquire, Inc., distributed by Harper & Row, 1963), pp. 71–72, concerning the first Vanderbilt races.

[44] Niemeyer, *Ransom E. Olds,* p. 92.

[45] Indianapolis *News,* July 3, 6, 27, 1907. Later in the year Frank Nutt, in his Haynes, won a series of reliability runs out of Chicago—to South Bend, to Rockford, to Ottawa, each approximately two hundred miles long. *Motor World,* December 5, 1907, p. 525.

[46] Kokomo *Dispatch,* June 26, 1912, quoted in Powell, "History of Elwood Haynes," pp. 106–107.

the fire of 1911 or the financial problems of 1923-1924. The firm was reorganized in 1905, and the corporate name was changed to the Haynes Automobile Company. V. E. Minich became the general manager of the company just before the Vanderbilt Cup elimination trials in 1905. His chief assistants were A. G. Seiberling, who later left the company from 1907 to 1912 to take over temporarily as the general manager of the Apperson Brothers Automobile Company, and H. H. Murden, who had been with the old company since working on the first car at the Riverside Machine Shop.[47] Calvin Haynes, Elwood's younger brother, also joined the office staff following the liquidation of his grocery business in Portland. Elwood retained the company presidency, but the new staff managed its affairs.

The company prospered under the leadership of men who devoted their undivided attention to the firm. In 1908, by which time the automobile had become a significant factor in the national economy,[48] the Haynes Automobile Company was one of the twenty or twenty-five largest automobile companies in the country. Ford was already the leading manufacturer, with just over ten thousand cars produced in 1908, while companies in the lower range of the top ten produced between one and two thousand automobiles.[49] As described by a Kokomo historian, Jackson Morrow, the Haynes automobile plant, with a capacity of 350 cars a year, consisted in 1908 of "three large and well constructed buildings, each forty by two hundred and seventy-five feet in size, and two stories high, besides a number of additional structures devoted to various uses, the floor space of the main structure being eighty thousand square feet." The Haynes Company was Kokomo's largest manufacturing enterprise, and between four hundred and five hundred persons were employed, receiving an annual payroll in excess of $200,000.[50]

Meanwhile Haynes returned to metallurgical research in 1905, but even so he remained interested in automotive applications for his research. In 1906 he contributed a short article to *Horseless Age,* entitled "Sulphur in Gasoline." An impurity recovered as black scales resembling flake graphite caused fuel lines to clog and engines to misfire. Haynes, showing the careful, scientific approach he used to analyze problems, described the way he had identified the source of the sediment ("the action of some sulphur compounds in the gasoline on the copper of the gasoline tank") and his proposed solution: "Since the scales are evidently formed after the gasoline is placed in the tank, no amount of straining or filtering will be of any avail. A method of preventing this annoyance, which has been more or less frequent, would be to screen the gasoline just before it leaves the tank and use an aluminum pipe for conveying it to the carburetor."[51]

The following year, too, Haynes wrote an account for the same journal in which he traced the development of new alloys for use in automobiles. The

---

[47] "Pioneer Maker—Elwood Haynes," in *Motor Age,* October 12, 1905, p. 34; *Automotive Daily News,* February 19, 1929, p. 12. The former article stated that Minich became the general manager so that "Haynes could devote more time to the mechanical details of the car." Actually he resigned in order to carry out some long-delayed metallurgical experiments.

[48] Chandler, *Giant Enterprise,* p. xii.

[49] *American Automobile Since 1775,* p. 38. The production tables in this publication, admittedly incomplete, list only the top fourteen or fifteen producers for 1905 to 1912, and even fewer than that for the earliest years. The Haynes Company's production is not listed at any time, even though it was among the leaders at the turn of the century, perhaps third, in fact, in 1900.

[50] Morrow, *History of Howard County, Indiana,* I, 248–49.

[51] *Horseless Age,* May 2, 1906, p. 638.

technical paper, based upon one Haynes read to the American Society of Mechanical Engineers, pointed out the problems faced by the earliest manufacturers in trying to use various types of high tensile, low carbon steel or Swedish iron, and then reviewed the history of new alloy adoption. His own company had successfully used nickel steel for an axle in the 1899 run of over one thousand miles to New York City, among other uses. To prevent gear teeth from breaking, the Haynes company used an iron, nickel, and chromium alloy at these and other stress points. Haynes then discussed an improved tool steel alloy, one that his iron-free Stellite would soon supersede, and vanadium steel, the alloy Henry Ford was to adopt with such great success for his automobiles. Haynes pointed to a recent discovery of a sulphide of vanadium "in an immense quantity in the Andes Mountains of South America" and reported that the American Vanadium Company was ready to "furnish the metal in the form of a ferro alloy . . . in any quantity desired." Later he discussed its properties and advantages—"the high elastic limit, strong contraction of area and splendid silky fracture, together with the large number of vibrations which the steel endures under dynamic stress, more strongly recommend this steel as almost ideal for many parts of the motor car."[52] He then explained the special uses of bronze and aluminum in the automobile, and concluded with a number of specific recommendations concerning the best alloys and steel to use in various parts: (1) for live rear axles, nickel steel (containing 4 to 5 percent nickel and less than 0.5 percent carbon); (2) for front axles, steering knuckles, and propeller shafts, vanadium steel; (3) for sliding gears, hardened nickel chrome steel; (4) for crank shafts, nickel steel or vanadium steel; (5) for frames, low carbon open hearth steel, mild nickel steel, or nickel chrome steel; and (6) for nearly all other parts, a good open hearth steel of low carbon (0.4 percent or less).[53]

In 1908 Haynes led the "historical section" in the mammoth New York City parade celebrating the first decade of the automobile, and additional attention was focused on the Haynes company when Bernice Haynes, Haynes's sixteen-year-old daughter, published an article in a national magazine describing how she had learned to drive. Her experiences had begun at the age of eight, when she was occasionally permitted to steer a car being operated by her father, and the following year she was permitted to circle a city block alone, driving "on the slowest speed." After this she had made a few short solo trips within the city, but her range was limited because she was unable to crank the engine herself. Once this task was performed, however, actual operation of the automobile was easy and safe. The article ended with a series of safe driving tips:

> When meeting a team on the road, it is best to go slowly, but not to stop unless the occupants of the vehicle demand it. One should turn out well to the right, far enough in front of the team so that the driver of the carriage may have plenty of time to get on the opposite side of the road and thus avoid any confusion. When passing a team from the rear, it is advisable after giving the occupants of the carriage a warning, to pass the vehicle slowly. With a high-powered machine this may be done with the high gear with very little noise. If the gear has to be changed, it should be done before reaching the horse, as the noise made by changing gears might frighten the animal.

[52] Elwood Haynes, "Materials for Automobiles," in *ibid.*, July 10, 1907, p. 52.

[53] *Ibid.*, p. 53. Haynes provided a table to accompany his article, giving the tested strengths of ten different metals and alloys ranging from aluminum and three types of bronze to nickel, nickel chrome, and vanadium steel.

Elwood Haynes Museum

Bernice Haynes at the wheel of a Haynes 1910 runabout in front of Kokomo city hall

When driving on crowded streets it is best to drive on the slow speed and be ready to stop instantly. A warning should be sounded at every corner.[54]

Given the growing popularity of the automobile in general, and of the Haynes in particular, the directors of the Haynes Automobile Company decided in 1908 to increase the capitalization and expand production to plant capacity. Several Kokomo citizens were added to the list of stockholders, and virtual control of the plant was handed over to the Kokomoans for the next few years. This was accomplished through a trusteeship, with three trustees authorized to vote the majority of the stock as a unit for a period of five years. The Kokomo trustees were Henry C. Davis and Richard Ruddell; Charles C. Cartwright was the lone Portland trustee. Under this arrangement, plant size and productivity increased. Near the end of the year, a Kokomo newspaper reported that 600 employees were capable of producing 400 cars a year (actual production for the 1908 and 1909 amounted to approximately 350 cars each year). The "oldest automobile factory in the United States" manufactured two grades of automobiles—the five-passenger, thirty-horsepower runabout selling for $2,500 and the seven-passenger, fifty-horsepower touring car priced at $5,500.[55] Two years later, Haynes became the first company to equip an open car with a top, a windshield, head lamps, and a speedometer as standard equipment.[56]

---

[54] Bernice Haynes, "How I Learned to Drive an Automobile," in *Automobile,* August 27, 1908, pp. 305–306. This was also the year in which the Kokomo Automobile Club was organized, with forty-six charter members, including Elwood Haynes, Calvin Haynes, and A. E. Starbuck, Haynes's nephew, who became a long-time friend and employee. Kokomo *Morning Dispatch,* June 2, 1908.

[55] Kokomo *Morning Dispatch,* November 12, 23, 1908.

[56] Eugene W. Lewis, *Motor Memories: A Saga of Whirling Gears* (Detroit: Alved Company, 1947), p. 244; see also "Elwood Haynes, America's Inventive Genius," in *Motor,* January, 1924, p. 257.

By then, additional fame had come to the Kokomo product through Booth Tarkington's highly successful play, *The Man from Home*. The hero was a man from Kokomo, Indiana, whose native intelligence permitted him to foil an elaborate scheme concocted by a group of indigent foreigners to defraud an American heiress, and the plot required an automobile on stage. Logically, perhaps, a Kokomo-made Haynes car was on nightly display during the play's two-year run.[57] In 1910, moreover, as former President Theodore Roosevelt was about to return from his African safari, he delighted Kokomo boosters by ordering a Haynes Model 19 to be ready for him upon his arrival home.[58]

Possibly the event most disturbing to Haynes during the first decade of the twentieth century was the Selden patent lawsuit (*Electric Vehicle Company and George B. Selden* v. *Winton Motor Carriage Company*), an attempt to force a royalty payment from all American automobile manufacturers under Patent No. 549,160. Selden had applied for a patent for an automobile in 1879, but it was not issued to him until 1895.[59] In 1899 Selden sold his patent to a group of Wall Street investors, including William C. Whitney and Thomas F. Ryan, who eventually formed the Electric Vehicle Company in order to develop a scheme for operating a fleet of electric cabs in various American cities. This plan was "a monumental failure," and John B. Rae believes this prompted the group to look elsewhere and "try to make what it could of whatever assets it had, including the Selden patent."[60]

Consequently, in 1900 the Electric Vehicle Company instituted proceedings against the Winton Motor Carriage Company, then one of the largest gasoline automobile manufacturers, charging infringement of the Selden patent. Winton's first instinct was to fight the suit, and a number of his fellow manufacturers joined in the effort. It is not clear exactly when Haynes first learned of the pending litigation, but correspondence late in 1902 between either Haynes or his brother and Judge Robert S. Taylor, a prominent Fort Wayne attorney familiar with patent law, indicates that the Hayneses had consulted with him and were reassured by his analysis of the situation. Their own study of the claims set forth in the Selden patent also convinced them that the claims were invalid. In an undated draft of a letter or memorandum Haynes wrote perhaps in 1901 (since it was written on Indiana Natural Gas and Oil Company letterhead, the firm Haynes left in that year) and perhaps intended for Alexander Winton, Haynes made the following points in refutation of the Selden patent: (1) that "the application of the gasoline engine steam engine or other prime mover to a new use does not constitute invention"; (2) that the use of a clutch for applying the power of a gasoline engine was not new; indeed, "this was the *usual* almost *exclusive* method" then being followed; (3) that "it is absolutely certain that Mr. Selden did not

[57] Booth Tarkington and Henry Leon Wilson, *The Man From Home* (New York: Harper & Brothers, 1908). An illustration of a scene in the play, facing p. 90, shows the Haynes car. For information on the stage history of the play, see Bennett Cerf and Van H. Cartmel (comps.), *S. R. O.: The Most Successful Plays in the History of the American Stage* (Garden City, N. Y.: Garden City Publishing Co., 1944), pp. xiv–xv; the play is reprinted on pp. 271–330.

[58] Kokomo *Daily Tribune*, June 4, 1910. In July, "delighted" with the car, Roosevelt purchased a second one, an exact duplicate of the first, for his daughter. *Ibid.*, July 16, 1910. The Haynes product made the news again later in the month, when a Haynes test driver was accused of speeding and reckless driving while performing his duties. It took two people to report the violation, the newspaper stated: "one to say, here she comes, and another to say there she goes." Indeed, the charge against the driver was not proven in this case, because of a lack of positive identification, but a warning was issued. *Ibid.*, July 23, 1910.

[59] For a detailed story of George B. Selden see William Greenleaf, *Monopoly on Wheels: Henry Ford and the Selden Automobile Patent* (Detroit: Wayne State University Press, 1961).

[60] Rae, *American Automobile*, p. 36.

invent the *gasoline engine* the *clutch* nor the combination of the two"; and (4) that prior to 1895, the date of the patent, "the writer [had] built a gasolene carriage . . . said to be the oldest now in existence." Haynes then referred to his correspondence with the editors of *Scientific American* in 1890, when he asked about the most suitable power for self-propelled vehicles, and was told that "steam is the most reliable power for carriages. Gasolene and electricity have not yet been made a success."[61]

Many of the same points were made in a letter Haynes wrote replying to Judge Taylor in December, 1902. Haynes was pleased with Taylor's discovery of "a great many of the weak points in the Selden patent," adding that "the weakness of the entire affair is more manifest to one who has made a study of the practical and essential details which enter into the construction of the modern automobile." He commented, in reference to Selden's claims regarding a clutch, that the true novelty would have occurred if "Mr. Selden had invented an engine and carriage propelled by a liquid hydrocarbon engine which did *not* require a disconnecting device" or clutch; "even up to the present time nothing has been invented."[62]

It is apparent that Haynes considered the patent wholly invalid, and he did what he could to assist Winton in preparing his defense. Judge Taylor was informed in December that "Elwood will now get in touch with other responsible [manufacturers] of Automobiles and agree on some plan to meet the Electric Company. As we are the pioneer manfgrs [*sic*] of automobiles in the country," Haynes's brother wrote, "other concerns naturally look to us to lead off."[63]

Although this claim was somewhat presumptuous, Haynes did make an affidavit in the case in which he spelled out at length and under oath the story of his first automobile. The full transcript of this testimony has not been found, but Charles E. Duryea reproduced portions of it when he sought to prove certain points in controversy concerning the early Duryea and Haynes automobiles, and these extracts survive. Duryea picked out and circulated Haynes's statement that his first car was unsatisfactory in several details (it was underpowered, difficult to steer, vibrated excessively due to the type of engine it used, and had small wheels), that changes were made in the Haynes "Pioneer" of 1893-1894 before its donation to the Smithsonian Institution, and that in general it was "just the opposite of satisfactory, it was positively dangerous."[64] Unfortunately, the rest of Haynes's statement is not available, but the reported remarks substantiate his other comments about chronology and his role in building the "Pioneer." Overall, however, Winton's defense suffered from inadequate financial resources, and the affidavits from Haynes and other pioneers in the industry failed to persuade the trial judge to nullify Selden's patent.

It is difficult to imagine how different the automobile industry would have been if this initial ruling had been reversed and had upheld Winton. Validation of the patent led to the formation of both the Association of Licensed Automobile Manufacturers and the Society of Automotive Engineers, with the members of ALAM paying a royalty of 1¼ percent on their list prices to the Electric Vehicle Company and George B. Selden; it also led to Selden's famous lawsuit against Henry Ford and his New York agent, C. A. Duerr.

---

[61] Elwood Haynes to [Alexander Winton?], n.d., Haynes Papers.

[62] *Ibid.*

[63] Walter M. Haynes to Judge Robert S. Taylor, December 8, 1902, Robert S. Taylor Papers, Indiana State Library.

[64] Merle J. Duryea Papers, *ibid.*

Ironically, Ford originally sought membership within ALAM but was turned down because he had not yet proved himself as an established manufacturer. As a result, he challenged both the association and the Selden patent, and was eventually sued by the Electric Vehicle Company for patent infringement.

The resulting trial was one of the most important in American legal history, both because of the thoroughness of the record compiled for consideration by the judges (a record, incidentally, which is an invaluable reference for the early history of the automobile in America) and because of its impact upon American economic life. Although Haynes neither testified nor submitted an affidavit in this suit, Elmer Apperson's statements in this matter put much of the early history of the Haynes-Apperson Company into the record. Apperson testified not only to the facts relating to the first automobiles built in Kokomo (saying that the first one, completed July 4, 1894, belonged to Elwood Haynes and was built "for his own pleasure"; the second one the two of them had built for the Chicago race "at our joint expense"), but also to the fact that his company, the Apperson Brothers Automobile Company, had signed a licensing agreement with the Electric Vehicle Company on March 5, 1903, and that under its agreement the company had paid royalties of over $2,000 a year for the first three years.[65]

The Haynes Automobile Company had also joined ALAM in 1903, although no record of the amount of its royalty payments has been found. It is unlikely that ALAM members who paid the royalties accepted Selden's patent as valid, but none was willing to face the prolonged and costly litigation required to break it.[66] There were, in fact, some advantages to the industry in the arrangements negotiated in the settlement of the Winton case that had given control of the patent to ALAM. Such control promoted stability within the industry, eliminated the "fly-by-night" operators whose legacies were "orphan" vehicles, and established cross-licensing and standardized parts agreements of major significance to the industry's future.[67] Still it is doubtful that many were unhappy when Ford won the patent suit on appeal after a protracted battle during which he became not only America's most famous but also its largest producer of automobiles. The district court in 1909 found for the Selden group, but the appeals court in 1911 reversed this ruling, holding that the patent was valid but was not infringed because its claims only covered the Brayton two-cycle engine, not the Otto-type four-cycle engine then in use.[68]

Ford's triumph paved the way for his domination of the automobile market during the next few years, but this was of less concern to Elwood Haynes than to other manufacturers. In the 1890s, the Haynes-Apperson Company product had been one of the best known in America; in the early 1900s, the company continued to produce a quality product as other manufacturers came onto the scene. But during the years of Ford's greatest achievements in mass production and his innovations in labor-management relations, Haynes personally was losing interest in automobiles and becoming increasingly involved in his metallurgical work.

[65] Selden Case Record, III, 1065, Automotive History Collection, Detroit Public Library.

[66] Rae, *American Automobile*, p. 36.

[67] See *ibid.*, pp. 38–41, and George V. Thompson, "Intercompany Technical Standardization in the Early American Automobile Industry," in *Journal of Economic History*, XIV (1954), 1–20.

[68] The appeals court decision appears at 184 Federal Reporter 893 (1911).

Chapter 9

Return to the Laboratory: A New Alloy Is Born

A newspaper reporter wrote of Elwood Haynes: "He is never happier than when shut off from the outside world in a laboratory, immersed in the mysteries of chemistry."[1] Haynes's daughter agreed with this assessment: "Father hated business, deciding who should do what," she remarked in 1970, "he much preferred his research."[2] Before 1905, however, his time for metallurgical research in improved laboratories was very limited. His occupations had required most of his energies for more than a decade after his graduation from Worcester Free Institute in 1881. Then, in the middle 1890s, when he settled into a somewhat routine job as manager of the Indiana Natural Gas and Oil Company's Kokomo plant, he had devoted his evenings and weekends to developing a horseless carriage. When this in turn led to the formation of a manufacturing company, Haynes had found little time for metallurgical research, even though Elmer Apperson took charge of manufacturing the Haynes-Apperson cars.[3] Haynes had been needed to handle other aspects of the business, especially the promotional work and arranging for new financing as necessary. He also sought both mechanical and metallurgical improvements in the Haynes-Apperson automobiles. The seven automobile patents Haynes obtained, either singly or with others, indicate some of this mechanical work; he seemed equally proud of his metallurgical work, never failing to point out that he had introduced the use of aluminum in automobile engines in 1895 or that he had used nickel steel in the automobile built in 1896. Indeed, it appears that the need for alloy steels in the automobile industry prompted Haynes's return to the laboratory and led, at least indirectly, to his most significant metallurgical discovery. It was while Haynes was searching for a suitable alloy for use as the contact points on spark plugs that he discovered the alloys he patented under the name Stellite. The name derived from the Latin word for star, *stella,* which Haynes

---

[1] Indianapolis *Star,* September 4, 1910.

[2] Interview with Bernice Haynes Hillis, Kokomo, Indiana, December 8, 1970. This view is also supported by a biographical questionnaire Haynes completed in 1924. He stated that his "favorite pursuit" was "Laboratory Research Work" and that his "dominating personal characteristic" was a "Very Modest Interest in Science and Invention, Particularly Metallurgy." 1924, Folder, Haynes Papers.

[3] Elwood Haynes to Charles E. Duryea, July 2, 1915, Automotive History Collection, Detroit Public Library.

considered appropriate because of the bright, nontarnishing surface of his cobalt-based alloys.

Haynes's interest in metals was one of long standing. In his youth, fascinated by an older sister's college chemistry book, he had conducted a number of experiments using makeshift equipment, including a homemade furnace in which he melted whatever bits of scrap metal he could find.[4] He had been able to continue and develop his interest in metallurgy in college; his senior thesis had been "The Effect of Tungsten upon Iron and Steel." In the course of this work he had made some of the first "high speed steel" in the United States, an alloy later patented by J. Maunsel White and Frederick W. Taylor that had important applications in the machine tool industry. There was no connection between Haynes's work and that of White and Taylor—i.e., the two research efforts were done independently and had different goals—, but their achievement indicates the potential significance of the work Haynes was doing on his own. He also began to investigate the influence of chromium on steel and steel alloys, a combination Haynes later discovered produces stainlessness; he had been prevented from exploring this field in Worcester because he had not included chromium in his original thesis proposal. His college research, limited initially to the influence of tungsten, nevertheless proved to be significant in Haynes's later metallurgical accomplishments.

The year's study at Johns Hopkins University in 1884-1885 had been an extremely important supplement to his previous work. His instructors, especially the outstanding chemist Ira Remsen, were eminent researchers as well as dedicated teachers. Haynes had learned new experimental techniques and laboratory procedures at Johns Hopkins; in later life he credited his Baltimore experiences with his eventual successes in metallurgy.[5]

During the 1890s Haynes had conducted his metallurgical experiments in a small laboratory that the INGO Company had permitted him to build on the floor above the gas company office. He installed a small furnace there, operated by natural gas, in which he melted his ingredients in tiny crucibles—"about the size of a coffee cup," according to his daughter[6]—and the alloy samples he produced there were sometimes quite tiny, making subsequent analysis difficult. He persevered in these experiments, usually conducted in the evenings after the children's regular bedtime story, and by the end of the decade he was obtaining very promising results. Eventually two companies would be established based upon his metallurgical discoveries of Stellite and stainless steel.

These were the tangible results of a search Haynes had undertaken tentatively as early as 1887 for a nontarnishable metal suitable for table cutlery. The family legend is that Haynes wanted to relieve his wife of the drudgery of polishing the silverware. In a biographical sketch approved by Haynes and published in 1919, Jacob P. Dunn reported that in 1887 Haynes began a series of metallurgical experiments in search of an alloy that "would resist the oxidizing influences of the atmosphere, and . . . take a good cutting edge." At first he tested various copper alloys but "after some years of trial" rejected them as unsuitable. He next worked with various rare metals, in-

---

[4] ["Haynes Autobiography,"] in *Haynes Pioneer*, July, 1913, p. 5. This first installment in the series contained drawings illustrating some of the crude apparatus Haynes used in his first experiments.

[5] Elwood Haynes to Frances Haynes, November 8, 1921, Haynes Papers.

[6] Interview with Bernice Haynes Hillis, December 8, 1970.

cluding tungsten, nickel, chromium, cobalt, molybdenum, and aluminum. Haynes made his fusions then in "small graphite crucibles, which were heated in a blast furnace of the Fletcher type, operated by natural gas." The first alloys that he produced in the late 1890s contained considerable amounts of carbon and silicon as impurities. But by 1898 he finally obtained a carbon-free alloy of nickel and chromium, having combined "the pure mixed oxides of the two metals with powdered aluminum, in a crucible lined with pure oxide of aluminum."[7]

As Haynes reported it, when these ingredients were heated sufficiently "the reaction was so violent that most of the metal was thrown from the crucible." Only a "few small pellets" could be recovered.[8] One suspects his family and business associates had reservations about these periodic explosions, but the experiments continued. The nickel chromium alloy possessed a "fine color," and when polished "exhibited a luster." Haynes also determined that when the chromium content exceeded 10 percent, "the alloy showed remarkable resistance to chemical reagents." Shortly afterwards Haynes also produced very small pellets of a cobalt-chromium alloy. This alloy, similar in appearance to the other, also was hard and could be scratched by a file. It occurred to Haynes that the metal might be used for cutlery,[9] but just at the point of significant discovery in 1901 Haynes was obliged to assume full-time management of his automobile business and consequently lost his laboratory at the gas company.

This hiatus lasted until September 1, 1905, when Haynes turned over the direction of his company to new managers. Then, for the first time since his graduate school days, he was free to engage in long periods of uninterrupted metallurgical research. The results were impressive.

He worked in a laboratory behind his house. There he repeated his previous experiments with nickel, chromium, and cobalt, hoping to find an alloy suitable for "electric contacts in the make-and-break spark mechanism" of his automobile.[10] By then, he was able to produce his alloys in small bar castings, five or six inches long, either a quarter or a half inch square. Carefully analyzing and testing these bars, Haynes was able to acquire a fuller understanding of the "very tough and malleable" alloys he had produced. He shaped some of the bars into razor, pocketknife, and table knife blades, and found them to be free of corrosion after months of constant use.[11] "One of these table knife blades has now been in use for more than two years in the kitchen," Haynes reported in 1910, "where it was used for all sorts of purposes, such as cutting bread, turning griddle cakes, peeling and paring vegetables, and for various other purposes such as are known to the culinary arts. After all this use and abuse, the knife shows not the slightest trace of tarnish, and has held its luster so well that when exposed to the sun it shows a reflection which dazzles the eyes."[12]

Haynes attempted to modify the properties of his alloys by varying the composition percentages and adding other substances. He learned to make

Return to the Laboratory: A New Alloy Is Born

119

---

[7] Dunn, *Indiana and Indianans*, II, 949; Elwood Haynes, " 'Stellite,' A New Alloy," in *Scientific American,* November 19, 1910, p. 398.

[8] Elwood Haynes, "Alloys of Nickel and Cobalt with Chromium," in *Journal of Industrial and Engineering Chemistry,* II (1910), 397 – 401 (reprint in Haynes Papers, paginated 1 – 9; the quotation is at pp. 3 – 4).

[9] *Ibid.*

[10] *Ibid.*

[11] *Ibid.*

[12] *Ibid.*

alloys of extreme hardness, including one which he formed into a small lathe tool. It showed cutting qualities comparable to that of high-speed steel and even surpassed this standard tool metal in light, rapid cuts when intense heat was generated. He emphasized in 1910 that he did not recommend this material as yet for lathe tools. Later, however, this became one of the most important early uses of Stellite, after Haynes had modified its composition through the addition of tungsten.

On April 25, 1907, after he felt sufficiently knowledgeable about their chemical and mechanical properties, Haynes applied for patents on two binary alloys. He engaged the Chicago firm of Poole and Brown, which had handled some of his previous automobile patents, to make the application. The allowance notice was dated November 7, and upon payment of the $20 fee for each one, the patents were issued on December 17, 1907—No. 873,745 covering the cobalt-chromium, No. 873,746 the nickel-chromium alloy.[13]

The initial petition for the former combination described a "novel metal alloy" of high and durable luster and sufficient hardness to make it suitable as a substitute for mild tempered steel in manufacturing "edge tools, . . . as table and pocket cutlery, physicians' and dentists' instruments, or standards of weight, measures, etc. etc." The alloy would take an "extremely lustrous polish, rivaling silver in this respect," and would resist "oxidation and all forms of corrosive fumes commonly occurring in the atmosphere." Similarly, it showed "no tendency to tarnish when exposed to the atmosphere of a chemical laboratory for a long period of time, and even retained its brilliantly polished surface when subjected to boiling nitric acid."[14]

Haynes in his patent application then described three methods of producing the alloy before listing the required specific claims for the invention: he specified a chromium content of between 10 percent and 60 percent, the remaining 40 to 90 percent of the alloy being cobalt. The application on the nickel-chromium alloy was similarly worded, specifying an anticipated use of the alloy "in the manufacture of tools and implements requiring a moderately sharp cutting edge" and, because of its desirable luster and other permanent qualities, in the production of "standards of weight, measures, and like uses." The chromium content of this alloy was specified as from 30 to 60 percent, and again three methods or processes of manufacture were outlined.[15]

These applications were initially rejected by Patent Office Examiner William J. Rich, on the ground that A. L. Marsh's patent (No. 811,859, issued February 6, 1906) anticipated Haynes, but Haynes overcame this objection by an affidavit to the effect that he had produced his alloys prior to the filing day of March's patent application (March 15, 1905) and by submitting dated samples.[16] Moreover, while the Haynes and Marsh alloys were of similar composition, their intended use was considerably different, since Marsh an-

---

[13] Patent Files, No. 873,745, No. 873,746, United States Patent Office, Department of Commerce, Washington, D. C.

[14] Patent File No. 873,745, *ibid.*

[15] Patent File No. 873,746, *ibid.*

[16] The need for sample pellets or bars produced before March 15, 1905 (i.e., the alloys made in the late 1890s) led to what must have been a feverish search of the Haynes household, laboratory, and factory. No sample of a cobalt-chromium alloy of pre-1905 vintage could be found, although other samples from the 1890s were located; fortunately, although "a large number" of the nickel-chromium alloys had been lost, one of sufficiently early date was located and submitted along with a number of more recent cobalt-chromium alloy samples. *Ibid.*

ticipated a use for his discovery not in edge tools but in electrical apparatus. There is some evidence that Haynes and Marsh subsequently made an agreement that Haynes would develop only the cobalt-base alloys, Marsh the nickel-base. No such agreement has been found, but Haynes dropped all experimental work with nickel alloys and went on to develop his cobalt-base tool metal. In a question and answer session following a paper Haynes gave in December, 1919, "Stellite and Stainless Steel," he was asked if Marsh's work with "Nichrome" was earlier, later, or simultaneous with his own. Haynes replied:

> I suppose I would be telling secrets out of school if I told that. I discovered the alloy and he discovered the resistance qualities in it. He uses it for resistance wire. We made a gentleman's agreement that neither would go into the other's field. That is better than to have a law suit.[17]

Stellite, as Haynes termed his patented alloys, was announced to the scientific and industrial world in 1910. In that year he attended the San Francisco convention of the American Chemical Society to read a paper. Entitled "Alloys of Nickel and Cobalt with Chromium," it opened with a brief résumé of the history of each metal. Haynes then recounted some of the details of his long years of experimentation with them and reported on the chemical properties and possible uses of his alloys. Although he noted that such promising items as chisels and lathe tools had been produced and tested, he was not yet ready to recommend his alloy for these uses. For the moment he predicted only that the uses of Stellite would include pocket and table cutlery, surgical instruments, chemical laboratory equipment, and standard weights and measures. He was unable to project the probable cost of Stellite on a manufactured basis but thought it would be only slightly higher than steel. At the conclusion of his talk, Haynes displayed several samples of Stellite to the audience.[18]

The paper aroused considerable interest in Stellite. One San Francisco newspaper featured the remarks of Haynes in its story of the American Chemical Society meeting, which was said to have been "jolted clear out of its rut of technical discussion" by Haynes's account of a new alloy. Another newspaper headlined its story: "New Alloy Dooms Steel in Making of Cutlery," the subhead reading "Elwood Haynes, Father of the Automobile, Erects Factory to Utilize Process."[19] Strangely, no mention of the Haynes address appeared in the Kokomo newspapers,[20] but other editors picked up the

---

[17] Elwood Haynes, "Stellite and Stainless Steel," in *Proceedings of the Engineering Society of Western Pennsylvania*, XXXV (1920), 482. By a strange coincidence, in the 1920s, shortly after the Marsh patent had expired, a Union Carbide metallurgist developed a nickel-base alloy for the Haynes Stellite Company, then a part of Union Carbide. Known as Hastelloy, the new product's unique property was its immunity to chemical corrosion. Produced in various grades today, Hastelloy is one of the most important products of the Stellite company's business. See Ralph D. Gray, *Stellite: A History of the Haynes Stellite Company, 1912–1972* (Kokomo, Ind.: Stellite Division, Cabot Corporation, 1974).

[18] Elwood Haynes, "Alloys of Cobalt with Chromium and Other Metals," in *Transactions of the American Institute of Mining Engineers* (1912), pp. 249–55. A shortened version of this paper also appeared in *Journal of Industrial and Engineering Chemistry*, V (1912), 189–91.

[19] Newspaper clippings, July 18, 1910, Haynes Papers.

[20] March Haynes, in 1929, stated that after his father had presented his paper in San Francisco, the "local newspaper reporters called us up about midnight to see what we knew of his new invention. They had received word of his paper through the Associated Press." General Folder, 1929, *ibid.* Yet a search of the two Kokomo newspapers for July, 1910, for the story proved

story, including the misleading reference to the factory, and Haynes was soon inundated with calls for the metal, which he was unable to supply.[21] One such request came from a Dr. Repin, head of the Pasteur Institute in France, who was seeking a suitable metal for surgical instruments.[22] Haynes also received a number of letters from owners of mining properties offering him chromium, nickel, and cobalt ores. The most significant contact of this type came from Thomas Southworth, an official of the Deloro Smelting and Refining Company near Cobalt, Ontario. The Deloro firm was seeking an outlet for its vast supplies of cobalt, then considered a nearly worthless, unsalable by-product in 'the production of silver. Its primary use prior to the development of Stellite was as a coloring agent in the manufacture of ceramics.[23]

Southworth explained in 1918 the roundabout way by which he first learned of Stellite. In 1910 a business associate in Wales sent him a clipping from an English newspaper that had reprinted an account from an Australian paper referring to Haynes's San Francisco address. Southworth immediately contacted Haynes directly, who thereupon visited him in Toronto and arranged to obtain a supply of cobalt. At the same time Southworth obtained a license from Haynes to produce Stellite in Canada and certain other countries. Apparently Haynes made these arrangements in exchange for, in addition to the customary royalty, assistance in developing Stellite cutlery. Some of this developmental work was done in Sheffield, England, although the cutlers there learned, as did Haynes and the American firms he engaged to produce pocketknives, that Stellite's hardness made it very difficult to work with in this way.

Manufacturers in both Ohio and Massachusetts worked on the production of Stellite knives in 1910 and 1911. Haynes himself made the necessary quantities of the alloy in his laboratory, where he was assisted by his brother-in-law Harry Lanterman, but he sent the castings to other firms for completing the knives.[24] As early as 1911, Haynes sold a few Stellite knives, of which he was extremely proud, and gave a number of them as Christmas gifts in 1911, delighting the recipients. In April, 1912, he was accepting quantity orders from sales agents, although difficult manufacturing problems still remained. Even Thomas Southworth of the Deloro firm, in consultation with his colleagues in Sheffield, found the existing Stellite composition impossible to process, and appealed to Haynes to make "new experiments in melting."

fruitless. A possible explanation is that on the day of Haynes's talk in California a sensational murder occurred in downtown Kokomo. A deputy sheriff shot a Negro trash collector following an argument over a fifty cent notary fee, and the papers gave extensive coverage to this event and its long aftermath.

[21] The Indianapolis *Sunday Star* carried a feature story on Haynes in September, 1910, reviewing his career as a scientist and a businessman. "He is a pioneer in chemistry as well as mechanics," it stated, citing as examples the automobile and Stellite. Haynes was reported as being "highly pleased" with the business outlook for the alloy. Indianapolis *Star*, September 4, 1910.

[22] Kokomo *Dispatch*, September 27, 1911.

[23] Roland S. Young, *Cobalt: Its Chemistry, Metallurgy, and Uses* (New York: Reinhold Publishing Corporation, 1960), pp. 2–4. See also the correspondence between Haynes and Southworth in 1912, Haynes Papers. The letters of 1910 and 1911 between these men have not been preserved. Regrettably, there are very few Haynes papers for the period from 1892 until 1912, when Haynes finally hired a personal secretary and began a file of his incoming and outgoing correspondence.

[24] See Canton Cutlery Company to Elwood Haynes, July 20, 1910, Haynes Papers; Humason & Beckley Manufacturing Company to Elwood Haynes, December 12, 1911, *ibid.*

The Sheffield cutlers had been "unable to drill" the necessary rivet holes because the alloy's "temper is so high."[25]

Fairly regular sales occurred during the year, nevertheless, and Haynes was unswervingly optimistic in the face of the production difficulties. Confident in the future of Stellite, he realized that new manufacturing procedures perhaps would be required but believed the results would be worth it. Although forced to reject many requests for purchases, he began to advertise through small printed circulars, in anticipation of planned expansion.

In March, 1912, he had to refuse a request for a quantity of Stellite, pointing out that "thus far, I have not made it for sale at all except in the form of table and pocket cutlery." Most sales were by mail order, which he handled personally, although in April the George W. Claffin Company of Providence, Rhode Island, temporarily served as the sales agent for Stellite knives in New England.[26] In May, Haynes described one of the Stellite products he manufactured as a "Gentleman's light three blade pearl handle pocket knife," but pointed out it was "not suitable for tough use. The large B[lade] of this K[nife] measures 1¾" from shank to point, & 2¼" over all. I expect shortly to make up a larger size . . . (2¼ x 2¾") @ $2.50 each. The metal used is hard, [but] will neither rust nor tarnish under any natural conditions whatever."[27]

In the winter of 1911-1912, while initiating the manufacture and sale of his Stellite knives made according to his original formula, Haynes was actively involved in seeking ways to improve the alloy. During this time Haynes made what, in retrospect, must be regarded as his most significant metallurgical discoveries. On the one hand, he learned that the addition of tungsten to his basic cobalt-chromium alloy rendered the metal incredibly hard without affecting its heat-, stain-, and corrosion-resistant qualities. This discovery eventually earned millions of dollars for Haynes. On the other hand, he became aware of the effect of chromium upon iron and steel—that is, he discovered that chromium in the proper proportions would render iron and steel rustless, or stainless. Patent applications on both discoveries were submitted, but only one was granted immediately. That the stainless steel idea would encounter difficulty was evident from patent attorney C. C. Poole's reaction to it. Haynes spent many hours during March and April, 1912, in correspondence with Poole, trying to convince him that he had made a patentable invention. Poole had hesitated in submitting the application because "chrome iron" and "chrome steel" were not new. Both had been known in the nineteenth century and various combinations had been patented. Haynes eventually persuaded his attorney that he had made new discoveries and a patent application was made, but, as Poole had anticipated, the patent office rejected "all claims of [the] chromium steel patent." Characteristically, this failed to discourage Haynes, who promised "additional experiments" and then "we will make new application."[28]

Although most of his attention at the moment was devoted to making Stellite according to his new formulae and testing the results, he informed

---

[25] Thomas Southworth to Elwood Haynes, April 19, 1912, *ibid.*

[26] The Claffin company ordered ten dozen Stellite table knives, pocketknives (both "gentlemen" and "ladies" models), and spatulas, but requested a one third discount instead of the regular 25 percent "for lines with established sales." This order was filled, the table knives being part of a lot of two hundred Haynes had produced, but production on a regular basis had not yet begun. George W. Claffin Company to Elwood Haynes, April 8, 1912, *ibid.*

[27] Elwood Haynes to W. A. Johnson, May 27, 1912, *ibid.*

[28] Elwood Haynes to C. Clarence Poole, May 13, 1912, *ibid.*

Poole that "some very interesting things are developing just now from my experiments with Stellite and chrome steel." A week later, he added, "I am very busy just at present with Stellite but as soon as I have finished the work in which I am now engaged I will take up the chrome steel matter again with you."[29] This later work led to a patent application in 1915 for stainless steel, but first he would explore those "very interesting things" in the development of Stellite.

The laboratory notebooks in which Haynes' carefully recorded his experimental work were copied in the 1920s. These data were used in an important court case, *Haynes Stellite Company* v. *Chesterfield Metal Company,* which upheld the validity of Haynes's Stellite patent No. 1,057,423.[30] The typescript of this record, now in the possession of the Cabot Corporation's Stellite Division in Kokomo, Indiana, reveals the slow, laborious process by which Haynes developed and then improved Stellite. It also indicates, by reading between the lines, some of the excitement and sense of discovery Haynes experienced as various tests were conducted on the sample bars.

124

As early as October 3, 1908, in fact, an alloy of tungsten, cobalt, and chromium was made, but he noticed nothing significant about it at that time. In 1911, in the course of a careful experimental program Haynes returned to these three ingredients, making in March of that year a cold chisel from the "very hard" bar he had cast. It "showed most remarkable cutting qualities," was difficult to roll or forge, and its very fine grain helped to give it an appearance "rivaling that of the finest tool metal." New combinations were made in April and tested for hardness, elasticity, and resistance to acid.[31] By February 16, 1912, he had an alloy of cobalt and chromium, with traces of tungsten, silicon, and molybdenum, which he thought would "make an excellent material for chisels," and added, "I am inclined to think it will make good lathe tools as it is." He continued making slight modifications in the composition, and on April 25 made a ternary alloy of cobalt, chromium, and tungsten. The bar was "*very hard* and brittle," took "a good polish," and would "readily scratch quartz"; "I believe it to be one of the *hardest* alloys I have yet made."[32] He immediately tested these and similar combinations in lathes at the Haynes Automobile Company. The results were striking. Operators were able to turn out a normal day's work by midafternoon, approximately a 50 percent increase in efficiency. William A. Wissler, a Union Carbide Corporation metallurgist who once worked for Haynes at the Haynes Stellite Company, wrote in 1939, "These and other tests showed that these cobalt-chromium-tungsten cutting tools were much superior to any then available, and in 1913 they were placed on the market."[33]

Haynes himself communicated the dramatic results of the lathe tool tests to his Canadian associates in May, but for reasons he explained he was unable to make any public announcements about the breakthrough. "I have some information regarding Stellite which I am sure will be very pleasing to you," he began. "I have been experimenting quite industriously on other

---

[29] *Ibid.,* May 13, 21, 1912.

[30] The district court decision, upholding the patent but finding no infringement, is found at 8 Federal Reporter (2d) 765–73; the appeals court decision, which reversed the lower court ruling, is at 22 Federal Reporter (2d) 635–38.

[31] Typescript, Early Notebooks of Elwood Haynes, Experimental Development of Stellite at Kokomo, Indiana, Elwood Haynes File, Stellite Division, Cabot Corporation, Kokomo.

[32] *Ibid.*

[33] Elwood Haynes, "Alloys of Cobalt, Chromium, and Tungsten," in *Metals Progress,* 1939, p. 131, in Haynes Stellite Company File, Indiana Division, Indiana State Library.

uses [besides cutlery] for the alloy & have recently succeeded in producing some most remarkable results from lathe tools made of this material." He then described the tests, and speculated upon their economic significance. The $11.00 per pound "high speed steel" used in the lathes at the automobile plant was not very satisfactory. In making some articles, such as "semi-steel wheels," the lathes had to be turned slowly and "even then the tool must be ground at least once for each wheel." After inserting a tool of Stellite made according to the new formula, the machine turned "just about twice as fast & completed 41 wheels without becoming dulled." In another test, an operator completed 26 wheels in ten hours with a steel tool; using Stellite he produced 24 wheels in five hours. He concluded that a Stellite tool "showed 41 times the endurance of the steel tool & did nearly twice the work in a given time," but he asked Southworth not to publicize any of this because "I am to read a paper before the International Congress of Applied Chemistry next September on Cobalt & its alloys" and "I am under obligations not to publish any data which is to appear in the paper previous to the time."[34]

Haynes then noted that the automobile plant had already decided to replace all its steel tools with Stellite ones (paying a price of $3.00 per pound). "It must not be supposed," Haynes cautioned, "that ordinary Stellite will give these results. This is a special alloy but its composition will be made known to you as soon as I am at liberty to disclose it."[35]

A month later Haynes reported again to Southworth on the enthusiastic, if initially incredulous, response to Stellite tools within the trade. Many high-speed steel salesmen refused to believe the men at the Haynes plant about Stellite's capabilities as a tool metal but changed their opinions after seeing the tools in service. Two men, in fact, solicited Haynes "most earnestly" to be allowed to sell Stellite, but he refused since no production facilities existed and his own plans for manufacturing and marketing Stellite were not yet formulated. He assured Southworth that when the time came Stellite tool metal "in large lots" would "sell readily at from $3.00 to $5.00 per pound" and offered to come to Deloro "just before or just after I read the paper" on Stellite. He proposed to "show some trustworthy person how to make the metal on a *small scale* just as I make it in Kokomo. I expect to make some rather exhaustive experiments upon turning tools within the next 2 or 3 weeks, & will let you know the results."[36]

By this time Haynes was ready to seek a patent on his improved Stellite alloys. The initial application submitted July 20, 1912, specified two ternary compounds—one of cobalt, chromium, and tungsten, the other of cobalt, chromium, and molybdenum; it also described a quaternary compound of all four metals. Rich, the patent officer, required separate applications on the ternary and quaternary alloys but promptly allowed them when received. The allowances were made on September 5 and 6, 1912, with the patents issuing on April 1, 1913. Patent No. 1,057,423 covers the cobalt-chromium-tungsten combination (with the tungsten ranging from 5 to 60 percent); Patent No. 1,057,828 covers an alloy of cobalt, chromium, tungsten, and molybdenum, again with the chromium group metals (tungsten and molybdenum) ranging from 5 to 60 percent.[37]

---

[34] Elwood Haynes to Thomas Southworth, May 7, 1912, Haynes Papers.

[35] *Ibid.*

[36] *Ibid.*, June 12, 1912.

[37] Patent File No. 1,057,423, No. 1,057,828, U. S. Patent Office.

When notified in early September, 1912, that the patents would be forth-coming, Haynes immediately began to arrange for manufacturing Stellite. By strange coincidence, at the time of his notification of allowance by the patent office, he was in New York presenting his paper on the new alloys before a session of the International Congress of Applied Chemistry.[38] In his talk Haynes referred to his paper of 1910, delivered in San Francisco, in which he had described his basic cobalt-chromium alloy. The alloy now "is modified to such a marked degree by the introduction of other substances," he reported, "that I have felt justified in reading another paper on this subject." He reviewed his experiments carried on since "1907 or 1908," when tungsten, molybdenum, and other elements were added. He still used a natural gas furnace for this work (although in 1912 he purchased an electric one for further experimentation),[39] making his fusions at first in graphite crucibles. The carbon in the graphite, however, contaminated the metal, so he constructed special crucibles for his later tests.[40]

126

Haynes then made his first public announcement on the lathe test results in machining the cast-iron wheels. Using high-speed steel, twenty-six wheels had been turned out in a ten-hour day; with a Stellite tool, forty-nine wheels had been completed. The steel tool, moreover, had been ground fifty times during the day; the Stellite tool "was dressed slightly by a carborundum whetstone, after its day's work was completed." With Stellite cutters in the boring-head of a cylinder-drilling machine, ten hours of work had been performed in three hours and twenty minutes. Haynes predicted that Stellite "will not fully supersede high speed steel in the machine shop, but in cases where rapid work is the main consideration, it will doubtless replace high speed steel."[41] Haynes's prediction proved correct, although exceedingly modest. No one could have anticipated the broad range of uses to which Stellite has been adapted. This, the widespread utilization of Stellite, was to be the legacy of the little business, the Haynes Stellite Works, Haynes estab-lished at the end of 1912.

---

[38] Earlier, in March, Haynes had written to several of his friends and business associates in Kokomo seeking their membership in the society. He mentioned the forthcoming meeting in New York but not that he was to give a paper there. When this was decided upon is not clear; Haynes referred to it in his letter to Southworth in May, and a letter from the president of the 8th International Congress in June reminded Haynes that his paper should be submitted to him by July 1. Charles L. Parsons to Elwood Haynes, June 20, 1912, Haynes Papers.

[39] Elwood Haynes to Professor Calhane, June 10, 1912, *ibid.*

[40] Haynes, "Alloys of Cobalt with Chromium and Other Metals," in *Transactions of the American Institute of Mining Engineers* (1912), p. 252.

[41] *Ibid.*

Chapter 10

The Haynes
Stellite Company

When Elwood Haynes learned in early September, 1912, that his Stellite tool metal patents had been allowed, he at once purchased property on South Union Street in Kokomo, near his automobile plant. There he built a small cement block building, hardly fifty feet square, installed a battery of gas furnaces, and began to produce Stellite on a commercial basis before the end of the year. Prior to this time, there had been a "mail order"[1] Stellite business in operation, offering pocket and table knives in small quantities, while Haynes continued both to improve the cutlery metal and develop a Stellite tool metal. The small amounts of binary Stellite for knife blades or sample tool bits were made in the laboratory, a barn behind the Haynes house.

The first tool metal Haynes produced had been tested, and then adopted for regular use, in his automobile factory in May, 1912. Tests early in the month produced "some quite remarkable results" when Stellite was substituted for high-speed steel in turning semi-steel wheels.[2] The automobile plant at once bought Stellite tools at $3.00 a pound for use wherever possible; a statement dated June 3, 1912, shows that the company purchased 25¼ pounds of Stellite (for $75.75) between May 27 and June 3. Haynes's daughter Bernice, who was attending Western College for Women in Ohio while the tool metal was being developed, was delighted at the automobile company's response. "You ought to advertize Stellite for lathe tools," she advised her father. "Just think what it would mean to get a dozen or more orders like the one from the factory. In fact, you ought to get several more right there in Kokomo. There are plenty of factories there that need lathe tools."[3]

Before acting on his daughter's suggestion and undertaking the commercial production of Stellite tools, however, Haynes obtained the patents upon his "new Stellite." In the meantime, he also presented his paper describing the modified alloys to the International Congress of Applied Chemistry in New York City. C. Clarence Poole, his patent attorney, had agreed to have Haynes read the paper while the patent applications were pending on condi-

---

[1] Elwood Haynes to "Mr. McWhirl," May 29, 1912, Haynes Papers.

[2] Elwood Haynes to Thomas Southworth, May 7, 1912, *ibid.*

[3] Bernice Haynes to Elwood Haynes, May 3, 1912, *ibid.*

tion that he not mention the applications or be too specific on certain points.

They need not have worried; the patent office acted to allow the applications while Haynes was in New York. Immediately upon his return to Kokomo, therefore, he set about to establish a small manufacturing plant. He also granted a broad license to a Canadian manufacturer, the Deloro Company, to manufacture and market Stellite in Canada and various other countries. From time to time Haynes dispatched workers from the Kokomo plant to assist their Deloro counterparts in their manufacturing procedures.

The work force at the Kokomo plant, termed the Haynes Stellite Works, at the outset consisted of only four people, all family members; but the business, if not the number of employees, grew rapidly. Haynes himself was both plant manager and furnace man; his brother-in-law Harry Lanterman was mold maker and furnace liner. Together they melted all of the Stellite, while March Haynes, the inventor's sixteen-year-old son, worked after school and on Saturdays grinding the bars. Mrs. Haynes filled in during 1912 as her husband's personal secretary, but she was succeeded in this position in December by Marie Huffer. The new girl was still a student at the Kokomo Business College and worked part time. In 1930, the former secretary recalled that her first office in the Stellite plant was just opposite "the little room where Mr. Haynes kept the different materials he worked with and weighed before taking them into the furnace room. . . ." She also remembered that Haynes "experimented almost every day" and that, after being in the furnace room with its "terrific heat and noise," he would "come hurrying in and write the results in a notebook in longhand."[4]

Only an occasional workman was added to the labor force during the first three years, and probably at no time did it exceed eight or ten men. When Miss Huffer resigned in March, 1914, Mrs. Clara E. Prestel moved across the street from the Haynes Automobile Company to become the Stellite Works secretary. She recalled in a letter to Haynes in 1923 that the entire "working force" when she began her new job consisted of Lanterman, March Haynes, and a "Mr. Sigfried."[5] H. B. Brewster, who worked at Stellite for one week in 1915, named three other non-Haynes family members who were with the company then. Brewster's job was to "shake out" the molds following a pour and then reclamp them; one of his partners operated the gas furnaces, and the other two men ground the bars produced and packed them for shipment.[6]

During this time Haynes appeared to be more interested in continuing his experimental work and in developing new and unusual uses for Stellite than in producing large quantities of metal for the market. Under Haynes's management the business grossed only $7,000 in 1913, $11,000 in 1914, and $48,000 in 1915. Three grades of the tool metal alloy were being produced using a battery of sixteen tiny gas furnaces. The crucibles used held fifteen-pound charges, which were melted in approximately ninety minutes. The small heats, the short life of the expensive crucibles (two or three heats), and the slow melting time caused Haynes to examine other types of furnaces. He first tried an electric resistance furnace which held a charge of eighty to ninety pounds, but its "complicated electrical arrangement among other things" made it as unsatisfactory as the gas furnaces.

128

---

[4] Deposition by Marie Huffer Englert, July 25, 1930, *ibid.*

[5] Clara E. Prestel to Elwood Haynes, February 18, 1923, *ibid.*

[6] Interview with H. B. Brewster, August 18, 1971.

As with the automobile company, Haynes handled the early advertising for Stellite personally. It consisted initially of a few printed cards, explaining what Stellite was and extolling its virtues both as a cutlery item and a lathe tool. These early cards and circulars identified Stellite as an alloy of semi-rare metals, containing none of the common metals such as copper, tin, lead, or aluminum. In 1914 Haynes wrote,

> It should be distinctly remembered that Stellite is not a steel and it is no more logical to call it by this name than to call brass or copper or diamonds steel. Steel is a compound of iron with other materials, and iron is always the predominating and essential constituent of all steels. Stellite is composed of the metal, cobalt, alloyed with other substances, and contains no iron. The name, stellite, is derived from the Latin word, stella, a star or strewer of light, and has no reference whatever to the word, steel. It was given this name because when the alloy is polished, it retains its brilliant luster under all atmospheric conditions.[7]

The Haynes Stellite Company

129

The outstanding properties of Stellite, in addition to its shiny appearance, were its freedom from corrosion and its hardness, even at the elevated temperatures reached in severe service applications—what the metallurgists call "red hardness." While these qualities gave Stellite its value as a tool metal, they also made it impossible either to forge Stellite tools or to harden them by heat treatments. "If they could be forged," Haynes explained, "it would be necessary for them to soften at a high temperature, which would, of course, destroy their cutting edge. Hence they are cast as nearly as possible into the desired form, then finished by grinding."[8]

Subsequently Haynes issued a twelve-page booklet describing his lathe tools in more detail, and he wrote articles and delivered papers regarding his metals before scientific and technical groups. In 1914, in his first article in *Iron Age,* Haynes discussed the "misunderstandings" which frequently arise "[w]henever any new material is proposed as a partial substitute for one already in use. . . . Exaggerated accounts of its capabilities are likely to be given, and . . . some of its purchasers are likely to be disappointed when it does not fulfill the exaggerated accounts." The trouble, however, usually stems from an "improper application" of the new device or material. "This was true," Haynes observed, "of aluminum, of the new abrasives, of the automobile, and of countless devices which have since won their way by sheer merit into extensive practical use." He then described Stellite and its unique properties and explained its most economical uses. "If, for example, a machine is running so slowly that a piece of carbon steel will take the cut without losing its hardness, then there will [be] no advantage in using the high speed tool," he wrote, "but the up-to-date manufacturer will see to it that his factory is equipped with the machinery that will give the best machines a chance to do their best work."[9]

Haynes provided several illustrations of Stellite's 50 to 100 percent superiority to steel tools in the volume of production per hour in regular machine shop use. Although not explicitly stated, these tests probably had been conducted in the Haynes Automobile Company plant. Haynes observed that the "best results" with Stellite occurred on "comparatively light cuts, mod-

---

[7] Elwood Haynes, "The Use of Stellite in the Machine Shop," in *Iron Age,* January 8, 1914, p. 149.

[8] *Ibid.*

[9] *Ibid.,* p. 148.

erate feed, and high speed." The tendency of the earliest Stellite tools to break had largely been overcome, both by strengthening the metal and by securing a perfectly snug fit of the tool bit in its holder. Haynes concluded his article by admitting that the cost of Stellite, because of the "comparatively expensive materials" in it, is "considerably higher than even the highest priced high-speed steel," but that "there were numerous instances in which it would pay well to use the Stellite." One government employee, after using a Stellite tool for a few days, asked how much it cost. Upon being told the price was $5.00 a pound, he replied, "I will give you $10 per lb. for it, if you will not cut my piece rate below the present figure."[10]

In the light of these informational and promotional claims, the demand for Stellite far exceeded Haynes's capacity to produce it. The problem was not in obtaining customers but rather in producing good quality Stellite in sufficient quantities for the growing demand. Suitable production techniques were not yet established, and satisfactory quality control checks were lacking. Stellite was a temperamental product, and further knowledge was necessary. But Haynes was unable to devote sufficient time of his own to the production process, and he was still unwilling to turn over the task to anyone else.

Haynes was away on extended trips during 1913 and 1914, and in 1915 he also began to take a much more active part in civic affairs. His fame as a pioneer in both mechanical and metallurgical areas began to spread, and the demands upon his time grew significantly. Haynes much preferred, moreover, to continue his research program investigating the properties of Stellite, "chrome iron," and "chrome steel" more thoroughly. This led to new patent applications in 1915, the first one in March being the revised "stainless steel" application he had promised in 1912 after "additional experiments."[11] Haynes also applied for a patent upon a new cutlery metal in May, 1915. Because the original Stellite, whether in its binary, ternary, or quaternary forms, was too hard to be worked into blades, edged, and fitted with handles, Haynes had persisted in his search for untarnishable tableware. In 1915 he finally hit upon a combination of Stellite and iron—something he came to call "Festel" metal. This name was taken from the chemical symbol for iron (Fe) and the first syllable of Haynes's previously patented alloy. He found that iron, ranging up to 50 percent of the whole (Haynes recommended 45 percent), rendered the resultant material malleable enough for the cutler while the nearly equal cobalt and chromium percentages remained sufficiently high to maintain the product's noncorroding, or stainless, qualities.

For assistance in filing his applications in 1915, Haynes retained the services of K. P. McElroy, a patent attorney in Washington, D. C., specializing in metallurgical work. McElroy proved to be a capable and effective advocate of Haynes's interests, and he was able to get all four of the claims in the "Festel" application accepted, despite Examiner Rich's objection to the fourth claim, the last and most general statement. McElroy was also to carry the "stainless steel" application of 1915 to a successful conclusion, even though it would require four years to do so. The "Festel" patent, No. 1,150,113, was allowed on July 15, and officially issued on August 17. The

[10] *Ibid.,* pp. 148–49.

[11] Elwood Haynes to C. Clarence Poole, May 13, 1912, Haynes Papers.

Kokomo *Daily Dispatch* report of this event was headlined: "New Alloy is Discovered by Elwood Haynes—From Stellite. Makes Handling of Stellite Easier."[12]

Despite the fruition of Haynes's new research work in 1915, probably the most significant event of the year in terms of Haynes's future was his decision to bring two partners into the Stellite business. This led to the formal establishment of the Haynes Stellite Company (the articles of incorporation bear the date October 26, 1915), the introduction of a small amount of outside capital, and the transfer of the day-to-day management of the company to a businessman with a reputation for salesmanship and aggressive leadership. The author of the reorganization plan is not known, but it appears likely that Richard Ruddell, one of Kokomo's leading bankers and an influential stockholder in the Haynes Automobile Company, developed it. Ruddell was intimately involved with a number of Kokomo industries, and he must have been aware of Stellite's outstanding commercial possibilities. He may have been the one to suggest both the more vigorous prosecution of the business and the man to do it—James C. Patten. Patten, Ruddell's son-in-law, had previously managed the Globe Stove and Range Company in Kokomo. An intense, hard-driving man (he was a boxer and an aviator in his spare time), Patten proved to be an effective manager of the Stellite company. Sales leaped at once to a monthly rate greater than the previous annual rate, and a million dollars' worth of Stellite was marketed from November, 1915, to November, 1916.

Haynes was given 200 of the 500 shares of Haynes Stellite Company stock in return for the business and an exclusive right to manufacture and sell Stellite in the United States. Haynes, who then held four Stellite patents (Nos. 873,745, 1,057,423, and 1,057,828 on cobalt-base alloys; No. 1,150,113 on "Festel" metal), was to receive in addition a monthly royalty payment based on the month's sales—15 percent if under $4,000 a month, 10 percent if over $4,000. His salary as president of the new company was a nominal $166.67, or two thirds of Patten's salary of $250. Ruddell, who would not be actively engaged in the business, received no salary at the outset. He and Patten, however, were the source of the small amount of capital required to finance an expansion of the plant. Both men purchased 100 shares of stock (at $100 per share), leaving 100 shares undistributed until December, 1916, when a stock dividend of 25 percent was declared. Haynes thereafter held 250 shares, or 50 percent, of the stock, with Ruddell and Patten dividing the remainder.[13]

A rapid expansion of the company followed incorporation. In November, 1915, the officers decided to "erect immediately" an addition to the original building which doubled the plant size; it was at this time that an order was placed for the Stellite company's first electric-arc furnace, manufactured by the Snyder Electric Furnace Company of Chicago. The electric furnace proved eminently satisfactory; it held charges of up to 125 pounds, reduced the melting time to thirty minutes, and rarely needed relining. Eventually Haynes purchased two additional Snyders of 500-pound capacity; together they produced more than four tons of Stellite in an eleven-hour day. In 1918, during the peak production required by World War I, the three furnaces

[12]*Ibid.*, August 21, 1915. See also Patent File No. 1,150,113, U. S. Patent Office.

[13]Haynes Stellite Company Minute Book No. 1, 1915–1916, Union Carbide Corporation Retired Records Center, Morrisville, Vermont.

produced all of the Stellite made in the United States.[14] In addition, Stellite hired a number of new employees and established a downtown office on the sixth floor of the Citizens Bank building, probably in late 1915. A photograph, taken in 1916 outside of the expanded original plant, pictures twenty employees of the company, including Haynes; at least seven other employees were not in the picture. This latter group included General Manager Patten; Bernice Haynes, now graduated from college and working both as company secretary and as her father's personal secretary; March Haynes, who assisted his father in various ways although his fellow employees considered him as merely an "errand boy"; and an office staff of from four to six others.[15]

132

Elwood Haynes Museum

Employees of the Haynes Stellite Company, 1916, Elwood Haynes at far left

During 1916 the initial property on the present site of the Stellite plant on the near southwest side of Kokomo was acquired from a canning company whose factory there had been destroyed by fire. The Stellite officers decided to erect a building, 60 by 120 feet, on the new property, where Stellite tools and castings would be finished. For the time being, all of the Stellite would continue to be made at the South Union Street plant.[16]

---

[14] Elwood Haynes, "The Development of Stellite," in *Iron Age*, October 10, 1918, pp. 886–88; Elwood Haynes to Perry Creager, May 7, 1918, Haynes Papers. A report published in 1919 indicated that the business had paid its expenses the first year, had earned 75 percent on its investment in 1914, and before the third year ended, during which incorporation occurred, had earned seven or eight times the investment. In 1919, the account concluded, the business was in a "highly prosperous condition." Kokomo *Tribune*, February 12, 1919. These two earnings reports, assuming both were accurate, indicate that Haynes's initial capital investment was between $6,000 and $7,000 annually.

[15] *Ibid.;* interviews with Cora W. Hicks, Lakeland, Florida, July 10, 1971; George Beatty, Kokomo, January 22, 1971.

[16] Kokomo *Daily Dispatch*, June 22, 1916; Haynes Stellite Company Minute Book No. 1, August 29, November 2, 1916, Union Carbide Retired Records Center. The "cobalt mineral lands" in

Haynes also decided to purchase a cobalt ore mining property outside Salmon, Idaho, in September, 1916, following a personal inspection of the site. There is a poignant and lengthy correspondence between Haynes and James W. Caples, the mine manager, describing Caples's struggles to overcome the nearly insuperable obstacles to developing the mine. The mine location was a poor one, without regular transportation into Salmon except by horse and wagon over virtually nonexistent roads, and a series of natural disasters also struck the valiant miner. Both he and Haynes persisted, the latter motivated as much by the desire to prove to his dubious partners that an alternate source of cobalt could be developed as by the immediate need for a supply. Patten especially objected to the time and energy Haynes expended in devising a process to recover cobalt from the Idaho ore, but Haynes was interested in the scientific challenge. He much preferred experimentation and testing to the routine of management and production tasks.

Later on, this persistence in research problems paid off handsomely for the company. During World War I, when the prices of cobalt and tungsten skyrocketed, Haynes was able to find cheap substitute sources for both metals. He used bichromate of sodium as a cobalt source, reducing its cost from $2.40 to less than $1.00 a pound, and he had even more dramatic success with tungsten. "When the price ran up to $10 a pound, Haynes decided that chemistry should lead him to a substitute," wrote a journalist who interviewed the scientist in 1925.

> Research disclosed that in certain mines in California there was a substance known as 'scheelite ore.' Haynes ordered several car loads and began to experiment with it in his tiny laboratory, which at that time was just 12 feet square. He finally succeeded in reducing this ore in his furnaces to a pure oxide of tungsten at a finished cost of $1.50 a pound. This discovery resulted in a saving that year of $150,000 in the manufacture of Stellite.[17]

Haynes became relatively prosperous as a result of his Stellite inventions. At the end of 1916, the first year of large-scale production, the business was in such a thriving condition that a dividend of 10 percent *a month* on all stock was voted, payable the last day of each month. This continued until July, 1918, when substantial annual salaries plus 12 percent of the net profits were approved for each of the company officers. Patten was to receive $12,000 a year; Haynes, $8,000; and Ruddell, $4,000. When C. C. Kerlin was elected assistant secretary-treasurer at this time, his salary was set at $5,000 a year, a figure that was doubled during 1919. Haynes subsequently reported that sales for 1918 approximated $3,600,000, with profits of $1,200,000. During the year, Haynes had casually remarked to a relative in Massachusetts that sales for the month were 66,000 percent above what they had been exactly five years before.[18]

The percentage payments on profits were revised in late 1918; thereafter, 5 percent of the gross sales went to Haynes, with 3 percent of the gross going

---

Idaho were purchased in September, 1916, for $17,500. Haynes Stellite Company Minute Book No. 1, September 6, 1916, *ibid.* See the Elwood Haynes-James W. Caples correspondence of 1916, 1917, and 1918 in the Haynes Papers for details concerning the problems involved in developing the mine and getting the ore to a shipping point.

[17] Foster, "How Elwood Haynes Came to Build First 'Horseless Carriage,'" in *Forbes,* March 2, 1925, p. 679.

[18] Haynes Stellite Company Minute Book No. 1, 1918, Union Carbide Retired Records Center; Elwood Haynes to George Haynes, August 15, 1918, Haynes Papers.

both to Patten and Ruddell. When the capital stock of the company was increased to $750,000 in March, 1920, preparatory to the transfer to Union Carbide, a 500 percent stock dividend was declared. By then, Richard Ruddell was dead, and his stock was held by his widow and their three children. During these highly prosperous years, employee wages went up considerably also. In 1915, seventeen and a half cents an hour was paid for an eleven-hour day, six days a week; in 1918, the going rate was from thirty to forty cents an hour, wages which were about equal to or slightly above the national average for industrial workers at the time.

These financial transactions reflect the enormous profitability and growth of the Stellite company, although precise figures on business and employment do not exist. Fortunately, however, Haynes reported on his affairs from time to time with remarkable candor to several of his close friends, and these statements are most impressive. Evidently the business grossed $1 million in sales in 1916 and 1917, jumped to about $3.6 million in 1918 before falling to $1 million in 1919 and slightly less in 1920 (a depression year). Indeed, Stellite sales did not achieve the 1918 peak again until 1937, and then not again until after the United States entered World War II.

The prosperity of the 1916–1918 period is partly explained by the relatively high prices Haynes was able to charge for his product (the three grades of tool metal were priced at $6.00, $7.00, and $8.00 a pound) but reflects even more the insatiable wartime demand for greater production, and hence for more efficient machine tools. A letter from Henry M. Leland of the Lincoln Motor Company, ordering 300 pieces of Stellite, indicates the urgency of this demand:

> Now Mr. Haynes, allow me to explain that we are trying to machine 850 steel cylinders for Liberty Aeroplane engines daily. We have to take heavy cuts off these forgings and the steel is so hard it is impossible for us to get high speed steel that will stand the work.
>
> As you probably know by reading the papers, it would be difficult to conceive how any greater pressure could be exerted in regard to any product than that which is being pressed upon us to get out quantities of the Liberty Motors.
>
> We have found that this stellite is very superior to the high speed steel or anything else that we have found. We can and will furnish you with a Priority A certificate if you require it and it will help matters. We are confident that the authorities in Washington will tell you that there is no other Government work that ranks ahead of this in importance.[19]

Another major use for Stellite during the war was in turning metal used in munitions—shells and shrapnel. Haynes often remarked that no less than 75 percent, and perhaps as much as 90 percent, of the shrapnel produced in the United States during the war was turned on machines equipped with Stellite tools. "People went so far as to say that they could not have afforded to make shells and shrapnel at the Government prices if they had been deprived of their Stellite tools," March Haynes told his classmates in 1919; and Elwood Haynes remembered that some machinists came personally to the Stellite plant to handcarry whatever Stellite was available back to their shops.[20] Haynes also reported that after the war some machinists carried their Stellite tools home with them at night for safekeeping; meeting their daily quotas without them would have been impossible.

[19] Henry M. Leland to Elwood Haynes, May 11, 1918, Haynes Papers.

[20] March Haynes, "Stellite," January 31, 1919, *ibid*.

134

Haynes seems not to have been concerned about the ultimate use of the wartime products the Stellite tools were used to manufacture. Perhaps this stemmed from his support of the war as a battle of democracy against autocracy, in President Wilson's words; perhaps, too, he realized that the weapons of war would have been produced with or without his product, although the costs would have been much higher.

The Stellite company also produced some 40,000 "lancets" or scalpels for the government during 1917-1918. These were used in field hospitals operating close to the front lines where the nontarnishing and lasting qualities of the alloy were important. An interesting experiment using Stellite as a reflecting mirror for telescopes was also made in 1918, something which partially anticipated the considerable use of Stellite as reflectors in Navy searchlights during World War II and afterwards.

For several reasons 1918 was an important year: war orders were heavy, good profits were obtained, and considerable plant expansion occurred. In July, 1918, the contracts for two major buildings, a foundry and a machine shop, each 60 feet by 132 feet, were let, and construction progressed rapidly.[21] Manufacturing operations continued at both locations during the war, with the Stellite truck, an old Ford, carrying the metal between the furnaces on South Union Street and the finishing shops on West Markland Street. The first building in use at the new site was the old strawboard factory, erected just after the natural gas boom hit Kokomo in 1886. It was used initially as the rough grind shop as early as the summer of 1917. Fred Hawkins, who made some of the runs between the two points, has suggested that a small fortune in Stellite was scattered along the way during the wartime rush.[22]

The year 1918 also meant enormous and well publicized profits for Elwood Haynes personally. As he readily admitted, his returns from Stellite far exceeded those from the automobile, even though he had been in the automobile business many more years. His combined income in 1918 from the Stellite company in Kokomo, royalties paid by the Deloro Company in Canada, and the automobile company exceeded $1 million; the bulk came, of course, from Stellite. Haynes alienated a number of his Stellite workmen at this time when he refused to carry out James C. Patten's suggestion that he give each employee a substantial year-end bonus and deduct the payment as a business expense. Haynes reportedly told one of his foremen, in explaining his reasons for the refusal, that "it doesn't pay to give the working man too much money—it makes him independent."[23] Instead, because of the heavy excess profits tax then in effect, Haynes made an enormous income tax payment to the federal government, nearly $500,000 for the year.

Andy Downhour had his first job with Stellite in the rough grind department, beginning in May, 1918, and he has vividly recounted his experiences there. "My first week was heart and back breaking," he stated. "Grinding Stellite bars was the hardest thing I had ever tried to grind. Many times I would have given up, only that I was making $3.00 a day, considered good money at that time, and was assured I could earn $4.00 a day." The doughty laborer also discussed the "crude and dangerous" methods of grinding:

---

[21] Kokomo *Daily Tribune,* July 10, 1918.

[22] Interview with Fred Hawkins, January 22, 1971. Data on the construction of the Strawboard Factory can be found in a special centennial issue of the Kokomo *Tribune,* October 30, 1950.

[23] Interview with Fred Hawkins, January 22, 1971. Similar versions of this story were encountered in a number of other interviews with former employees of the Haynes Stellite Company.

Iron Age, October 10, 1918

Gas-fired crucible furnaces, Haynes Stellite Company

Iron Age, October 10, 1918

Snyder electric furnaces, Haynes Stellite Company

Iron Age, October 10, 1918

Pouring molten Stellite into ladle, Haynes Stellite Company

"Sometimes my fingers were ground almost to the bone. Injuries everyday were common, and no First Aid then. Our backs were near the breaking point each evening, arms and hands numbed so much that next morning we had to rub them to get going again." After a short while, however, "a simple method was worked out to reduce the strain on back and arms and to eliminate near all danger to hands and fingers. This method increased the Production to about double."[24]

Additional details about the manufacturing procedures followed at the time are available from a speech prepared very carefully by March Haynes, who had been trained by his father in 1918 to combine the Stellite ingredients and do the melting.[25] At the time he delivered the speech in 1919 he

---

[24] Quarter Century Club Newsletter, April, 1951, Archives File, Stellite Division, Cabot Corporation, Kokomo.

[25] "Rough Draft," June 28, 1929, Haynes Papers. This letter fragment was apparently the draft for a letter March Haynes wrote to Francis P. Gormley, Union Carbide's general manager of the Haynes Stellite Company, in response to a request for detailed information about the early history of Stellite's development and manufacture.

was enrolled in a special school in Milwaukee, Wisconsin, taking courses designed to overcome emotional problems, and he delivered the remarks to his classmates in a speech course. There was an obvious effort to impress and perhaps overawe his fellow students, but the account of the production process, which March sent to his father to check for accuracy before its delivery, is the most thorough one available:

> First, the raw materials are weighed very carefully in their required proportions, and then mixed thoroughly together. The mixture is placed in an electric furnace and the current turned on. This produces a dazzling white heat, and the metals melt rapidly. We have three electric furnaces, one small one and two larger ones. Stellite melts at about 2500–3500° F.
>
> After the metals have been in the furnace long enough to melt and thoroughly alloy with each other they are ready to pour. The metal is first poured into a large ladle, holding about fifty pounds. This ladle has a handle at each side, and two men hold it. The oxide or slag is scummed from the top, and then it is poured into another ladle, and then into the molds. These molds are made of graphite, machined to the size bars we wish to cast. These bars are green in appearance, the color being caused by the oxide of chromium. However when the bar is ground, the green color is removed, and the bar is bright.[26]

March Haynes pointed out that there were "two grades of malleable Stellite"—soft malleable, containing only cobalt and chromium, and hard malleable, containing also a "small amount of tungsten to increase its hardness." Even the soft malleable Stellite was "much harder to forge than steel," and could not be forged by the usual methods. "It must be forged at a red heat, with light rapid blows of the power hammer," March explained, adding that both grades could "be cut hot on a punch press by using Stellite pocket knives." He then described how scalpels, which "must have a hard, sharp edge," were manufactured from hard malleable Stellite. After the initial forging and shaping of the metal, "it is then carefully ground to the required form, going through at least eight different operations before it is ready to polish. Each grinding operation is done with a finer-grained wheel than the one previous." The blades were then sandblasted, reground to remove the sand, and polished.[27]

Stellite's accomplishments were receiving wide attention by 1919. A. E. Winship, the editor of the *Journal of Education* published in Boston, met Haynes in Kokomo and toured his factories. "We shall always remember with intense satisfaction," he began, "the week we spent at Kokomo, Indiana, at the Teachers' Institute, in September, 1919, because it was there and then that we came to know about stellite, to see it made and used." Winship praised Haynes as the creator of "a metal which the Lord neglected to make; a rustless, tarnishless, corrodingless metal; harder than any creation in steel; harder than any creation by man or by nature except the diamond." Moreover, its discovery "came just in time to increase efficiency in the making of munitions of war to such an extent as to make it almost literally true that stellite won the war." We once worshipped, Winship continued, "at the shrine of Bessemer tool steel," but the high-speed steel of White and Taylor, which cut "tool steel as easily as I could whittle a cedar shingle" gave us a "new object of mechanical worship." Then, in Kokomo, when

138

---

[26] March Haynes, "Stellite," January 31, 1919, *ibid.*

[27] *Ibid.*

I saw an almost endless shaving which stellite planed from high speed steel I literally exclaimed "What hath man wrought!" . . . Stellite makes steel of any kind look silly, and even silver plays no honorable part in comparison, for no fruit acid discolors it; no exposure dims its lustre; no heat distempers it, for it has not temper. Stellite gave Elwood Haynes more fame and fortune in a day than the automobile has given him in a quarter of a century.[28]

But the major development of the year, insofar as the future of the Haynes Stellite Company was concerned, was the increasing interest Union Carbide and Carbon Corporation officials were taking in the Indiana company. Corporate attention had been focused on Stellite by its huge orders for various ferroalloys from the Electro Metallurgical Company, one of the original companies in the Union Carbide merger of 1917. This led to direct negotiations early in 1919, by which "a group of eastern capitalists," as the Kokomo *Daily Tribune* termed it, attempted to purchase the company. In fact, according to an apparently authoritative report published in the local press, a firm offer of approximately $3.5 million was made to the Stellite officers. At this point, Haynes and his son March, along with Patten, Ruddell, and attorney Conrad Wolf, visited New York, evidently to make final arrangements, but the deal had to be called off. The excess profits tax imposed during the war was still in effect, which meant that 80 percent of everything above the capitalization of the company (still only $50,000) would go to the government, or more than $2 million. "There was no way to get around the enormous grab the government would have made from the purchase price," one of the men, probably Wolf, was quoted as saying. "The law is that way and there is no way to sidestep it," he continued. "Furthermore, Mr. Haynes, Mr. Ruddell and Mr. Patten are not the type of men who resort to evasions of the law in business matters." Neither were the travelers displeased at the outcome; they had never been enthusiastic about disposing of the company and were delighted to retain the business for themselves and for Kokomo. Plans for additional plant expansion, in fact, were announced by Richard Ruddell upon his return home.[29]

These plans were promptly carried out; a substantial plant of four modern manufacturing buildings, soon flanked on the south with three wooden structures, was available for use by the summer of 1919. There was, in addition, the adjacent strawboard factory. By the end of the year, with approximately 125 employees, Haynes was pushing ahead with the manufacture of Stellite for specialties—tableware, pocketknives, jewelry—rather than for tools.[30] Haynes seemed especially fond of the idea of producing decorative as well as practical items, even though irksome production and quality control problems accompanied these efforts. A particularly blistering letter from William C. Smith, sales manager of the L. D. Caulk Company, a dental supply house, in November, 1919, complained of slipshod workmanship on three different types of instruments, including pliers, and one irate customer suggested that Haynes should have his cutlery department manager "put the edge on the knife instead of on the letter" he had written in response to an earlier complaint.[31]

---

[28] A. E. Winship, "Stellite," in *Journal of Education,* XC (1919), 546.

[29] Kokomo *Daily Tribune,* January 8, 13, 1919.

[30] See [Elwood Haynes], *The Story of Stellite* (Kokomo, 1920?), a rather immodest, finely illustrated account of the development of the Stellite company. This publication clearly indicates that the "inventor's dream" originally was stainless cutlery.

[31] William C. Smith to Elwood Haynes, November 5, 1919, C. M. Falconer to Elwood Haynes, April 19, 1920, Haynes Papers.

Stellite

NOT STEEL – BUT ITS MASTER

Stellite lathe tools are harder than the hardest of high speed steel tools.

Stellite tools are immune to heat up to a temperature of 1800 F.

Up to that point, the hotter they get the tougher they get, and the better they cut.

These facts are known to manufacturers everywhere, for Stellite has been in successful use in thousands of American manufacturing plants for five years. Stellite speeds up production, does away with vexatious delays, cuts costs and gets the job done.

Stellite tools not only permit speeds and feeds never before considered possible, but they last much longer between grindings.

The manufacturer (large or small) who puts Stellite to work will find an increased production and a decreased cost.

Let us tell you more about this wonder metal.

Patentees and Sole Manufacturers

The Haynes Stellite Company

Dissension grew among Stellite's officers during 1919. The decision to maintain local control and to expand operations considerably had been mutually satisfactory, but Patten in particular became increasingly upset over the way in which the business was being managed, or rather mismanaged, by Haynes. Deciding to force a showdown, Patten addressed a long, intemperate, even embittered letter to Haynes on June 25, 1919. It is one of only two letters in the rather full collection of Haynes Papers which are unrelievedly critical of the man.[32]

Patten's complaints centered upon the tight control Haynes maintained over many facets of the Stellite business, his failure to modernize the plant more completely, to develop new uses for Stellite, or to seek new marketing outlets, and his reserved, often supercilious attitude toward all his employees. "You regard and treat us like a lot of children just out of a kindergarten," Patten charged. He was particularly sensitive to the point that he was general manager in name only, not in fact. "You invited me to go in this business with you to manage it," Patten stated, but "I have been as near being manager of this business as I have the Speedway." Patten charged that everything he did was either criticized or, worse, ignored, and that he was unable to get Haynes's full attention:

> I can't even talk to you and get you to concentrate on the subject long enough to be understood. Sometimes I think you are merely absent minded; other times I think you either don't want to know or don't care. . . . You found fault with the last Chrome-Tungsten contract, without reading my letter to you on the subject, and by not paying any attention whatever to my verbal report to you. . . .

He also charged that, during the entire three and one half years he had been with the company, "neither you or your son have ever voluntarily given me one item of information concerning the business. I have had to go to you every time. Neither you or your son ever considered me sufficiently important to tell me if you were going out of town—even on a protracted trip."[33]

Patten was also dissatisfied with Haynes's liberality in granting the Deloro Company exclusive sales territories outside the United States (thereby limiting their own market), the terms under which royalty payments went to Haynes, the unwarranted expenses involved in Haynes's continuing efforts to get cobalt from the Idaho mine, and the restraints he was unwittingly placing upon real growth. "You don't seem to realize that Stellite is a big thing, . . . [that it] is no one man's job. Frankly, I am ready to quit," Patten said. "You and your family, perhaps rightly, consider this your business, and what you do or don't do is your own affair." Yet, with four Haynes family members on the payroll and with a royalty based on sales, not profits, "you have a good proposition whether the company makes money or not." Patten, however, as a stockholder, wanted the company operated so that a profit would be realized. "I started in this business full of great expectations," he lamented, but "now I am disappointed and honestly [wish] that I had staid out of it. My time has been wasted and three and one half years lost."[34]

---

[32] In addition to James C. Patten's letter is one from Edward Lurker, a former Stellite company salesman, who believed Haynes had failed to live up to certain promises made him and sought a financial settlement, but no further information about this complaint has been discovered. Lurker to Elwood Haynes, November 4, 1920, *ibid.*

[33] James C. Patten to Elwood Haynes, June 24, 1919, *ibid.* The letter in the files is a typewritten copy of the original.

[34] *Ibid.*

The response Haynes made to Patten's charges is not known. He apparently refrained from making a similarly intemperate and hasty reply in writing and discussed the situation with Patten in a private conversation. Perhaps they agreed to resume purchase negotiations with Union Carbide officials. In the meantime, the business continued and Haynes pursued his long-standing desire to manufacture Stellite cutlery.

One of the last publications of the Haynes Stellite Company before its acquisition by Union Carbide was a pamphlet entitled *The Story of Stellite,* which gives a brief history of the alloy and its development over the years by Elwood Haynes, "a chemist and metallurgist of international reputation . . . the discoverer and patentee of stainless steel, and . . . the father of the gasoline automobile. . . ." (Haynes exercised considerable license and no modesty in such unsigned, promotional literature.) As the booklet pointed out, the "very first expression" of Stellite was in the form of tableware—"this was indeed the inventor's dream," but a more urgent need for Stellite intervened. Consequently the first commercial use of Stellite was in the form of "lathe machine tools," and some facts concerning wartime production and uses were spelled out. The production of scalpels during the war led to the marketing of Stellite surgical and dental instruments in May, 1918, and this was followed by the manufacture of Stellite pocketknives. Finally, in 1919 came "the latest expression" of Stellite—fine tableware. "This is the development that has always stood first in the inventor's mind," Haynes pointed out, and the booklet concluded with glowing descriptions of Stellite cutlery: "Stellite is the metal eternal."[35]

Despite the inventor's fixation on cutlery items and a neglect of other products that seemed shocking to Patten, Union Carbide officials retained their interest in the alloy. Convinced that Stellite had a future, the corporation searched for a way to acquire the manufacturing rights. Attorney Conrad Wolf was given the credit (and a $50,000 fee) for arranging the method by which the desired transfer could be made without excessive tax losses. The negotiations were troubled not only by the growing estrangement between Haynes and Patten but also by the death of Richard Ruddell, whose heirs refused to accede to the proposed stock transfer.[36] The final agreement provided for exchanging the stock of the Haynes Stellite Company for Union Carbide and Carbon Corporation stock, a transaction quietly concluded in the early months of 1920. Ownership officially transferred on April 10, although it was not announced until a week later.[37]

The indications are that Haynes received approximately 25,000 shares of Union Carbide stock, with an additional 2,000 shares forthcoming if the basic Stellite patents could withstand an expected legal challenge. Patten and the Ruddell heirs divided another 12,500 shares. When the Ruddells refused to accept the stock, Haynes agreed to buy it from them. Because of the complicated arrangements and the fragmentary evidence available, it is difficult to know the exact purchase price agreed upon by the parties involved. Perhaps the published speculations of approximately $4 million were a bit high. Union Carbide stock had no assigned par value, but in August, 1919, it was

142

---

[35] [Haynes], *The Story of Stellite.*

[36] Richard Ruddell, founder of the Citizens National Bank of Kokomo, had come to the city in 1882. A merchant until 1889 when he organized the bank, he served as its president for more than thirty years. Also associated with the Globe Stove and Range Company, Ruddell died in January, 1920. Kokomo *Dispatch,* January 16, 1920.

[37] Kokomo *Daily Tribune,* April 19, 1920; Francis P. Gormley to Elwood Haynes, March 14, 1921, Haynes Papers.

selling at $80 a share, and in April, 1920, at only $72.25. There was, moreover, an undisclosed cash payment, probably a nominal amount to cover the plant inventory, so the precise figure may never be known. It was, however, a satisfactory arrangement for Haynes. He received more than $500,000 in Union Carbide dividends in the interval between the transfer in April, 1920, and his death five years later. In April, 1925, his Union Carbide stock (not including the 6,250 shares purchased from the Ruddells) was worth approximately $1.6 million (the stock during the month ranged between $65.38 and $67.25).

Still another variable in the transaction concerned the outcome of litigation known as the Chesterfield case (*Haynes Stellite Company* v. *Percy C. Chesterfield and Chesterfield Metal Company*). This case, involving alleged infringement of Haynes patent No. 1,057,423 (the ternary Stellite alloy), had far-reaching implications for the future of the Haynes Stellite Company, but Union Carbide's payment of an additional 2,000 shares of stock to Haynes was also contingent upon the outcome of the suit. The case was initiated in 1922, when an infringement complaint was filed in Detroit, where the Chesterfield company was producing tool metals suspiciously similar to Stellite. The Chesterfield product contained additional "ingredients" to those specified by Haynes, but it was believed these items had no beneficial influence upon the resulting alloy. Not until April, 1925, did the case come to trial; in fact, Haynes died while it was underway. He had, however, participated in the considerable efforts made by the Stellite company to present the evidence establishing the facts of Haynes's discovery, the properties of Stellite, the results of extensive tests, and the charge of infringement against Chesterfield.

Two fat volumes were required to hold the exhibits prepared for the trial and the record of the proceedings when these were consolidated for transmittal to the appeals court. Despite the complexity of the issues and District Court Judge Tuttle's admitted inexperience in patent litigation, the judge followed his usual practice of rendering his decision immediately upon hearing the final pleadings. Tuttle ruled that only four of the eight claims in the Haynes patent were valid and then declared them not infringed.[38] He also readily granted an appeal to the Circuit Court of Appeals in Cincinnati. There in 1927 Tuttle was reversed, and the Haynes patent was, in effect, validated. The appeals court, however, limited itself to a consideration of Claim 8 only, the broadest one in the patent; this had the dual effect of giving the Haynes Stellite Company victory in the case and of relieving Union Carbide from its obligations to make an additional stock payment to the Haynes estate (the agreement specified that all of the patent claims must be upheld). A lawsuit filed by A. E. Starbuck, administrator of the estate, to force the contingency stock payment failed.[39]

The Haynes Stellite Company as a division of the Union Carbide Corporation for fifty years, and then as a division of Cabot Corporation, became one of Kokomo's largest and most important manufacturers, compiling particularly outstanding records of service to the country in times of national emergencies. The company's performance immediately following its acquisition by Union Carbide, however, indicates that some of James C. Patten's

[38] The Chesterfield case is reported at 8 Federal Reporter (2d) 765 and 22 Federal Reporter (2d) 635. A petition for a rehearing by the Circuit Court of Appeals was denied in 1928. 25 Federal Reporter (2d) 719.

[39] Legal Papers, 1927–1953, Stellite Division, Cabot Corporation, Kokomo.

criticisms concerning its previous management were justified. A major thrust of Union Carbide's early operation of the Stellite company involved the development of new products, the installation of quality control procedures, the continued modernization of facilities, and the acquisition of new, qualified personnel. For these reasons and others (including new accounting procedures which charged a portion of the costs of certain administrative and experimental activities in New York against the Stellite company, as well as the general business depression of 1920-1921), the Stellite company failed to show a profit for the parent company until 1925. Union Carbide Corporation management was not discouraged by the poor initial results, confident that the new procedures, products, and emphases within the company would be productive.

During these years, Haynes continued to have laboratory privileges at the company, with the understanding that any product improvements he was able to make would belong to the company.[40] There is still a considerable folklore among the employees and former employees at Stellite about Haynes and his research techniques. The professional scientists were often bemused at Haynes's apparently amateurish—at times even dangerous—practices, but they came to have a great respect for his instincts and rule-of-thumb knowledge. Subsequently Haynes and a brilliant research scientist from the Electro Metallurgical Company, Frederick M. Becket, were honored by Union Carbide Corporation; in 1954, it named its research collection at Niagara Falls, New York, the Haynes-Becket Library.[41]

[40] Another understanding between the parties at the time of the merger was that Harry Lanterman, Haynes's brother-in-law and long-time assistant in the development of Stellite, was to have a job with the company for as long as he desired. Interview with George Beatty, Kokomo, January 22, 1971.

[41] Interviews with John R. Brown, Kokomo, July 7, August 16, 1971, and F. T. McCurdy, Clearwater, Florida, July 30, 1971; William A. Wissler, "Elwood Haynes, Scientist and Inventor," n.d., address in Haynes Papers. All three men were metallurgists who worked closely with Haynes in the late 1910s and early 1920s. For a report on the library dedication see *Carbide Courier*, March, 1954, Archives File, Stellite Division, Cabot Corporation, Kokomo.

144

Chapter 11

Did Haynes Discover Stainless Steel?

In contrast to his remarkable successes in developing and marketing Stellite, Haynes had a much more difficult time in obtaining patent rights to, and sharing in the commercial development of, stainless steel. The story of Haynes and this alloy is more nearly analogous to his experiences with the automobile than with Stellite, except that he did not personally manufacture stainless steel. Rather he and Harry Brearley, an English metallurgist who independently discovered stainless steel some time after Haynes had done so, combined their interests in the American Stainless Steel Company, a personal service corporation which licensed various steel companies in the United States to produce stainless steel under the Haynes and Brearley patents.

The analogous situation with automobiles is that both the new alloy and the new self-propelled vehicles were under development on both sides of the Atlantic and that a large number of metallurgical experimenters, most of whom were employed by iron and steel companies, shared in the development of the chromium-iron alloys which came to be known as stainless. The analogy is broader still, for Haynes, through his independent investigations and without a company laboratory, was among the first metallurgists in the world to recognize the commercial significance of sufficient quantities of chromium upon iron, and he was the first to apply for a patent in the United States covering these discoveries. Haynes's application in 1912 anticipated Brearley's by more than three years but was rejected upon grounds that the alloys described were not new. Haynes readily conceded that point, but he had based his patent request upon his recognition of the stainlessness of such alloys.

In order to understand the history of the development of stainless steel, one must not concentrate solely on the roles of Haynes and Brearley and the company they organized; other pioneers in the production of various stainless steels available on the market today played important parts. Carl Zapffe, a metallurgical consultant and writer who is perhaps the leading authority on the subject of stainless steel development, divides the credit for discovery among ten or twelve men, selecting six individuals as the true pioneers. Zapffe has also divided the process of development into three phases or "classes of discoveries"—(1) "constitution" or composition of the alloys, (2) "corrosion resistance," and (3) "industrial usefulness"—and credits one or more of the six pioneers with priority in each classification.[1]

Table 2*

ZAPFFE'S DISCOVERERS OF STAINLESS STEEL

Investigator	Discovery
Guillet, L.	Compositions and primary metallurgical
Portevin, A. M.	characteristics of the stainless steels—
Giesen, W.	martensitic, ferritic, and austenitic
Monnartz, P.	Stainlessness and the passivation phenomenon (also commercial utility of the chromium grades)
Brearley, H.	Commercial utility of the chromium grades
Maurer, E.	Commercial utility of the chromium-nickel grades[2]

*Source: Carl A. Zapffe, "Who Discovered Stainless Steel?" in *Iron Age,* October 14, 1948, pp. 122–28.

Various chrome-bearing steels were produced in the nineteenth century (following Louise-Nicolas Vauquelin's discovery of chromium in 1797) but these alloys had either too little chromium or, when the chromium content was raised, too much carbon to be stainless. Among the nineteenth century producers of chromium steel was Sir Robert Hadfield, an eminent British metallurgist whose 1892 report on some of his findings in this area marked a significant milestone. Hadfield had produced various steel alloys containing as much as 16.47 percent chromium but had limited his analyses to alloys containing not more than 9.18 percent of chromium, which falls below the stainless range. Moreover, the carbon content in Hadfield's alloys ranged from 1 to 3 percent. Consequently, as Zapffe reports, Hadfield "reached the conclusion that chromium impairs the corrosion resistance of steel!"[3] This perhaps retarded European investigators in their recognition of the true significance of chromium content above 10 or 12 percent in terms of corrosion resistance,[4] but careful study of other aspects of such alloys resumed in the first years of the twentieth century.

As the above table indicates, Zapffe considers the work of Guillet and Portevin in France, of Monnartz in Germany, and of Giesen in England be-

[1] Carl A. Zapffe, *Stainless Steels: An Elementary Text for Consumers* (Cleveland: American Society for Metals, 1949), p. 13; see also Carl A. Zapffe, "Who Discovered Stainless Steel?" in *Iron Age,* October 14, 1948, pp. 120–29. Dr. Zapffe, a metallurgical consultant, has carefully reviewed the literature on the history of stainless steel development, but he had little opportunity to consider Haynes's contribution beyond the Haynes patent of 1919 and his article published in 1920, since the Haynes Papers have only recently been opened to scholars. It appears, however, that Dr. Zapffe did not examine the rather fat Patent Office files pertaining to the early litigation upholding these patents, i.e., the Ludlum case. See below for exact citation to all of these references.

In contrast to the six pioneers whom Zapffe credits with the three phases of stainless steel development, as listed in Table 2, a slightly altered group of six metallurgists were considered to be the pioneers in the 1940s. Zapffe surveyed a group of six specialists to obtain their list of "pioneers" in the stainless steel field. Their top choices, each with six votes, were Harry Brearley, Benno Strauss, and Eduard Maurer. Elwood Haynes received five votes, Frederick M. Becket four, and C. M. Johnson three. *Ibid.,* p. 122.

[2] Zapffe, "Who Discovered Stainless Steel?" in *Iron Age,* October 14, 1948, pp. 121, 123.

[3] *Ibid.,* p. 123.

[4] Zapffe observed that the most remarkable aspect of this story is not that stainless steel was discovered in the early twentieth century but that it was not discovered before. Zapffe, *Stainless Steels,* p. 6.

tween 1903 and 1910 as that which led to the discovery and metallurgical analysis of the modern stainless steels, although he recognizes too that these men, with the exception of Monnartz, "made no point" of their corrosion resistance qualities.[5] Moreover, when "the great patent suit" of *American Stainless Steel Company* v. *Rustless Iron Corporation* was litigated,[6] evidence was provided that C. Dantsizen, a metallurgist employed at the General Electric Research Laboratory in New York, had experimented with low carbon chromium alloys in the stainless range as early as September, 1911. His work resulted in using such alloys in steam turbine blades as early as 1914. Similarly Eduard Maurer and Benno Strauss, at the Krupp Works in Germany, produced various chromium-nickel steels, "the other great branch of stainless steels," after 1910 and developed their commercial potentials.[7]

The names of Brearley and Haynes do not appear among the pioneers in Zapffe's first classification regarding the discovery of stainless steel. Zapffe also believes that neither man deserves inclusion in the second category involving the recognition of corrosion resistance properties of chromium alloys. He credits this to Monnartz alone, citing his "monumental paper" of 1911. In his third category, Zapffe attributes to both Monnartz and Brearley the discovery of the "commercial utility of the chromium grades." He grants only a "prominent role" to a few others, including Haynes, in the early development of the stainless steels. Their discoveries, he concludes, "seem necessarily secondary even though in some cases the work might have been truly performed without foreknowledge of the investigations here cited."[8]

Quite clearly this was true of Haynes, whose independent discovery of stainlessness in chromium-iron alloys stemmed directly from his earliest metallurgical researches. As early as 1887 Haynes had begun to seek a corrosion-resistant alloy suitable for cutlery items. In the course of his intermittent work along these lines, he developed not only his iron-free Stellite alloys but also made very significant findings concerning chromium-bearing iron and steel alloys. The series of experiments he conducted in 1911 and 1912 was among the most important he ever performed. The intensive work of that period resulted in both his improvement of the previously patented Stellite alloys by adding tungsten or molybdenum and in his stainless steel discovery.[9] He immediately attempted to patent both findings but ran into

---

[5] Monnartz patented a stainless composition in Germany in 1910, and published a long paper on such alloys in 1911: "The Study of Iron-Chromium Alloys with Special Consideration of Their Resistance to Acids," in *Metallurgie*, VIII (1911), 161ff., as cited in Zapffe, "Who Discovered Stainless Steel?" in *Iron Age*, October 14, 1948, p. 129. The Monnartz paper was cited as a "reference" by Patent Office Examiner William J. Rich when he denied, initially, both the Haynes and the Brearley patent applications. The patents were subsequently granted more in terms of articles which could be produced from stainless alloys than upon the alloys themselves.

[6] This case involved two patents, owned by the American Stainless Steel Company, which were invalidated by the court. 2 Federal Supplement 742 (1933); 71 Federal Reporter (2d) 404 (1934). An earlier case, *American Stainless Steel Company* v. *Ludlum Steel Company,* upheld on appeal the validity of both the Haynes and the Brearley patents. 290 Federal Reporter 103 (1923).

[7] Zapffe, "Who Discovered Stainless Steel?" in *Iron Age*, October 14, 1948, p. 126.

[8] *Ibid.,* p. 128. Earlier authorities, it should be noted, have given the work of Haynes and Brearley more prominence in this regard. See, for example, J. H. G. Monypenny, *Stainless Iron and Steel* (New York: Chapman & Hall, 1931), pp. 18–27; Ernest E. Thum (ed.), *The Book of Stainless Steels: Corrosion Resisting and Heat Resisting Chromium Alloys* (2d ed. Cleveland: The American Society for Metals, 1935), chapter 1; and Donald G. Clark, "Recent Developments in Stainless Steel," *Yearbook of the American Iron and Steel Institute* (1925), pp. 262–68.

[9] Portions of the "Laboratory Book" in which Haynes recorded his experiments and findings were typed for use as an exhibit in patent litigation. A copy of this typescript, covering the period from June 15, 1899, to May 25, 1915, is in the Elwood Haynes File, Stellite Division, Cabot

difficulty on the latter. Consequently he put this work aside while he concentrated on setting up the Haynes Stellite Works and introducing that alloy to the market. Later, spurred on by rumors of a similar development in England, Haynes resumed his stainless steel investigations and renewed his patent application.

Haynes described his stainless steel work less frequently and less fully than his work on the automobile and on Stellite—he had less direct interest in its manufacture—but his public and private accounts are both adequate and consistent, and they are supported by the primary evidence. In a 1925 letter in which Haynes tried to bring his college roommate Stephen Roberts up-to-date on his activities (Roberts was living in Australia), Haynes had a few things to say about his discovery of stainless steel, which he clearly dated. "Later (1911)," he began, "I formed an alloy of Iron and Chromium, which showed remarkable resistance to rust or tarnish and could be worked into pocket and table cutlery and adapted to various other industrial applications." This alloy, which came to be known as stainless steel, was "rediscovered by and [sic] Englishman named Brearley, in 1914."[10]

Haynes's most thorough report on this subject came in a speech delivered in Pittsburgh in 1919, describing his 1911 experiments and quoting at length from his laboratory notebook:

> *November 15, 1911.* While I have known for some time that chromium when added to iron or steel, influences or modifies their properties in a marked degree, I am now engaged in gaining a definite knowledge of,
> a. The effect of chromium on the resistance of steel and iron to chemical and atmospheric influences.
> b. The effect of chromium on the hardness of iron and steel.
> c. The effect of chromium on the elasticity of iron and steel.
> d. The effect of chromium on the cutting qualities of iron and steel.
>
> The preliminary experiments which I have already made along this line indicate that the effect of chromium on iron and steel is much the same as on cobalt and nickel.
>
> I have already prepared the following alloys:
> a. Alloy 20-C. 79.4% iron, 20% chromium, 0. 6% carbon.
> b. Alloy 15-C. 84.4% iron, 15% chromium, 0. 6% carbon.
> e. Alloy 5-C. 95.0% iron, 5% chronium.
> f. Alloy 10-C. 90.0% iron, 10% chromium.
> g. Alloy 15-C. 85.0% iron, 15% chromium.
> h. Alloy 20-C. 80.0% iron, 20% chromium.[11]

He continued these experiments during the winter of 1911-1912, and in April, 1912, made various items from the chromium-iron alloys, including cold chisels, wood chisels, and auger bits.[12] When properly heated and annealed, the tools were sufficiently hard to take "keen" edges and "showed fine cut-

148

Corporation, Kokomo. Pages 24–69 of the 93-page typescript cover Haynes's experiments in 1911 and 1912.

[10] Elwood Haynes to Stephen F. Roberts, January 17, 1925, Haynes Papers.

[11] Haynes, "Stellite and Stainless Steel," in *Proceedings of the Engineers' Society of Western Pennsylvania,* XXXV, 469–70. The manuscript copy of this speech in the Haynes Papers is dated November 20, 1919.

[12] In 1931 the American Stainless Steel Company returned to March Haynes one of his father's cold chisels made in 1912. This item had been used as an exhibit in the Ludlum case. C. S. Bunting to March Haynes, May 29, 1931, Haynes Papers.

ting qualities." Haynes also learned, to quote directly from the laboratory book entry for April 8, 1912, that "They hold their luster in the air under all conditions."[13]

Haynes had elaborated upon the significance of this latter finding and the testing program which preceded his initial application in April, 1912, for a stainless steel patent in a letter to his patent attorney in Washington, D. C. in 1925. "It does not always follow," Haynes wrote, "that if an alloy resists acids that it will resist atmospheric influences, nor does it follow that a pellet of metal which will resist both acids and atmospheric conditions can be worked into useful forms. A long series of experiments are [*sic*] usually necessary to determine these points." That had been the purpose of the experimentation in 1911-1912, to determine the properties of stainless steel before applying for a patent. Haynes recognized one limitation: "The only thing which I did not discover was that within certain chromium limits, heat treatment enhanced the *stainless* quality of the steel." He had discovered, however, that a chromium content above 20 percent rendered the steel "highly resistant to both atmospheric influences and acids. This was claimed in the body of my patent, as you will remember."[14]

Haynes pointed out that "the discovery rests not on the possibility of adding to the steel other elements which may render it more or less immune to corrosion, more easily or less easily workable, but upon the fact that immune chrome-steels must contain more than eight percent chromium . . . ." Indeed, for certain purposes, a chromium content of up to 60 percent was possible. Haynes included as part of his basic discovery the facts that "such steels are distinctly workable and useful, whether subjected to heat treatment or not [Brearley had specified the necessity of such treatment]; [and] furthermore, that the proportion of carbon may be raised as high as two per cent. without materially interfering with the untarnishable qualities of the alloy. . . ." He freely admitted that Brearley, his English counterpart, had "discovered practically the same properties in chrome-steel, and I am practically certain that his discovery was made independently of any discoveries made by me." He explained that Brearley's patent had been approved because it contained "a provision that it was necessary to polish and harden the steel in order to render it immune. This, however, was later found not to be correct," and subsequently "practically all of the claims" in Haynes's prior application "were granted by the Patent Office."[15]

Again, the primary sources give full corroboration to this account of discovery. A faded, dog-eared, yellow notepad contains the only copy of Haynes's outgoing correspondence for this period, but the entries here not only verify his statements but indicate the range of activities at this busy period in Haynes's life. Haynes still had no personal secretary, and it appears that Mrs. Haynes took dictation from her husband in the yellow notepad, from which she typed up the letters (retaining no other copies). Perhaps, also, due to the significance of this correspondence and his desire for secrecy, Haynes preferred to have his wife, rather than a hired secretary, handle these matters.

A lengthy correspondence with C. Clarence Poole, in March, April, and May, 1912, resulted from Haynes's efforts to patent his stainless steel dis-

Did Haynes Discover Stainless Steel?

149

---

[13] Haynes, "Stellite and Stainless Steel," in *Proceedings of the Engineers' Society of Western Pennsylvania*, XXXV, 471.

[14] Elwood Haynes to K. P. McElroy, January 20, 1925, Haynes Papers.

[15] Haynes, "Stellite and Stainless Steel," in *Proceedings of the Engineers' Society of Western Pennsylvania*, XXXV, 471–73.

coveries at that time. The first existing letter relating to this (although not the first such exchange) is dated March 15, in which Haynes sets out some of the "peculiarities" of the alloy and some of the "points to be covered by a patent." His first "points" were that "there is no absolutely rust-proof steel in use at the present time" and that considerable attention was being given either to rust-proofing iron and steel or finding comparatively cheap substitutes for iron and steel among various nonferrous or noncorroding alloys.[16]

"While it is known to some chemists and metallurgists," he continued, that chromium "exerts a beneficial influence so far as corrosion is concerned when alloyed with other metals, I have never known any one to suggest using a steel or iron containing [a] high percentage of Cr [chromium] for any of the above purposes." Moreover, these alloys were "well adapted for non-corrosive cutlery, provided the percentage of Cr lies between 4% & 5%,"[17] but they must also be capable of taking and holding a keen edge. "I have demonstrated," he contended, "that these alloys possess these qualities in addition to their non-corrosive features."[18]

Haynes suggested, furthermore, that stain-free cooking utensils could be fabricated from his alloys, although he had not produced any such items, and then he described his other experimental compositions. "What I claim as my invention," he summarized, "is 1. A non-corrosive alloy consisting of iron or steel & chr[omium], containing at least 4% of Cr. 2. A non-corrosive alloy of iron or steel & Chr[omium] containing from 4% to 50% of Cr. 3. A non-corrosive alloy of iron or steel with chromium & and a metal of the chromium group," and he concluded the letter by arguing for the patentability of his findings. The three requisites of a patent, that a discovery be "new[,] novel, & useful," were clearly present:

> The discovery of the distinctly non-corrosive qualities of the above alloys is surely new or some one would have suggested their use in the arts. . . . Such an alloy is novel, since . . . the immunity to atmospheric influences is only possessed by gold, & the metals of the platinum group, while recently I have added to these the alloys of nickel and cobalt with chromium. . . . That such an alloy will be useful, admits of little question, since it can be drawn into rods, rolled into sheets, worked into tools as well as manufactured into utensils of various kinds & at the same time it is comparatively cheap.[19]

Haynes followed this lengthy persuasion with others of like tenor. On April 8, 1912, he responded to Poole's request for more precise "limitations" of the alloy by citing the experience of Taylor and White in patenting their "high speed" lathe tools early in the twentieth century. Dr. John S. Unger

---

[16] Elwood Haynes to C. Clarence Poole, March 15, 1912, Haynes Papers.

[17] Haynes later revised these figures, and the patent as issued covered a chromium content of from 8 to 60 percent. The Brearley patent, by contrast, covered alloys with a chromium content of from 9 to 16 percent. Standard stainless steel today contains between 12 and 30 percent chromium. It is instructive to compare Haynes's admittedly broad patent claims of 4 to 50 percent, later 8 to 60 percent, and his basic claim that these amounts of chromium produced stainlessness with more recent definitions of stainless steel. The following statement appears in a 1951 publication of the Allegheny-Ludlum Steel Corporation, one of the nation's largest stainless steel producers: "The stainless steels are basically alloys of chromium and iron. When chromium, a metallic element, is added to iron in excess of 10 percent, it imparts throughout the entire body of the metal remarkable resistance to corrosion and heat." The statement continued that other elements, such as nickel, are added to the alloy to get special characteristics. *Stainless Steel Handbook* (Pittsburgh, 1951), p. 11.

[18] Elwood Haynes to C. Clarence Poole, March 15, 1912, Haynes Papers.

[19] *Ibid.*

credited these tools, composed of alloyed tungsten, chromium, and steel, with "revolutionizing" the machining of steel. They permitted a four- to five-fold increase in cutting efficiency and dominated the market until they were superseded by Stellite.[20] Taylor and White, however, never benefited properly from their discovery, according to Haynes, because of too limited specifications. Competing steel firms were able to use their findings but, by showing that the steel tools could be heated to a higher temperature than the maximum stated in the patent, they were able to avoid infringement and, therefore, royalty payments.[21]

Haynes continued his discussion of the Taylor and White alloy by remarking that, "so far as I am aware, I was the first to produce tungsten-ch[romium] steel." This had occurred in Worcester, in 1881, while doing his senior thesis, "The Effect of Tungsten upon Iron and Steel." Then, some twenty years later, the two Bethlehem Steel Company men discovered their method of tempering tungsten steel and an important use for it, "and I would not question for one moment their right to this discovery," Haynes stated, "notwith[standing] the fact that I was probably the first to produce the alloy." They had discovered new attributes and a new use for a known alloy, and were entitled to their patent. By limiting too sharply the heat-treating temperatures, however, Haynes believed they made a grievous mistake. Their steel, he wrote, "has saved millions of dollars in machine shop practices within the last five years & the reward coming to the discoverers was really very meager when compared with the results attained."[22]

In another exchange, following Poole's submission of a list of citations which apparently indicated anticipation of Haynes's discovery, the inventor answered them seriatim, again noting his discovery was not the alloy itself but some of its properties. He observed, moreover, that "I did not obtain my knowledge of the chromium alloys by reading what others had done but by direct experiment upon the alloys themselves." Then Haynes repeated his observation that nonrusting or nontarnishing alloys could not be purchased because no such alloys were known to exist. "If one should go to the hardware store & ask for a rustless hatchet, chisel, or any other article made from steel," Haynes concluded, "he should at once be told that no such articles are manufactured in the world. . . ."[23]

Whether or not this convinced Poole, he proceeded to submit the patent application in April, 1912. Perhaps Haynes himself was not entirely convinced, or at least wanted corroboration on this point, for only two days later he caused inquiries to be made to the major steel companies in the country concerning the market availability of a nonrusting or nontarnishing steel alloy. In order to conceal his authorship these inquiries were sent under another signature and mailed either by a brother in Portland or a friend in Indianapolis—the rough draft of a request to both is in the yellow notebook. As Haynes indicated in his 1920 paper, all the replies to his intermediaries pointed out that no rustless alloys were available. Haynes's disappointment must have been great when Poole wired him early in May that "all claims are rejected," but he gave no outward sign of this. Because

---

[20] Unger was the program chairman at the session where Haynes delivered his paper in 1919. He made his remarks concerning high-speed and Stellite lathe tools as he opened the discussion on the paper. Haynes, "Stellite and Stainless Steel," in *Proceedings of the Engineers' Society of Western Pennsylvania*, XXXV, 475.

[21] Elwood Haynes to C. Clarence Poole, April 8, 1912, Haynes Papers.

[22] *Ibid.*

[23] *Ibid.*, April 10, 1912.

of his increasing involvement with Stellite, he laid the stainless steel matter aside temporarily after promising Poole that they would make a new application after additional experiments.[24]

The new application did not come until March 12, 1915, two months before Haynes also filed for a patent on the cobalt-chromium-iron alloy called "Festel Metal." The stainless steel application antedated by several days the similar but more limited stainless steel application filed by Harry Brearley on March 29, 1915, although Haynes freely admitted that "rumors" of a stainless steel discovery in England prompted his reapplication at that time. Both the Haynes and Brearley applications were rejected initially, and both men submitted revised forms in 1916. The Brearley petition was filed with the Patent Office on March 6; following a second rejection, Brearley (who was in England) submitted a lengthy affidavit responding to the examiner's objections and citations and requested reconsideration. The affidavit contained several extracts from newspaper articles describing the "Rustless Cutlery" and "Rust-Proof Steel" Brearley had invented, as well as copies of letters from prominent metallurgists. Sir Robert Hadfield, whose 1892 paper was one of the references used by Examiner Rich to prove anticipation, pointed out in his letter to Brearley, dated May 10, 1916, that neither in 1916 nor previous to hearing of and testing "your stainless cutlery did I consider that low-carbon high-chromium steels, such as you are using, could be made into bright articles of cutlery which would remain untarnished in contact with vinegar and acid foods." Moreover, Hadfield pointed out, the carbon content of his alloys was too high to "produce stainless cutlery blades of the same quality as now being made as a result of your investigations."[25] Accepting the arguments presented by Brearley and his counsel, the Patent Office decided to "allow" the patent in June; it was formally issued on September 5, 1916. The office continued its rejection of the Haynes application.

By reason of his patent office success, Harry Brearley is popularly recognized as the inventor of stainless steel. A brilliant and dedicated research metallurgist, Brearley became involved in a prolonged controversy with his employer, the Thomas J. Firth Company, over the terms under which the new stainless steel would be marketed. This led to a number of Brearley statements and publications which have added considerable detail to the story of his major metallurgical discovery and, quite likely, to his fame in connection with it.

"If I am asked if I invented stainless steel," Brearley wrote in 1924, "I answer, 'Yes.' " He acknowledged the help of others in developing useful products, initially cutlery, from the new alloy, and in obtaining his foreign patents. Because of the Brearley-Firth disagreement, his discovery was not patented in Great Britain. Thus he explained the circumstances under which stainless steel had been developed in the course of an autobiographical statement.[26]

Harry Brearley, born in 1871 the son of a steel melter at the Thomas Firth & Son firm in Sheffield, went to work for the same company as a boy. He

---

[24] *Ibid.,* May 13, 1912. This pledge was repeated later, after Haynes had received the full patent file from Poole. "I am very busy at present with Stellite but as soon as I have finished the work in which I am now engaged I will take up the chrome steel matter again with you." *Ibid.,* May 21, 1912.

[25] Patent File No. 1,197,256, U.S. Patent Office.

[26] Sheffield (England) *Daily Independent,* February 2, 1924; Harry Brearley, *Knotted String: Autobiography of a Steelmaker* (London: Longman, Green and Co., 1941), pp. 22–23.

worked his way up, serving briefly as works manager for the Firth plant in Riga (during the Russo-Japanese war and the Russian Revolution of 1905) before returning to England to establish a research laboratory operated jointly by Firth's and John Brown & Company. In May, 1912, Brearley was working on ways to prevent "erosion and fouling in rifle barrels" and suggested a number of steels which would curtail the corrosion. In subsequent testing of the new alloys he had recommended, he learned that a low carbon, high chromium alloy would not etch, and later he found that it did not rust in a damp atmosphere. Unable to interest the Firth company in developing new uses for the new steel, he turned to the R. F. Mosley Company, a cutlery firm, and had a few table knives made. Difficulty in working the steel made it seem useless for cutlery purposes, but when Brearley personally supervised the heat treatment given the alloy (an item carried by Firth on its list as Firth Aeroplane Steel), the batch was made into satisfactory knives. Following this breakthrough, the Firths and Brearley still disagreed about sales and promotion of the alloy (Brearley thought heat-treated blanks ready to be processed by the cutlers should be furnished in order to provide a satisfactory product for the consumer) and Brearley resigned from the firm in late 1914.[27]

At this point John Maddocks, a seventy-five-year-old Londoner whom Brearley did not know, approached the steelmaker and offered his services in obtaining an American patent for Brearley's discovery. Maddocks, a stranger to Brearley, explained that "he knew America well, and had had considerable experience with patents." Brearley agreed to the proposal on the condition that Maddocks undertake it at his "own trouble and expense." The result was the March 29, 1915, application covering the chromium-iron alloy, but, in Brearley's words, "he failed to get a patent on the steel as such." The next year, however, with Maddocks's encouragement and "the kindly aid" of Sir Robert Hadfield, the late Dr. J. E. Snead, and Mr. F. W. Harbord (all of whom wrote letters for Brearley which he used in his affidavit included with the new patent application), a patent was ultimately obtained for an article with "stainless properties." Brearley, personally, had given little time to the application, since he had taken a new position in 1915 as the works manager at Brown Bayley's Steel Works, and there were unusually heavy demands upon him at that time because of the war. Indeed, he was forced to refuse Maddocks's suggestion that the two of them visit the United States "to dispose of" the patent rights obtained in September, 1916. Instead, they offered the patent to the Firths, who had plants in the United States and might be as well able to make use of it as any other American steel manufacturer. After some skirmishing about the former agreement between Brearley and Firth, the Firth-Brearley Stainless Steel Syndicate was organized to handle the American patent as well as the sale of "Firth-Brearley Stainless" in Great Britain.[28]

While these events were taking place in England, Haynes and his patent attorney, K. P. McElroy of Washington, D. C., were at work making slight modifications in their initial application and checking out the references

---

[27] Harry Brearley, *Stainless Steel: The Story of Its Discovery* (a twenty-four page pamphlet reprinted from the Sheffield *Daily Independent,* February 2, 1924), especially pp. 22–23.

[28] *Ibid.,* pp. 19, 22–23. Amicable relations between the parties named in the syndicate title failed to last very long. Much to Brearley's chagrin, the Firths soon dropped the dual label and "again began to advertise themselves as discoverers, inventors, and originators." *Ibid.,* p. 23. It was this situation which prompted Brearley to publicize his role in the development of stainless steel.

cited as anticipations of the Haynes invention. Communications from Haynes and McElroy to William J. Rich, the patent office examiner, were submitted in April, 1915, and again in April, 1916, following a second rejection. The April 21, 1916, letter argued that Examiner Rich had not been specific enough in explaining why he considered the Haynes alloy to have been anticipated, and stated that Rich evidently believed the alloy to be ferrochrome. This was not the case—rather it was a binary alloy of iron and chromium, "containing enough chromium to give it noble characteristics and enough iron to make it workable." Again the claims were promptly rejected, this time on the basis of a new reference—two 1911 articles by Professor Monnartz in *Metallurgie*.[29] The initial Haynes-McElroy response to this citation of June 2, 1916, is missing from the Patent Office file, but there was a second and major response on December 11, 1916. By this time the Brearley patent had been issued; consequently part of the Haynes-McElroy strategy was to add the three Brearley claims to their patent application for the purpose of obtaining an interference. These new claims were also rejected by Rich, and the sides squared off into a battle over how to interpret the words "hardened and tempered." To Rich, these indicated a process and he would not allow the words (part of the Brearley claims) to be added by Haynes. To McElroy (and Haynes), however, these words merely indicated the nature of the final product, not a process. In their original petition they had mentioned that the alloy would take a high polish and receive and retain a good cutting edge. "This of course means nothing more or less," McElroy argued, "than that the alloy can be tempered and hardened."[30]

Rich's adamancy induced Haynes and McElroy to try new tactics in 1917, when (on February 9) a number of amendments to the petition were submitted—including a significant title change from "Noble Alloys" to "Wrought Metal Articles"—with corresponding modifications to claims 1 through 4 in the original application. The three Brearley claims were then repeated, and new claims 8, 9, and 10 were added. Lengthy "remarks" accompanied these amendments, particularly focusing upon the Monnartz reference. McElroy argued that the German scientist had not disclosed anything useful in the practical arts, that he was chiefly interested in scientific considerations. McElroy admitted that Monnartz's work was "of great interest, indeed very great interest," but maintained it had nothing to do with practical inventors. Haynes, he pointed out, "is intent on making a useful article" and was not concerned with "curves of fusion of the various alloys or their resistance to this or that mixture of nitric acid and salt. What he is concerned in is making useful edged tools." Noting that Brearley had submitted affidavits concerning the usefulness of his product, McElroy offered the same to Rich if he desired them.[31]

When Rich again rejected the claims, particularly claims 5 through 10, Haynes and his attorney resorted to the appeal process of the Patent Office. Their case was heard on May 17, 1917, by the Board of Examiners-in-Chief, after briefs had been submitted by both parties. Rich explained the reasons why he had rejected all references in the Haynes application to "hardened

154

---

[29] Patent File No. 1,299,404, U. S. Patent Office.

[30] *Ibid.* Haynes, of course, remained in Kokomo during the long months of the patent application appeal, keeping in touch with his attorney through correspondence. Haynes once summarized his conception of the issue in these words, ". . . as I understand this controversy, it is largely a question as to whether the steel will be stainless without tempering or polishing. To this, I will answer without hesitation, 'Yes.'" Elwood Haynes to K. P. McElroy, August 2, 1918, Haynes Papers.

[31] Patent File No. 1,299,404, U. S. Patent Office.

and tempered" articles, whereas Haynes (through McElroy) explained that a "hardened and tempered" article was clearly implied in the original application and that this point was made explicit in the amended one. Haynes undoubtedly invented the same alloy as Brearley, they argued, and specified among its uses that of cutting tools. Since Brearley's patent did not disclose any heat treatment process, there was nothing in the one that was not in the other. The proper way to interpret the Brearley claims, therefore, was that the words "hardened and tempered" were merely adjectives describing the quality of the alloy. The appellants concluded Brearley's alloy "is hard and it has a temper. It is the same as the Haynes alloy and article. The inventions are so undoubtedly the same so there should be an interference . . . and since these inventions are exactly the same, the burden of proof should be placed upon Brearley, he having the latest filing date."[32] The Board in its decision of June 2, 1917, agreed with these points and reversed the examiner on all points except claim 6.[33] This was enough to gain the interference, and it was granted on July 31, 1917.

The records are not sufficient to reconstruct the next steps, but the general outline is clear enough. Rather than risk the expense and delay of litigation to determine who had priority in the discovery of the fabrication of useful products from the steel, if not of the stainless steel itself, the Haynes and Brearley interests (now controlled by the Firth-Brearley Stainless Steel Syndicate) were merged. Both turned over their rights to the stainless steel invention to the American Stainless Steel Company. Haynes briefly explained his business relationship with Brearley: "We compromised rather than enter into a legal battle and merged our patents into a corporation known as the American Stainless Steel Company," made up of the patentees and "most of the prominent alloy steel manufacturers of the United States. . . . The company is comparatively new but is already paying very good dividends on the money invested."[34]

Both Elwood Haynes and Harry Brearley sincerely believed they had discovered stainless steel, knowing as only they could the thought processes and experiments which led to the discovery. Both men initially sought to patent the discovery as a stainless alloy, only to be informed of partial anticipations. Consequently both modified their applications to cover articles produced from their stainless alloys. As Zapffe has pointed out, others had produced low carbon chromium steels before, and Monnartz had subjected such steels to thorough metallurgical analysis, but it was left to later practitioners to convert the new alloy discoveries into useful products. As it happened, the two men who did this, Brearley and Haynes, also made independent discoveries of the alloys and their resistance properties. Brearley was the first to produce a stainless steel cutlery on a modest scale and bring it to world attention; in a more quiet way, laboring alone, Haynes had anticipated Brearley's work by nearly two years. Because Haynes insisted upon his legal rights, he and Brearley shared equally in the stainless steel royalties paid to the American Stainless Steel Company.

---

[32] *Ibid.*

[33] This claim contained the word "tempered" as used by Brearley in his second claim. The appeals board refused to permit Haynes to make the claim in view of a Haynes statement in the original patent application that the alloys hardened "without tempering." Haynes and McElroy appealed directly to the commissioner of the patent office to get this ruling reversed, but the appeals board was upheld on this point. *Ibid.*

[34] Haynes, "Stellite and Stainless Steel," in *Proceedings of the Engineers' Society of Western Pennsylvania*, XXXV, 469–70. The manuscript copy of this speech in the Haynes Papers is dated November 20, 1919.

Chapter 12

Haynes and the American Stainless Steel Company

157

The American·Stainless Steel Company was organized in July, 1917. The firm, a Pennsylvania corporation with headquarters in Pittsburgh, was set up initially to handle the Brearley patent rights in the United States. Its organization came three weeks before Haynes obtained his interference with the Brearley patent, and the five original directors of the company were eastern steel men and attorneys, including Lewis J. Firth of McKeesport, Pennsylvania, whose firm controlled the Brearley patent in America.[1] Haynes did not transfer the rights expected to flow from his patent application to the stainless steel company until March, 1918.

Very little is known about the details of the negotiations which led to the merger of the Haynes and Brearley patent rights. A letter Haynes wrote to a friend and Stellite associate in Canada contains the most complete account of this transaction in the Haynes Papers. In May, 1918, he informed Thomas Southworth, perhaps for the first time, of his work in developing stainless steel. He continued that, after he had successfully contested the Brearley patent "on the grounds of prior invention and prior application, . . . the Brearley people came to me and offered a compromise, which finally resulted in the formation of a Patents Holding Co., which pays us a royalty of about 4½ percent each, on all steel manufactured by the various steel companies of America, licensed to make steel under these patents."[2] The exact terms of the merger agreement remain unknown, but Haynes and his son March were added to the board of directors along with three other persons, making in all ten directors. In addition, Haynes obtained a sizable interest in the company (probably between a fifth and a third) as well as royalty payments from it.

Following this agreement, which in effect merged the ownership of the Brearley patent and the pending Haynes patent, the interference which had

---

[1] Professor Robert Doherty to author, May 7, 1971. The company was originally capitalized at $150,000. The other directors were F. A. Bigelow of Reading, Pennsylvania; Edward S. Kinsley of South Bethlehem, Pennsylvania; H. A. Brown of New York; and James W. Kinnear of Pittsburgh. Kinnear, an attorney, was elected president of the company.

[2] Elwood Haynes to Thomas Southworth, May 2, 1918, Haynes Papers. Haynes, of course, did not manufacture stainless steel himself, although obviously he intended to do so eventually. "Haynes & Son" was one of the licensees of the American Stainless Steel Company. They never worked this license, as Haynes's manufacturing efforts remained devoted to automobiles and Stellite alloys.

been so laboriously gained was dissolved. Moreover, the patent application itself was now modified by dropping the new claims, 5 through 10, for which Haynes and McElroy had fought vigorously. Marshall A. Christy of Pittsburgh, the distinguished patent attorney retained by the American Stainless Steel Company, also rewrote the Haynes claims 1 through 4. Haynes Patent No. 1,299,404 was finally issued on April 1, 1919. It should be noted, however, that the Haynes claim for a chromium content of from 8 to 60 percent was not modified. This, coupled with the Brearley patent specifying a chromium content of from 9 to 16 percent and certain heat treatment processes, gave the stainless steel company great leverage. Placed together, the two patents were a formidable barrier to any manufacturer who sought to produce stainless steel in America without paying the admittedly high royalties set by the American Stainless Steel Company.

The company's successful lawsuit against the Ludlum Steel Company attests to this, as does the rate of returns earned by the company during its seventeen- or eighteen-year life. In 1930, according to a newspaper report, thirty-five large companies were manufacturing stainless steel products. "With one exception," the report continued, "all the steel made in these plants is under the Haynes patent." The exception was the Rustless Iron Corporation of Baltimore, producer of approximately 40,000 tons annually, and the stainless steel company had "recently filed suit" against it "for infringement of patents."[3]

Information about the American Stainless Steel Company is difficult to uncover today, since it intentionally maintained a low public profile and none of its papers seem to have survived. A considerable number of items in the Haynes Papers, including occasional board meeting minutes, serve to give some indications of its operations. James W. Kinnear of Pittsburgh, a prominent corporation attorney, was selected as the first president of the company and he served until his death in 1922. He was succeeded first by James C. Neale, also of Pittsburgh, and then by A. E. Starbuck of Kokomo.[4] The board consisted mostly of steel company executives whose firms were involved in the manufacture of stainless steel as licensees of the holding company, but it was specified that Haynes and the Firth-Brearley syndicate would each control two seats on the ten-man board.[5]

---

[3] Kokomo *Dispatch,* January 3, 1920. This case, mentioned in the preceding chapter, was lost by the stainless steel company. The patents involved had been acquired by the company in the 1920s but were declared invalid. Carl A. Zapffe has called this a "great" patent suit, and indeed its massive record put many facts about metallurgical research upon corrosion and heat-resistant alloys into the public record. Attorney Charles Neave, in his opening remarks at the trial, commented that the briefs prepared by both sides in the case, totaling 552 pages, were "absurdly long," and the trial transcript ran to more than 200 pages. By the time of the decision (1933, reaffirmed 1934), the American Stainless Steel Company was in the process of closing its doors, since the Brearley and Haynes patents were about to expire. Zapffe, "Who Discovered Stainless Steel?" in *Iron Age,* October 14, 1948, p. 125; *American Stainless Steel Co.* et al. v. *Rustless Iron Corporation of America,* 2 Federal Supplement 742; 71 Federal Reporter (2d) 404.

Haynes, who died in 1925, was personally involved in only the Ludlum case, but this was the major test upon which continuation of the stainless steel company depended.

[4] Following Kinnear's death, the president's office was not filled until a favorable ruling in the Ludlum case had been obtained (April, 1923). President James C. Neale was succeeded by A. E. Starbuck in 1928. Starbuck, a close family friend who married Elwood Haynes's niece, had been associated with Haynes in the automobile business for eighteen years. The secretary-treasurer of the Haynes Automobile Company for many years, Starbuck became the administrator of the Haynes estate in 1925 and was given the opportunity to watch over, in an unusually direct way, one of the major assets of the estate during his tenure at the American Stainless Steel Company. He died suddenly in Pittsburgh on April 15, 1930, at the age of fifty-nine. General Folder, 1930, Haynes Papers; Kokomo *Dispatch,* April 16, 1930; Kokomo *Tribune,* April 16, 1930.

[5] In 1924, one of the few years for which a board roster has been found, the following persons were directors: F. A. Bigelow, Harry Brearley, E. B. Clarke, Lewis J. Firth, L. Gerald Firth, Elwood

March Haynes, a rather brash young man of twenty-two when he first joined the board, enjoyed the frequent trips to Pittsburgh with his father to attend the board meetings. Interested in a business career rather than science like his father and his sister (a Western College for Women graduate in 1915), March attempted to play prominent roles in all of his father's business enterprises—automobiles, Stellite, and stainless steel. His father always encouraged him and generously praised his son's help; others have been less complimentary about the contributions March Haynes was able to make.

His associates always considered him a bit odd, or different, someone who did not work well with others. While many ascribed this simply to youthful arrogance or to an elevated sense of his own and his family's importance, in time his problems with daily relationships came to be recognized as stemming from emotional difficulties. The boy's parents never admitted to others, and perhaps not even to themselves except indirectly, that their son was less than perfect, even when March failed to complete high school, but in 1919 they quietly arranged for him to participate in a special education program in Wisconsin. Earlier March had worked at odd jobs in both the automobile and Stellite enterprises, primarily the latter, and in 1922-1923 he attended a business college, the Babson Institute in Massachusetts.[6] Elwood Haynes recognized no deficiencies in his son, and he paved the way for March to hold responsible positions in the family's companies, including one of the two board memberships allocated to the Haynes interests by the American Stainless Steel Company.

As Haynes confided to his friends, the company paid "very good dividends" almost from the very start. The list of licensees in 1918 included Bethlehem Steel, Carpenter Steel, Washington Steel and Ordnance, and Crucible Steel. The Ludlum Steel Company of Watervliet, New York, however, was not among the licensees, and when it began to market its own stainless steel alloys, tradenamed "Neva-Stain" and "Silchrome," the basis for a lawsuit was at hand. These alloys were composed of high chromium, low carbon, iron, and silicon, and had been patented in 1919 by P. A. E. Armstrong, a Ludlum company metallurgist.[7]

In mid-1920 F. A. Bigelow, president of the Carpenter Steel Company and a director of the American Stainless Steel Company, transmitted to Haynes an analysis of the new Ludlum alloy for his comments. Haynes replied immediately that he considered it "clearly an infringement" of the fundamental Haynes patent and suggested that their only recourse was to bring suit against the parties involved to determine the rights of the holders of the two stainless steel patents. Haynes noted that Armstrong had added certain metals to his basic, patented chromium and iron formula, and that the resulting combination, containing more than 8 percent chromium, was practically stainless. The addition of other ingredients, such as silicon, carbon, nickel, cobalt, molybdenum, or tungsten, did not materially affect its stainlessness. His patent, he explained, was based upon the combination of

Haynes, March Haynes, E. S. Kinsley, J. A. Madrens, and James C. Neale. "President Neale to the Stockholders of the American Stainless Steel Company," January 22, 1924, Haynes Papers.

[6] March Haynes (1896–1968) married in 1923, and his wife died in May, 1925, just a month after his father's death. Hospitalized for the emotional strain, March soon recovered and led an active life. He remarried in 1928, and his only child, Elwood March, was born in 1929. Haynes remained in Kokomo until the 1950s, when he moved to California. He died there in January, 1968. Haynes (ed.), *Walter Haynes and His Descendants*; Kokomo *Daily Tribune,* May 23, 1925, January 15, 1968.

[7] Elwood Haynes to Stephen F. Roberts, January 17, 1925, Haynes Papers; General Folder, 1920, *ibid.* This folder contains the Ludlum Steel Company's announcement regarding Patent No. 1,322,511 on "Stable Surface Alloy Steel."

iron and chromium, and was "independent of all other metals, whether added in inappreciable or larger quantities. Neither does it take into account the methods of *working* or heat-treating same. Any article made of a combination, therefore, which involves a steel containing more than 8% chromium is an infringement against the patent."[8]

When all the directors considered this matter, their decision was first to attempt a settlement through negotiation, the alternative being a lawsuit against Ludlum and its customers, but the Ludlum company rejected all such overtures. It announced "to the trade," moreover, its willingness to defend any suit "at our own expense" based on the use of the unlicensed "NEVA-STAIN cutlery steel," and released portions of its correspondence with the stainless steel company demanding royalty payments and threatening a lawsuit if the payments were not made.[9]

In the face of this intransigence, the American Stainless Steel Company began preparing its case to present to the courts. In July, 1920, Haynes recounted his early stainless steel experiments of 1911 and 1912 to patent attorney Christy. He explained his experiment-recording procedures and how the authenticity of his recorded remarks could be verified not only by the chronology of the experiments themselves but also by a witness to the secret testing program—Harry Lanterman.[10]

Christy filed the suit, *American Stainless Steel Company* v. *Ludlum Steel Company,* in the federal district court in New York on December 31, 1920. When President Kinnear reported this step to the board of directors in March, 1921, he expressed his confidence in an early victory. During the previous month, Haynes and Lanterman had spent a day in Pittsburgh going over the various defenses which had been offered in the Ludlum company answer. The results of that session, Kinnear stated, made him more certain than ever about a favorable decision. He then explained to the board the plans for conducting the suit. They involved retaining Professor William Campbell of Columbia University, an eminent metallurgist, to run some additional experiments for them, and asking Harry Brearley to come to New York (at company expense but without additional compensation) and testify at the trial. Kinnear added, however, that "We shall depend largely upon the testimony of Mr. Haynes in this Case, both as an expert and in regard to his early work in developing Stainless Steel."[11] Charles Neave, a member of the

---

[8] Elwood Haynes to F. A. Bigelow, November 13, 1919, *ibid.*

[9] General Folder, 1920, *ibid.* The cutlery trade is aware, the announcement stated, that the American Stainless Steel Company is in the habit "of threatening our customers of NEVA-STAIN steel with suits on patents controlled by them and relating to articles made from a straight ternary or three part alloy of iron, carbon and chromium. We submitted this matter to our patent counsel . . . and they each advised us that our right to make NEVA-STAIN cutlery steel and the rights of our customers to manufacture it into cutlery and other tools are not affected in any way by these patents."

[10] Elwood Haynes to Marshall A. Christy, July 8, 1920, *ibid.* Haynes, of course, dated his experiments; he also designated each series by a letter (in alphabetical order). Individual experiments within a series were numbered consecutively. Lanterman, the witness, was a trusted friend and brother-in-law who assisted Haynes in all of his work for nearly a quarter of a century. Haynes told Christy that Lanterman was "a man of absolute integrity, and of the highest character in every respect." See also Elwood Haynes to Marshall A. Christy, July 17, 1920, *ibid.*

[11] "President's Report to the Directors," American Stainless Steel Company, March 14, 1921, *ibid.* See also Elwood Haynes to James W. Kinnear, November 3, 1921, March Haynes to Elwood Haynes, November 5, 1921, *ibid.* Haynes was unable to attend the November, 1921, meeting of the board, but his son attended and reported on its developments. There is some evidence that the Ludlum company attempted an out-of-court settlement in December, but no details are known. See James W. Kinnear to Elwood Haynes, December 30, 1921, *ibid.*

bar where the case was initiated, was retained as Christy's associate, and Maxwell Barus was a third attorney for the plaintiff.

The case came to trial in the early months of 1922, with the distinguished jurist, Learned Hand, on the bench. Both Haynes and Brearley appeared, evidently at different times, to give testimony, but a brief illness caused Haynes to leave New York early, before he had made all the points he had intended.[12] Brearley, however, testified at length, as he recorded in his autobiography (although this account contains some obvious and self-serving overstatements and he neglected to point out that the final outcome in favor of the American Stainless Steel Company came only upon appeal in 1923).

According to Brearley, when he arrived in the United States, "the U.S.A. patent holders were in the dumps and about to compromise; but, on hearing what kind of evidence I could give, the leading counsel became very optimistic." Under the expert interrogation of Attorney Neave, Brearley communicated his information and his opinions to the group, and they agreed upon what constituted acceptable evidence and what did not. Consequently, Brearley reported, "on the opening day I was in the witness box for three hours and enjoyed every minute of it. I had nothing to conceal from the cross-examining counsel, and understood the subject in dispute and the value of his direct evidence better than he." In fact, he boasted, "I was therefore able to draw from him, by incomplete answers, some questions I wanted him to ask. He got so cross with me that he was reproved by the judge. . . ." The English metallurgist concluded his account of the Ludlum case by quoting a portion of the appeals, not the district court, decision which, as he noted, had so greatly "pleased the patent owners."[13]

Brearley's comments, although interesting and valuable, failed to indicate that Judge Learned Hand had dismissed the case, declaring the patents valid but not infringed by the Armstrong alloys being marketed by Ludlum. The Hand decision, delivered April 13, 1922, "apparently hinged on the silicon content of the Ludlum steels," according to the *Iron Age* reporter, who then quoted a portion of the judge's opinion: "The issue . . . is whether the addition of silicon, which obviates the necessary additional heating of the plaintiff's composition beyond its critical point, makes the resulting article an infringement. Obviously this could not be. . . . Granting that the addition of silicon would not avoid infringement, it does not create it."[14]

---

[12] One of the points Haynes did make was that polishing was not essential in producing stainless steel. Displaying both a hatchet (with a polished edge) and a hammer (without such polishing), he pointed out to Judge Hand that both were made of the same stainless steel alloy. See James W. Kinnear to Charles Neave, New York, February 11, 1922, a copy of which is in *ibid.* There is no evidence that Haynes and Brearley ever met, even though Brearley, in his autobiography, states that he went to America "in 1921" for the lawsuit. Brearley, *Knotted String*, p. 139. Neither man ever mentioned in writing that he met the other.

[13] Brearley, *Knotted String*, pp. 139–41. On this American visit, Brearley also toured a number of New England cutlery factories, tested some stainless iron heats at the Firth-Sterling Works, "talked to a meeting of manufacturers [the American Stainless Steel Company board of directors, Elwood Haynes being absent] about the attractive properties of the material," and lectured at the Massachusetts Institute of Technology before he returned to England and again became embroiled with Firth's over their respective rights concerning stainless steel. *Ibid.*, pp. 141–44. When March Haynes reported on the progress of the trial and the March, 1922, meeting of the board to his father, he mentioned both attorney Neave's summation of the case and Brearley's talk. He passed along Kinnear's impression that Neave had "killed [the] Armstrong argument regarding the prior arts" and made other necessary points "in good shape," and stated that a decision was expected in three to four weeks. After Kinnear's report had been received, Haynes simply remarked that Brearley spoke to the board on the "wonderful possibilities" of stainless iron. March Haynes to Elwood Haynes, March 9, 1922, Haynes Papers; see also, "Stainless Iron— A New and Striking Product," in *Scientific American,* December, 1921, p. 99.

[14] *Iron Age,* April 20, 1922, p. 1109.

This ruling caused considerable dismay among the American Stainless Steel Company family initially, but within a week, after a more careful review of the complicated and rather technical decision, President Kinnear regained some of his optimism. "Since I wrote you [about the decision]," he informed Haynes on April 21, "our metallurgists studying the decision say it is more in our favor than we thought, and that the range of Stainless Steel which covers most of our cutlery steel is absolutely protected." Nevertheless, he asked Haynes to study the decision himself and report his reactions to the board the following Tuesday.[15]

Kinnear apologized for calling such a "hasty meeting" at which he expected "some drastic measures" to be taken, but he explained that "some radical action" concerning the licensees was vital, "as Ludlum is already flooding the country by letter and telegram advertising this decision and offering Stainless Steel at very low rates."[16] For his part, in the meantime, Kinnear sent a standard letter to all licensees of the company, expressing his disappointment at the outcome but pointing out that Ludlum could take but little comfort in it. "Our patents are not vitiated," he emphasized, quoting from an attorney's review of the decision, and he announced plans to appeal the decision as soon as possible.[17]

Haynes attended the April 25 board meeting held in New York, and reported upon his reactions to Judge Hand's decision and the proper steps for the company to take. The board minutes do not reflect Haynes's exact response, but it agreed in substance with Kinnear's earlier statements. However, since Haynes embarked upon a short trip immediately thereafter to keep "out of reach of the telephone and telegraph," his first recorded comments on the decision came on May 15. At that time Haynes sought to encourage Kinnear and some of his disheartened fellow directors. Talk of dissolving the company and giving up the patents was utter foolishness, he thought, since both continued to have great value; "all sorts of articles can be made to advantage from Stainless Steel" within the limits protected by the decision, he counseled, and he also believed an appeal would modify Hand's decision, "which it seems to me is not altogether satisfactory."[18]

The company continued in existence, of course, making such modifications in its licensing agreements as necessary, and the royalty receipts increased substantially in 1922 beyond those of 1921 despite the initial Ludlum case decision.[19] In July, shortly before leaving for Europe on the first extended vacation of his life, Haynes communicated to Kinnear some of his further reflections upon the matter. Believing that the company had proceeded on the "wrong basis" in the initial trial, Haynes set out the points which he felt should be emphasized upon appeal. He stressed the idea that

---

[15] James W. Kinnear to Elwood Haynes, April 21, 1922, Haynes Papers. Kinnear had written Haynes on April 18, expressing his regret at the outcome and stating that the "technical" decision had given Armstrong "considerable advantage." When he subsequently heard from Maxwell Barus, Neave's partner on the case, that "your patents are not entirely vitiated by this decision," Kinnear forwarded a copy of this letter, along with Hand's decision, to Haynes. *Ibid.*, April 18, 19, 1922.

[16] *Ibid.*, April 19, 1922.

[17] James W. Kinnear to "Haynes & Son," April 20, 1922, *ibid.*

[18] Elwood Haynes to James W. Kinnear, May 15, 1922, *ibid.* See also Harry Brearley's long review of the Hand decision, also dated May 15, 1922, which agrees substantially with Haynes's analysis. A copy of the Brearley report was enclosed in James W. Kinnear to Elwood Haynes, June 2, 1922, *ibid.*

[19] In 1921 the company's royalties amounted to $72,000; in the first three quarters of 1922, they topped $50,000. The cost of the Ludlum litigation to date, prior to the appeal being filed, was $27,830.25. March Haynes to Elwood Haynes, October 24, 1922, *ibid.*

neither patent covered any "process for either polishing or tempering the alloys" and repeated his contention, earlier presented to his patent attorney, C. Clarence Poole, that the "primary invention" was "the discovery that *stainless* articles can be made from an alloy consisting essentially of 8 percent or more of Chromium and 92 percent or less of Iron." Carbon was not an essential ingredient, but with 0.6 percent or more carbon such articles might be tempered or hardened by slightly modifying the manufacturing process. Finally, with a chromium content of from 10 to 18 percent, with the carbon at 0.6 percent, "the stainless quality of the article may be enhanced by a suitable heat treatment. This latter feature is covered by Mr. Brearley's patent only, but he gives no specific method for hardening the article."[20]

Haynes ended this statement with a criticism of patent office procedures. "I do not like to complain," he wrote, "but it seems to me that it is the practice of the Patent Office to grant as *little* protection as possible to a basic invention, and as *much* as possible to subsequent applicants. This practice inevitably leads to litigation."[21]

Upon receipt of this letter, the company officers considered petitioning Judge Hand to reopen the case to allow further testimony. Some points, Kinnear explained to the board, had not been fully developed, and some new facts regarding stainless steel had been learned since the trial. Kinnear died, however, before this step was taken, and the board of directors decided in October, 1922, to appeal Hand's decision rather than seek a rehearing. They decided, too, to dissolve the company if the appeal were lost.[22]

Both Haynes and Lewis J. Firth, who represented Brearley and the Firth-Brearley Syndicate, opposed the latter decision, but Haynes also objected to Firth's proposed concession concerning royalties. Firth believed the company's 15 percent royalty was too high, causing among other things consumer discontent, and he suggested as a more "reasonable" figure only a 5 percent royalty. This would also reduce the possibility of infringement. Haynes, however, believed that inventors were seldom paid more than the "minutest fraction" of what their inventions were really worth to manufacturers and to the public. Recognizing, however, the need for some concession, he suggested a 10 percent royalty if the appeal succeeded, an 8 percent charge if it failed. The two men agreed in their concern over a lack of vigorous and effective management of company affairs: its patents were being infringed "with impunity" and the advertising program designed to acquaint the public with stainless steel and its authorized manufacturers had been allowed to lapse.[23]

No action was taken on any of these concerns until following the most welcome and satisfactory decision handed down by the Circuit Court of Appeals on April 16, 1923. As the attorneys exuberantly wired Haynes the following day, "Haynes and Brearley both held pioneer patents valid and infringed."[24] It was in this decision, too, that Judge Hough credited Haynes with priority in discovering the basic properties of stainless steel. "The object of both patentees," he observed,

---

[20] Elwood Haynes to James W. Kinnear, July 12, 1922, *ibid.*

[21] *Ibid.* Haynes added that he was not being critical of company attorneys Christy, Neave, and Barus, who had done "splendid work" in the case, but failure to make the above points inevitably had led to "confusion in the mind of the Court."

[22] March Haynes to Elwood Haynes, October 24, 1922, *ibid.*

[23] Lewis J. Firth to Elwood Haynes, March 15, 19, 22, 1923, *ibid.*; Elwood Haynes to Lewis J. Firth, March 17, 20, 1923, *ibid.*

[24] Fish, Richardson & Neave to Elwood Haynes, April 17, 1923, *ibid.*

is the same, and may be shortly described as a desire to produce what has for some years been increasingly well known under the tradename "stainless steel." Although Brearley's patent date is earlier, his date of application is later, and it may be summarily held that Haynes' is the generic and Brearley's the specific patent.

He then launched into a brilliant review of the history of steelmaking, stressing the ancient problem of producing a steel which was resistant to corrosion, now solved. He discounted the supposed anticipations by other investigators, and ended by according to both Haynes and Brearley "pioneer" status in one branch of the steelmaking art, thereby reversing the lower court decision. The defendant, he reasoned, has, "omitting silicon . . . produced stainless steel; with the silicon added, it has also produced 'stainless steel' therefore, in respect of infringement, the silicon is immaterial no matter how beneficial it may be."[25]

This decision, while most welcome, was of course not the end of the matter. The recommendations of attorney Maxwell Barus concerning future courses of action indicated the steps yet necessary to recover damages and prevent additional infringements. "[A] great many questions as to scope are still undecided," he pointed out, particularly with regard to Ludlum's unhardened and unpolished articles such as automobile valves, and these questions "are sure to come up during the accounting which will follow the decree." He then outlined what would follow: the lower court, following the appeals court mandate, would appoint "a Master to take an accounting of profits and damages" and order "an injunction . . . against further infringement." Following this, the master would order the defendant to file an account. Such accounts, Barus noted, were "usually extremely incorrect and inadequate so that it is usually necessary to file exceptions to the account and then proceed with the examination of the defendant's books and of witnesses. . . . Probably defendant's account will be limited to sale of polished articles, such as cutlery." He observed further that "patent accountings are always very long drawn out affairs" and predicted that it would be "a year or possibly two" before the master's report would be completed and filed. Then, the case could be reargued before the district court upon exceptions to the report, with appeals to the circuit court also possible. He predicted, however, that Ludlum would soon offer a settlement, for their position is a "very unhappy" one, and he recommended a "stiff attitude" in negotiations with them.[26]

Barus proved to be an accurate prognosticator; the events transpired much as he had predicted, although even more slowly. As expected, the Ludlum firm considered their valve steel unaffected by the court rulings and made their accounts accordingly. The special master accepted this version (Haynes complained at one point that there seemed to be "a studied attempt on the part of the master to aid Armstrong in his effort to evade both the Brearley and Haynes patents" and that he seemed to be in collusion with Ludlum to make the terms of the settlement as small as possible),[27] and District Court Judge Thacher, in a decision dated February 4, 1926, upheld the master's ruling on the valve steels.[28] This decision merely limited the extent of the settlement made with Ludlum, the exact terms of which are

---

[25] 290 Federal Reporter 103; the quotation appears at 105 and 109.

[26] Maxwell Barus to F. A. Bigelow, April 20, 1923, Haynes Papers.

[27] Elwood Haynes to Marshall A. Christy, August 6, 1924, *ibid.*

[28] 16 Federal Reporter (2d) 823.

unknown, and of course had no effect upon the validity of the basic stainless steel patents.

The business of the American Stainless Steel Company remained good throughout the 1920s. Haynes's relation with the company during the final years of his life, after the appeals court had upheld his patent, was a genial one. He remained on the board of directors and continued to advocate a generally hard line on the matter of prices, royalties, licensees, and court action against supposed infringers.[29] He also strongly urged a much more liberal policy on advertising. New licensing agreements were drawn up in the summer of 1923, with new classifications and new royalty rates for the different types of stainless steel. The royalties in 1923 ranged from 10 to 13.3 percent, and dividends totaling 100 percent ($300,000) were paid during the year. (These payments had been suspended pending the outcome of the Ludlum litigation.) Less spectacular but good dividends on a greater volume of business were declared for the rest of the decade.[30]

It is regrettable that more information concerning the American Stainless Steel Company is not available and that the secondary literature contains almost no references to it. It is a topic well worth additional study, and the material in the Haynes Papers is sufficient for a good start. Only partial income figures for the company during the first half of the 1920s have been found, but evidently Haynes was fairly well pleased with the company's earnings. For the latter half decade, an income, expenditures, and dividend statement has been located (see Table 3). Incomplete figures for subsequent years indicate continued high earnings into the 1930s, with a 36½ percent dividend in 1932, a depression year, on profits of $300,000.[31]

Table 3

American Stainless Steel Company Financial Statement, 1925 – 1929*

Year	Income	Expenditures	Dividends
1925	$197,847.29	$114,046.58	24%
1926	$241,575.06	166,511.29	24%
1927	$242,311.19	166,466.63	24%
1928	$268,927.26	82,359.37	24%
1929	$310,356.01	61,482.04	24%

* Source: General Folder, 1929, Haynes Papers.

Haynes's last communication with the directors and attorneys of the American Stainless Steel Company dealt again with his unceasing efforts to gain judicial recognition for the full range of claims he had set out in his patent and to have his role in developing stainless steel given greater publicity. In mid-1924, when Haynes reviewed a paper on stainless steel to be published in the handbook of the American Society for Steel Treating, he

[29] Haynes, for example, did not concede the court ruling excepting Ludlum steel valves, their "Silchrome" product, and he sought to have a reconsideration made. See especially Elwood Haynes to Marshall A. Christy, February 1, September 6, 1924, Haynes Papers.

[30] June, July, September, 1923, folders, *ibid.* See especially the new classification table at September 18, 1923.

[31] This figure is known because of office staff complaints to the board in January, 1933, objecting to a 20 percent ($3,500) salary cut in the face of the 36½ percent dividend declaration. Moreover, as the letter pointed out, the life of the company was necessarily limited, with liquidation expected in either 1936 or 1938, depending upon the outcome of the lawsuit against the Rustless Iron Corporation. J. C. C. Holding to March Haynes, January 31, 1933, *ibid.*

was dissatisfied only with the author's "historical statement" and its emphasis upon British origins. He suggested the following modification:

> What is now termed Stainless Steel was first discovered by an American inventor and its resistance to corrosion fully set forth. A patent was afterwards obtained in the United States on articles made from this material containing from 8% to 60% of Chromium. The properties of the alloy were afterward independently discovered by an English Metallurgist who demonstrated that its stainless qualities were enhanced by heat treatment so long as the chromium content did not exceed 16%. He was also granted a United States patent on the above discovery. Both of these patents are now the property of the American Stainless Steel Company and have been adjudicated and upheld by the Appellate Court.[32]

The company would be involved in a second major litigation in the early 1930s, the above-mentioned Rustless Iron Company case. In this suit, decided in 1933, the American Stainless Steel Company failed to have two other patents it owned covering different types of stainless alloys upheld.[33] This may have contributed to the demise of the company shortly afterwards (the date is uncertain), but it would have dissolved when the Haynes patent expired in 1938 in any event.[34]

Haynes, of course, did not live to see these final acts. During the brief heyday of the American Stainless Steel Company's affairs, however, he considered the company earnings no more than he and Brearley deserved. For Haynes, moreover, the company was visible, tangible proof of the value and importance of his metallurgical wisdom, and he viewed its royalty and dividend payments as his just reward.[35] As pointed out before, Haynes fought hard for every claim to which he felt entitled, and when a patent office examiner, or the board of examiners-in-chief, or a district court judge, or a special master appointed by the district court attempted to limit his claims, he counseled a vigorous response.

Perhaps critics will deplore this mercenary streak in Haynes, a man often praised for his generosity and charity, but he believed that inventors as a class failed to be rewarded properly. He did what he could to prevent what he considered a similar injustice from happening to the stainless steel inventors-patentees.

166

---

[32] Elwood Haynes to Owen Parmiter, July 3, 1924, *ibid.* Parmiter, author of the paper and a Firth-Sterling company metallurgist, declined the wording offered; rather than raise what was evidently a touchy subject on all sides, he deleted the remarks about Brearley that had prompted Haynes's rebuttal. Owen Parmiter to Elwood Haynes, July 10, 1924, *ibid.*

[33] 2 Federal Supplement 742. The Circuit Court of Appeals affirmed this decision in June, 1934. 71 Federal Reporter (2d) 404.

[34] The Haynes Papers contain very few items dated after Haynes's death in 1925, and there are no records there concerning the final years of the American Stainless Steel Company. The last listing for the firm in the Pittsburgh city directory appeared in 1935. Professor Robert Doherty to author, May 7, 1971.

[35] In fact Haynes did not personally control all of his stainless steel shares; he had divided them equally with his wife and children.

Chapter 13

Manufacturing Haynes Automobiles, 1910–1920

The automobile industry was firmly established in the nation by 1910. James J. Flink, in his book on the "automobile revolution" in America, considers its first phase to have lasted from 1895 until 1910.[1] Earlier, when David Beecroft surveyed "The Progress of 25 Years" within the automobile industry, he discerned five periods in its development through 1924, the first three lasting until 1905, by which time "the vehicle and the organizations" had been developed. Period four, which he dated from 1908 to 1912, "provided the complete vehicle and the means for volume manufacture."[2] Already the industry was concentrated in the Great Lakes states, especially Indiana, Ohio, and Michigan.[3]

Within Indiana the automobile industry had consisted of only one firm in 1899, the Haynes-Apperson Company, and only 11 companies were underway in 1904 with products valued at $1,639,000. By 1909, however, there were 67 automobile establishments, including body and parts suppliers, manufacturing products valued at $23,764,000, more than fourteen times the 1904 figure.[4] In 1919 the respective figures were 172 establishments, with $179,065,000 as the value of their products.[5]

---

[1] See Flink, *America Adopts the Automobile*, p. 10.

[2] David Beecroft, "The Progress of 25 Years," in *Automobile Trade Journal*, December 1, 1924, p. 19. As Flink has emphasized, Ford's Highland Park plant, which opened its doors on January 1, 1910, epitomized the shift to "volume production of a static-model, reliable car for the masses . . . ." Flink, *America Adopts the Automobile*, pp. 4–5. See also Rae, *American Automobile*, and compare Boas, "Locational Patterns of American Automobile Assembly Plants," in *Economic Geography*, XXXVII (1961), 219–24. Boas considers 1914 as the dividing year between "the period of experimentation and the widespread entry of small manufacturers: and the establishment of a more stable, mature, and large-scale industry." *Ibid.*

[3] See the tables in Boas, "Locational Patterns of American Automobile Assembly Plants," in *Economic Geography*, XXXVII, 222–23, depicting the industry's concentration in 1900, 1910, and 1920.

[4] Dunn, *Indiana and Indianans*, II, 946. He added that a number of other businesses classified under other headings also manufactured automobile accessories, including tires. In 1912 an Indiana newspaper reporter called the Haynes company "the recognized pioneer of motordom. . . . Since then automobile factories have sprung up in about every city of size in the Hoosier state until Indiana is now recognized as second only to Michigan" in motor vehicle production. Kokomo *Tribune*, August 30, 1912.

[5] Phillips, *Indiana in Transition*, p. 315.

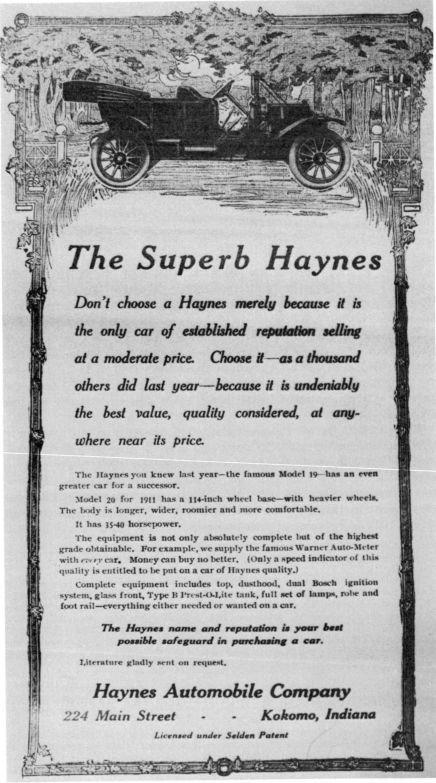

The Superb Haynes

Don't choose a Haynes merely because it is the only car of established reputation selling at a moderate price. Choose it—as a thousand others did last year—because it is undeniably the best value, quality considered, at anywhere near its price.

The Haynes you knew last year—the famous Model 19—has an even greater car for a successor.

Model 20 for 1911 has a 114-inch wheel base—with heavier wheels. The body is longer, wider, roomier and more comfortable.

It has 35-40 horsepower.

The equipment is not only absolutely complete but of the highest grade obtainable. For example, we supply the famous Warner Auto-Meter with *every* car. Money can buy no better. (Only a speed indicator of this quality is entitled to be put on a car of Haynes quality.)

Complete equipment includes top, dusthood, dual Bosch ignition system, glass front, Type B Prest-O-Lite tank, full set of lamps, robe and foot rail—everything either needed or wanted on a car.

The Haynes name and reputation is your best possible safeguard in purchasing a car.

Literature gladly sent on request.

Haynes Automobile Company

224 Main Street - - Kokomo, Indiana

Licensed under Selden Patent

On the national level, in 1909, the industry produced over 127,000 vehicles valued at $193.8 million and was ranked twenty-first among United States industries. By 1919, despite a considerable weeding out of manufacturers, the automobile industry produced over 1.6 million vehicles, valued at more than $2.3 billion, and it ranked among the top five industries in the nation. By 1925, when more than 4 million cars and trucks were built, the automobile industry was the largest in the nation.[6]

The Haynes company played a role in these developments, although after 1910 it was an increasingly minor one compared to the giants in Detroit. The Haynes automobile, nevertheless, established itself in the medium to high price range, leaving the mass market to Ford and his would-be competitors, and it developed a loyal and growing clientele throughout most of the 1910s. Annual sales of the Hayneses, reported at approximately 1,000 units in 1910, rose to the company's all-time peak of 7,100 in 1916, and averaged 3,800 a year through 1920. Sales peaked again in 1921, reaching 5,900 for the year, but a decline, gradual at first but then precipitous, began in 1922.[7]

TABLE 4

Haynes Automobile Company Sales, 1906−1924*

Year	Sales	Year	Sales	Year	Sales
1906	300E	1913	1,400	1919	3,746
1907	300E	1914	1,700	1920	3,800
1908	350E	1915	5,500	1921	5,900
1909	350E	1916	7,100	1922	5,600
1910	1,000	1917	5,500	1923	4,300
1911	1,000E	1918	2,200	1924	1,500
1912	1,200E				

* Source: James Dalton, "How the Eighteen Biggest Failures Rose and Fell," in *MoToR,* November, 1925, pp. 30−31; Haynes Papers, *passim.*

For a brief period in 1911, it appeared that the Haynes company would not survive the year. A disastrous fire swept through the plant on February 28, destroying several buildings and causing damage in excess of $750,000, but the owners decided immediately to rebuild "a larger, modern and better equipped factory" upon the same site.[8] The fire had begun in the washroom of the "erecting department," immediately below the paint room. A short-circuited wire ignited a gasoline-filled pan, and the "flames spread with startling rapidity." Several second floor workmen had to leap from the windows for safety, and a paint shop employee perished in the flames.[9]

---

[6] Federal Trade Commission, *Report on the Motor Vehicle Industry* (Washington, D.C.: U.S. Government Printing Office, 1939), pp. 7, 9.

[7] Dalton, "How the Eighteen Biggest Failures Rose and Fell," in *MoToR,* November, 1925, pp. 30−31; Indianapolis *Star,* July 16, 1910. Incidental references in Haynes Automobile Company literature, particularly random references to motor numbers, are in keeping with the general totals indicated here and in Table 4.

[8] *MoToR,* April, 1911, clipping in "Companies" file, Automotive History Collection, Detroit Public Library.

[9] Kokomo *Dispatch,* March 1, 1911. The company afterwards complained of "considerable delay" and inefficiency on the part of the Kokomo fire department in responding to the crisis, which resulted in the suspension and ultimate resignation of the fire chief. Less than one third of the $750,000 loss was covered by insurance. *MoToR,* April, 1911, clipping in "Companies" file, Automotive History Collection; Kokomo *Dispatch,* March 10, 1911.

In a report on the fire published by *MoToR* magazine, the extent of the damage was detailed, but so were the company's ambitious rebuilding plans. No completed cars had been destroyed in the fire, as recent sales had exceeded production and there was no backlog. In addition, since the factory had been running at maximum capacity at the time of the fire, huge quantities of stock had been stored in tents and temporary structures outside the factory. These temporary quarters were immediately converted for production, so that the manufacturing process was resumed "with comparatively little interruption. The fire occurred on Tuesday, and on Saturday afternoon the first cars built from the ground up since the fire, were completed and [road tested]." In April it was predicted that the "thoroughly modern and up-to-date plant" being built on the site of the old one would be in operation within the next two months.[10]

The possibility of relocating the plant in another community had been considered briefly as an alternative if local financing was not forthcoming. "Many offers from Indiana towns and cities to build the plant away from Kokomo" were received within twenty-four hours after the fire, but Haynes announced his intention not to move. "Kokomo is good enough for us," he said. Nevertheless, when representatives from Warren, Ohio, met with Haynes and his directors in late March, offering a stock subscription and fifteen acres of free land, the company had to consider it.[11] Nearly $200,000 of new capital was needed to rebuild in Kokomo, and the directors decided to try to raise this amount by selling shares of preferred stock. Consequently, a subscription drive, heartily backed by the local newspapers, took place during the last week in March. Its success was announced on March 28, by which time $160,000 had been obtained.[12]

Haynes himself, of course, took an active role in getting the company refinanced and planning its modernization, and the new plant was in full operation by September, 1911. Since Haynes had long since transferred the routine management of company affairs to others, he retreated to his laboratory as soon as possible following the fire crisis. His research time was crucial in 1911; Haynes was on the threshold of his most important metallurgical discoveries and was anxious to continue his program of experiments. From time to time Haynes participated in such promotional work as the advertising department requested, responded personally to the occasional complaints he received concerning bad workmanship or service, and frequently attended the annual automobile shows in Indianapolis, Chicago, and New York.[13] There were, in addition, increasingly large numbers of invitations to speak, and he accepted a great many of them. His topics included not only the automobile story and his new alloys but also general scientific and moral themes. He avoided strictly political subjects except for prohibition and local option laws, which he strongly supported.

Another major company reorganization in 1912 helped Haynes divorce

---

[10] *MoToR*, April, 1911, clipping in "Companies" file, Automotive History Collection.

[11] Kokomo *Dispatch*, March 2, 25, 1911.

[12] Eventually the entire issue of preferred stock was taken up, and a year after the fire Haynes wrote to a friend in Washington, D. C., that the rebuilding "on a larger scale" was complete, and that the company was "now producing more cars than ever." *Ibid.*, March 28, 1911; Articles of Incorporation, Haynes Automobile Company, Archives Division, Indiana State Library; Elwood Haynes to N. A. Cobb, April 12, 1912, Haynes Papers.

[13] See, for example, the Indianapolis *Times*, February 16, 1954, for a story about the 1913 Indianapolis Automobile Show. The accompanying photograph depicts the Haynes company exhibit in the left foreground.

himself more completely from management decisions than he had been able to arrange in 1905. A. G. Seiberling was brought back after five years at the Apperson Brothers Automobile Company, and this proved to be a wise step. Hired initially as factory manager, Seiberling was soon promoted to general manager, succeeding C. B. Warren, and he supervised the remarkable achievements of the next few years. "The growth of the Haynes Automobile Company since 1912," it was reported in 1918, "has been one of the sensations of industrial Indiana."[14] From a production average of five cars a day in a plant of 150,000 square feet in 1912, the company grew to one capable of producing forty cars a day, and plant space had increased to 400,000 square feet by 1918. The capitalization had grown too, from $600,000 (plus $200,000 in preferred stock) in 1912 to $3,500,000 six years later.

Other new personnel added in 1912, or shortly thereafter, included George Strout as sales manager, R. T. Gray as advertising manager, and A. N. Wilhelm as factory manager (succeeding Seiberling); all three carried out their assignments aggressively and well. A number of technical improvements were made upon the Haynes product in 1912, including electric lighting and starting (as perfected by Charles F. Kettering in 1911 for the Cadillac company), and this trend toward greater comfort continued in 1913 with the introduction of electric shifting.[15] The latter improvement was announced during the summer of 1913 to be standard equipment on all three 1914 models, although manual shifting continued to be available as an option. The company reported that the Vulcan Electric Gear Shifter, developed by its own engineers, had been tested for months, that one test had required over five hundred shifts in a single day, and that the device was both simple and reliable. On a circle above the steering wheel were seven buttons, one for each gear (three forward, one reverse, and neutral), the starter, and the horn. To engage the gear desired, the driver merely depressed the clutch, pushed the proper button, and the change occurred automatically. A contact plate on the clutch permitted gear changes only when the clutch was disengaged and precluded the danger of stripping the gears.[16]

Strout and Gray accompanied their promotion of the new technical improvements with a vigorous campaign seeking greater recognition for Elwood Haynes as an automotive pioneer. In 1912, to remind the public of the historical significance of their product, the company adopted a new trademark and slogan, which subsequently appeared as the hood ornament on all Haynes automobiles: "Haynes: America's First Car."[17] The following

---

[14] Kokomo *Sunday Dispatch*, January 6, 1918.

[15] Indianapolis *Star*, August 30, 1912, July 1, 1913.

[16] *Ibid.*, July 1, 1913; *The Automobile*, June 19, 1913, clipping in "Companies" file, Automotive History Collection.

[17] This slogan proved upsetting to Charles E. Duryea, who insisted that Haynes had been anticipated by the Duryeas. Duryea damaged his case, however, by claiming a date some seventeen months earlier than the actual first run of the Duryea vehicle. Unable to prove his April, 1892, date (September, 1893, is now accepted as correct), he was unable to prove the anticipation. It should be noted that the Haynes advertising department stretched a point by using the year 1893 as the date for the beginning of the Haynes. This, of course, was when Haynes purchased the marine gasoline engine and began to construct the "Pioneer," but the automobile was not tested until mid-1894. Duryea also pointed out that the Haynes company began using its trademark on June 25, 1912, although it was not registered (No. 95,909) until August 24, 1914, and he noted that the words "Haynes" and "America's First Car" were disclaimed. In other words, only the shape of the design and the drawing of the car were trademarked. Duryea Papers, Automotive History Collection. See also the notice describing the "decidedly distinctive" new name plate in *Motor Age*, November 6, 1913, in "Companies" file, *ibid.*

year, when a new registration law was enacted, the Haynes Automobile Company requested and received Indiana License Number 1, but the state would not allow them to use the license in their advertising.[18] Meanwhile Strout and Gray collected sworn affidavits from persons who were formerly associated with Haynes or Apperson and were familiar with the Riverside Machine Shop in the 1890s; all, of course, gave Haynes the primary credit for designing and building the "Pioneer" of 1893 – 1894. These sworn statements were presented to the public in a double-page advertisement in the Indianapolis *Star* on July 1, 1913, the day the Indiana-Pacific automobile caravan left Indianapolis for the west coast. Their obvious purpose was to support advertising claims that Haynes was the "father of the American automobile" and that the Haynes was indeed, "America's First Car."[19]

Elwood Haynes's national fame grew in the mid-1910s, and this was perhaps most clearly indicated to the inventor when he consented, after much importuning, to travel to the west coast with a caravan of Indiana-made cars and trucks in 1913, not only to boost the state's industrial prowess but also to dramatize the need for improved roads and highways. Haynes had championed the "Good Roads Movement" in the United States for almost as long as he had been building automobiles. "The first thing that impressed me after the road trial of the little car [in 1894]," he said in 1913, "was the importance of the highway itself."[20] He had repeatedly stated that automobile usefulness and speed were limited only by the state of the roads, and he called for improvements by county and state (not federal) authorities. In a 1910 interview granted to the Indianapolis *Star* magazine, Haynes had been especially critical of the road building methods employed in Indiana. Given their inefficiency and wastefulness, he commented, "The wonder is our roads are as good as they are." When repairs were undertaken, he described the procedure "as a lick and a promise, without method and devoid of satisfactory results." Haynes then had spelled out the details of his plan to establish "a department of state government" to look after roads. He favored a superintendent of highways, just as there was a Superintendent of Public Instruction for education, with local officials in each county responsible for the roads in their jurisdiction. "Road materials," he added, "should not be placed on roads by farmers, as now, but in sheds along the road," from which they would be "placed by the county supervisors."[21]

While Haynes was making these statements, a substantial movement calling for improved roads was underway throughout the United States. The initial thrust in this direction, following the advent of the railroad and its near monopoly of intercity passenger travel, came from bicyclists in the late

---

[18] The Apperson Brothers Automobile Company also had asked for License No. 1, on the grounds that a member of their company had built the first automobile in Indiana, but Secretary of State Ellingham's decision was not based on the rival priority claims. The Haynes company request had been received first, and it was honored upon the condition given above. Kokomo *Daily Tribune*, June 30, 1913.

[19] Affidavits had been obtained from William Wrightsman, P. A. E. Armstrong, E. E. Sanders, E. G. Shortridge, and William Adrian. All but Sanders, an associate with Haynes for twelve years in the natural gas business, had been employed at the Riverside Machine Shop at the time Haynes approached Apperson with his unusual request. Indianapolis *Star*, July 1, 1913.

[20] *Ibid.*

[21] *Ibid.*, September 4, 1910. In this same interview, Haynes also favored an end to the 20 miles per hour speed limit. "There is not one automobilist in forty who does not run faster than twenty miles," he averred, "and the state sets a bad example when it enacts a law that is certain to be violated with impunity." His preference was for a law punishing "furious driving," letting each case be judged according to the evidence submitted. "Laws," he repeated, "should not be enacted just to be broken," an interesting statement from one who championed prohibition.

1880s and 1890s. In 1892 the National League for Good Roads was formed, and the following year Congress established the Office of Public Road Inquiry within the Department of Agriculture, endowing it with a $10,000 appropriation. One historian locates this appropriation as the beginning of the modern good roads movement.[22] Later the League of American Wheelmen organized the National Good Roads Association, but results by the end of the decade were meager. Four years into the new century "only 151,664 of the nation's 2,151,000 miles of roadways had been improved with gravel, shell, oil, or some other substance. The rest, nearly 2,000,000 miles of them, were dirt; rough, rutted, often impassable, these were the farmers' farm-to-market roads."[23] These were also the surfaces upon which the nation's increasing number of automobiles were forced to run.

Many forces inspired the spread of the good roads movement in the early years of the twentieth century. The initiation of rural free delivery by the United States postal service may have brought the greatest sense of urgency to the movement, but the Office of Public Road Inquiry, the good roads associations, and the rise of the automobile also contributed. The automobile interests focused attention on hard-surfaced major interstate and transcontinental highways, an emphasis that ignored the farm-to-market road improvements desired by farmers.

Haynes supported both types of road improvements—rural and interstate. In 1912 he accepted the chairmanship of a local Good Roads Committee, and in 1914 he noted with pride the way automobiles were increasingly being used by farmers, including bringing them to church on Sundays.[24] His most noted contribution to improved roads and highways in America, however, was his endorsement of the Lincoln Highway proposal in a personal and dramatic way. The Lincoln Highway was the brainchild of Carl G. Fisher, an Indianapolis businessman who was also involved in building the Indianapolis Motor Speedway and later in developing Miami Beach, Florida. The highway was to run all the way across the continent from New York to San Francisco. In 1913, to publicize the need for such a highway as well as to demonstrate the reliability of automobiles on both good and bad roads, the Indiana Automobile Manufacturers Association decided to drive several of their vehicles from Indianapolis to San Francisco and then on to Los Angeles. A caravan of twenty-two Indiana-built cars and two trucks were to leave from "the circle" in Indianapolis on July 1. After considerable hesitation, primarily because of his reluctance to abandon his metallurgical experiments and his new Stellite business for so long a time, Haynes decided at the last minute to join the tour.[25] The company had already entered two cars, a four-cylinder and a six-cylinder model, and four men were to travel in

Manufacturing
Haynes Automobiles,
1910–1920

173

---

[22] Wayne E. Fuller, *RFD: The Changing Face of Rural America* (Bloomington, Ind.: Indiana University Press, 1964), p. 182; see also Frederic L. Paxson, "The America Highway Movement, 1916–1935," in *American Historical Review*, LI (1946), 236–53, and John Chynoweth Burnham, "The Gasoline Tax and the Automobile Revolution," in *Mississippi Valley Historical Review*, XLVIII (1961), 435–59.

[23] Fuller, *RFD*, p. 178.

[24] Chicago *Inter-Ocean*, January 30, 1914.

[25] This decision was announced in the Indianapolis *Star* magazine, June 29, and in the Kokomo *Daily Tribune*, June 30, 1913. The latter paper praised the decision, mentioning that Haynes "is almost universally acknowledged to be the man who created the first American automobile" and that he had "earned a vacation." Two Apperson cars were also on the tour. For a brief and sympathetic treatment of Carl G. Fisher, see Jane Watts Fisher, *Fabulous Hoosier: A Story of American Achievement* (New York: R. M. McBride & Company, 1947), especially chapter 7, "The Lincoln Highway."

Elwood Haynes

Elwood Haynes in Denver, 1913, on automobile tour from Indianapolis to Los Angeles

each vehicle. Haynes was joined in Car No. 12 by C. A. Branston, of Cambridge, England, and by two company employees, Robert Crawford, the assistant sales manager, and L. R. Wagner, the designated driver.[26] According

---

[26] Indianapolis *Star,* July 1, 1913. In addition to the manufacturers' representatives, a number of newspapermen and civic organization officials joined the tour. Carl G. Fisher, representing the Lincoln Highway Association, and representatives from the United States Bureau of Public

to Strout, "the presence of Elwood Haynes on the tour is one of immense importance to the Indiana automobile manufacturers, who are proud of their fellow Hoosier, from whose crude little horseless carriage of 1893-1894 has sprung the big powerful six-cylinder car of today."[27]

The planned itinerary led westward by way of St. Louis, Kansas City, Denver, Salt Lake City, Lake Tahoe, San Francisco, and Los Angeles. A reporter from the Indianapolis *Star* filed almost daily reports, and his published accounts are the best source of information about the eventful six-week journey. Haynes, who announced by the time the group reached Terre Haute that he liked the idea of it "better and better as the miles are reeled off," was unquestionably the star attraction. He was in great demand as a speaker to the crowds that gathered to greet the travelers at various stops along the way, receiving even more attention than the governors who often accompanied the tour across their states. In its summary of the trip, the Indianapolis *Star* reported that Haynes, " 'The Father of the Automobile,' as he is called, has addressed many audiences throughout the tour and his presence has added weight. His picture has appeared in almost every paper in every city through which the party has passed, and he has been honored as no other man on the trip."[28] Twenty of the twenty-two vehicles that started westward reached Los Angeles safely on August 2, two cars having dropped out at St. Louis and San Francisco "as planned."[29]

Some difficulties had been experienced in Utah and Nevada, where the sun, heat, and dust aggravated the problems of poor roads and faulty maps, and the tour was once described by the *Star* reporter as "an endurance contest" with "the cars scattered out along the route," but the caravan regrouped for its triumphant drive into the Golden Gate city at the end of the month. This event was marred by a fatal accident involving one of the "tour escort" cars; later, in Santa Barbara, near the end of the long trip, L. R. Wagner, while driving Car No. 12 with Crawford and W. B. Cochrane of Los Angeles as passengers, struck and killed a small boy. The car was traveling no more than ten miles an hour, but the child was accidentally pushed into its path by his companions. A tour truck was also hit by a streetcar in Los Angeles.[30]

Elwood Haynes's personal summary of the tour was published in the Indianapolis *Star* magazine on August 10, 1913. Terming it "pleasant" and "successful" in both of its purposes, he reviewed the road and weather conditions encountered, the receptions accorded the tourists, the natural beauty of the country, particularly in the Rockies and beyond, and other highlights. "The performance of Indiana machines," he concluded, "was highly creditable, and I feel compelled to say in all sincerity that Indiana has established a great prestige in the minds of the people along this road

---

Roads and the Indiana Chamber of Commerce were also present. "The tour is for the Indiana makers," the paper explained, "but its secondary work will be the furthering of the good roads projects." *Ibid.,* June 29, 1913.

The second car in the Haynes group, No. 13, carried the Haynes company sales manager, George H. Strout, W. J. Morgan, T. L. Tencher, and F. R. Wagner.

[27] *Ibid.,* June 29, 1913.

[28] *Ibid.,* August 10, 1913. Such a story from the San Francisco *Examiner,* July 30, 1913, was reprinted in the *Haynes Pioneer,* September, 1913, pp. 8–9. The following month this journal reported that Governor George H. Hodges of Kansas, who had accompanied Haynes on the trip across the state, ordered two Haynes "6's," exact duplicates of Car No. 12, on the tour. *Ibid.,* October, 1913, p. 3.

[29] Indianapolis *Star,* August 4, 1913.

[30] *Ibid.,* July 27, August 3, 1913.

regarding the character of its products"; unsurprisingly, he was also pleased with the performances of the Haynes cars.[31]

Englishman C. A. Branston's report on the trip to the Haynes Automobile Company, while not contradictory to the Indianapolis *Star* version or the Haynes summary, gives another perspective. Branston's telegram immediately upon arriving in Los Angeles reveals something of the Branston viewpoint:

> Arrived in land of sunshine—and dust. Unlike Kokomo, alcoholic beverages plentiful, thank goodness! but Haynes, Crawford, and Wagner are teetotalers. Horrible! Due to your kindness have been able to gather numerous impressions of American roads, chiefly in the shape of bruises on various parts of my anatomy. Rockies fine—Salt Lake City ditto. The lake smelly. The desert beastly. Reno ripping—am returning there shortly. Haynes cars unfortunately ran so well that I have no interesting photographs to take home. When are you organizing your next trip? I want to go.[32]

The Indianapolis *Star* reporter confirmed the lack of suitable beverages on portions of the trip. He wired that the group all drank "William Jennings Bryan cocktails" (milk) outside of Grand Junction, Colorado, and that later some "real buttermilk" was obtained.[33]

Exploiting the Haynes publicity, his automobile company began a new advertising campaign which also included the introduction of an attractive and well-edited monthly magazine, *The Haynes Pioneer.* Its features, illustrations, and frequent retrospective views of the company in the absence of the company records themselves constitute a major source of information about the Haynes company.[34] Haynes was a frequent contributor to the journal, recounting stories about his first car, the early days of the automobile, and himself. Indeed, the very first numbers carried short autobiographical sketches by Haynes concerning his boyhood chemical experiments, his education, and his experiences with the Portland Natural Gas and Oil Company. The series was not continued for long, but the Silver Anniversary Number carried Haynes's oft-repeated account of "How I Built the First Automobile" as well as many other stories concerning the "Pioneer" and its construction and early operation.

At the same time that the company began publication of *The Haynes Pioneer,* it was decided to compile a book describing the history of the Haynes Automobile Company, the achievements of its founder, and, in greater detail, the newest Haynes cars (Models 26, 27, and 28). Ostensibly written by Elwood Haynes, identified as the "Inventor and Builder of America's First Automobile," *The Complete Motorist* was published early in 1914. Supposedly designed to explain everything about the modern automobile to the general reader, it was in fact a brief autobiographical account of Haynes, a statement of his business philosophy, a puffery of the Haynes Automobile Company, and a thorough introduction to the new Haynes cars and their electric starting and shifting features.

---

[31] *Ibid.,* August 17, 1913.

[32] *Haynes Pioneer,* November, 1913, pp. 16–17.

[33] Indianapolis *Star,* July 16, 1913.

[34] There is no known complete run of the journal, which was published regularly from mid-1913 until the 1920s. The file in the Haynes Papers begins with Volume I, No. 2 (August, 1913), and has many gaps. The Indiana State Library and the Detroit Public Library have several random issues, including the particularly valuable Silver Anniversary Number, July, 1918.

George H. Strout, the new sales manager, wrote the introduction to the book praising Haynes as an inventor who should be ranked with Stephenson and Fulton in the transportation field and who, in addition, had just invented "a new metal which is harder than steel. . . . He can both dream and do."[35] This was followed by an autobiographical chapter, "The Horseless Carriage," in which Haynes quickly reviewed his early life and then described his first experiences with the automobile. He noted the recent "tremendous" growth of the automobile industry in America, which for "years after the first car was put into operation" had failed "to develop at all." He then praised his associates in the Haynes company as men of "vast experience and great talent."[36]

This chapter was the only portion of the book which Haynes personally wrote, for the balance of the work differs greatly in language and style and is clearly a public relations statement. Haynes, nevertheless, permitted the book to be issued in his name and must bear the responsibility for the exaggerated claims it contained. Some sections, such as those dealing with "The Care of the Haynes Car" or "The Vulcan Electric Gear Shift," were unexceptionable and informative, especially Chapter Seven, "Expert Advice on Haynes Equipment." This contained no fewer than nineteen statements by automobile parts manufacturers whose products were used in the Haynes, including Goodyear tires, Willard batteries, Timken-Detroit axles, Stewart-Warner speedometers, Fedders radiators, and bodies (open and closed) manufactured in Union City, Indiana, and Amesburg, Massachusetts.

The final chapter of the book, however, which purported to tell something of Haynes's business philosophy as well as his purposes in writing the book, is both maudlin and uncharacteristically promotional. Yet it bears examination because it contains the most blatant claims that Haynes made for his automobile work. Although he believed them to be true at the time, it is interesting to note that ten years later, given the outraged response which some of the Haynes claims elicited from other automobile pioneers, particularly Charles E. Duryea and Elmer and Edgar Apperson, Haynes planned to write a carefully researched and comprehensive book on the history of the automobile. Encouraged by an editor at the Bobbs-Merrill Company of Indianapolis, Haynes was to correspond with a number of his fellow pioneers in the automotive field in order to verify specific dates and facts concerning their first machines. The many conflicting reports he received in response to his first inquiries must have overwhelmed him, for he would write no more than three pages on the advantages of the rolling wheel before quietly abandoning the book project.[37]

Haynes professed a disinterestedness and desire to search for the truth in *The Complete Motorist*: "Even if this book should demonstrate to you that some other type of car is better for you individually, I believe I should feel highly complimented. Because it would prove that I had discussed auto-

---

[35] Elwood Haynes, *The Complete Motorist* ([Chicago] Privately printed. [Wells and Co., 1914]), pp. 5–6. The book was privately printed and "Issued to the Followers of America's Cleanest Sport." The book was reprinted in 1977 by the Haynes Apperson Festival, Inc.

[36] *Ibid.*, pp. 7–15.

[37] See John R. Carr to Elwood Haynes, November 16, 1923, Elwood Haynes to Bobbs-Merrill Company, January 1, 1924, Haynes Papers, for a sampling of book project correspondence. In response to the questionnaire, Henry Ford's letter, for example, claimed an 1892 vehicle although it is now established that he built his first gasoline automobile in 1896. E. G. Liebold to Elwood Haynes, June 4, 1924, *ibid.* Liebold was Ford's secretary and handled much of his personal correspondence.

Elwood Haynes

Elwood and Bertha Haynes being driven by their son March in 1914

mobiles and not the Haynes."[38] But his later assertions deny this point, and the repeated protests that the book was not intended as a commercial message made the reverse point emphatically. The closing paragraphs of the book began:

> I do not wish to be accused of undue pride or unmerited assurance in my knowledge, but . . . because of the fact that I first produced a horseless carriage and that I have brought forward and perfected practically every fundamental automobile improvement or advance in the automobile . . . I was fitted to tell what points one should look for, or guard against, in buying an automobile.[39]

"I have not tried to sell the Haynes car," he reiterated. "I am proud enough of my work, sure enough of my principles, confident enough of the service, to know that the Haynes car sells itself." Emphasizing, then, that the Haynes was not a "commercial proposition" with him, but rather his contribution "to the great work of the world," he reviewed all of the innovations and improvements he claimed for himself and his company, including aluminum alloy engines, nickel steel axles, a throttling carburetor, electric ignition, the

---

[38] Haynes, *Complete Motorist*, p. 75.

[39] *Ibid.*, pp. 76–78.

magneto, and finally the electric gear shift. These had been either developed or first introduced "not for commercial reasons," a refrain used to begin each new category of achievement, but "because the Haynes is my life-work."[40] This last remark is perhaps the most incredible in the book, and proof of unacknowledged authorship, because in all of his other writings Haynes gives priority to metallurgical research, truly his "life-work."

Sales of the 1913 model, which featured electric lights, a self-starter, and, towards the end of the model year, a new six-cylinder engine, climbed to 1,488 cars and taxed plant capacity.[41] With the 1914 models, the new six-cylinder engine was continued, the Vulcan electric gear shifter was introduced, and sales mounted rapidly. Over 1,700 cars were sold in that year, and this figure jumped to 5,500 in 1915 and to 7,000 in 1916.[42]

In July, 1914, the company began marketing its "Light Six," a most popular car, and soon nothing but these six-cylinder models were in production at the plant.[43] The Haynes company's first sixes had been of the big bore (4½ inches), long stroke (5½ inches) type, and were both cumbersome and uneconomical, but these defects were largely overcome in a newly designed and lighter short-stroke engine introduced in its 1915 models. Throughout much of that year and into 1916, the Haynes factory operated day and night to keep up with the unprecedented demand.[44] As many as 100 cars a week were turned out during 1915, and this number increased the following year after substantial plant expansion. A four-story machine shop, a three-story paint shop, and a large test barn were added late in 1915, and new administrative headquarters were erected, thereby releasing an additional 9,000 square feet to the first assembly department.[45]

As A. G. Seiberling described the new plant, when the building plans were first announced in April, 1915, it was to incorporate "the principles of progressive production and progressive assembly."[46] Although the end result was a far cry from the continuously moving assembly line which Henry Ford installed in his huge plant in Detroit, the new design represented a marked improvement over the previous system. There were to be six major buildings and several smaller structures, designed so that chassis, painted and trimmed, and engines, thoroughly tested and tuned, would emerge into the final assembly building after the least possible travel. Then, as the chassis, to which the wheels and tires had been added, rolled slowly along a track, the final installations were made. Extensive railroad sidings delivered the stock to the departments where they were to be used.[47]

---

[40] *Ibid.*

[41] *Haynes Pioneer,* October, 1913, p. 5.

[42] *Ibid.*; Kokomo *Daily Tribune,* May 24, 1915. According to the story, the Haynes company had sold all of its anticipated 1915 "Light Six" production by April 1, 1915. During these years the company accounted for one third of the total output of motor cars in Indiana, a state second only to Michigan in automobile production.

[43] See the Kokomo *Sunday Dispatch,* September 19, 1915, for a long article describing the current operations at the Haynes plant. Labor conditions for the five hundred employees were termed "ideal." The plant was considered of the "most modern design, fireproof and daylight construction throughout," with good equipment on hand. "The Haynes is not an assembled car," the article emphasized but was totally designed and manufactured "in the Haynes factory under the direct supervision of the engineers and inspectors."

[44] On September 30, 1915, the Kokomo *Daily Dispatch* contained an article describing the Haynes Automobile Company in a special series on Kokomo plants working at night.

[45] Kokomo *Daily Tribune,* May 27, 1915; Kokomo *Daily Dispatch,* September 22, 1915; Kokomo *Sunday Dispatch,* September 26, 1915.

[46] "New Plant for Haynes," clipping, "Companies" file, Automotive History Collection.

[47] *Ibid.*

These construction plans and the continued growth of the Haynes company were sources of great civic satisfaction. The Haynes automobile had not only added significantly to Kokomo's economic life but also had given the city a measure of national fame. "One cannot go down into the midst of this plant and see all those men busy making the Haynes automobile, to be shipped all over the United States," reported one newsman in 1915, "without feeling that all the pride Kokomo has for the machine itself and the company's amazing progress is amply justified."[48] In that year the Haynes car was among the "top 20 sellers"—number 19—in the nation, and even greater developments were expected.[49]

The "Light Six," which had marked the Haynes company's departure from producing a relatively high-priced product to one more modestly priced, was largely responsible for the sales increase. (A company publication later said the "entire credit" for the company's success was due to the "famous Haynes Light Six."[50]) In 1917, the company entered its fourth year of producing this model and introduced a new twelve-cylinder line, with its advertisements featuring "America's Greatest Light Six" and "Light Twelve." These models ranged in price from $1,485 for a five-passenger open "Light Six" to $2,750 for a seven-passenger "Light Twelve" sedan.[51]

Late in 1915, in the midst of this prosperous period, Theodore Dreiser had returned to Indiana and visited the Haynes Automobile Company in the course of his travels (in a Pathfinder automobile) through his native state. These encounters resulted in a hastily written, often vitriolic travel narrative, *Hoosier Holiday*, published in 1916. First Dreiser recorded his generally favorable impression of the Haynes plant.

> At Kokomo, we had a most interesting experience. We met the man who made the first automobile in America, and saw his factory . . . which was employing, at the time we were there, nearly three thousand men and turning out over two thousand cars a year, nearly a car apiece for every man and woman in the place. I saw no children employed.

Dreiser was far off on his figures here; 1915, in fact, was one of the years of peak production for the Haynes Automobile Company and more than 5,000 units were manufactured by fewer than 1,000 employees. His biographical information on Haynes was also faulty, but when Dreiser moved from the realm of factual background information into a description of the factory as it appeared to him, more weight can be given his words. He was most impressed by the sights and sounds and smells of the factory and by the end results. "We pay very little, comparatively, for what we buy," he remarked, "considering the amount of time spent by thousands in supplying our idlest wants."[52]

The author found the Haynes plant to be "a fascinating spectacle," its lights aglow, the air permeated with "a friendly odor of smoke and hot mould sand and grease and shellac and ground metal," and the "great

---

[48] Kokomo *Daily Dispatch*, September 30, 1915.

[49] Some startling news regarding a proposed sale of the company was published in the latter part of 1916, but it failed to materialize and no additional information on this point has been located. See the Kokomo *Dispatch*, August 19, 23, 24, September 6, 20, and November 3, 1916.

[50] Special Supplement, Kokomo *Sunday Dispatch*, September 26, 1920.

[51] *Haynes Pioneer*, September, 1917, p. 1; see also such national journals as the *Saturday Evening Post* for 1916 and 1917.

[52] Theodore Dreiser, *Hoosier Holiday* (New York: John Lane Co., 1916), pp. 351–53.

rooms" filled with "droves of men . . . in jeans and jumpers, their faces and hands and hair stained brown or black with oil and smoke, their eyes alight with that keen interest which the intelligent workman always has in his work." The magnitude of the undertaking was equally impressive. "I never saw so many automobiles and parts of automobiles in all my life," Dreiser exclaimed, and "never imagined that there were so many processes through which all parts of a machine have to be put to perfect them, or that literally thousands of men do one little thing to every machine turned out." He was particularly intrigued by the mechanics "hovering over automobile motors attached in rows to gasoline tanks and being driven at an enormous rate of speed for days at a time without ever stopping, to test their durability and speed capacity."[53]

Following a tour of the plant, Dreiser and his companions met and conversed briefly with Haynes, an "affable and courteous" man, about his experiences in the automobile industry. Haynes told them his first automobile sale was to a doctor in Chicago who still had the car, although he had built the first car "with the idea of having one for myself, really." Following its completion, he borrowed enough money to begin manufacturing, taking in a partner. In response to Dreiser's "And then what?" he said, "Well, the machine was a success. We just grew. In a few months we were behind on our orders, and always have been since."[54]

Haynes's appearance both attracted and repelled Dreiser: "He was relatively undersized, quite stocky, with a round dumpling-like body, and a big, round head which looked as though it might contain a very solid mass of useful brains. He had the air of one who has met thousands, a diplomatic, cordial, experienced man of wealth." Dreiser thought that Haynes "looked quite sickly and preoccupied," and commented upon his habit of "folding both arms over his stout chest, and then lifting one or the other forearm and supporting his head with it, as though it might fall over too far if he did not." He also remarked upon Haynes's "grey-blue eyes, the eyes of the thinker and organizer." At first the men discussed the automobile and its comparative development in Europe and America, and then Haynes abruptly changed the subject:

> "But I'm not nearly so interested in automobiles as I was," he observed smilingly, at the same time diving into his pocket and producing what looked like a silver knife. "My son and I . . . have invented a thing which we call stellak [sic], which is five hundred times harder than steel and cuts steel just as you would cut wood with an ordinary knife."

Dreiser also quoted Haynes as saying that the alloy contained a certain quantity of steel, and that " 'All the processes are patented,' . . . as though he imagined we were looking too curiously into the workshop . . . and might desire to steal his ideas." In response to Dreiser's comment that there might be a "real fortune" in "stellak," Haynes agreed, "a kind of lust for money showing in his face, although he was already comfortably rich and daily growing richer as well as sicker."[55]

Dreiser concluded this account with some reflections on the emptiness of a materialistic culture, imputing to Haynes no other motives than the accumulation of wealth. But his analysis of Haynes is in conflict with almost every other published account and a host of unpublished reminiscences. The obvious errors in Dreiser's statements, particularly that "stellak," a non-ferrous alloy, contained steel and that it was "five hundred times harder than steel" (a false and meaningless statement), suggest what reliance should be given the Dreiser interpretation.

The year 1916 was notable for a promotion, unique at the time, undertaken by the company to find the oldest Haynes car still in operation. An 1897 model was discovered in Bound Brook, New Jersey, and the company ran a series of advertisements asking "Is this . . . the oldest Haynes in use?"

---

[53] *Ibid.*, pp. 352–53.

[54] *Ibid.*, p. 355.

[55] *Ibid.*, pp. 354, 355–56. For other, more flattering descriptions and assessments of Haynes see W. J. Morgan, "Motor Men I Have Met," in *Morgan's Message*, February, 1925, p. 13; W. A. P. John, "Looking Backward," in *MoToR*, January, 1922, p. 260.

They offered to exchange a new "Light Twelve" for the oldest Haynes located, the transfer to take place as part of the Good Roads Day program in the Indiana Centennial observation on October 12, 1916. Eventually an 1897 car slightly older than the New Jersey model was discovered in Jeffersonville, Indiana. It belonged to Edward J. Howard, president of the Howard Shipbuilding Company, who had purchased the car personally from Haynes in Kokomo in the summer of 1897. Governor Samuel M. Ralston presided over the presentation ceremony, which immediately preceded a speech by President Woodrow Wilson. The governor remarked that President Wilson's "employers" owned the very first car Haynes had built, on exhibit at the Smithsonian, and then gave Howard the keys to his new Haynes.[56]

The exuberance and prosperity which this type of activity reflected was soon dampened by United States entry into World War I. Automobile production after April, 1917, was drastically curtailed, although enough orders and supplies were on hand to make the year's total production (5,500) only 1,600 below that of 1916. The figures for 1918, when only 2,200 cars were sold, more truly reveal the decline in business caused by the war, but some alternative forms of production in support of the war effort were conducted. A. G. Seiberling went to Washington on several occasions in search of war contracts; among those received was one for four thousand truck motors.

When the war ended Seiberling and others made vigorous efforts to retain Haynes's share of the peacetime automobile market. The boom of 1919 and 1920 reflected war-delayed demand and boosted total automobile industry sales to 1,651,625 (1919) and 1,905,560 (1920), compared with 943,436 in 1918.[57] Although a letter from Haynes himself to an old Portland friend in November, 1919, expressed real doubts about the immediate future of the automobile industry,[58] the boom prompted yet another Haynes expansion program, the most ambitious one yet. By September, 1920, the company had completed a new four-story assembly building, 500 feet by 150 feet, complete with a moving final assembly line.[59] The Haynes company also embarked on one of its most ambitious and expensive advertising programs, led by its new advertising manager Gilbert U. Radoye, who joined the firm in 1919 after considerable experience with other companies. Radoye organized a new sales promotion department and claimed that his messages reached forty million newspaper readers each month and an additional twenty-three million magazine subscribers. His motto, published in *Haynes Successful Selling* magazine, was "Early to bed, early to rise, demonstrate every hour—and advertise."[60]

It is probable that Radoye's zealous approach touched off a new priority dispute with the Appersons, which flared up again in 1920. This clash, largely

---

[56] Kokomo *Dispatch,* October 7, 1916; *Haynes Pioneer,* November, 1916, pp. 6–7. Following the President's address, Howard's new and old cars were taken to the Indianapolis Motor Speedway and "raced." The 1897 model, according to the report, did "very well for itself" and ran 20 miles per hour.

[57] Chandler, *Giant Enterprise,* p. 4. In the Haynes company's rush to reconvert their plant to peacetime production, some customers felt they had been ill-treated. See Rodney Hallam to Elwood Haynes, July 12, 1919, and Elwood Haynes to "The Ever Tight Piston Ring Company," July 9, 1919, Haynes Papers. Haynes simply referred these complaints to company managers.

[58] Elwood Haynes to E. E. Sanders, November 21, 1919, Haynes Papers.

[59] Kokomo *Dispatch,* May 20, 1920.

[60] *Haynes Successful Selling,* October 27, 1923, p. 1. John Ryan, a commercial photographer for the Haynes company, worked closely with Radoye during these years. He described the man as a "feisty little Frenchman," hardworking, meticulous, and talented. Interview with John Ryan, Kokomo, July 18, 1971.

the product of the rival advertising departments of the companies and not of the principals involved, was beneficial at least in the quantity of factual data it put into the public view, particularly in the form of affidavits and testimonies.

It is not clear which company initiated the advertising war of 1920, for conflicting advertisements for both firms appeared on the same day—June 12, 1920. It appears, however, that Gilbert U. Radoye's activities were responsible for the outburst. One of his schemes was to release a film depicting the history of the automobile and Elwood Haynes's unique role in it. Radoye personally wrote and produced such a film in 1920, which unfortunately has not survived, and it may have been that some of the claims in it prompted the Apperson company's response. Radoye had notified Haynes in May, 1920, following his return from New York where he had been working on the film project, that "very soon we will get out some advertising which will 'clinch' the first car matter."[61] On the other hand, the Appersons had attempted some time early in 1920 to have the Smithsonian Institution revise its label on the Haynes "Pioneer," and these efforts may have touched off the controversy.[62]

Perhaps Radoye's "clincher" was a statement from Richard H. Lee, special counsel for the National Vigilance Committee of the Advertising Clubs of the World, whose slogan was "Truth in Advertising." Lee had been approached by the Haynes company to investigate whether or not its advertising claims, and even the Haynes plaque in the Smithsonian, were misleading or untruthful. Lee's reply to A. G. Seiberling was that "the credit for building the first car belongs to Mr. Elwood Haynes," and this statement appeared in a Haynes company advertisement carried in the Indianapolis *Star* on June 12, 1920.

The same day the Apperson Brothers Automobile Company placed a full-page advertisement in the Kokomo *Daily Tribune* giving "The Exact Facts Concerning Who Actually Built the First Mechanically Successful American Automobile." There is actually little disagreement in the "facts" as stated by the Apperson or the Haynes men, but the inferences drawn from them differ considerably. The Apperson advertisement implies more of a partnership than an employer-employee arrangement, and, after admitting that Haynes initiated the idea for the car, it suggests that the *three men* (Haynes and Elmer and Edgar Apperson) together discussed and developed the idea, with the Appersons doing the mechanical work of construction and assembly. The offending Smithsonian placard, however, did not even mention the Appersons, stating instead that the 1893-1894 "gasoline automobile" was *"built* [italics added] by Elwood Haynes."[63]

The Apperson charges were answered by the Haynes Automobile Company with "A Sworn Statement by Elwood Haynes," which was widely circulated, and the company also reprinted a number of the affidavits of workmen associated with Haynes and Apperson in the 1890s to substantiate its position. Seiberling prefaced his release of the Haynes statement with a strong defense of his employer's claims. "I want to say emphatically," he wrote, "that no other person has any right to lay claim to any of the honors which go with the inventing, designing and building of America's first mechanically successful automobile, because all credit rightfully belongs to Elwood Haynes alone." And he drew this analogy:

[61] Gilbert U. Radoye to Elwood Haynes, May 14, 1920, Haynes Papers.

[62] "A Sworn Statement by Elwood Haynes," *ibid.*

[63] Kokomo *Daily Tribune,* June 12, 1920.

Suppose that you had hit upon a great enterprise. Say you are an architect. You conceive, design and originate a new idea in skyscraper construction. You advertise the fact to the world that you are the inventor, designer and builder of this skyscraper. Some years later two of the laborers who actually placed the steel girders with their own hands become wealthy. They see the opportunity to capitalize wrongly on your brains, so they advertise that they are the actual builders of the skyscraper. You can see what position this puts you in. The public is partially deceived, and the credit, which[rightfully belongs to you, is somewhat absorbed by the untruthful claims of those you hired to build a reality.[64]

The article then carried the Haynes affidavit, which essentially repeats the story of Indiana's first automobile as Haynes had told it so often and so consistently. Haynes recognized that

there may have been some slight changes in the plans, to enable the workmen to follow them more easily, and if these minor changes constituted the designing and building of the car, then certainly the credit for it belongs to the Appersons. But if the engineering plan enabled them to carry out my ideas and instruction—the idea, the designing and the drawings and the general plan—then it seems to me the credit is mine.

He added, perhaps a bit ungenerously, "It would have been practically the same machine if built in any other machine shop in the world or by any other workmen." Haynes also claimed to have proposed the design for the famous Haynes-Apperson double-opposed motor, something which the Apperson company claimed for its founders.[65]

The controversy, of course, did not end there, and to some extent it still continues. The truth, it seems clear, lies somewhere between the extreme statements made by both parties in 1920, but Haynes deserved to be and generally has been recognized as the primary mover in the developments which led to his first car in 1893-1894. This was the collective judgment of his fellow townsmen, who became increasingly aware of Haynes's national and even international prominence in the postwar days. In 1919 Haynes was honored by the Kokomo Chamber of Commerce, a group Haynes had helped to establish in 1914, and a permanent memorial to the man and his inventions was to be erected in 1922.[66]

The Haynes company also built at least fifty dwellings for its employees in 1920. The company employed more than eighteen hundred persons and was Kokomo's largest and most famous business enterprise. Under Seiberling's leadership the Haynes firm had prospered, and sales were twenty times greater in 1920 than they had been in 1912 when he rejoined it. Indeed, the only dividends ever issued by the Haynes firm were paid during Seiberling's tenure, and between 1913 and 1920 "every stockholder who was in the business when Mr. Seiberling took charge, ha[d] received his original investment back in cash dividends." When a newspaper reporter asked Elwood

---

[64] "A Sworn Statement by Elwood Haynes," Haynes Papers.

[65] *Ibid.*

[66] See the *Haynes Pioneer,* April, 1914, p. 3; Kokomo *Daily Tribune,* February 13, 1919. The front page photograph in the newspaper was captioned, "Kokomo's First Citizen," and the write-up pointed out that the banquet was Kokomo's "first formal expression of appreciation to its fellow townsman who has attained international distinction as a scientist and inventor." The program included five adulatory speeches by business associates and friends on Haynes as a scientist, inventor, manufacturer, citizen, and man. In making his response, Haynes began with a story concerning an alleged meeting between General Grant and Mark Twain. He quoted Twain's remark following the effusive introductions, "General, I'm embarrassed, aren't you?"

The NEW Series HAYNES BROUGHAM

ROMANCE, social distinction, traveling luxury—these distinguished the Brougham in the old days of fine coaches and colonial manners.

In creating the new series Haynes Brougham, all the richness of appearance and supreme comfort of travel have been restored, with the added improvement of motoring flexibility and power.

The charming lines of the body appeal as much as do the wide doors, the deep-upholstered divan which forms the rear seat, the exquisite fittings and all the other thoughtfully incorporated conveniences which are so greatly admired by car connoisseurs. Exteriorly the new series Haynes Brougham conveys an expression of richness, exclusiveness and dignity. The new series Haynes Brougham seats comfortably five passengers.

The Haynes, America's first car, now exhibited by the Government at the Smithsonian Institution, National Museum, Washington, D. C., was invented, designed and built by Elwood Haynes, in 1893.

The beautiful Haynes Brochure, descriptive of all the new 1920 and new series Haynes character cars, will be mailed to you upon request. Address Dept. 466.

THE HAYNES AUTOMOBILE COMPANY
KOKOMO, INDIANA · · · · U.S.A.

HAYNES
CHARACTER CARS
Beauty ∿ Strength ∿ Power ∿ Comfort

1893 ∿ THE HAYNES IS AMERICA'S FIRST CAR ∿ 1920

Country Life, April, 1920

Haynes to account for the success of his automobile company in 1920, he responded simply, "Mr. Seiberling."[67]

Nevertheless, when Seiberling recommended that year that the Haynes company produce a small car, selling for less than $1,000, the board of directors rejected the suggestion. The least expensive car the company had ever produced was its 1915 Model 30, which had sold for $1,485, and for the company to have decided to produce a small, cheaper automobile would have required a drastic change in policy.[68] The 1920 advertising campaign,

---

[67] Kokomo *Dispatch,* September 26, 1920.

[68] A. G. Seiberling to Wallace S. Huffman, June 28, 1951, personal papers of Wallace S. Huffman; Kokomo *Tribune,* December 17, 1963. The newspaper account was an interview with Ross

for instance, stressed "Cars of Character" and appealed to the upper middle class. According to the Haynes "creed" that accompanied many of its advertisements in the 1920s, the company was determined to "build well, to build faithfully, to create intelligently, to hold character above any other consideration," enabling it to achieve "the four essential factors of car character: Beauty, Strength, Power and Comfort." Advertisements also featured a new five-passenger Brougham, a "sociable car" with swiveling front seats, and the new seven-passenger Suburban, which boasted either a single or a double closed compartment: a glass screen between the front and rear seats could be raised and lowered to make either an appropriate chauffeur-driven car or a family car.[69]

The Haynes people were obviously proud of their new plant and its product and published a special eight-page newspaper supplement in the fall of 1920 to celebrate themselves. Designed to acquaint the reader with company history, the backgrounds of the company's managers, the layout of the new assembly plant, and the new Haynes models, the publication was full of fascinating details. Much of the information was collected by an outsider, a Kokomo newspaper reporter whose by-line was simply "Jane," who had spent literally weeks going through the plant. She interviewed company officers and the entire management staff, including some thirty foremen, and wrote her account from a real or assumed bias of complete ignorance about things industrial and mechanical.

"Jane" began with a long, remarkably full and accurate biographical sketch of Elwood Haynes, followed by a somewhat shorter but revealing description of general manager A. G. Seiberling and even briefer comments about dozens of other Haynes Automobile Company employees. She toured practically every department in the plant, and her wide-eyed innocence apparently prompted each foreman to explain his department's work in simple but full detail. "Jane" reported that the forge shop, where fourteen air hammers pounded incessantly, "sounds like hell let loose," and she found the milling department "a wilderness of machines . . . with their overhead belts and their smell of oil and grease and their click-click and chang-chang and bing and slap and whirr-whirr noises going every second." The machine shop, where the parts for Haynes automobiles except for bodies and some casting were produced by the company's own furnaces, was "enormous and bewildering," but the new assembly plant, "a mammoth place," was even more confusing. She did her best, however, to describe the stamping presses in the sheet metal department, the parts, motor, transmission, and chassis assembly operations, and the simultaneous work in the "finishing departments," where the imported bodies were puttied, painted (repeatedly), padded, and polished to prepare them for the final assembly. This last operation took place on the second floor of the building, where the chassis, fitted with wheels and tires, were placed on carriers mounted on tracks. Moving along at a slow but steady pace, various items were added so that, at the other end of the floor a complete car emerged. "Testers" drove each finished vehicle down the ramp for final inspection and washing prior to shipment.[70]

In 1920 the Haynes automobile, "America's First Car," and Elwood Haynes's place in the history of the automobile both seemed securely estab-

---

Garrigus, editor of the Vincennes *Sun-Commercial* and a former employee in the advertising department of the Haynes Automobile Company.

[69] Kokomo *Dispatch*, September 26, 1910.

[70] *Ibid.*

lished. The company was prepared to build more cars than ever in its expensive new plant, and Haynes had won wide recognition as the inventor and builder of the 1894 car. In fact the Haynes automobile was to disappear within a few years, and Haynes's reputation as an automotive pioneer was to prove almost equally ephemeral.

Chapter 14

Crisis in the Automobile Company, 1921–1925

The postwar boom of 1919-1920 led to the bust of 1920-1921. The inflationary spurt had driven prices up nearly 100 percent since 1916 and had led to general overexpansion in the business community. The resulting recession created a severe crisis for the automobile industry, affecting even the giant Ford and General Motors companies. According to automotive historian Edward D. Kennedy, "the year's end [1920] found the industry in a state of almost complete paralysis, with only Ford running at anything approaching a normal pace."[1] Ford had to do this in order to survive, and he managed it only by forcing his cars on his dealers and requiring prompt cash payment from them upon delivery. In this way Ford would emerge from the crisis in a stronger competitive position than ever, owning 55 percent of the market. Whereas other manufacturers, including Haynes, would be unable to get the required loans, Ford used his dealers' credit, in effect, to obtain the capital he needed to continue production.[2]

"The automobile's first depression could hardly have been more complete," Kennedy continued, and, if 1920 was a bad year, 1921 was even worse.[3] For the first time the ability of the industry to produce automobiles had exceeded the ability of the public to purchase them. Competition from a growing used car market, moreover, threatened the continued expansion of new car sales, a situation that was largely responsible for the general adoption of new models annually.[4] Kennedy concluded that the automobile industry "price-cut" its way out of the depression.[5] In the squeeze between the high prices paid for materials and equipment in 1919 and 1920—the year the Haynes company remodeled and expanded—and the low prices received for automobiles in the next few years, many automobile companies failed. Among them were a number of the industry's pioneers: Apperson, Winton, Dorris, Maxwell, and also Haynes.

---

[1] Kennedy, *Automobile Industry,* p. 120.

[2] Chandler, *Giant Enterprise,* especially pp. 13, 87–92, 97.

[3] Kennedy, *Automobile Industry,* p. 129. See also Calvin Haynes to Edward Haynes, January 16, 1922, Haynes Papers. He reported that used cars worth $1,000 a year before were then worth only $500.

[4] Rae, *American Automobile,* pp. 79–80.

[5] Kennedy, *Automobile Industry,* p. 137.

The Haynes company's dual mistakes of acquiring a high-priced inventory and undertaking a huge expansion program in 1920 were not yet apparent in 1921. Although it was a bad year for the industry, Haynes production was up. At one point the assembly line reached a maximum production rate of sixty cars a day and in a banner week shipped 301 automobiles.[6] The company had decided to hold the line on prices and had even issued formal guarantees to its customers on this point, and the new Model 50, slightly smaller than the standard 1921 Haynes Models 47 and 48, was selling very well.

The company had begun to build its own automobile bodies in 1920 and boasted that their cars were at least "90% Kokomo made." In April, 1921, the Haynes company was reported to be the first of the big automobile manufacturers to announce a return to normal conditions.[7] Seiberling attributed this to the demand for the Haynes 50s. Many dealers, in fact, unwilling to wait for ordinary shipment by rail, came to the factory to take delivery. There were more than a hundred such "drive-aways" the first week in April, all going to dealers in Illinois and Iowa.[8] The Model 50s, listed at $1,985, were powered by the Haynes "Light Six" engine, and they boasted both a "brilliant Brewster green finish" and "genuine leather upholstery."[9] The larger, standard Haynes cars for 1921, Models 47 and 48, had a wheel base of 132 inches and were powered by either a six (Model 47) or a twelve (Model 48) cylinder engine; the six listed for $2,935 to $4,250, the more luxurious twelve for $3,635 to $4,950. These cars were all finished in "coach green," except for the bright red "special speedsters."[10]

In August, updated versions of these models were prominently displayed in Chicago's "Pageant of Progress." For the Haynes company, the pageant permitted a preview of its 1922 line. Model 55 was the successor to Model 50; Model 75, with its size optional, was the successor to both Models 47 and 48. Over a hundred of these cars, the first trainload of 1922s shipped by the company, paraded along the Windy City's municipal pier. Mayor "Big Bill" Thompson rode in the "honor car" with Elwood Haynes, A. G. Seiberling, and Sidney Smith, the cartoonist for the Chicago *Tribune*.[11] One man, obviously very much impressed by what he had seen, wrote a congratulatory message

190

---

[6] Kokomo *Dispatch*, June 19, 1921. Walter M. Haynes had complained to his brother Elwood when Seiberling was brought in that their brother Calvin, the previous general manager, was being made the "scapegoat" in the matter, but he must have been pleased at the results of the change. Walter Haynes retained, however, a distrust and a resentment of Seiberling, whose lifestyle was unlike that of the Hayneses, and he was quick to blame Seiberling for the reversal of fortunes the company suffered in the 1920s. Calvin Haynes for his part went to San Francisco, where he became the west coast distributor for Haynes automobiles. He remained in California following the company's demise and died there in 1949. In 1951 Seiberling commented upon Calvin Haynes's attempt to use grocery store methods (he had been a wholesale grocer in Portland before going to Kokomo) in the automobile business. Walter M. Haynes to Elwood Haynes, May 8, 1912, Haynes Papers; A. G. Seiberling to Wallace S. Huffman, June 28, 1951, personal files of Mr. Huffman, Kokomo, Indiana.

[7] Kokomo *Dispatch*, April 3, 1921.

[8] *Ibid.*; see also *ibid.*, April 8, 1921.

[9] *Ibid.*, May 20, 1920, April 3, 1921. The headlines for the latter story in the "Special Automobile Edition" read, "New Haynes is a Big Sensation in Auto World."

[10] "Prices of the New 1921 Haynes Character Cars," 1921 folder, Haynes Papers. All models except the speedsters had wooden wheels and cord tires, although wire wheels, standard on the speedster, were available at $150 extra; disc wheels were $250 extra. In 1922, after race driver Howard Wilcox drove a Model 75 speedster around the Indianapolis Motor Speedway track at 75 miles per hour, the company designated the car its "blue ribbon" special. Each car sold thereafter had a blue ribbon attached to the steering wheel bearing a message from Wilcox. "Companies" file, 1922, Automotive History Collection, Detroit Public Library.

[11] General Folder, 1922, Haynes Papers. The story of the pageant, circulated by the Haynes advertising department, carried a picture of the mayor, Haynes, and Seiberling.

to Haynes. "After looking over our great 'Pageant of Progress' and the new 1921 [*sic*] 'Haynes' there," he stated, "I feel that perfection has been reached in automobile achievement. I wish to congratulate you on your Success in bringing to us such a marvel of motordom, and send you my personal regards to the Inventor of America's First Car." Hereafter, he promised, he would "consider you in a Class with Edison, Carnige [*sic*] & others that have done and are doing things that make America Great."[12]

Five months later the new 55s and 75s were exhibited at the New York Automobile Show, the company calling them the product of twenty-eight years of experience. The "new improved Haynes 55 . . . is not, in any sense of the word, an experiment. It is a combination of proved transportation units, tried and verified, part by part, built and rebuilt, subjected to every conceivable test of the most rigid character by Haynes engineers throughout a long period." The company literature also called the Haynes 55 "the typification of the ideal medium-weight, medium-priced automobile, the crowning achievement of more than a quarter of a century of motor car manufacture."[13]

The price on the new 55s, moreover, was $200 below that of the 50s, which prompted at least one complaint and a refund request from a purchaser of the 1921 model. Haynes, as usual, referred the matter to Seiberling for his disposition, and so notified the buyer, but he responded further by saying that "you got a wonderful value for your money when you purchased our Model 50. It is a splendid machine and so far as I am aware everyone who had purchased this model is highly pleased with its operation and sterling qualities." Haynes then candidly pointed out that the price reduction on the 55s "was at our expense." Even at slightly reduced labor costs, the company was "not making any money on either [1922] model," although as the cost of materials decreased they hoped "to make some profit a little later on."[14]

Evidently these hopes were realized, even though the profit was quite small. Sales in 1922 started off briskly. A weekly production schedule of thirty cars was set up in January.[15] The first quarter report indicated total sales of 1,177 cars, up 68½ percent over the comparable period for 1921; sales amounted to 2,592 cars by the end of May and ended at 5,915 for the year. This generated a gross income of $9,497,039, an amount remarkably close to the company's total assets as of June, 1922.[16] At the outset of the

[12] Lewis H. Winterson to Elwood Haynes, August 15, 1921, *ibid*. Haynes replied to Winterson on August 21, sending along some data on the new 75s. The car could climb hills at nine miles per hour in high gear, or reach sixty-five miles per hour on the open road in the same gear.

[13] New York *Evening Telegram,* January 9, 1922. The Haynes company, of course, appeared regularly at the New York, Chicago, and Indianapolis automobile shows. For the 1921 show in New York, the company took along the 1897 model it had obtained from Mr. Howard in 1916 and displayed it after Mayor Hylan had been given a ride down Broadway in the antique. Clipping, January 12, 1921, Haynes Papers.

[14] Elwood Haynes to Walter H. Brown, September 5, 1921, Haynes Papers.

[15] W. R. MacConnell to A. E. Starbuck, January 7, 1922, *ibid.*

[16] "Financial Statements," June, 1922, "Manufacturing Costs," 1922, General Folder 2, 1922, *ibid.* The latter document indicates manufacturing costs of only $3,678,251.51, but this must have been a partial accounting. The "manufacturing profit" for April, 1922, when over 10 percent of the sales for the year were recorded, was given at $142,059.53. This would indicate earnings of perhaps as much as $1,500,000 for the year but not four times that much. The figures for May, when over 12 percent of the year's total was sold, show earnings of only $35,137.05. If these figures held for the year, they would mean an annual profit in 1922 of only $422,000. The latter amount is probably closer to the actual figure; Elwood Haynes later remarked that company earnings for the period from 1914 to 1920 equaled $4,000,000.

year, the company was behind on some "200 small accounts," amounting to $40,000, despite a $25,000 loan from Haynes to the company during the previous year. As a result, in spite of the good sales record for 1922, the financial situation was far from satisfactory, and greater sales were needed to get the company back into the black.

Ironically it was in the midst of this financial turmoil that Elwood Haynes was honored in a memorial celebration by the city of Kokomo. The idea for a memorial may have come from W. A. P. John, a writer whose long interview with Haynes was published in *MoToR* in January, 1922. At least John publicized the lack of a marker to commemorate Haynes's famous first automobile trip. During the course of John's interview, he had been taken to the spot where, twenty-seven years before, the first run had been made. When asked where the marker was, "Mr. Haynes smiled. 'There isn't any,' he answered." This prompted John to suggest that

> some group—either the citizens of Kokomo, a city which owes an incalculable debt to the genius of Elwood Haynes, or the representative builders of automobiles in America—might well spend a few hundred dollars to commemorate in some enduring form an event whose importance has equal parity with Fulton's first trip up the Hudson, or with the transmission of the first message by telegraph.[17]

Whatever its origin, the plan to stage a Fourth of July celebration in honor of Elwood Haynes on the twenty-eighth anniversary of his first motorized trip along Pumpkinvine Pike mushroomed. Initially publicized by the Haynes Automobile Company, the official sponsors for the extravaganza became the Indiana Historical Commission and the Hoosier State Automobile Association. Representatives of the State of Indiana, the National Automobile Chamber of Commerce, the Indiana Federation of Women's Clubs, and the city of Kokomo also participated. The local Chamber of Commerce band provided music, Battery A of the 150th Field Artillery unit of the National Guard fired a twenty-one-gun salute, and a solitary airplane thrilled the crowd of 7,000 with its aerial acrobatics at the close of festivities.[18]

Dr. George L. McIntosh, president of Wabash College, delivered the featured address, reviewing the history of transportation. He placed Haynes as the "inventor" of the automobile in the company of Alexander Graham Bell and Thomas A. Edison, calling them "the three great living American inventors."[19] Following this a granite monument bearing a plaque, made appropriately enough of Stellite, was unveiled. Its text reads as follows:

> In Commemoration of Elwood Haynes of Kokomo, Indiana, the inventor, designer, and builder of America's first mechanically successful automobile, in the year eighteen hundred and ninety three. This tablet marks the road, and starting place, where Elwood Haynes on July 4, 1894, seated in America's First Car, made the run. Here, too, was the birthplace of a new era of transportation, the nucleus and beginning of the now gigantic automobile industry, 1893–4.

---

[17] John, "Looking Backward," in *MoToR*, January, 1922, p. 89.

[18] July, 1922, folder, Haynes Papers. This folder contains a number of items printed both preceding and following the celebration. See especially the attractive eight-page brochure, "In Honor of Elwood Haynes," which provides a full report on the dedication ceremonies and is profusely illustrated.

[19] Press Release, July 5, 1922, *ibid.*

The sponsors' news release concerning this occasion reported that Haynes responded to this lavish praise with his usual "fine modesty" and told amusing stories about his early work with the "Pioneer." And, of course, he thanked his fellow townsmen.[20] They and others had combined to make July 4, 1922, one of the happiest days in the life of Elwood Haynes. A scientist and inventor honored in his adopted hometown while still alive, Haynes appreciated the rarity of the situation and was deeply touched by the tributes he had received.

This event was given considerable attention in the state and national press, and Pathé News was on hand to record its highlights on film. President Harding did not attend but sent a message which was read to the crowd. The federal government responded in other ways, too; the Smithsonian Institution made a rare concession and permitted one of its permanent exhibits, Haynes's first car, to be taken to Kokomo for display during the anniversary observation. Indiana Congressman Fred Purnell, whose photograph sitting in the car was widely reprinted, had helped arrange the special exhibit, and the presence of the "Pioneer" undoubtedly added to the impressiveness of the occasion. Unfortunately, the vehicle suffered considerable damage during its journeys in 1922. A large number of persons climbed in, on, and around it during its period of public display, and it appears that Haynes Automobile Company employees also drove the car around in the garage during its temporary storage in Kokomo.[21]

Five months later, in December, 1922, in an effort to lift their dangerously sagging sales, the Haynes Automobile Company announced a "new sales policy," i.e., an increased number of dealers and outlets and a substantial price cut. The smallest Haynes touring car was now priced at $1,595, and its seven-passenger touring car or speedster was $2,395. A company news release predicted an increase of 9,000 sales in 1923 to make a total of over 14,000; instead, sales dropped by 1,600 to only 4,300 for the year.[22]

Indeed, 1923 was the year in which the bottom dropped out of the Haynes company. The financial condition of the company steadily worsened, and it was unable to meet its obligations as bank loan payments became due. In desperation the company introduced a small car, the Model 60, priced at only $1,295, in June, 1923, but it was too little and too late. Moreover, a chief competitor, Buick, had introduced its new small car a week before the Haynes, and it sold for only $1,200. Haynes wrote in some bewilderment to his brother in October that it was incredible the company "could get into such an awful mess, within so short a time."[23]

At first a remedy was sought through a proposed merger with two other automobile companies. All three companies—Winton of Cleveland, Dorris of St. Louis, and Haynes of Kokomo—were pioneers in the industry, and it was hoped that their combination into the Consolidated Motors Corporation, to be capitalized at nineteen million dollars, would solve the immediate problem. Each company had a "well defined appeal and place in the market," and the product of each would continue. Both the Haynes and Dorris company stockholders agreed to the proposal in June, 1923, but the Winton people

[20] *Ibid.*

[21] Don H. Berkebile to author, January 11, 1971; interview with Fred Hawkins, Kokomo, January 22, 1971.

[22] Calvin Haynes to Elwood Haynes, January 1, 1922, Haynes Papers; New York *Times,* December 12, 1922; *Automobile Topics,* December 9, 1922, p. 323.

[23] Elwood Haynes to Walter M. Haynes, October 20, 1923, Haynes Papers.

Elwood Haynes addressing the crowd in Kokomo at commemoration ceremony, July 4, 1922

delayed, and in September the merger plans were abandoned.[24] It is doubtful, in any case, that combining three financially troubled companies would have helped.

By the fall of 1923, instead of a merger, plans were well underway to refinance the Haynes Automobile Company. This attempt was made urgent and more complicated because of the lawsuits filed or threatened by various of the company's creditors. Unless the creditors agreed to an extension of the repayment period based upon the refinancing plan, bankruptcy was imminent.[25] The preferred stockholders also had to authorize a bond issue before it would be permitted, but as March Haynes explained to his sister, "Your preferred stock is not worth much unless we sell bonds and get enough new money in the concern to continue manufacturing."[26]

The financial crisis also prompted a major personnel reorganization. A. G. Seiberling, whose relationship with the Portland Hayneses had never been good, was increasingly blamed by them for the company's misfortunes despite his earlier successes. Other complaints were directed at Radoye and his high-handed treatment of dealers. Consequently, following an emergency board meeting in September, for which Calvin Haynes was called in from San Francisco, both Seiberling and Radoye were fired.[27] S. E. Burke succeeded Radoye as sales and advertising manager at once, but the identity of the new general manager was kept secret until a refinancing meeting was held in November, 1923.

The company appeared to have a future if the refinancing plan could succeed. The plan rested upon the citizens of Kokomo pledging to buy at least a million dollars' worth of Haynes Automobile Company bonds; the company directors had already pledged themselves to raise an additional half million from their own resources; and outside sources were expected to take up another million in bonds. A vigorous campaign to sell the bonds was mounted in December, following its authorization by the stockholders in November. "The people of the city are taking hold of the movement with great earnestness," Haynes explained to a disgruntled investor in Kentucky, and he expressed his hope that its success would permit the company to "pay ultimately dollar for dollar with interest to all concerned."[28]

The efforts to "Save the Haynes" in 1923 were indeed vigorous. A bond campaign committee, with headquarters in the YMCA building, was organized, staffed largely by Haynes company personnel—directors, officers,

---

[24] Kokomo *Dispatch*, June 17, 1923; *Automobile Topics*, May 26, 1923, p. 120; compare Kennedy, *Automobile Industry*, p. 155; Philip Hillyer Smith, *Wheels within Wheels: A Short History of American Motor Car Manufacturing* (New York: Funk & Wagnalls, 1968), p. 87.

[25] See J. W. Johnson to Charles N. Gillette, October 6, 1923, Haynes Papers, requesting assistance in getting a bank loan extension (insistence on immediate payment would drive the company into receivership); and Ernest F. Brandon to Elwood Haynes, October 26, 1923, *ibid.*, notifying Haynes that the Equitable Trust Company loan of $122,500, "guaranteed by you," was overdue.

[26] March Haynes to Bernice Haynes Hillis, November 14, 1923, *ibid.* Letters to the preferred stockholders had been sent in July, inviting them to exchange their stock, on which dividends were last paid in 1921, for common stock in a new organization, but this met with resistance. See, for example, Anna D. Green to Elwood Haynes, August 29, 1923, *ibid.*

[27] Charles F. Headington to Elwood Haynes, August 20, 1923, Bernice Haynes Hillis to March Haynes, November 6, 1923, *ibid.* Headington, Haynes's brother-in-law, was the brother of Ernest Headington, the Haynes agent in New York.

[28] Elwood Haynes to Sarah L. Humphrey, November 8, 1923, *ibid.* Mrs. Humphrey, a widow, had asked Haynes for preferential treatment. "You of course understand that we can not discriminate in favor of any creditor or stockholder," he replied, "but must treat all alike." A number of such personal appeals, however, particularly after the company had failed, added considerably to the anguish that accompanied the bankruptcy.

and volunteer workers—and community business leaders. J. W. Johnson, a
director and head of the Kokomo Iron and Steel Company, was chairman of
the committee; Elwood Haynes was its treasurer; and sixteen other members
were listed on the letterhead of the committee's special stationery. Mack A.
Brown, of the local Chamber of Commerce, wrote one of the several appeals
of the committee "to Kokomo Folks." In a two-page letter, Brown emphasized the value of the Haynes plant to the city of Kokomo—"a money
maker" in the past now struggling to overcome its losses in the "1921
business slump." An average of 1,300 persons were employed there daily,
earning an average weekly payroll of $32,035.66; moreover, the Haynes com-
pany had paid 8 percent of the city's tax revenues over the previous five
years.[29]

Some pledges were obtained immediately, and the hard and persistent
labors of the committee steadily brought more. By the year's end, the committee was still short of its million dollar goal, but a series of last minute
meetings and appeals, particularly in plants around the city, brought the
committee to within $45,000 of the top. Fund raising continued the first two
days of the new year, and when a gala victory celebration was held on the
evening of January 2, 1924, $2,000 more than the goal had been raised.[30] A
jubilant crowd swarmed to the automobile plant to hear the speakers and
share in the excitement. "It was a great night for Kokomo," reported the
Kokomo *Tribune*. "Sedate, hard-headed men of affairs forgot their dignity
and effervesced with gleeful triumph that found a safety-valve in whoops of
joy, whistling, singing that was pretty awful, and the vigorous thumping of
one another upon the back. Such antics at another time," the paper predicted, would have led to a "riot call." When speeches were requested, a
number of committee officers responded. As Haynes rose to speak, he was
greeted with "one of the greatest ovations in all the history of his long and
honored career." "Words are inadequate," he began, "to express my fullness
at the consummation of this greatest achievement. Nothing in reason is
impossible in this community. You have demonstrated it. I thank you one
and all from the bottom of my heart." Following these remarks Hayden
Eames was announced as the new general manager; he spoke briefly and was
cheered enthusiastically.[31] All of the speakers predicted success in marketing the remaining bonds and in restoring the company to solvency.

Eames came to Haynes highly recommended. He had been general manager of three other automobile companies—Pope, Garford, and Studebaker.
One of Eames's associates at the Pope company, Hiram P. Maxim, described
him memorably:

> Hayden Eames was an intensely interesting character. No man who met him
> ever forgot him. He was one of those blue-eyed, handsome thoroughbreds they
> raise in the State of Maine more frequently than anywhere else I know of. He
> stood erect, looked you over in a stern way, and had you on the defensive in the
> first few minutes. He had graduated from the Naval Academy at Annapolis, had
> been to sea, had seen considerable navy diplomatic service as aide to the
> admiral of one of the fleets, and had been about everywhere on earth. He was a
> great reader, remembered everything he had read, and had the most amazing
> vocabulary ever bestowed upon mortal man. His emotions were just barely
> under control all the time. To hold himself in leash required a superhuman
> effort day and night. He was profane to a degree, but intellectually and poeti-

[29] "To Kokomo Folks," Haynes Automobile Company Folder, Huffman Collection.

[30] March Haynes to Bernice Haynes Hillis, January 2, 192[4], Haynes Papers.

[31] Kokomo *Daily Tribune*, January 3, 1924.

cally so; never was he vulgar. When he lost his grip on his emotions he would launch forth into an epic of profanity that was nothing short of inspiring. Many times have I listened to one of his profane perorations with the same enraptured feeling which I enjoy when listening to great music. Eames' energy defied description. He fairly boiled from morning to night. Until you became accustomed to him he would tire you out—it would wear you down to a nervous frazzle merely to be in his presence for half an hour.[32]

The enthusiasm which swept the January 2 celebration carried over in the daily operations. Before the end of the month the conditions for receiving the pledges had been fulfilled, the first call was made on the pledges, and the company had more orders for cars than it could fill. Eames announced that the company, which months earlier had "hung precariously upon the verge of bankruptcy," was then on the road to recovery. "I've brought a number of sick industries out of the hole," he added, "but none ever revived so quickly as the Haynes Automobile Company is doing."[33]

But this diagnosis was overly sanguine. The new Model 60s, upon which the hopes of the company were based,[34] did not sell well, and an uncharacteristic "hard sell" campaign directed by S. E. Burke was unproductive, perhaps even counterproductive because of the financial outlay it required.[35] The dual factors of high price and poor design on the 60s were largely responsible for the poor reception—only 1,500 sales for the entire year. As company treasurer A. E. Starbuck emphasized in April, 1924, "our problem now is a sales problem and not a financial one, for the finances will take care of themselves if we can only sell our product."[36]

Because the cars were "moving rather slowly" and the dealers were slow in paying their drafts, additional bond sales were required in April. These were handled by the Edward Miller Company, whose president requested a statement concerning Haynes's character from his minister, evidently planning to use it in his sales approach. The Reverend Hurd Allyn Drake's reply was an unqualified endorsement:

Elwood Haynes is the kind of man who would sell his own house from over his head before he would see anyone suffer loss through any fault of his. He has spent the best years of his life in Kokomo and is, not only our most prominent, but also our best loved citizen. His integrity has never been questioned and his character is such as to inspire universal confidence.

As to his business ability, the outstanding success of the Haynes Stellite Company is evidence of his careful painstaking policies. Mr. Haynes is not a plunger and is not anxious for spectacular results. In my judgement the best thing that has happened to the Haynes Automobile Company in connection with its refinancing campaign is the reentrance of Mr. Haynes into active personal participation in the management of this, our greatest industry.[37]

---

[32] Maxim, *Horseless Carriage Days,* p. 28. This book was dedicated to Hayden Eames.

[33] Kokomo *Daily Tribune,* January 30, 1924. Production for the first week in February was set at eighteen per day, after a rate of only four a day "for months." *Automobile Topics,* February 2, 1924, p. 1301.

[34] Fred C. Headington to Elwood Haynes, September 6, 1923, Elwood Haynes to Fred C. Headington, September 17, 1923, Haynes Papers.

[35] See *Motor Age,* December 20, 1923, p. 8, and January 7, 1924, p. 197, for examples of the new campaign. Burke was promoting a new "Haynes Merchandising Plan" (with details to be available upon request) which "positively cannot fail to jump your sales ahead," but he admitted that automobile dealers had not responded. *Ibid.,* p. 197.

[36] A. E. Starbuck to Ernest W. Headington, April 28, 1924, Haynes Papers.

[37] March Haynes to Charles F. Headington, April 17, 1924, Hurd Allyn Drake to E. M. Miller, April 14, 1924, *ibid.*

When Haynes learned of these developments, he immediately ordered Miller not to use the Drake letter in seeking bond sales. He did, however, review for Miller the company's history from its difficult recovery following the 1911 fire through "an unprecedented period of success and prosperity." This had been followed by an $8 million "overpurchase of material" during a time of inflated prices, which accounted for the company's "present rather limited activities." Despite still being "heavily in debt," the company, Haynes believed, had a "fighting chance, under careful management" to recuperate fully. He closed by clarifying Drake's final point—that not he but an executive board, working with "the most competent manager that could be obtained," was directing company affairs.[38]

Even so, Haynes was directly and almost daily involved in the refinancing and reorganization efforts of mid-1924. It was his practice to come to the office in the late afternoon, accompanied by his dog Duke, and handle the necessary correspondence by dictation. Despite his financial worries, he remained cheerful and approachable, ever accessible to anyone for at least a brief conversation.[39] During these months he made repeated personal loans to the company, guaranteed loans tendered by others, and paid the assessments made upon the company directors for himself as well as assisting his brother Calvin and the Headingtons in paying theirs. All the directors divided the responsibility of paying the assessments upon A. G. Seiberling, a director no longer able to make any payments whatsoever. Haynes, pointing out that he had "put a large amount of money in the automobile business since the first of the year," was unable to make a personal loan to a relative in 1924 (he had perhaps $125,000 of such loans outstanding upon his death the following year), and he continued to concentrate on company affairs.[40] In May, 1924, he wired an urgent request to Calvin Haynes in San Francisco, saying that he was needed at the factory and asking him to come to Kokomo for at least three months.[41] Calvin, however, who had once acted as the general manager of the company, declined the invitation. Although he wanted to help, he considered the operations "too big." "I know my limitations better than anyone else," he said.[42]

By summer 1924, the situation was critical. Hayden Eames's leadership of the Haynes company had turned out to be anything but successful; he was accused of having foolishly squandered the money so laboriously raised in the bond drive of 1923-1924, and his departure from the company in July, 1924, preceded its bankruptcy by only two months. During the summer of 1924, Charles F. Headington, Haynes's New York agent, in particular had voiced his objections to Eames, Burke, and "the entire crowd of mere Money Spenders." He preferred to return to family management; "[let us] quit this awful overhead expense, and let's get to selling and making cars. We have as good a car as any made in the United States."[43] In Kokomo there were desperate efforts to keep the company afloat in June, July, and August. Almost $3 million in cash was needed to meet the immediate demands. At

---

[38] Elwood Haynes to E. M. Miller, April 17, 1924, *ibid.*

[39] Interview with Zuma Marquis, Kokomo, January 2, 1971.

[40] Elwood Haynes to Walter Headington, June 23, 1924, Haynes Papers. He did send a "gift" of $100 to his nephew at that time.

[41] Elwood Haynes to Calvin Haynes, May 9, 1924, *ibid.*

[42] Calvin Haynes to Elwood Haynes, May 9, 1924, *ibid.*

[43] Charles F. Headington to Elwood Haynes, July 21, 24, 1924, *ibid.;* see also *ibid.,* July 23, August 7, 11, 1924.

one point Elwood Haynes approached Henry Ford, suggesting that his purchase of the Haynes plant would serve to "fill the gap between your small car and the Lincoln, and would enable you to respond to the market for a car of almost any class," but Ford's perfunctory reply merely stated that he was unable to consider the proposition.[44]

The following month another plan to save the company was drawn up by Burns and Burns, a Philadelphia firm about which Haynes subsequently received alarming reports of disrepute. The plan called for new bond issues and creditors accepting as payment in full fifty cents on the dollar, but it fell through.[45] This plan would have required the directors personally to take up loans amounting to $594,000, as well as providing $500,000 in new money; the merchandise creditors were to accept bonds in the new company for 50 percent of their claims, and a new general manager would be appointed in whom the creditors had confidence.[46] Although Hayden Eames had been dismissed in July, his appointed replacement, referred to only as a "secret executive . . . of the highest and broadest standing," would not be announced until the stockholders authorized the refinancing plan at their meeting called for September, 1924.[47]

Haynes was not confident of success. He wrote to a Portland acquaintance in August that "the future does not look at all hopeful." In all probability the common stockholders would realize nothing more on their holdings, and Haynes himself stood to lose not only all his "holdings in the company, but a great deal more which I have advanced from time to time, in an effort to prevent disaster."[48] Indeed, the expected collapse came in September, just days before the new reorganization and refinancing plan were to be considered. Two minor creditors and the Chicago firm hired by Eames to sell bonds in April, 1924, filed suit in federal court seeking a receivership for the Haynes company. As a consequence all manufacturing stopped at the Haynes plant on September 2, 1924, where three hundred men had been working three days a week; only thirty-five remained on hand to operate the service department.[49]

Thus it was a meeting of Haynes company creditors, not stockholders, that took place on September 5. There was some discussion of a merger with the Apperson company, holding forth the prospect of the reappearance of a Haynes-Apperson automobile, but this was not possible, given the embarrassed financial condition of both companies. Instead the suit for receivership proceeded, and the Haynes company was declared bankrupt in October; the trustee appointed by the court to handle company affairs was Robert L. Tudor. He supervised the liquidation of the manufacturing stock (handled in part by assembling two hundred more cars in December, 1924,

---

[44] Elwood Haynes to Henry Ford, June 4, 1924, E. G. Liebold to Elwood Haynes, June 16, 1924, Henry Ford Office File, 1921, Ford Archives, Dearborn, Michigan.

[45] This plan is described in some detail in *Automobile Topics*, July 26, 1924, p. 1016. See also the telegrams from New York and Philadelphia, dated July 16 and 18, to Haynes company officers regarding Burns and Burns's lack of standing in financial circles. One report said the company was "absolutely no good. Have reputation of big fake promoter. Better watch your step." Ernest W. Headington to A. E. Starbuck, July 18, 1924, Haynes Papers.

[46] *Automobile Topics*, August 20, 1924, p. 216. There are numerous letters and drafts of proposed financing plans in the Haynes Papers, but the records are insufficient to clarify them completely.

[47] *Ibid.*

[48] Elwood Haynes to Amy Moore, August 30, 1924, Haynes Papers.

[49] Kokomo *Daily Tribune*, September 3, 1924.

The Haynes brothers: l. to r., front row, Sumner, Walter, and Fred Headington, a business associate; back row, Calvin, Elwood, Edward

and January, 1925, from the materials on hand), two or three attempts to resume regular operations under leasing agreements, and the final disposition of the plant and equipment. A sale of these assets was scheduled for January 22, 1925, but all of the bids received were rejected. Reset for February 19, 1925, the bondholders then bid the amount of their bonds and acquired the plant for $750,000. They also bought the inventory and other materials not covered by the mortgage for an additional $125,000 in cash, but their efforts to operate the plant soon failed.[50]

In the meantime, the directors were faced with the responsibility of paying off the company loans which had been guaranteed by them. These loans amounted to nearly $500,000, with Haynes responsible for almost 20 percent of this amount ($94,774). In addition, Haynes had lost $60,000 in preferred stock and all of his common stock, valued in 1920 at $275,700, and "substantial" amounts on the bonds he had purchased in the drives of 1923 and 1924. Three "outside bank loans," totaling $385,000, were the most pressing debts of the company directors in the fall of 1924, and $100,000 in payments were delayed until February, but Haynes was conscientious in trying to meet his obligations as they came due, as well as in helping out a number of the other

---

[50] March Haynes to James B. Helme, March 27, 1925, Haynes Papers; *Automobile Topics*, February 14, 1925, p. 19, February 28, 1925, pp. 202, 205. Tudor sold and leased some of the Haynes company buildings in 1926; final disposition of the matter, with a tiny distribution of assets to the creditors, came in 1933.

directors. The bondholders, of course, had to seek a distribution of the company assets for their returns, which proved to be very small, and all of the stock, both preferred and common, became worthless. All in all, Elwood Haynes lost "hundreds of thousands of dollars in cash, besides the loss of all my holding in the company." He estimated it would take him two to three years to get back on his feet financially.[51]

In summary, the real trouble had begun in 1920 when, despite inflated prices, the company stocked an eight million dollar inventory and undertook a one million dollar building expansion program, for which the money had to be borrowed. With the price deflation in late 1920, the company ran into financial distress from which it was unable to extricate itself. Although the "Million Dollar Bond Campaign" was nominally successful and six hundred thousand dollars were actually received on the pledges, the new management, in March Haynes's view, "wasted" the money.[52] Forced into bankruptcy in 1924, the company and its assets were sold to the bondholders in February, 1925, and subsequently liquidated.

In 1951, A. G. Seiberling gave his analysis of the company failure. He noted that "the appearance of volume or mass production in the early twenties caused the business to wane" and that all small manufacturers like Haynes failed. No one, he felt, was to blame, although "the blame was placed on me" and the "reward for twenty years of arduous labor" was "to have my life absolutely ruined." Even though he had little respect for Eames, his successor, he recognized that no one could have saved the plant under the policies followed. He added, however, that if the company had carried through with his idea for a small car selling at under $1,000 in 1920, it might have been a different story. Walter M. Haynes, however, "got in his handiwork and killed the deal." Seiberling considered Haynes's banker brother a "genuine menace" in company affairs; he may have known how to run a $25,000 bank, but his manufacturing ideas were "radical" and disastrous to the company. In fact, Seiberling considered the entire board of directors incapable of managing the business after it had grown so large, although he exempted Elwood Haynes from this general indictment. An "honorable, fair and square" man, he "was very proud [of] the name Haynes and its connection with America's First Car. Personally," he added, "I always felt that these matters had more or less to do with his rather premature passing."[53]

Undoubtedly Haynes was deeply affected by these events, financially as well as psychologically. His personal losses were great, far exceeding the amount earned from the automobile business from the beginning, and it pained him to see his friends, who had invested in his company because they had faith in him personally, lose their investments. "Taking it all together," Haynes wrote in a bald understatement in April, 1925, just six days before his death, "this Haynes Auto Business has certainly been a trial to us all. . . ."[54]

Haynes rejected the idea, however, that he was a fit object for sympathy or pity. He took solace in the knowledge that he had done all that was possible to avert the company's collapse and had "sacrificed several hundreds of thousands of dollars which I had made from another source," and he counted his blessings in other areas. His family was well, both his children were married and living nearby, and he fully expected to recoup financially

---

[51] Elwood Haynes to E. S. Shumaker, December 9, 1924, Haynes Papers.

[52] March Haynes to James B. Helme, March 27, 1925, *ibid.*

[53] A. G. Seiberling to Wallace S. Huffman, August 4, 1951, personal files of Mr. Huffman.

[54] Elwood Haynes to Walter M. Haynes, April 9, 1925, Haynes Papers.

in two or three years. With his son handling his business affairs, he had once again frequent opportunities for experimental work.[55]

Throughout it all, Haynes remained cheerful and optimistic, and he tried to communicate these feelings to his family. "I trust we will all live just as happily and just as long," he wrote to his brother, "as if this calamity had not occurred. It is, as you know, a part of life's philosophy not to spend our time in worry, but to make the most of life while it lasts."[56] Despite these brave words it was no mere coincidence that Haynes's death would come the same year as the demise of his automobile company.

---

[55] Elwood Haynes to the Rev. A. E. Allen, January 14, 1925, *ibid.*

[56] Elwood Haynes to Calvin Haynes, January 17, 1925, *ibid.*

202

Chapter 15

The Man as Moralist

Since the 1919 Kokomo Chamber of Commerce banquet honoring Elwood Haynes, it had been customary for Kokomo newspapers to refer to Haynes as "Kokomo's First Citizen." This appellation was not explained, but no explanation was needed. Obviously the man's role in Kokomo was more than that of a successful businessman and manufacturer, or even of a famous scientist and inventor. He was a participant in the civic and religious, and to some extent the political, life of the community, and his philanthropies were legion. Haynes had come a long way since his entry into Kokomo in December, 1892, as spokesman for an unpopular gas monopoly. Much notoriety accompanied his work with automobiles and, later, alloys which led to the establishment of two of the largest manufacturing companies in Kokomo. This brought him increasing public attention and eventual national fame.

The changes in Haynes's personal lifestyle, habits, and outlook were remarkably few as his influence and wealth grew. For more than twenty years he lived in a small cottage originally acquired from the gas company. In 1916 Haynes finally succumbed to his family's desire for a larger home. Unable to find an existing place suitable to all, Haynes purchased a large lot on South Webster Street, adjacent to Highland Park, and built a handsome two-story brick house, with a full basement equipped as a laboratory. The Haynes family also remained devoted to the church and played a large role in its ministry. Haynes had transferred his membership to the First Presbyterian Church in Kokomo in May, 1892, months before he actually moved there, and he was elected to the board of elders in 1895. He held that office for the rest of his life, while also serving the church in many other capacities, and he contributed generously.[1] For many years he taught an adult Sunday School class, and Mrs. Haynes was the church organist, playing at both the Wednesday evening prayer meetings and the Sunday services. The Hayneses, considered "old-fashioned" by many, lived and dressed simply, did their own household chores, and were friendly to all.

---

[1] According to a story passed along by some of his fellow elders to a subsequent minister of the First Presbyterian Church, Haynes would come around at the end of the year, "find out how much the church needed to pay off its bills . . . and then would write a check for the whole amount." Harry P. Walrond to author, December 17, 1970. See also *"The Unfinished Story": A Brief History of the First Presbyterian Church of Kokomo, Indiana, 1868 – 1968* (privately printed, n.p., n.d.).

In 1922 they invited their niece, Margaret Haynes of Maybell, Colorado, to live with them while she completed her high school education in Kokomo. She remembers that she was treated with the "greatest kindness and consideration" although "there was little social life." She wrote:

Uncle Elwood spent a great deal of time in his basement workshop. He did take time to talk to me of his work, my interests, and various things. Although they were wealthy, my Aunt and Uncle practiced small economies in their daily lives. Probably force of habit from leaner years. However, they were very generous with charities, both private and public, but shunned public acclaim. I would say they succeeded in being happy in spite of their wealth.[2]

These traits never ceased to amaze and bemuse writers who sought interviews with Haynes. He often surprised callers by answering the door himself. One young writer, a new staff member of the *Haynes Pioneer,* had these impressions upon first meeting the company founder and president. He was "robust and round-faced," with a "keen sense of humor. . . . Not haughty, not familiar, not bubbling over with affected cordiality—[he was] just a plain, ordinary citizen with a big heart, who doesn't seem to realize that he had accomplished anything out of the ordinary. . . ."[3]

Admittedly this account was intended for a Haynes company publication, but its descriptions were not dissimilar from those of disinterested persons. W. A. P. John spoke of his "genuine delight" in meeting Haynes.

His is a charming and winning simplicity. So unassuming is he that unless you knew who he was and were acquainted with his achievements, you would pass him as one of the moderately successful business men of a small town. His conversation is always lucid, and his mind is so nimble and active that it required nimble and active questions to keep him from diverting the conversation. I judge that he has a marvelous memory for details, because he rattled off dimensions and data on experiments that he made 25 years ago. His deeply tanned face is the playground for mobile expressions, and his gray mustache and hair belie the youthfulness of his interests. . . . A man simple in his tastes and modest in his achievements, who cherishes spiritual happiness and cultural contentment far above the dollar. That is Elwood Haynes.[4]

In like fashion, W. J. Morgan, an automobile industry leader who had accompanied Haynes on the Indiana-Pacific Tour in 1913, considered the inventor "one of the most lovable men we have ever met. Courtesy and thoughtfulness for others are his strong characteristics."[5] Conrad Wolf's remark at the 1919 banquet honoring Haynes, that Haynes still wore the same size hatband as he did when he was far less prosperous, was quoted with approbation by Haynes's younger brother Edward who added: "I am pleased to note that there are no snobs in the Elwood Haynes Family."[6]

---

[2] Margaret Haynes Rambolt to author, June 10, 1971. Mrs. Rambolt concluded by saying she was "proud to have had such a famous Uncle, but more gratified still to have known him as a kind and unassuming person. . . ."

[3] "Elwood Haynes—America's Genius," in *Haynes Pioneer,* July, 1919, p. 11.

[4] John, "Looking Backward," in *MoToR,* January, 1922, p. 260.

[5] Morgan, "Motor Men I Have Met," in *Morgan's Message,* February, 1925, p. 13. Morgan added that the trip to Los Angeles had given him "a splendid opportunity to study the really great student and inventor." *Ibid.,* p. 14. See also William Fleming French, "And So He Did It Himself," in *Illustrated World,* May, 1922, pp. 388–90, 459, 461–62; and Foster, "How Elwood Haynes Came to Build First 'Horseless Carriage,' " in *Forbes,* March, 1925, pp. 679–82. The latter article closed with the following exchange: " 'What is the most worth while accomplishment of your life?' 'Retaining the affection and esteem of those with whom I have been associated.' And, looking at him, I knew it was true." *Ibid.*

[6] Edward Haynes to Elwood Haynes, November 15, 1919, Haynes Papers.

Haynes's unpretentious manner, his approachability by all, and the sincerity of his religious belief are also evident from the support he gave to other churches and denominations besides his own. He was singled out in 1920 for the generous support he had given to "the rural program of the interchurch world movement,"[7] and he made a number of publicly unacknowledged gifts to individual ministers, churches, and religious organizations. His greatest interest and activity outside of his own church, however, related to the Winona Lake Bible Conference and its evangelical work. Haynes served as a trustee of the Winona Assembly, which was located in Kosciusko County, Indiana, near Warsaw, and in 1924 he was elected as its second vice-president. Haynes attended summer programs and occasionally spoke on various aspects of Christian life and stewardship at Winona, sharing the speaker's platform with such men as William Jennings Bryan and "Billy" Sunday.[8]

The Young Men's Christian Association was another major interest of Haynes's. He was instrumental in reviving the "Y" in Kokomo in the early years of the twentieth century, and for a time he presented regular monthly lectures to the boys of the city. Very little is known about these talks, but a newspaper account describes his remarks in a similar situation. In 1915, on the occasion of Thomas A. Edison's birthday, Haynes spoke to a gathering of sixth, seventh, and eighth grade pupils at Kokomo's Central School. The headlines pointed out that "one great inventor" was paying tribute "to another," and that Haynes was "frequently cheered" during his talk. The reporter covering the talk stated that Haynes spoke "with an ease which betokened past experience in teaching" and that his remarks were well received by an "eager audience." In closing, Haynes invited the boys present to attend his regular lectures at the "Y" and expressed his regret that there was no provision for girls at these meetings.[9] This concern was more than a platitude, for Haynes helped establish the YWCA in Kokomo some years later. In 1919, Haynes was elected to a year's term as president of the Kokomo YMCA, an office he agreed to fill for another year in 1920. Culminating a successful membership drive under Haynes's prodding leadership, on November 26, 1920, the Haynes Automobile Company employees treated 175 community boys to a swim, a Thanksgiving Day meal, and a movie at the Victory Theater.[10]

The cause to which Haynes devoted the most time, aside from his family, research, and business interests, was prohibition, which grew from its nineteenth century roots into one of the major reform movements of the early twentieth century. A number of states—twenty by 1919, including Indiana—had adopted statewide prohibition prior to ratification of the Eighteenth

---

[7] Kokomo *Dispatch,* September 29, 1920. These remarks were made by Dr. Edgar L. Williams, executive secretary of the Church Federation, at the group's meeting in Indianapolis on September 24, 1920.

[8] See Elwood Haynes, "Speech at Winona," June 9, 1923, Haynes Papers. This talk was prepared for delivery early in July at a "Consultation Christian Citizenship Conference." In 1910 the Sundays, who had been coming to Winona since the 1890s, bought a home and took up residence there. *Winona Lake Yearbook, 1924,* in *ibid.*; William Gerald McLoughlin, *Billy Sunday Was His Real Name* (Chicago: University of Chicago Press, 1955), p. 157.

[9] Kokomo *Dispatch,* November 22, 1915. See also Sarah Jane Pyle, "Elwood Haynes [as an Orator]," 1962 Folder, Haynes Papers. This account, an analysis of Haynes's techniques and success as a speaker, concluded that he was effective without being dynamic or flamboyant. He spoke easily and fluently, without hesitation and often without notes, and he was in great demand as a speaker or presiding officer. He used analogy and illustration effectively, as well as a humor often subtle but occasionally quite broad, as when he resorted to German or Negro dialect stories.

[10] Kokomo *Tribune,* December 6, 1920.

Amendment in that year, but it had taken an enormous effort by a variety of organizations, including the sometimes antagonistic but powerful Prohibition party and the Anti-Saloon League, as well as the boost given the movement by the wartime situation, to bring about the shortlived national reform.[11]

Haynes, it will be recalled, had been an early convert to the prohibition banner, and he remained its loyal supporter throughout his lifetime. He refused to get caught up in the internecine warfare which sometimes threatened the cause, and gave generously of himself and his resources to the Anti-Saloon League and the Prohibition party, to the Flying Squadron and the Intercollegiate Prohibition Association, and to many other groups and organizations opposed to the liquor traffic. He became most upset, in fact, at a "prohibition victory dinner" in January, 1919, when one group attempted to arrogate to itself credit for a development in which many had participated. The Prohibition party, he remarked indignantly to his brother, also a dedicated prohibitionist and a state party leader, had not even been mentioned during the dinner, nor had the contributions of such organizations as the Sons of Temperance, the Murphy Movement, and the WCTU been recognized.[12]

Haynes's support of prohibition was confined to local activities until 1916. He continued, as he had done in his youth at Portland, to give occasional talks on the evils of drink and the dangers (scientifically demonstrable) of alcohol, to support local or county option laws in the absence of anything better, to sign remonstrances against saloonkeepers when asked, and he invariably voted the Prohibition party ticket. He became a close friend of J. Frank Hanly, governor of the state from 1905 to 1909, a Republican, and a prohibitionist. During Governor Hanly's "reform" administration, a number of significant political and social reform measures were enacted.[13] Finally, in the last months of his term, Hanly prevailed upon a special session of the legislature to adopt a county option law, as opposed to the less drastic local option law. This action split the party, and James E. Watson, the Republican candidate for governor in 1908, attributed his defeat to the prohibition label which Hanly had so firmly, if only temporarily, attached to the Republican party.[14]

Hanly, in fact, soon left the Republican party to embrace the Prohibition party openly, and he became its presidential candidate in 1916. An able platform speaker, Hanly originated and managed the Flying Squadron Foun-

---

[11] For brief and readable recent analyses of this reform see James H. Timberlake, *Prohibition and the Progressive Movement, 1900–1920* (Cambridge: Harvard University Press, 1963), and Andrew Sinclair, *Prohibition: The Era of Excess* (Boston: Little, Brown, 1962). See the older D. Leigh Colvin, *Prohibition in the United States: A History of the Prohibition Party, and of the Prohibition Movement* (New York: George H. Doran Company, 1926), and Peter H. Odegard, *Pressure Politics: The Story of Anti-Saloon League* (New York: Columbia University Press, 1928). The dissertation by Mary E. Harshbarger, "Elwood Haynes: Scientist with a Social Conscience," provides an excellent summary of the prohibition movement within Indiana and Haynes's relationship to it. For a good treatment of the powerful impact of prohibition and other cultural forces upon midwestern politics in the late nineteenth century see Richard J. Jensen, *The Winning of the Midwest: Social and Political Conflict, 1888–1896* (Chicago: University of Chicago Press, 1971). Haynes in many ways fits the typical description of the "pietist" (as opposed to the "liturgical") who pressed for prohibition during this time.

[12] Elwood Haynes to Sumner W. Haynes, January 21, 1919, Haynes Papers.

[13] Phillips, *Indiana in Transition*, pp. 97–101.

[14] *Ibid.*, pp. 100–101; James E. Watson, *As I Knew Them: Memoirs of James E. Watson Former United States Senator from Indiana* (Indianapolis: The Bobbs-Merrill Company, 1936), p. 19. See also Hanly's famous and oft-repeated address, part of which was presented to the Indiana legislature in its special session, entitled "The Liquor Traffic, Why I Hate It." A short passage from it is quoted in Phillips, *Indiana in Transition*, p. 100; a longer extract appears in Colvin, *Prohibition in the United States*, pp. 415–16.

dation, an organization whose speakers toured the country campaigning against the liquor traffic, and he established a prohibition newspaper, *The National Enquirer.*

It was this man who was responsible for Haynes's candidacy for the United States Senate in 1916. Haynes consented to join Hanly on the Prohibition ticket, although he made it clear he would not wage a statewide campaign. He did, however, mount something approaching a campaign in his own county, and of course Haynes supported the party's fund-raising efforts with thousands of dollars. His contributions to the state campaign included the use of a new Haynes automobile, dubbed the "Prohibition Flyer." It was used by party officials to make a tour of the state, beginning in August in Indianapolis (after a grape juice christening ceremony at Monument Circle). The "Flyer," which reached Kokomo on September 12, accommodated a tour group consisting of J. Raymond Schmidt, chairman of the state committee, R. S. Hiatt, a "saxophone artist," Clifford Boling, the "chauffeur and whistler," and one or more speakers.[15] Haynes's personal campaign activities included holding rallies at nearby Greentown and Galveston in August, at several other places in September and October, and in making several appearances with Hanly and Ira Landrith, his Texas-born running mate, when their coast-to-coast train passed through Indiana. Haynes also made a vigorous last-minute campaign tour of Howard County.

The national tour arrived in Kokomo on October 18, a bitterly cold day, but the small audience gave a warm welcome to the group and interrupted their oratory with applause and many "old fashioned campaign whoops." Haynes, "always immensely popular in Kokomo," received "much applause and cheers from the crowd" while introducing Hanly, who gave a "forceful address."[16]

Only six days before, Haynes had been in Indianapolis on the occasion of the "Good Roads Day" observation, at which time a 1916 Haynes had been exchanged for an 1897 model, the oldest one found in the United States. President Wilson was on hand to hear the "thunderous cheers" for Haynes upon his introduction by Governor Ralston, who also described Haynes's work in developing the automobile and in promoting good roads.[17] Haynes promptly resumed his prohibition campaign, however, and made what appears to be his most important speech on the subject in Kokomo on October 26. He argued for the constitutionality of the reform and spoke out against local option in favor of state action, insisting that "if the liquor business can be suspended in one part of the state it should be suspended in all parts." He also viewed prohibitionism as an economy measure, particularly vital in view of reduced support at the state's penal and charitable institutions, and countered the argument that a prohibition vote is a lost vote. A person should vote his sentiments, he maintained, and if enough people register a vote in favor of prohibition, either one or both of the old parties will take it up or else the Prohibition party will be elected.[18]

As mentioned, Haynes closed his campaign with a whirlwind tour of the county. Eight automobiles carried approximately forty "prohis," including a musical group, the Snow quartet, on what was at least a twelve-stop itiner-

---

[15] Kokomo *Dispatch,* September 8, 1916. The speakers included Sumner W. Haynes of Portland, Elwood's older brother, who had himself campaigned for the governorship in 1908 and for the United States Senate in 1914.

[16] *Ibid.,* October 19, 1916.

[17] *Ibid.,* October 13, 1916.

[18] *Ibid.,* October 26, 1916.

ary. Haynes spoke at each point, pleading not for personal votes but for party support. Privately, the county prohibitionists had no expectation of carrying Howard County, but they did hope for their largest vote ever. This was accomplished, with Haynes's 505 votes in the county nearly 200 more than that of the Prohibition party candidate in 1914. Statewide, however, Haynes received only 15,598 votes, and hard-campaigning William H. Hickman, the other Prohibition party candidate for the Senate (both Indiana seats were open), received 16,095 votes, including 467 from Howard County. Two reasons were given for the disappointingly light prohibition vote in the state—Haynes had refused to make, or permit others to make for him, a personal honor or home pride argument for votes; secondly and more importantly, the contest between the two major parties was very close, and people were reluctant to forego recording their votes for Wilson and Hughes and the major parties.[19]

A week following the election, the Hayneses entertained some thirty Prohibition party workers in their new home. The program consisted of songs and readings, including short speeches by Haynes and two others. The group was praised for having nearly doubled the Prohibition vote of 1912, and the guests left at a late hour "with feelings of love and gratitude for Mr. and Mrs. Haynes."[20] A limited postmortem on the election came two days later, when Haynes addressed a group of businessmen at the YMCA. Speaking on "Christian Citizenship, or After the Election, What?" Haynes reviewed man's rapid technological progress over the past 150 years, and then revived the question of whether Prohibition votes were lost votes. "I expect that a lot of you men here this afternoon," he said, "voted for Hughes. Well! You lost your vote because Hughes is defeated. Again. Doubtless a number of you voted for Wilson. Well! You lost your vote because Hughes carried Indiana." Haynes went on to say that "drink and war" were the "two great evils" facing America, but he predicted these matters would be solved during the next four to eight years. In his historical review, Haynes, who had been introduced as Kokomo's "great scholar and scientist," pointed out the distinction between knowledge and wisdom, invention and discovery: "Invention is the making use of discovery the same that wisdom is the making use of knowledge."[21]

Following his efforts in the 1916 election, Haynes was not actively involved in the prohibition movement other than continuing sizable contributions until 1918, when Indiana's new statewide prohibition law was to go into effect.[22] He was most generous with the Prohibition party and the Anti-Saloon League, the latter a lobbying organization of the Protestant churches. The Reverend E. S. Shumaker, once called "the most powerful man in the state," headed the Indiana branch of the ASL and made repeatedly successful appeals to Haynes for additional funds. Irving Leibowitz said that Shumaker in 1919 merely "cracked the ecclesiastical whip" in order to get state ratification of the Eighteenth Amendment. His organization, he continued, "unlike its ally, the Ku Klux Klan, sought no members—only donors—

[19] *Ibid.*, November 11, 1916. Indeed, the election was so close that the Kokomo *Dispatch* on November 8 had announced the victory of Hughes over Wilson.

[20] *Ibid.*, November 12, 1916. See also Ida Whitaker Cedars, "Campaigning with Mr. Elwood Haynes," typescript dated December 1, 1962, Haynes Papers.

[21] Kokomo *Dispatch*, November 12, 1916; Kokomo *Tribune*, November 13, 1916.

[22] See especially the correspondence between Virgil Hinshaw, chairman of the Prohibition National Committee, and Elwood Haynes for 1917 and 1918 in the Haynes Papers. This details many aspects of what Hinshaw, on November 24, 1917, termed Haynes's "extreme generosity."

and it was eminently successful. It was built around and in the evangelical pulpits and styled itself the 'church in action.' "[23]

Haynes estimated in 1920 that his prohibition donations over the previous four or five years amounted to $40,000 or $50,000.[24] In 1918, moreover, he began to speak in various parts of the state extolling the virtues of prohibitionism. His greatest labors, and his most extensive correspondence in defense of prohibitionism, came following the passage of the amendment and adoption of the Volstead Act providing for its enforcement. Perhaps this was a function of Haynes's greater leisure time, following the sale of the Stellite company to Union Carbide, but it was also an indication of how intensely Haynes wanted the "noble experiment" to succeed. Whenever Haynes learned of a public statement challenging either the wisdom or the legality of prohibition, he sought to answer it. He even took up the hopeless task of attempting to persuade Indiana Senator James E. Watson, a notorious "wet," to adopt his way of thinking, and he also tried to modify the views of people ranging from William Howard Taft and Nicholas Murray Butler to individuals unknown to him who had expressed themselves on the matter. An example of Haynes's thinking on prohibition issues is contained in a letter to F. Lyman Windolph of Lancaster, Pennsylvania. Haynes concentrated upon three points in this letter—the legal question, the effects of alcohol on the human body, and prohibitionists as a group. Haynes had absolutely no doubts about the authority of the government to prohibit the manufacture and sale of intoxicants. He argued that there was an enormous and long-standing precedent for laws of this type and that such legislation constituted no threat to human liberty. He admitted that those who argued for the right of the individual to make and drink anything he wanted had a point, since one's personal liberty was at stake, but such liberty "should be properly restricted to the individual, and not even extended to his own children."[25]

Haynes also had no doubts about alcohol's deleterious effects, both physiological and social. As a chemist, he viewed alcohol, not as an " 'agent of Satan,' but simply as a highly dangerous narcotic" which had adverse effects upon the brain. When taken in large quantities, "it seems to exert a paralyzing effect upon the will-power, thus causing a man to lose to a certain

---

[23] Irving Leibowitz, *My Indiana* (Englewood Cliffs, N. J.: Prentice-Hall, 1964), pp. 182–83. Odegard, in his classic study of the Anti-Saloon League, quoted an Alabamian on the source of ASL power: "They won the churches and the army controlled by them. . . . They figuratively hit us politicians over the head with a steeple." Odegard also pointed out that all thirteen Hoosier congressmen had opposed the prohibition amendment in 1914. The ASL "declared war on them," ten of the thirteen were defeated in 1916, and in 1917 all thirteen voted for the amendment. Odegard, *Pressure Politics*, pp. 23, 98.

[24] Elwood Haynes to D. Leigh Colvin, December 17, 1920, Haynes Papers. Haynes also called for better co-ordination among the organizations of the prohibition movement and registered a mild complaint with one correspondent about the number of groups calling upon him and the resulting overruns in his budget for "benevolences." (At the time Haynes was committed to purchasing the Ruddell family's shares of Union Carbide stock and was consequently short of cash.) "At the beginning of the year 1920," he wrote, "I made out a budget for contributions for the year, and though the year is not yet three-quarters gone, I find that I have paid out more than twenty-five per-cent more than the budget already, and calls are coming just as urgently as if I had not paid anything. Add to the above the remaining pledges I have already made, and still to be filled, and it is easy to see that my contributions will run more than fifty per-cent ahead of the budget." Elwood Haynes to Elton R. Shaw, September 15, 1920, *ibid.*

[25] Elwood Haynes to F. Lyman Windolph, June 30, 1920, *ibid.*; F. Lyman Windolph, "Two Sins Against Tolerance," in *Atlantic Monthly,* CXXV (1920), 473–78. Haynes, in a 1921 speech, said the money paid for liquor in one year would amount to a gold bar one and a quarter miles high; the money spent for enforcing prohibition, one third of 1 percent as much, would amount to a "tiny speck." Elwood Haynes, "Speech on Prohibition," August 16, 1921, Haynes Papers.

degree his self-respect and logical control of himself." He estimated that fully 30 percent of his early associates, presumably those in Portland, had "been ruined by drink," either quickly or gradually over the years. "You have doubtless heard the story," he continued, "of the school boy who wrote the essay on 'Pins.' In conclusion he said that pins had saved a good many lives. The teacher asked Johnny to explain what he meant by this statement. He replied, 'By not swallerin' 'em.' The same may be said, broadly speaking, regarding the medicinal qualities of alcohol."[26]

Haynes challenged the stereotyped image of the straitlaced prohibitionist. Rather than being a "lot of fanatics" trying to compel others to submit to their particular views, Haynes said, perhaps rather self-servingly, that he did not know "a more honest, logical, and reasonable people than the leaders in the prohibitory movement." And, he hastened to add, "the writer mingles with all sorts and classes of men," corporation directors, millionaires, men of distinction in literary and scientific circles, as well as laborers, and the statement still stood.[27]

Haynes also responded to Nicholas Murray Butler, president of Columbia University, following an address delivered by Butler in January, 1923, to the Ohio State Bar Association. In Butler's speech entitled "Law and Lawlessness," he had lamented the growing crime rate in the United States, but he argued that the impracticality of some laws (and he cited the Fifteenth and Eighteenth Amendments as examples) forced the lawlessness. Haynes, in a five-page letter, immediately challenged Butler's reasoning and proclaimed the benefits of prohibition. Butler responded not only by sending Haynes the full text of his remarks but also by forcefully restating some of his views.

One of the most difficult things in the world is to get the modern human being, and particularly the modern American, to listen to the truth or to face a fact. He lives in a world of illusion and prejudice, and to tell him the truth first mystifies him, then irritates and finally infuriates. All that I did in my address was to state a few perfectly obvious facts and to let them speak for themselves. . . . If you have any notion that the Eighteenth Amendment to the Constitution has brought to an end the manufacture and sale of intoxicating liquor in this country, you are certainly living in a world of illusion. All it has done is to change the channels of the trade, to make it surreptitious instead of open, to make it lawless instead of law-controlled, and to deprive the Government of immense revenue and of a means of effectively controlling it. . . . Constitutional prohibition is the greatest enemy of temperance and of the controlled and regulated liquor traffic that has ever been devised. It has set back both movements probably a hundred years, and in addition is perhaps the single most effective agency making for lawlessness in the world today. There are no more earnest supporters of the Eighteenth Amendment than those who in all parts of the country are making fortunes, small and large, by the illicit manufacture, sale, and transportation of alcoholic liquors.[28]

Haynes undertook a point-by-point refutation of Butler's arguments in his reply. He noted that, as a scientist, he had sometimes been disappointed when the facts were not as he might have wished, but that "I am not in the habit of becoming 'infuriated.' " He called Butler's comparison of crime in Canada with crime in Cook County (Chicago), Illinois, "decidedly unfair" and an attack upon prohibition. He admitted that the Eighteenth Amendment had

---

[26] Elwood Haynes to F. Lyman Windolph, June 30, 1920, Haynes Papers.

[27] *Ibid.*

[28] Nicholas Murray Butler to Elwood Haynes, February 19, 1923, *ibid.*

not ended the manufacture and sale of alcohol but insisted that it had had beneficial results, such as a lower crime rate, and he enclosed a newspaper clipping to reinforce the latter point.[29] Butler called off the debate at this point, after repeating his basic contention: "Constitutional prohibition is the greatest obstacle which the cause of temperance and control of the liquor traffic has ever had to face. It has made us a nation of hypocrites and lawbreakers. If persisted in, it will destroy the Republic."[30]

Haynes received a similarly negative reply from the Reverend Roland Sawyer, a member of the Massachusetts state legislature, to whom he had written following Sawyer's call for repeal of the Eighteenth Amendment. Sawyer's argument was both a practical and philosophical statement about the role of law in society. "The place of law," he maintained, "is to catch up and hold for the future, the progress of the present. Hence it comes at the end, and not at the beginning of a reform. You can not reform by law—but when a majority is ready for a reform, then you can put it into law and hold it." He said that the country was ready for only a limited change, the abolition of the saloon and the sale of hard liquor. By attempting too much, the whole movement was endangered. "Haste makes waste," he charged, and "overeagerness has done us much harm—the quicker we right about-face and get out of the hole, the better it will be. The public is not ready for ENTIRE prohibition—and it will not support the law."[31]

Haynes responded to these points and rejected them as based on expediency rather than principle. "If the Volstead Act should be repealed," he asserted, "it will, in my opinion, be the greatest piece of folly that Congress has ever committed." A saloon keeper had admitted to Haynes personally that his was the "meanest business on earth," and Haynes's recent experience in serving on a federal grand jury in Indianapolis had confirmed his views on the evils of drinking and its relationship to crime. He also considered the "foreign population" and "ignorant outlaws" responsible for the repeal demand, and he was unwilling to accede to their request. "We have placed our hands upon the plow," he concluded; "let us have the courage to move forward, and not turn back."[32]

If Haynes failed to modify Butler's or Sawyer's views, the converse was also true. In 1924 Haynes reacted to an "Easy Chair" column in *Harper's* mentioning prohibition and sought to have the magazine publish an essay of his own in rebuttal. An editor warily requested a summation of his "general views" before agreeing to this, although he recognized that, coming "from a man in your position," Haynes's ideas "would be certain to command attention." Haynes submitted his précis in April and his completed article in May, but it was not published.[33]

Haynes provides no exception to the classic model of the prohibitionist. A midwesterner of middle-class background and outlook, a devout Protestant churchman, a manufacturer aware of occasional time losses and absenteeism in his plants because of alcoholism, and a scientist whose experiments had "proved" the dangers of the narcotic, Haynes also came from a family in which an active interest in prohibitionism had been present from

---

[29] Elwood Haynes to Nicholas Murray Butler, March 3, 1923, *ibid.*

[30] Nicholas Murray Butler to Elwood Haynes, April 6, 1923, *ibid.*

[31] Roland D. Sawyer to Elwood Haynes, January 23, 1923, *ibid.*

[32] Elwood Haynes to Roland D. Sawyer, January 27, 1923, *ibid.*

[33] Elwood Haynes to Thomas B. Wells, April 15, 1924, Thomas B. Wells to Elwood Haynes, April 17, 1924, Elwood Haynes to Thomas B. Wells, April 22, May 23, 1924, *ibid.*

his childhood. Yet he was more sophisticated than many of his fellow prohibitionists and saw the wisdom, once the Eighteenth Amendment had been achieved, of moving away from the Prohibition party in national elections and into whichever party adopted the stronger stand on preserving the victory. For this reason, Haynes abandoned a lifelong practice of voting the Prohibition ticket in 1920. Instead, after much discussion and deliberation, he decided to cast his vote for Republican candidate Warren G. Harding. Moreover Haynes was not strongly nativistic, another trait generally attributed to prohibitionists, despite his concern about America's "foreign population" being responsible for a disproportionate share of crime and for leading the fight for the repeal of prohibition. "I have no objection to a foreigner, just because he is a foreigner," Haynes wrote in 1923. "In fact, if he were abused by a crowd of Americans, I would take off my coat and stand by the foreigner, but I see no reason why we should repeal our laws which have been passed by a majority of the people of the United States and under the regular procedure laid down. . . ."[34]

Similarly, Haynes refused to countenance the tactics of the Ku Klux Klan, which was particularly strong in Indiana and which, in Leibowitz's term, was the "ally" of the Anti-Saloon League. Haynes denounced the Klan in no uncertain terms. "The organization known as The Ku Klux Klan," he wrote to a friend in Chicago in 1921, "claims that one of its principal objects is to bring such officers [those who connive to prevent or nullify laws they have sworn to uphold] to justice, by taking the law into their own hands. The methods adopted by The Ku Klux Klan, however, are so reprehensible that the average loyal American repudiates them with scorn."[35] Whether Haynes was equally outspoken publicly is not known, but it is clear that he was not a member of the organization, although Kokomo was a Klan stronghold in the 1920s.[36]

Haynes was not concerned with the end alone, but also with the means to that end. Supremely devoted to the cause of prohibition, he persevered in it throughout his lifetime. This meant that "any substance, such as alcohol or tobacco, which interfered with the maximum performance of the mind and body was to be avoided. Persons lacking strength of character were to be assisted by laws enacted to aid in the procuring of a better tomorrow."[37] Haynes's untimely death during the "noble experiment" at least spared him the pain of witnessing the ultimate failure of this cherished reform.

Although his commitment to prohibition had occupied him both before and after World War I, the greater leisure time he enjoyed in the immediate postwar period permitted him to take up a number of other causes too, and he assumed several frequently burdensome civic responsibilities. Except perhaps for his advocacy of United States membership in the League of Nations and a limited pacifism, the new concerns stemmed logically from his previous work. His interests in children, in teaching and teaching methods, and in vocational training were whetted by his service on the state board of

---

[34] Elwood Haynes to Roland D. Sawyer, January 27, 1923, *ibid.*; this passage was also quoted by Harshbarger, "Elwood Haynes," p. 105.

[35] Elwood Haynes to Alice Hyatt Mather, October 1, 1925, Haynes Papers.

[36] For an interesting account of the huge statewide rally held in Kokomo on July 4, 1923, with Indiana Grand Dragon D. C. Stephenson dramatically arriving by airplane before the assembled masses, see Robert Coughlan, "Konklave in Kokomo," in Isabel Leighton (ed.), *The Aspirin Age, 1919–1941* (New York: Simon and Schuster, 1949), pp. 105–29.

[37] Harshbarger, "Elwood Haynes," pp. 143–44.

education from 1921 until his death in 1925.[38] Appointed by the governor in 1921, Haynes accepted the post with relish. He had long been an advocate of improved educational opportunities at all levels, from elementary schools through colleges and universities; now he had a chance to give new meaning to some of his educational convictions. He eventually became the chairman of the committee on vocational training, and he served on the committee on attendance and on a science textbook committee.[39] In 1921 Haynes helped finance a campaign designed to make the state superintendent of public instruction an appointive rather than an elective office (this required a constitutional amendment), and he was widely quoted in the fall of that year, during a legislative session, when he advocated liberal support for the state's educational institutions. "Never employ a man, not in this day of the world," Haynes had declared, "who is not a college graduate to attack any problem that requires an original process. It isn't safe. . . . The so-called practical man might stumble onto a process, but it isn't likely at all that he would. In this day and age it requires scientific knowledge to attack any new and original problem. . . ." Indeed, Indiana University officials requested Haynes's permission to publish these statements for use in making their budget presentation to the state legislature.[40]

Haynes was also associated with two other educational institutions as a member of their boards of trustees—Western College for Women at Oxford, Ohio, the school from which his daughter had graduated in 1915, and Taylor University, at nearby Upland, Indiana, a small denominational school. His wealth rather than his educational philosophy was probably responsible for his appointment to both boards, but Haynes served conscientiously and, in time, did make substantial cash contributions to both institutions, as well as to his alma mater in Massachusetts.

He retained great fondness for the "Tech" and his associates there, and he attended as many of the 1881 class reunions as possible. In 1914, after Haynes had achieved some national recognition, he had been honored by the school for his achievements both in "mechanics" and "chemistry." In subsequent years Haynes regularly included generous gifts to the "Tech" among his benevolences. Other persons and projects which benefited from his philanthropy were C. V. Haworth's publication detailing Howard County's participation in World War I; a young chemist suffering from tuberculosis whom Haynes sent on recuperative travels; the city of Portland, to which Haynes and his brothers donated land for a city park; various students seeking a college education; and several individuals to whom Haynes loaned money.[41] Haynes once expounded on the problems of philanthropy to W. W. Boyd, president of Western College for Women, who wrote often seeking financial support for his institution. "I have, as you are doubtless aware,

---

[38] For a brief history of the development and membership of the state board of education see Fred Swalls, "An Evaluation of the Indiana State Board of Education and Its Function" (Ph.D. dissertation, Indiana University, 1950), pp. 37−41. From 1913 to 1933, there were thirteen members on the board, seven *ex officio* and six appointed by the governor to represent different "publics." Haynes was the member representing "employers."

[39] See Harshbarger, "Elwood Haynes," pp. 129−32, for a somewhat more detailed account of Haynes's service on the school board.

[40] Oscar H. Williams to Elwood Haynes, August 4, 1921; Clipping, Paoli (Ind.) *News,* December 7, 1921; Frank R. Elliott to Elwood Haynes, March 29, 1922, Haynes Papers.

[41] These examples came from a reading of the Haynes Papers. See especially Elwood Haynes to Walter M. Haynes, June 17, 1919, and clipping, Portland *Commercial-Review,* April 5, 1921. C. V. Haworth's book was *History of Howard County in the World War* (Indianapolis: Burford, 1920).

numerous calls for funds from various sources, to which I think I have given a reasonable response," he wrote, but "it is a notable fact in my own experience that as soon as one gives what he considers a reasonable amount to any given cause, the people representing it, instead of being satisfied, usually come promptly back for more, so the calls for funds in a little while become almost incessant."[42]

Another cause which Haynes enthusiastically supported, in this case more with time and energy than money, was adoption of the metric system. Both his scientific and business interests led him to a determined advocacy of this project. "We and Great Britain," he observed in 1924, "are the only civilized nations in the world at the present time, who have not definitely adopted this system. And we are, therefore, at a decided disadvantage in selling our wares in foreign countries."[43] Convinced as to its desirability, Haynes was not bashful in presenting his arguments at every opportunity. In January, 1923, he spoke on the subject to the Indiana State Board of Education (for which he received a letter of commendation from the New York office of the American Metric Association), and at year's end he spoke before a meeting of the association. His greatest effort in behalf of this cause, however, had come two years earlier, when he testified before a congressional subcommittee. Haynes appeared before members of the Senate Committee on Manufactures on October 12, 1921; his testimony included a dramatic demonstration in problem solving, comparing the difficulty in using metrics and non-metrics to determine cylinder volumes. "Ten times as many figures were needed with our present system," Haynes reported afterwards. He also made the point, based upon his own experiments in teaching the metric system to school children in Indianapolis, that students could learn it easily and would have the advantage of being familiar with it when they encountered it in the business world. Moreover, scientific research is conducted using the metric system.[44]

Haynes's crusade for this reform was part of a strong national movement following World War I. In a burst of activity at that time, thousands of people from the professions, business, and politics, in addition to numerous associations and clubs, were supporting the movement, and they generated a flood of publicity.[45] Congress received 105,000 petitions from individuals and groups, and memorials from five states, seeking action. The senate committee which held hearings in October, 1921, was one of several congressional committees investigating the matter, all of which recommended positive action, but the desired law did not materialize in the 1920s. Advocacy of the metric system seemed to be another "lost cause" to which Haynes devoted considerable time and labor, but he was not discouraged by the lack of popular support. As Haynes brashly explained to Alfred Reeves, the general manager of the National Automobile Chamber of Commerce, whose association was opposing the switch to metrics, ignorance and prejudice were responsible for its negative outlook. The advantages of the met-

[42] Elwood Haynes to W. W. Boyd, October 23, 1919, Haynes Papers.

[43] Elwood Haynes to Alfred Reeves, November 12, 1924, *ibid.*

[44] *Ibid.*; Harshbarger, "Elwood Haynes," p. 33; United States Senate, 67th Congress, 1st Session, *Hearing Before a Subcommittee of the Committee on Manufactures . . . on S. 2267* (Washington, D. C.: U. S. Government Printing Office, 1921). A copy of this government publication is in the Haynes Papers. See also Elwood Haynes to Howard Richards, December 26, 1924, *ibid.,* for a description of Haynes's methods of teaching the metric system to school children.

[45] J. T. Johnson (comp.), *The Metric System of Weights and Measures (20th Yearbook, The National Council of Teachers of Mathematics,* New York, 1948), p. 41.

ric system, however, "become more apparent with its use," and he was confident about its ultimate adoption.[46]

Next to prohibition, Haynes's greatest interest in the postwar world was in preserving peace. Not only did he fervently hope for, and work for, the success of the League of Nations, he also assisted those institutions, old and new, devoted to world peace. If it seems inconsistent on Haynes's part to have supported the war effort, and to have done so in unintended but dramatic fashion through use of his Stellite tool metal, so too were the American people inconsistent in the 1910s and 1920s.[47] Haynes was, however, one of the original sponsors of the League to Enforce Peace, organized in 1915, and he continued to support numerous antiwar organizations following 1918. It should be recalled that when the United States entered the war most peace organizations called upon their memberships to support the war. Haynes did so, agreeing with President Wilson that there were such things as a "just war." "While I despise war as a means of settling quarrels," Haynes wrote in 1918, "I feel that there have been times when the better element of the world has been obliged to protect itself against the encroachments of ambitious men or nations who have sought to usurp the power to rule others by means of military force."[48]

Haynes, however, in December, 1918, declined an invitation to join the Navy League, an organization working for continued high level military appropriations and naval expansion. "I would not have you infer . . . that I do not believe in military force," he responded, and referred to his having "done something" to aid the government in the recent war, but now he preferred to give his support to an international organization devoted to peace rather than a national organization seeking heavy armaments. "I firmly believe that a League of Nations can be formed," he continued, "and I earnestly hope that such a League may be formed, which will be able not only to decide all international questions of the future, but back up its decisions with military forces if necessary."[49] League Secretary W. S. Townsend remonstrated with Haynes, indicating that now the Navy League was interested in building up the national merchant marine, but Haynes, although sympathetic with this goal, was not convinced by Townsend's arguments and at any rate preferred to assist in getting the League of Nations established.[50]

---

[46] See, for example, the Indianapolis *Star,* October 3, 1971; *National Observer,* January 5, 1974.

[47] Harshbarger, "Elwood Haynes," pp. 110–28. The author is indebted to Miss Harshbarger who thoroughly studied this aspect of Haynes's life, for the conclusion presented above. See also Merle E. Curti, *Peace or War: The American Struggle, 1636–1936* (New York: W. W. Norton & Company, 1936), and Robert Ferrell, *Peace in Their Time: The Origins of the Kellogg-Briand Pact* (New Haven, Conn.: Yale University Press, 1952).

[48] Elwood Haynes to Rodger Everett Reed, July 5, 1920, quoted in Harshbarger, "Elwood Haynes," p. 117. These sentiments were expressed to a nephew, a conscientious objector, who had been court-martialed and imprisoned. Since he refused to accept any army pay, he had requested his uncle to support his "bare necessities at $7.00 per month." Haynes enclosed a check for $84 in the letter. *Ibid.*

[49] Elwood Haynes to W. S. Townsend, December 16, 1918, quoted in *ibid.,* p. 119.

[50] *Ibid.,* pp. 119–20. In similar fashion, Haynes declined to serve on a committee considering the "Relation of Chemistry to National Defense." "I can not conscientiously serve on any committee," he wrote, "which contemplates a subject involving a hostile attitude toward the Nations of the World. Long study has forced me to the conclusion that the consideration of such questions in time of peace lead to distrust and finally to hostility on the part of other Nations. We can never lay a firm foundation for universal peace among Nations by such means." He added that he was not a pacifist, "in the sense that term is frequently employed. I believe in force, military if necessary, to quell the individuals who insist upon war to settle disputes." Elwood Haynes to "Mr. Jordan," March 12, 1925, Haynes Papers.

This he did throughout 1919 and 1920, largely through correspondence with editors, public officials, and friends. By the time of the election of 1920, Haynes was convinced that United States membership was inevitable, regardless of which presidential candidate was elected. Consequently, he voted for Harding rather than Cox because he considered the Republican candidate more likely to enforce the Volstead Act. When the United States ultimately rejected League membership and it became evident that the Harding administration was content with this decision, a new organization, the League of Nations Non-Partisan Association, was established in December, 1922, to seek a reconsideration. Haynes immediately joined and would have served as the presiding officer at one of its meetings held at Winona Lake in August, 1923, but a business conflict prevented it.

The activities described above—Haynes as a Presbyterian, as a prohibitionist, as a pedagogue, philanthropist, and peacemaker—provide some of the bases for his reputation as a "first citizen." His interests were a blend of the common and the uncommon, the popular and the unpopular. But he was not swayed by considerations of popularity. He was a man whose successes in most personal endeavors had given him a supreme self-confidence in his own judgments, but these qualities were tempered by a humanitarianism. Although delay or failure in achieving many of his social goals may have been disappointing, Haynes was never discouraged or defeated.

Chapter 16

Kokomo's First Citizen

It would be possible to paint a picture of Elwood Haynes in his final years with tragic shadings. His automobile company had failed, his rights to both his stainless steel and Stellite discoveries were challenged by patent suits, many of his cherished dreams for social and educational reforms were unfulfilled, and his personal wealth, which amounted to considerably more than a million dollars in 1920, had diminished so drastically that he was forced to borrow against future dividends and royalties in 1924. Yet such a portrait would be both misleading and incomplete. There was no underlying sense of tragedy or failure within Haynes during the early 1920s. These years, indeed, were among the happiest and most active of his life. He accepted his many trials with the same good grace and equanimity with which he had accepted his triumphs, remained confident in himself and the future, and often experienced moments of joy and the satisfaction of accomplishment and recognition.

Some of Haynes's activities in the 1920s have already been described—labors on behalf of more effective prohibition enforcement, service on the state board of education, sponsorship of the metric system for the United States. He was also a member of the federal grand jury in Indianapolis in 1921, whose unusually heavy docket included a number of prohibition violations. When the jury was impaneled in December, 1920, the district attorney announced that hundreds of witnesses had already been subpoenaed and that he expected the jury would set a duration record investigating, in addition to the "usual cases," an alleged coal conspiracy and several "whiskey rings" in the state. He anticipated a session of two months; in actuality, the jury was not discharged until April 26, 1921, after three months of service. During that time, although no details of the grand jury deliberations are available and Haynes himself subsequently made only the most general references to its investigations, Haynes had so impressed his fellow jurors that he was presented a "gold-headed cane" by them.[1]

Haynes was also an aviation enthusiast for at least the last twelve years of his life. In 1913 he supported an "Aviation and Athletic Meet" held in Kokomo. His automobile company contributed 73 cars to a 250-car parade which welcomed the flyers to town, and George W. Beatty, the featured

---

[1] Kokomo *Daily Tribune*, December 8, 1920, April 26, 1921.

American aviator in the show, was Haynes's house guest during his stay in Kokomo.[2] If Haynes had been invited then to go up with Beatty, he declined; George H. Strout of the Haynes company, however, made a twelve-minute flight. Haynes did make a highly publicized flight in 1919, when a team of officers from the army air service visited the "Haynes Aviation Field"—land made available to flyers by the Haynes Automobile Company—located a few miles from the Kokomo Aviation Company's field.[3]

A large crowd witnessed the thirty minute adventure, as the open cockpit Curtiss biplane "swooped and maneuvered thousands of feet in the air, now diving, now climbing, now racing swiftly across the sky." Haynes remarked upon returning safely to the ground, "It certainly was a fine trip and I'm glad I made it. There wasn't a disagreeable sensation in the whole ride."[4] He later wrote a fuller account of his reflections upon the flight in connection with an article he published in the *Haynes Pioneer* on "The Evolution of the Aeroplane." After quickly reviewing the highlights in the history of flight, Haynes pointed out that a successful flight across the Atlantic (in a plane he had recently seen in New York) had been completed. He stressed his own complete sense of safety and security in the open air, partially based upon his "great faith in the reliability and efficiency of the gasoline motor."[5] Haynes made at least one more flight. In 1920 he flew from Kokomo to Fountain City, Indiana, covering the seventy-nine miles in forty-nine minutes, a speed of just under 100 miles an hour; he visited the Reverend Aaron Worth, an elderly former minister in Portland, and Orville Wright, one of Worth's distant relatives. Haynes quoted Worth as saying he was overjoyed at having "the two greatest inventors in the world" visit him on his birthday. Haynes also remarked that his return to Kokomo via interurban car required five hours.[6]

Haynes nevertheless continued to prefer the automobile to the airplane, and he became more and more interested in the early history of the automobile as time passed. Undoubtedly this interest was spurred not only by his participation in the story, but also by the intermittent controversy over the first actual builder and seller of automobiles in the United States. This question had arisen again following adoption of the Haynes Automobile Company's advertising slogan in 1912, "America's First Car." The dispute was investigated without resolution by David Beecroft and Charles E. Duryea in 1915, reappeared in 1920 when the Appersons challenged the display card text on the 1893-1894 "Pioneer" at the Smithsonian, and attained new intensity following the huge celebration (and the attendant national publicity) in Kokomo on July 4, 1922, honoring Elwood Haynes for his automobile invention. The Duryea family, particularly Charles, objected to the Haynes claims, sought clarifications and retractions, and eventually persuaded the Smithsonian Institution to revise its label of the "Pioneer."[7] All of these factors, as

218

---

[2] *Haynes Pioneer*, July, 1913, pp. 18–19.

[3] Haynes was the president of the aviation company, which later became the Curtiss-Indiana Company, and in 1923 he accepted the Kokomo chairmanship of the National Aeronautics Association. General Folder, October, 1921, May, 1923, Haynes Papers.

[4] *Haynes Pioneer*, October, 1919, pp. 1–2.

[5] Elwood Haynes, "The Evolution of the Aeroplane," in *ibid.*, pp. 3, 13. The English aviators Alcock and Brown flew from Newfoundland to Iceland in 1919.

[6] Elwood Haynes, "Trip to Fountain City by Aeroplane," n.d., General Folder, 1921, Haynes Papers. A telegram from a Curtiss company official to Haynes establishes the date of the flight as April, 1920. W. W. Mountain to Elwood Haynes, April 10, 1920, *ibid.*

[7] See especially M. J. Duryea, "The Haynes—Indiana's First Car," in *Antique Automobile*,

well as Haynes's desire to know the truth, led to his decision to write a book on the subject.

He communicated these intentions to the Bobbs-Merrill publishing house in Indianapolis, whose editors were enthusiastic about the idea and considered his initial outline a "splendid" one. In November, 1923, a contract was drawn up for "The Story of the Automobile" and was submitted to Haynes, but evidently he never formally accepted it, despite Bobbs-Merrill's assurances of full co-operation and unpressured deadlines. "Write as you have time and inclination," John R. Carr suggested.[8] Even without having signed the contract, Haynes drew up and submitted on New Year's Day, 1924, a ten-chapter outline which evidently pleased the editors, and the following month Haynes stated that he hoped to begin writing the book within thirty days, devoting all of his "spare time" to it.[9] But the book was never written. It appears that Haynes did not get beyond page two of his opening chapter, for only an intriguing fragment, intended as part of the introduction to chapter 1, remains among the Haynes Papers.

The correspondence between Haynes and some of his fellow automobile pioneers about the proposed book may account for Haynes's failure to get beyond the point where the automobile appeared in his text. It may be, too, that the increased attention required by the automobile company crisis caused Haynes to abandon his writing plans. Furthermore, the array of confusing and contradictory data which Haynes received in response to a questionnaire he sent to Henry Ford, Alexander Winton, and others must have dampened his enthusiasm for the project. Haynes had posed these seven questions:

1. When did the idea of building a "Horseless Carriage" first enter your mind?
2. When did you build or caused [sic] to be built your first machine?
3. With what kind of an engine was it equipped?
4. Did it have a clutch mechanism, or other disconnecting device?
5. Approximately how many miles was it driven all told?
6. In what town or city was it operated?
7. Is the machine or a drawing of it still in existence?[10]

Winton, who later claimed to have made the first automobile sale in America, gave full and candid answers to Haynes. He indicated he had built his "first motor car in 1895 & 6." It had a two-cylinder gasoline engine, one positive and two friction clutches, and "was run about 200 miles in Cleveland & vicinity." He still owned it, as well as one of the single-cylinder cars he first marketed (at a date unspecified here).[11] Henry Ford, however, replying through his secretary, claimed a first machine of steam, built in 1889 and

---

December 19, 1943, p. 19, and the Merle J. Duryea Papers, Indiana Division, Indiana State Library. The text change in the label on the "Pioneer" points out that

> About two years after the trial, certain changes were made which were embodied in the machine as it now stands. The original one horsepower motor was replaced by one of 2 horsepower; the original steering mechanism . . . was discarded . . . ; and the original 28-inch cushion tire wheels were replaced by the present 36-inch pneumatic tire wheels.

This whole question boiled again in March, 1939, following a Lowell Thomas radio broadcast from Kokomo, in which the Haynes claims were restated. See *ibid.* for photostatic copies of news reports on the broadcast and the response to it.

[8] John R. Carr to Elwood Haynes, November 16, 1923, January 3, 1924, Bobbs-Merrill Company Papers, Lilly Library, Indiana University, Bloomington.

[9] Elwood Haynes to John R. Carr, January 1, 1924, Elwood Haynes to H. H. Howland, February 14, 1924, *ibid.*

[10] These pages, undated, appear in the General Folder, 1924, Haynes Papers.

[11] Elwood Haynes to Alexander Winton, May 28, 1924, *ibid.*

consisting only of the engine. "The second," Haynes was informed, "was a gas engine and was built in 1892"; it "was driven by a friction belt." Ford operated this car "principally in Detroit and the vicinity," running it some 3,000 to 5,000 miles. Still in running condition, it was then being driven and exhibited "along side of its ten millionth brother. . . ."[12]

Whether Haynes accepted Ford's chronology as accurate or not is unclear—the correct date for Ford's first car is 1896—but this response either convinced Haynes of the difficulties and the potential for future disputes in pursuing his book or else caused him to lose interest in an extended account of the automobile in America, since his own work, about which he had planned three of the ten chapters in the book, apparently had been anticipated and therefore would have less historical interest.

In retrospect, 1922 proved to be the banner year in Haynes's life. He was given outstanding honors and recognition early in the year, and he capped it off with a four-month tour of Europe. In June he received three honors. On June 2 he was in Worcester, Massachusetts, to accept the prestigious John Scott Medal for his achievements in "Stellite, stainless steel, and chrome-iron." The award had been provided for in a fund to the city of Philadelphia for honoring "ingenious men and women who make useful inventions." Following its customary practice, the award committee arranged to have the medal (and an $800 check) bestowed during the commencement exercises at the recipient's alma mater.[13]

Five days later Haynes was in Bloomington, Indiana, to receive an honorary degree from Indiana University.[14] Haynes, one of five men recognized by the school with LL.D. degrees in 1922, heard President William Lowe Bryan read the following citation to him:

The world knows you best as the maker of the first automobile in America.... You will have no less enduring remembrance as a scientist and as an inventor of metals of capital importance in the industrial arts. As a mark of this, your work has just been crowned by the city of Philadelphia upon the recommendation of the University of Pennsylvania, the American Philosophical Society and the American Academy of Sciences. In recognition of these achievements and of your enlightened ideas and your civic courage, Indiana University confers upon you the degree, doctor of laws.[15]

Haynes attended another commencement on June 14, addressing the graduating class of the Babson Institute. March Haynes had attended the school in Wellesley Hills, Massachusetts, during the previous year and com-

[12] Alexander Winton to Elwood Haynes, June 3, 1924, E. G. Liebold to Elwood Haynes, March 14, 1925, June 4, 1924, *ibid.* See also Charles E. Duryea to Elwood Haynes, March 14, 1925, *ibid.* He too claimed an 1892 date for his first car, a year too early, and said his second one was built in 1893. See also the entertaining pamphlet by H. I. Phillips, "In the Not-So-Good Old Days: A History of the Automobile," reprinted from the New York *Sun*'s Silver Jubilee Automobile Issue, January 3, 1925. Ernest Headington sent the humorous account to Haynes, pointing out that not much mentioned there would be relevant to the contemplated book, "but it does hit the high spots from the view point of the public." General Folder, 1925, Haynes Papers.

[13] Kokomo *Dispatch,* May 11, 1922; *Automobile Topics,* June 24, 1922, p. 486; Ira N. Hollis to Elwood Haynes, May 11, 1922, Haynes Papers.

[14] Haynes had been notified of the university's decision in March; earlier in the month, in an apparently unrelated development, Haynes had agreed to speak to the Indiana University student body in May at one of its regular weekly convocations. William Lowe Bryan to Elwood Haynes, March 29, 1922, H. G. Childs to Elwood Haynes, March 4, 1922, Haynes Papers.

[15] *The Indiana Alumnus,* June 18, 1922, p. 6. A copy of this publication is in the Haynes Papers. The other four recipients were Amos William Butler, Lotus Delta Coffman, Ernest Hiram Lindley, and John Taliaferro Thompson. *Indiana University Faculty Newsletter,* April, 1972, pp. 1–6.

pleted its business leadership training program. The experienced twenty-six-year-old had been pleased with the course and felt better qualified to assist in the management of his father's affairs afterwards. Elwood Haynes addressed Babson's graduates on the subject of "The Relation of Science and Invention to Our Modern Industries."[16]

Of course the most highly celebrated recognition of Haynes came the following month, when Kokomo honored its adopted citizen on July 4th. Following the hectic days of June and July, Haynes and his wife left Kokomo for their first extended vacation trip aboard.[17] They motored to Indianapolis, took the train to New York City, and sailed aboard the *Aquitania* in early August. Haynes made infrequent reports home on the progress of their travels, which took them from Great Britain into Belgium, Germany, France, and Italy. The indications are that neither one was impressed by their European hosts and the Old World landmarks they encountered and that they wished to be home long before their itinerary had been completed. Haynes kept a close watch on business developments through regular contacts with his son, while Mrs. Haynes's activities abroad required, among other things, the shipment home of "Two cases of marble, etc., from Venice."[18] Haynes admitted afterwards that he preferred traveling in America, and he took a number of short pleasure trips in the 1920s. In April and May, 1922, he and Mrs. Haynes had driven south to Florida, returning via Decatur, Alabama, where Mrs. Haynes had lived for several years as a child.

Haynes disliked to spend much time away from his home, his laboratory, and his manifold interests in and around Kokomo. He wanted to be in constant touch with his three major businesses, for there were important developments in each during the early 1920s, and he also tried to resume something approaching systematic laboratory experiments. Although the financial problems caused by the troubled status of the automobile company delayed the long-planned construction of a large laboratory on property adjoining his home, in 1923 he purchased a new small electric furnace, which he installed temporarily in the basement of his home, and he spent many long and happy hours in this makeshift workshop. Given the other demands upon his time, it is not surprising that Haynes failed to complete the experiments he had planned and made no more major discoveries. By habit and experience, Haynes was quite secretive about the exact nature of the work he was engaged in during his final years, but it involved looking for new alloys as well as investigating the possibility of making artificial gemstones.[19] (It is mere coincidence, however, that the company which acquired the Haynes Stellite plant in 1920 has recently begun to market a wide variety of artificial gemstones.[20])

Haynes was interested in a number of mechanical improvements too, and he gave financial support and technical advice to a young inventor, Eugene Bournonville, working to improve a rotary gas engine (Haynes had invented

---

[16] Elwood Haynes to President G. W. Coleman, May 15, 1922, Haynes Papers.

[17] Bertha Haynes also went abroad in 1926-1927 following Elwood's death, and had traveled with her husband in the Caribbean in 1919.

[18] American Express Company to Elwood Haynes, January 8, 1923, *ibid.* See also Elwood Haynes to "Mr. Souder," August 11, 1922, Elwood Haynes to March Haynes, September 6, 1922, *ibid.*

[19] Margaret Haynes Rambolt to author, June 10, 1971; Foster, "How Elwood Haynes Came to Build First 'Horseless Carriage,'" in *Forbes,* March 1, 1925, p. 679.

[20] H. R. Morrison to author, March 15, 1971. Mr. Morrison was at the time the manager of the Marketing Communications Department, Linde Division, Union Carbide Corporation.

his own rotary engine in 1903). He also promoted the development of an improved farm tractor, but the Haynes Tractor Company, organized in 1921, never progressed to the production stage.[21]

Haynes also accepted a great many speaking engagements and was as willing to describe the remarkable qualities of either Stellite or Haynes automobiles as he was to discuss educational or business philosophies. He delivered a lecture on Stellite before the Sigma Xi scientific honorary at Purdue University in April, 1921 (which may have been responsible for the thesis on Stellite planned by two Purdue students in the fall of that year),[22] the same month in which he spoke about his first automobile at the Indiana Society of Chicago's "Hoosier Industrial Exposition." He shared the speaker's rostrum with two of Indiana's most popular humorists, writer George Ade and cartoonist John T. McCutcheon, and afterwards was complimented on his talk, his modesty, and the "good reception" which greeted his remarks.[23]

In 1923 Haynes was particularly busy as a speaker. He began the year with a national radio address from New York on the automobile (which caused considerable pride among Haynes dealers and owners, at least in the northeastern part of the United States).[24] Later he lectured the boys in a YMCA Bible study class upon the evils of smoking, spoke again in Bloomington at a business symposium, and appeared in Marion, Indiana, on behalf of Taylor University. There he extolled the value of the type of Christian education available at such institutions as Taylor, and suggested that society's problems could only be solved through "the application of the principles of Jesus Christ." Haynes also revealed to his Marion audience, in response to a question, that his first automobile "was never much account" and that he had driven it approximately 1,000 miles only "with much labor and vexation of spirit," a remark somewhat reminiscent of Alfred P. Sloan's comment that his first car (not a Haynes) had "taught me how to swear!"[25] Perhaps Haynes's last appearance before a Kokomo audience came in early 1924, upon the occasion of a tabernacle revival led by the Reverend Bob Jones. Haynes had consented to introduce Jones the first day of the planned five-week rally, but his own introduction at the morning session as "Kokomo's first citizen" led to a "prolonged tumult of applause in appreciation of Mr. Haynes' activity in everything promoting the city's best interests, and it was some time before he could speak" his words of introduction to the overflow crowd.[26]

There is, of course, another, more somber story concerning Elwood Haynes in the 1920s. Despite his reputation for enormous wealth during his later life, Haynes's fortune had declined significantly. The value of his total assets dwindled steadily from an estimated $1.2 million in July, 1920, to approximately half that much in later 1923, with most of his resources either in nonnegotiable securities or in shares of stock which represented the sale

[21] *Automobile Topics*, July 23, 1921, p. 887; *ibid.*, October 29, 1921, p. 874.

[22] Kokomo *Dispatch*, April 17, 1921; Professor A. P. Poorman to Elwood Haynes, October 14, 1921, Haynes Papers.

[23] Kokomo *Dispatch*, April 17, 1921; W. H. Rankin to Elwood Haynes, April 14, 1921, Haynes Papers.

[24] *Automobile Topics*, January 13, 1923, p. 904; *Journal of Worcester Polytechnic Institute*, XXVI (1923), 157; see also Ernest Headington to Elwood Haynes, January 17, 1923, Haynes Papers, reporting on the local reaction to the radio talk.

[25] Kokomo *Daily Dispatch*, April 2, 1923; Elwood Haynes, "The Relation of Education to the Manufacturing Industry," June 19, 1923, Haynes Papers; clipping, January 17, 1923, *ibid.*; Sloan and Sparkes, *Adventures of a White Collar Man*, p. 36.

[26] Kokomo *Daily Tribune*, February 4, 1924.

price of his alloy company and patents. He also had significant sums tied up in outstanding loans to friends and business associates, many of which were never repaid. Haynes tried, nevertheless, to maintain his normal high level of gifts and benevolences, to be generous in meeting requests for money from his extended family, and to shore up the sagging fortunes of the Haynes Automobile Company. The results were considerable financial worry during the 1920s and complicated financial problems for his heirs when he died intestate in 1925.

The worry had been compounded by an Internal Revenue Service claim for additional taxes, based on IRS refusal to recognize a valuation of $1.8 million on his Stellite and stainless steel patents, which Haynes wanted to depreciate over their seventeen-year life. The IRS believed that only out-of-pocket expenses incurred in obtaining the patents—in Haynes's case, only comparatively small attorney and registration fees—should be used to determine the original value of the patents. Haynes contested the government claim, and obtained statements from Leo H. Baekeland, the famed inventor, and Professor Charles L. Parsons, then probably the best known chemist in the United States, upholding his view on valuation, but no settlement had been reached by April, 1925.[27]

The Stellite patent infringement suit—the Chesterfield case—also consumed a great amount of Haynes's time and energy during 1924 and 1925. Anxious to win the case not only to claim a sizable additional stock payment but also to substantiate his reputation as an inventor and his conviction that he was right and justified, Haynes aided the Union Carbide company in replicating his experiments, amassing test data, and preparing its case. Haynes was as proud of the development of Stellite as of anything else he had done, considering it the "most natural outcome" of his life's work. When the Chesterfield case finally came to trial in Detroit in 1925 (the suit had been filed in 1922), Haynes testified briefly and soon returned to Indiana. His son remained in Michigan to send back daily reports. Judge Tuttle, rendering his opinion expeditiously, failed either to uphold the patent in all claims or to declare infringement. Reversing this judgment the following year, the appellate court decision gave Haynes the limited victory he would have taken as vindication of his labors, but the court's refusal to rule on all eight claims in the patent relieved the Union Carbide company of the obligation to pay an additional five thousand shares of stock to the Haynes estate.[28]

At the beginning of 1925, however, it had appeared that the year might be a particularly good one. There was still hope that the Haynes Automobile Company would be rescued from its receivership and that manufacturing on a full scale would resume. During January and early February, several cars were still being assembled from the materials on hand, and a bondholders' committee was looking for the requisite capital to carry on. In the meantime,

---

[27] John J. Kennedy to Elwood Haynes, September 19, 1924, Leo H. Baekeland to Elwood Haynes, September 21, 1924, Haynes Papers. Baekeland, who invented "Bakelite" and "Velos" photographic papers, was also the author of articles critical of the patent office. See his "The Abuses of Our Patent System," in *Scientific American Supplement,* June 1, 1912, pp. 346−47, and "The Incongruities of American Patent Litigation," in *ibid.,* November 23, 1912, pp. 322−23. Parsons served as secretary of the American Chemical Society from 1907-1945. Eventually Haynes's position on the value of his patents was accepted by the Internal Revenue Service.

[28] Since the court had upheld the broadest claim, Claim 8, and had declared infringement and awarded damages, A. E. Starbuck sued Union Carbide for the stock payment as administrator for the Haynes estate, but the suit was unsuccessful. Mrs. Haynes had stressed the importance of the case to Starbuck, since it involved "hundreds of thousands of dollars," but the court ruling in 1928 ended the matter. General Folder, 1928, Haynes Papers.

Elwood Hayr

Automotive pioneers honored in 1925

Haynes's role as one of America's automobile pioneers was given additional national recognition.

On January 6, 1925, the National Automobile Chamber of Commerce, in conjunction with the New York Automobile Show, honored a number of "old-timers" at a special pioneers' banquet. The occasion was the twenty-fifth year of the show, and eleven living persons were recognized at the "Silver Anniversary Dinner" as those who had "contributed most to the mechanical development of the motor car." In addition to Haynes, the "honor roll" consisted of John D. Maxwell, Edgar L. Apperson, A. L. Riker, John S. Clarke, Rollin H. White, H. H. Franklin, Charles E. Duryea, Charles B. King, Alexander Winton, and R. E. Olds.[29]

Haynes was delighted with the dinner and the opportunity to renew a number of old acquaintances and make a few new ones. Perhaps they even encouraged him to resume his project for a history of the automobile in America, for he mentioned it to at least one of the "pioneers," Charles E. Duryea. Duryea subsequently wrote Haynes about his own early work, and, despite the earlier acrimony about the tag on the "Pioneer" in the Smithsonian, Duryea encouraged him in his writing.[30] In a later letter to Haynes, the general manager of the NACC congratulated Haynes upon his award for "distinguished service to the industry." "You must have been highly

[29] Ralph C. Epstein, *The Automobile Industry: Its Economic and Commercial Development* (New York: Shaw, 1928), frontispiece. R. E. Olds did not attend the dinner. The eleventh person in the group photograph is Charles Clifton, the official host for the dinner.

[30] Charles E. Duryea to Elwood Haynes, March 13, 14, 1925, Haynes Papers.

pleased," he added, "at the enthusiastic reception given to you when your name was called."[31]

The trip to New York had taken a toll, however, for Haynes returned exhausted and suffering from the flu. He was confined to his bed for the next ten days, one of the few times in his life he had ever been bedridden, and was forced to miss the January meetings of the board of the American Stainless Steel Company and the Indiana State Board of Education. He was sitting up and able to dictate a few letters on January 17, including a long autobiographical résumé he sent to a former college roommate living in Australia. In a remarkably full and candid letter he undertook to review his activities since 1881, inviting his friend to reciprocate.[32] Just what had put Haynes in the reminiscing mood is not clear; it may have been the pioneers' banquet or perhaps the recent loss of another Tech classmate. At age sixty-seven perhaps he began to have a sense of his own mortality. Haynes began by noting that only about half the members of the class of '81 were still living, and predictably he remarked that when he had attended the fortieth anniversary reunion at Worcester in 1921, although "I anticipated changes in their appearances, I could hardly realize that the white-haired men who greeted me were the Classmates with whom we had gone through the Tech." The subsequent pages reviewed Haynes's careers as teacher, gas man, automobile and alloy manufacturer, and concluded with some family details. "Mrs. Haynes and I, as well as the children," he wrote, ignoring his present condition, which he did not consider serious, "have all had excellent health."[33]

Within a few days, Haynes tried to resume his normal activities, particularly the final preparations for the Chesterfield trial and the last-ditch efforts to revive the automobile company. His income tax appeal was scheduled for a hearing in Washington, D. C., in March. Understandably, given the press of financial and business affairs, Haynes was unable to shake off the flu quickly. Nevertheless, he fulfilled a few speaking commitments in the first months of the year and even spent a number of partial days in his laboratory. In mid-March, he left for an extended recuperative tour of the South, first going to Washington for the tax hearing. From there he and Mrs. Haynes journeyed down the east coast to Raleigh, North Carolina, then into Georgia and to Savannah, and later on into Florida, planning to sail to Cuba and return by way of New Orleans. On April 1, however, Haynes wired from Jacksonville that they were starting home the next day and would arrive on the 3rd. He had become, he said later, "rather worse than better" on the trip.[34]

March Haynes, who had kept his father in touch with a number of pressing business matters during the abbreviated trip, was alarmed at the news. He told a friend on April 6 that his father had returned but was "not feeling at all well." Haynes had again taken to his bed but expected to go to Detroit soon to attend the Stellite "trial." His travels and his trials, however, were nearly over. The last two letters he wrote, both directed to relatives in Portland, were dictated on April 9. In a note to his brother Walter, Haynes answered some questions concerning the automobile company refinancing, admitting that the automobile business had been "a trial to us all, and in

[31] Alfred Reeves to Elwood Haynes, January 10, 1925, *ibid.*

[32] Elwood Haynes to Stephen F. Roberts, January 17, 1925, *ibid.*

[33] *Ibid.* Haynes's other correspondence on January 17 and in following days concerned the financial problems of the automobile company.

[34] Elwood Haynes to Mrs. Edward Haynes, April 9, 1925, *ibid.*

Elwood Haynes in later life

addition I have a number of other matters of my own which are giving me concern." He said he was "now recovering from a double dose of the flu," and expected to be up and about soon. To his sister-in-law, he replied, not altogether accurately, to an objection she had raised about Haynes not being properly credited for his first car that he had never contested for its priority and that it was enough merely to state the facts. He also remarked that he was feeling better since returning home.[35]

But Haynes's condition worsened rather than improved after the 9th, and his heart action became erratic. On Monday, April 13, his two Kokomo physicians called in a heart specialist from Indianapolis, but the suggested therapy was ineffective. Haynes spent much of the day sitting up in the chair in his room, where he was most comfortable, surrounded by his immediate family. By midafternoon the end was obviously near. He died around 5:00 PM, just one day short of being 67½ years old.

The news of his death stunned the community and led to a great out-pouring of tributes from around the state and nation. Haynes's contributions in four areas—automobiles, metallurgical development, moral and civic leadership, and charity—were usually mentioned in eulogies. Howard C. Marmon, an Indianapolis automobile manufacturer, said that if Haynes were not the father of the automobile industry, "he was as near to it as any man I know about." The New York *Times* editorial on Haynes's career also stressed his automotive achievements.[36] Frederick E. Moskovics, an engineer with the Stutz Automobile Company, called Haynes a metallurgist "second to none in the world," adding that his "was one of the most beautiful characters it has been my privilege to know"; he was "truly a lovable man." President William Lowe Bryan of Indiana University stressed Haynes's record of moral leadership. In addition to becoming "great by the mastery of certain chapters of science and their application," which led both to "great fortune and the recognition of universities, learned societies, and men of business," Bryan praised Haynes as a man who "stood unafraid for the old-fashioned moral-ities which he knew to be far more necessary for us all than his most wonderful new-fangled invention."[37] And William Fortune, an officer of the American Red Cross, and others praised Haynes as an outstanding citizen and benefactor. Will H. Arnett, secretary of the Kokomo Chamber of Commerce, reinforced this latter point. "No one will ever know," he said, "the extent of his generosity, for although his public benefactions were many, most of his good work was performed directly for those in need."[38]

Moving tributes to Haynes were also included in the minutes of the Indiana State Board of Education, the First Presbyterian Church of Kokomo, the American Stainless Steel Company, and elsewhere,[39] but the most pro-found evidence of public grief was demonstrated during the funeral on April 16. Hundreds of persons, many more than could be accommodated inside the church, came to pay their respects to the deceased. In addition, Mayor James Burrows called for a complete cessation of all businesses and indus-tries in the city during the time of the funeral services.

---

[35] March Haynes to Hugh Hill, April 6, 1925, Elwood Haynes to Walter M. Haynes, April 9, 1925, Elwood Haynes to Mrs. Edward Haynes, April 9, 1925, *ibid.*

[36] Indianapolis *Star,* April 14, 1925; New York *Times,* April 15, 1925.

[37] Indianapolis *Star,* April 14, 1925.

[38] Kokomo *Daily Tribune,* April 14, 1925.

[39] The "elsewhere" includes the local chapter of the Knights of the Ku Klux Klan, which adopted resolutions noting the passing of Kokomo's "First Citizen," a world-renowned "scholar, scientist, inventor and Christian." Kokomo *Dispatch,* April 17, 1925.

Haynes's sudden and unexpected death had a devastating effect upon his family, especially upon March. He knew that his father's financial affairs were in disarray and that there was no will. The troubled financial picture became even worse when, on April 21, Judge Tuttle announced his decision of non-infringement in the Chesterfield case. March Haynes, appointed the administrator of the estate, was in Detroit to hear the judge deliver his decision and was deeply disappointed with it. "The judge talked for an hour in making his final decision," March wired his family, but "neither side could tell the final outcome until his last sentence which was to the effect that Chesterfield had not infringed the Stellite patents," although the patents themselves were not invalidated. "We will appeal," he continued, noting that the attorneys were confident of success on appeal.[40] Yet the death of his father, the unfavorable court ruling, and the unusual administrative burdens suddenly thrust upon the young man proved too much. He suffered a nervous breakdown while in New York early in May, and he remained hospitalized for several months. While March was recuperating in New York another tragedy hit the Haynes family at the end of May when his wife Hazel contracted pneumonia and died suddenly.[41]

In the meantime, A. E. Starbuck, the former treasurer of the Haynes Automobile Company and a relative, was appointed to replace March Haynes as administrator. He and Glen H. Hillis, a young Kokomo attorney and Elwood Haynes's son-in-law, labored throughout the year and beyond in settling the estate.[42] Its tangled situation was complicated by the automobile company's failure and Haynes's guarantee of many of its loans; the estate, moreover, included a large number of outstanding, virtually unsecured loans and a miscellaneous securities portfolio. Both represented Haynes's investment philosophy, which was characterized by friendship and philanthropy rather than business judgment. As Haynes rather confusingly told a business associate, an officer of the Hunt Porcelain Company of Kokomo, in 1919, "I took hold with you principally because I believed that there was a basis for a good business, but primarily because I wished to assist you and Mr. Hunt in the enterprise."[43]

The major portion of the estate, of course, consisted of Union Carbide company stock acquired in the sale of the Stellite company, American Stainless Steel Company stock obtained in the transfer of the stainless steel patent, and a substantial number of municipal and government bonds. Although the estate had been diminished by recent misfortunes and considerable labor was involved in its settlement, Haynes left his family with a modest fortune and the likelihood of a good income in the future.[44]

---

[40] March Haynes to "Mother, Bernice, and Hazel," April 21, 1925, Haynes Papers.

[41] New York *Times*, May 5, 7, 24, 1925; Kokomo *Daily Tribune*, May 8, 23, 1925. Haynes was unable to return to Kokomo for the funeral of his wife.

[42] Hillis had married Bernice Haynes in 1921 while he was in law school at Bloomington, Indiana. He subsequently became a prominent Kokomo attorney and was the Republican party candidate for governor in 1940. The Hillises had four children: Margaret, Elwood, Robert, and Joseph. Margaret Hillis is the choral director of the Chicago Symphony Orchestra. Her brother Elwood Haynes ("Bud") Hillis, has represented the Indiana Fifth District in Congress since 1970.

[43] Elwood Haynes to M. E. Louth, January 14, 1919, Haynes Papers. Haynes's other stock included shares in the Stevenson Gear Company, the Springfield Clay Products Company, the Kokomo Malleable Iron Company, and banks in three cities—Kokomo, Portland, and New York. He held almost no insurance; a $1,000 policy was paid up in 1918, at which time he declined to take out any more because the rates were "too high" and he considered his future prospects as "good." "Trial Balance," July 31, 1920, *ibid.*

[44] Howard County probate court records for 1925 indicate that the estate had total assets of $694,226.82, total liabilities of $397,667.77, and that Administrator A. E. Starbuck was authorized

Mrs. Haynes, a warm, gracious, unassuming person with a sly humor, whose independence and limited demands upon her husband had made her the perfect helpmate, lived until 1933. She continued to live simply, her chief self-indulgence a world cruise she undertook in 1926-1927 with her son. Ever the devoted mother and grandmother, she took great pride in her growing family, which included by 1933 several grandchildren, only one of whom her husband had lived to see.

For more than sixty years after Elwood Haynes's death his legacy has been an enduring one. He remains both Portland's and Kokomo's most famous and honored citizen, and no decade has passed without a significant recognition of the man. In 1932, on the seventy-fifth anniversary of his birth in Portland, the birthplace of the inventor was marked with impressive ceremony. The little house on the corner of High and Commerce streets no longer stood, but a marker was erected on the site. Among the speakers on the program were Sumner W. Haynes, an older brother, Hurd Allyn Drake, minister of the First Presbyterian Church in Kokomo, and C. V. Haworth, a Kokomo educator and historian who had had many intimate associations with Haynes from the 1890s. Haworth reviewed Haynes's entire career but stressed his personal characteristics of warmth, good humor, strong convictions, and generosity. The three thousand persons who were on hand for the occasion also heard a message from President Hoover and watched four of Haynes's grandchildren unveil the marker.[45]

Twelve years later, in January, 1944, the *U. S. S. Elwood Haynes* was launched at Permanente Yards near San Francisco, California. The vessel, a 10,500-ton "Liberty ship," had been built in less than a month. Because of the wartime travel restrictions, only Calvin Haynes, still living in San Francisco, and two Haynes Stellite Company officials represented the man being honored by the ship's name, but the Stellite representation was considered particularly appropriate since Stellite "has played a very important part in the war program."[46]

Haynes was also honored posthumously in the 1950s, first by the 1954 establishment of the Haynes-Becket Research Library at the laboratories of the Union Carbide Corporation in Niagara Falls, New York, honoring two outstanding scientists associated in different ways with the corporation, and second by the 1955 dedication of the Elwood Haynes School in Kokomo. In 1959 the Howard County Historical Society acquired the Elwood Haynes Papers, an event for which Wallace S. Huffman was largely responsible, and the house built by Haynes in 1916 was dedicated as the Elwood Haynes Museum in May, 1967. The Haynes Papers have since been transferred to the museum, which offers not only an insight into the life and career of Haynes but also depicts some aspects of the industrial history of Kokomo.[47]

---

on September 13, 1926, to sell $224,500 worth of bonds and securities to pay the claims allowed by the court. In subsequent developments, the suit against Union Carbide failed, but in 1928 a tax court ruled that Haynes's $1,800,000 valuation of his patents was a conservative one and that no further tax liabilities were justified. General Folder, 1926, 1928, *ibid.*

[45] *Indiana History Bulletin,* X (1932), 119−20; *Journal of the Worcester Polytechnic Institute,* XXXVI (1933), 41−42. See the Haynes Papers, 1932, for copies of the addresses by Haworth, Drake, and Sumner Haynes. Earlier on July 4, 1925, the Howard County Historical Society marked the site of the first Haynes home in Kokomo at the corner of Washington and Mulberry streets. The cottage in which he lived from 1892 until 1916 had been moved to 407 South Armstrong Street to make way for the commercial development of the downtown location. Kokomo *Tribune,* May 28, 1967.

[46] Kokomo *Tribune,* January 26, 1944; see also *ibid.,* January 8, 1944.

[47] The museum dedication and opening occurred May 28, 1967; see *ibid.,* May 29, 1967.

These recent events serve to underscore the fact that Elwood Haynes was indeed an extraordinary man. His remarkable career consisted of significant national contributions as well as local and state services. Haynes's scientific insights and abilities put him on the leading edge of a series of mechanical and chemical discoveries. His contemporary fame rested upon a popular misunderstanding of his actual contributions to the development of the automobile, but his most enduring legacy, as he himself predicted, has been his metallurgical discoveries, particularly Stellite.

Haynes, despite the image created by the local press, was not a paragon of all the virtues. He had his faults and his limitations, was "old-fashioned" and conservative socially and religiously, and his scientific approach was more amateurish and utilitarian than professional and pure; yet his scientific instincts were amazingly good, and he often confounded the professional researchers with whom he worked. If "Old Elwood—he always had gravy stains on his vest—"[48] was occasionally ridiculed as hopelessly outmoded and prudish in social intercourse by some, he was praised by others for the courage of his convictions and the resolute dignity he brought to his causes. He attempted to live a life of moral rectitude and would have considered it praise beyond value to be described, as he was so frequently by his eulogists, as a true Christian gentleman.

Haynes's reputation has suffered in recent years as the man's real achievements have been ignored after a long period of exaggerated and misplaced praise. Today he deserves a wider recognition, based not only upon a realistic assessment of his automotive work but also upon his noteworthy achievements in the field of metallurgy and for the cause of humanity. A teacher, scientist, and manufacturer, a social and political reformer, a churchman and a citizen, Elwood Haynes excelled in the art of living well and fully.

---

[48] This comment was made to the author by a former Stellite Company employee who knew Haynes only after the company had been acquired by Union Carbide.

A Note on the Sources

There is a vast amount of material relating to Elwood Haynes, beginning with the valuable but incomplete group of Haynes Papers now housed at the Elwood Haynes Museum in Kokomo, Indiana. These papers include the correspondence of Haynes, both incoming and outgoing after about 1913, a few business papers, and some miscellaneous items, but there are huge gaps in the correspondence file except for the last dozen years of Haynes's life. The business records of the three companies Haynes was most intimately connected with—the Haynes Automobile, Haynes Stellite, and American Stainless Steel companies—are not in the Haynes Museum and apparently have been destroyed. There are a few Haynes manuscripts and photographs in the Archives Collection of the library at Indiana University at Kokomo. The remaining Haynes sources are widely scattered among contemporary newspapers and journals, scientific, technical and legal reports, and various specialized library collections such as the Automotive History Collection at the Detroit Public Library or the historical files of the Stellite Division, Cabot Corporation, in Kokomo.

Two of the more surprising results of my search for information about Haynes were that he, both as a young teacher and later as a businessman in three Indiana communities—Portland, Greentown, and Kokomo—had his activities regularly reported in the local press and that he was a prolific author. His name appears on the title page of only one book, the frankly promotional *The Complete Motorist* (c. 1913-1914, reprinted 1977), and it was partly if not largely the product of the Haynes Automobile Company advertising department, but there is no doubt about the Haynes authorship of more than a score of published papers, many of which appeared in trade journals such as *Horseless Age* or *Iron Age* or in various scientific and technical journals. Haynes also presented a number of informal talks and formal papers before academic and professional scientific groups, for some of which copies are in the Haynes Papers.

There is no substantial secondary literature on Haynes as an automobile pioneer, despite his widely acknowledged early participation in the thoroughly studied automotive industry. Most books on the subject take only the most perfunctory notice of Haynes, usually lumping him with a group of other automobile pioneers, and none of the secondary accounts, including the recent and generally well done book issued by the editors of

Automobile Quarterly, The American Car Since 1775 (2d ed. New York, 1971), provide information about Haynes's production figures. The early trade journals of the industry began in 1895, however, and contain considerable information on Haynes and his cars, including articles and company advertisements by him. The most convenient place to examine these journals is at the Detroit Public Library's extraordinary Automotive History Collection, which also offers an extensive clippings file on individuals and companies and countless other automobile references.

Similarly, there is little in the way of interpretative secondary accounts on Elwood Haynes as a metallurgist who developed significant new alloys, but one may supplement the Haynes Papers with contemporary scientific and industrial journals to learn about Haynes, Stellite, and stainless steel. The Haynes Stellite Company, now a division of Cabot Corporation, is still in Kokomo and its historical records and patent files yield rich rewards to the diligent researcher. Unfortunately, nothing like this exists for the stainless steel story, since the American Stainless Steel Company was dissolved in the 1930s, although the corporate records of the licensees of the patent holding company, which with one exception have not been examined, may contain some of the missing files.

Court records of the litigation involving Haynes, beginning with the natural gas suit and continuing through the Selden (automobiles), Chesterfield (Stellite), and Ludlum (stainless steel) cases, are available in Indianapolis, Detroit, and Cincinnati. These records proved to be extremely useful, as did the complete patent files maintained by the U. S. Patent Office in Washington, D.C., which contain the original application, the resulting correspondence and, in some cases, affidavits and other information.

Other valuable sources of information on Haynes and his achievements, his character, and his personality are the people who knew him and worked with him. Many of these people were interviewed for the press or otherwise left personal reminiscences of their experiences and impressions. For this study I not only used these accounts, but also had the good fortune to be able to interview personally approximately forty people who had been associated with Haynes in various capacities. This group included Bernice Haynes Hillis, Haynes's daughter; C. V. Haworth, an educator and friend who lived to be over 100 years old and whose historical interests did much to perpetuate the memory of Haynes; F. T. McCurdy, one of the first metallurgists Haynes hired to work for him at the Stellite plant; and dozens of other automobile and Stellite company employees.

Specific citations identifying the most useful of the books, articles, manuscript records, and interviews used in preparing this study appear in the footnotes.

Index

chemistry department, 38, 41; role in
natural gas boom, 39–53; early ideas
about autos, 44, 52, 61, 67; duties as
gas company superintendent, 44–45,
47–48, 50, 65; marries Bertha Lanterman, 45; invents devices to improve
gas service, 45, 65; and children, 48, 97
(see also March Haynes; Bernice
Haynes Hillis); moves to Greentown,
51; tests law prohibiting pumping
natural gas, 53, 55–66; as Kokomo gas
manager, 64–66, 118; publishes article
on natural gas (1895), 65; research
during natural gas employment,
65–66; Apperson contributions to first
car, 71, 72 (see also Edgar Apperson;
Elmer Apperson; Haynes-Apperson);
decides to manufacture autos with
Apperson, 80; and "Pioneer," 73–75,
ill.,78; and Chicago race (1895), 79–81;
leads parade of historic autos (1908),
80–81; claims "first" auto, 81, 103, 184,
218; and early auto manufacturing,
83–95; uses aluminum in auto engine,
84–85, 86, 117; role in Haynes-
Apperson Co., 85, 89; makes first
1000-mile auto trip, 91; as auto manufacturer (1900–1910), 97–116; family
home, ill., 98; and carburetor patent,
99–100; leaves Apperson (1901),
103–104 (see also Apperson Brothers
Automobile Co.); writes Haynes-
Apperson Co. catalogs, 107; and Vanderbilt Cup race (1905), 109; and Glidden tours, 110; as businessman,
110–11, 117–18, 128, 141; quits managing auto company (1905), 111; writes
scientific articles, 111–12; continues
metallurgical experiments, 112, 117,
118–19, 128, 130, 144, 221–22; and
auto patents, 114–16, 117; discovery
of Stellite, 117–26; and Stellite patents,
120–26; and Haynes Stellite Co.,
127–44; describes Stellite, 129; applies
for "Festel" patent, 130; profits and
salary from Stellite, 133, 135; purchases cobalt ore mine, 133; attitude
towards workers, 135; criticized by
Stellite manager, 141; and sale of Stellite Co., 142; and stainless steel patents, 130, 145, 149–55, 158, 162–64;
writes Story of Stellite, 142; and discovery of stainless steel, 145–55; describes uses of stainless steel, 150;
merges stainless steel patent with
Brearley, 155; and stainless steel manufacture, 157–66; profits from Stainless Steel Co., 159; judge gives priority
in stainless steel patent, 163; opposes

lower royalties on stainless steel, 163;
asks greater recognition for stainless
steel work, 165, 166; and auto co.
(1910–1920), 167–68, 170–71; priority
stressed in auto ads, 171; and good
roads movement, 172–73; national
fame grows, 172, 193; tours to San
Francisco (1913), 173–76; writes autobiography, 176; plans history of auto,
177, 219–20; Dreiser's impression of,
182–85; honored by Kokomo groups,
185, 192; and demise of auto co.
(1921–1925), 189–202, 223–24; at-
tends Chicago auto show (1921), 190;
reviews auto co. history (1911–1924),
198; asks Ford to purchase Haynes Co.,
199; Seiberling's estimate of, 201;
financial loss in auto co. (1920–1925),
200, 222–23; lifestyle of, 203; descriptions of, 204; supports churches,
205; and Winona Lake Bible Conference, 205; runs for Senate as Prohibitionist, 207; moves to Republican
party, 212; and League of Nations, 212;
and nativism and Ku Klux Klan, 212;
serves on State Board of Education,
212–13; on college education, 213; as
philanthropist, 213–14; advocates
metric system, 214; advocates peace,
215; and Navy League, 215; serves on
federal grand jury, supports aviation,
217; last years, 217–30; travels with
Bertha, 221, 225; as lecturer, 222; plans
tractor production, 222; disputes with
IRS, 223; and Chesterfield case, 223;
honored at New York auto show
(1925), 224; ill health (1925), 225;
reminisces about life, 225; death of,
227; eulogized, 227; death devastates
family, 228; estate settled, 228; post-
humous honors, 229; see also Haynes
Automobile Co.; Haynes-Apperson
Automobile Co.; Haynes Stellite Co.
Haynes, Frank, 5, 10, 36; ill., 200
Haynes, George, 18
Haynes, Hazel, dies (1925), 228
Haynes, Henry (grandfather of EH), 5
Haynes, Henry (uncle of EH), 18
Haynes, Hilinda Sophia Haines, 22, 23;
death of, 4, 38; married Jacob March
Haynes, 5; as mother, 7; anxieties
about EH, 7, 9; and WCTU, 7
Haynes, Jacob March, 23; and Portland, 4;
sketch of, 5–7; ill., 6; slender re-
sources of, 13; scolds EH for poor
grades, 17; upset by EH's involvement
in student/faculty dispute, 22; proud of
EH's education, 25; advocates teacher
training school in Portland, 29; and